In *A History of Canadian Catholics* Terence Fay relates the long story of the Catholic Church and its followers, beginning with how the church and its adherents came to Canada, how the church established itself, and how Catholic spirituality played a part in shaping Canadian society. He also describes how recent social forces have influenced the church. Using an abundance of sources, Fay discusses Gallicanism (French spirituality), Romanism (Roman spirituality), and Canadianism (the indigenisation of Catholic spirituality in the Canadian lifestyle).

Fay begins with a detailed look at the struggle of French Catholics to settle a new land, including their encounters with the Amerindians. He analyses the conflict caused by the arrival of the Scottish and Irish Catholics, which threatened Gallican church control. Under Bishops Bourget and Lynch the church promoted a romantic vision of Catholic unity in Canada. By the end of the century, however, German, Ukrainian, Polish, and Hungarian immigrants had begun to challenge the French and Irish dominance of Catholic life and provide the foundation of a multicultural church. With the creation of the Canadian Catholic Conference in the postwar period these disparate groups were finally drawn into a more unified Canadian church.

A History of Canadian Catholics is especially timely for students of religion and history and will also be of interest to the general reader who would like an understanding of the development of Catholic roots in Canadian soil.

TERENCE J. FAY is in the faculty of the Toronto School of Theology for St Augustine's Seminary, the University of Toronto.

McGILL-QUEEN'S STUDIES IN THE HISTORY OF RELIGION

Volumes in this series have been supported by the Jackman Foundation of Toronto.

SERIES TWO   In memory of George Rawlyk
Donald Harman Akenson, Editor

A History
of Canadian Catholics

Gallicanism, Romanism,
and Canadianism

TERENCE J. FAY

McGill-Queen's University Press
Montreal & Kingston · London · Ithaca

© McGill-Queen's University Press 2002
ISBN 0-7735-2313-8 (cloth)
ISBN 0-7735-2314-6 (paper)

Legal deposit second quarter 2002
Bibliothèque nationale du Québec

Printed in Canada on acid-free paper that is 100%
ancient forest free (100% post-consumer recycled),
processed chlorine free, and printed with vegetable-
based, low VOC inks.

McGill-Queen's University Press acknowledges the
support of the Canada Council for the Arts for its
publishing program. It also acknowledges the financial
support of the Government of Canada through the Book
Publishing Industry Development Program (BPIDP) for
its publishing activities.

**National Library of Canada Cataloguing
in Publication Data**

Fay, Terence J., 1932–
   A history of Canadian Catholics: Gallicanism, Romanism
   and Canadianism
   (History of religion)
   Includes bibliographical references and index.
   ISBN 0-7735-2313-8 (bound).
   ISBN 0-7735-2314-6 (pbk.)
   1. Catholics – Canada – History.   2. Catholic Church –
   Canada – History.   I. Title.   II. Series.
   BX1421.2.F38 2002   282'.71   C2001-903454-7

This book was typeset by Dynagram Inc.
in 10/12 Baskerville.

Contents

Preface

Many colleagues and students have let me know that an outline history of the Canadian Catholicism is needed now. Thus, *A History of Canadian Catholics: Gallicanism, Romanism, and Canadianism* was conceived to utilize published research to create the first comprehensive history of Catholics in Canada. A history of Canadian Catholics is desperately needed to provide on overview for students and interested readers, but a history based on primary sources is not yet possible. An abundance of sources for a synthetic history are readily available in the more than sixty volumes of the Canadian Catholic Historical Association's *Historical Studies*, other related journals, and in the various monographs published on Canadian church history. This history aspires from available sources to assess, analyse, and interpret the significant events of Catholics in Canada over four hundred years. The main themes of Canadian Catholic history are distilled and communicated in the strong narrative style of the volume.

Let me express my gratitude to the late Professor Paul Crunican who gathered the first secondary source materials from which I began this study. Since that time I have greatly augmented Crunican's materials and revised them many times to provide this preliminary synthesis of Canadian Catholicism. I am grateful to my colleagues in the Canadian Catholic Historical Association, Mark G. McGowan, Edward Jackman, OP, Brian F. Hogan, CSB, Richard Lebrun, Vicki Bennett, and Brian Clarke who provided helpful and timely advice on the subtle issues of Canadian church history. I thank Michael Power, William F. Ryan, SJ, Bishop Attila Miklósházy, SJ, and Msgr Joseph O'Neill, who have all reviewed the manuscript. They raised questions and supplied me with helpful suggestions that enriched this work. I am most grateful to Gilles Chaussé, SJ, James D. Cameron, and Margaret Brennan, IHM, who read particular chapters. Their understanding of the areas they reviewed strengthened the text. I am especially indebted to Mark McGowan, who read with great care and reflection and made excellent suggestions in reshaping whole sections of the manuscript, and to the editors of McGill-Queen's University Press, Donald Akenson, Roger Martin, Joan McGilvray, and Claire Gigantes who showed great interest and gave steady support through the production of manuscript. I take full responsibility, however, for any shortcomings that may remain.

I want to express my gratitude for the church histories by Thomas Bokenkotter, James Hennesey, SJ, and Jay Dolan, which inspired this work. I thank my Jesuit community and friends at Our Lady of Lourdes Parish in Toronto and the faculty of St Augustine's Seminary for their enthusiasm and support. Students at the Toronto School of Theology of the University of Toronto also enriched this volume with their interest and comments. Most especially, I am grateful to the Jesuit Fathers of Upper Canada and the Jackman Foundation for their encouragement and financial support.

Introduction

Formal Christianity has existed in North America for four hundred years. Some Amerindians explain that Christ was known among the native people in their own terms centuries before the Europeans arrived.[1] Christianity over four centuries has played a major role in shaping both Euro-Canadians and Amerindians in North America. From the first meeting in Canada between the Amerindians and the French Catholics, Christians have been present in most of the settlements of both the native people and the French colonists. Gallicanism (French spirituality), Romanism (Roman spirituality), and Canadianism (the indigenization of Catholic spirituality in the Canadian lifestyle) emerged through the four centuries of Canadian Catholic history.[2]

Early Christians in Canada struggled to live the gospel and show their concern for others in the face of overwhelming numbers who adhered to other belief systems. Side by side, native Christians and French missionaries preached the Word, taught catechism, cared for the sick, and fed the hungry. French Catholics inspired others by their sacrifices but also displayed their personal weaknesses and manifested their cultural imperatives. Amerindians, industrious in the fur trade, succeeded in preserving their culture. In time, however, having welcomed the Europeans, they were disillusioned to find their lands taken and themselves marginalized.

Catholic missions had an impact on family, politics, and artistic endeavour in North America. They instilled the Christian idea of the golden rule, the beatitudes, and sacrificial love. They struggled to carry salvation to the faithful, provide education, and supply health care. They built churches, schools, hospitals, and cemeteries across the land. Their strong affirmation of life, based on the Ten Commandments and the didache (an early Christian Manual on morals and Church practice), has given a creed for Canadians to live by. From the Christian prayer of the hours, the Canadian crest was inscribed with "a mare usque ad mare."[3] Christian influence through four centuries has had a strong influence on the Canadian nation. Catholic officials and professionals from the seventeenth century to the present have helped to guide the Canadian nation. The percentage of Catholics in Canada today hovers around forty-six percent and influences Canadian national policy.

Yet it was not abstract wisdom that ushered the Canadian Catholic community down through the corridors of time but the Roman church, which was organized into metropolitan provinces, dioceses, and parishes. These units, like the fleets and ships of the Royal Navy, were run by well-educated and carefully selected bishops and clergy. At their head the bishop of Rome gave leadership in matters of faith and morals and enjoyed primacy of jurisdiction over fledgling Canadian dioceses. The twenty-one ecumenical councils of the Catholic church from Nicaea (AD 325) to Vatican II (1962–65) formulated Catholic teachings and guided the truths that Catholics believed. Roman Canon Law outlined the rights of Catholics and condemned vices. The clergy and laity in conscience were expected to follow the commandments, the Scriptures, church teachings, and the prescriptions of canon law. Through the rite of Christian initiation, new members were instructed in the Christian tradition handed down, as Catholics believe, from the apostles through the Scriptures and Christian practice. After instruction, neophytes were socialized into the community. The policies of the Canadian Catholic church were decided by diocesan synods and plenary councils of the Canadian bishops within the guidelines of the Roman communion.

Gallican clergy and laity through the first two centuries influenced the Canadian nation. Out of love for the Amerindians, the first French Jesuits arrived on the shores of Canada to initiate the Canadian missions. They left behind their language and European ways and learned to paddle canoes, eat native food, sleep in native longhouses, and communicate in native ways. They founded Sainte Marie in Huronia as a centre of European inculturation into Amerindian culture. Many Hurons became Christian and formed an important segment of Amerindian Christianity. Dying in many ways to their European past, the Jesuits emerged in the new land of the Hurons to live their lifestyle.

As the Jesuits entered into the Huron culture, the French laity trickled ashore at Montreal to found an evangelical community at the crossroads of the Amerindians. Maisonneuve led the first party to establish the missionary outpost in 1642, and Marguerite Bourgeoys with friends from Troyes opened the first school for both Amerindian and French colonial children. Jeanne Mance, often in poor health herself, opened a second Canadian hospital in Montreal to care for the sick. Kateri Tekakwitha travelled from her village on the Mohawk River to Kahnawake south of Montreal to inspire the Amerindian Christian community with her sense of humour and goodness. Bishop Laval was appointed to Quebec to pull this disparate church into order and to keep it in harmony but independent of the royal government. This spirit of doing great things for God has continued in Canada through the centuries. Brother André healed the sick, Governor General Georges and Madam Pauline Vanier inspired the Canadian nation, and Cardinal Paul-Emile Léger carried Canadian assistance to Africa. The visit of John Paul II to Canada in 1984, and to the native people at Fort Simpson in 1987, brought hundreds of thousands of Canadians to street corners and the playing fields to see the pope, to enjoy the enthusiasm of a spectacular event, and to attend the communal celebration of Eucharist.

After the English Conquest, Bishop Briand guided the Canadian church through an oppressive time with good humour, loyalty, and Gallican subtlety. By his cooperative spirit, he guaranteed that the episcopal succession would be handed down to the present. After the beginning of the nineteenth century, Bishop Plessis, again through agreeableness, loyalty, diplomacy, and Gallican feistiness in defence of the Church, expanded the episcopate from one to six sees, an external symbol of internal growth of the Canadian Catholic church.

Underorganized in missionary periods, the Canadian church in the nineteenth century was centralized by the bishops under the direction of the Roman See. Bishop Bourget with ultramontane zeal and loyalty organized not only parish spirituality and devotions but also schools and social services. He threatened French Canadian politicians who avoided adherence to his loyalist theology. During the last half of the nineteenth century, Roman and Canadian Catholicism in tandem pursued a narrowly focused theological tradition and devotional practice. The Second Vatican Council lifted these constraints, which had hobbled the spiritual and intellectual expansion of Catholics and encouraged personal growth and social involvement.

The immigration of the Scottish and Irish laity and clergy to Canada in the eighteenth and nineteenth centuries upset the Gallic control of the Canadian church. The immigration of the Germans, Ukrainians,

Poles, and Lithuanians at the end of the nineteenth century ended the bipolar French-English dominance and Canadianized Catholics. The Catholic church in composition rapidly became multicultural. The laity, clergy, and bishops were pluralistic in their understanding of church affairs and began forming a Canadian church with a distinctive Canadian ecclesiology.

The Canadian Catholic church, following a decade of observer status at the Canadian Council of Churches, opted for full membership in the landmark decision of 1997. The Catholic church accepted representation not according to the number of its adherents but rather in proportion to the representation of the other major denominations, namely, the United and Anglican churches. Like these other churches, the Catholic church embraced aboriginal rights, land claims, and self-government. Other joint projects of the Canadian churches have shown a mutual concern for the economy and the development of the North.[3] The Canadian Catholic church throughout the twentieth century fostered its Canadian identity.

One of the strong features of Christianity since the turn of the century has been its promotion of social thought. The Protestant social gospel preached by Salem Bland in *New Christianity* and Catholic social thought introduced by Leo XIII in *Rerum Novarum* placed these churches on the side of the downtrodden and the marginal. The Christian churches were inclined to support the demands of trade unions, lobby for extension of the social safety net, and seek out the needy in the cities, countryside, and reserves to provide them with the necessities of life. Of recent years, the welfare of migrants and refugees are a constant concern for the churches.

Christian schools were a mammoth undertaking. They provide a viably alternative school system to the uniformity of government schools. Hundreds of thousands of students across Canada have been educated in the Catholic school system from the primary grades to high school. Lay boards administer the schools, and religious sisters, brothers, and lay teachers provide the instruction. Religious orders have founded Catholic colleges on most provincial university campuses and graduated many laity who today are staffing and administering them. To Christian students, religious colleges offer a believing intelligentsia to guide them in the integration of the sciences and faith in their life.

As Canadian Catholics attempt to shape Canadian society, Canadian social and intellectual life shapes Canadian Catholics. The Second Vatican Council challenged Catholic homes, workplaces, universities, marketplaces, and churches. Study groups, base communities, Christian life communities, diocesan synods, councils, and committees considered contemporary Canadian life, discussed Christian practice, and decided where the future lay for Christians in Canadian society. Catholic church leaders accepted their responsibility to guide Catholics in Canada and the Canadian nation. The bishops do not pretend to have ready answers but feel the need to ask questions about where we the Canadian people are going. They raise questions in Rome as to whether we as a church can offer women fuller equality in church affairs; they ask the business community whether it can pay its workers more fairly; and they ask the Canadian government whether it is ready to offer the Amerindians adequate land, aboriginal rights, and self-government.

The Canadian Catholic church offers an alternative and coherent vision of life in contrast to the ephemeral nature of civil policies, commercial interests, and a purely secular outlook. The development of Canadian Catholic coherence will be examined in the context of the *Gallican period* of missionary and mystical origins, the *Roman period* of nineteenth-century ultramontane loyalty, and the *Canadian period* with the flowering of multicultural communities in the twentieth century and the dynamics of the post-conciliar world.

Traditional Catholic historiography likes to see Canada's zealous inhabitants and wonder-working Jesuits performing heroic deeds while bearing French culture and Catholic Christianity to the Amerindians.[4] We like to believe that these inventive adventurers, though they laboured under the double yoke of royal absolutism and Church control, carried out their tasks of evangelization with great determination. What is needed, however, is a contemporary vision for our day, a vision, says Cornelius Jaenen, that is "a more penetrating and constructive overview" of the church's role in New France.[5] This volume uses the published insights of new history to construct an integrated and candid overview of Catholics in Canada.

A History of Canadian Catholics

PART ONE

Gallicanism

1 Missionary Origins
of Catholic Church in Canada

Catholic Christianity was first brought to North America when the Spanish Dominicans and Franciscans settled in Mexico in the early sixteenth century. The friars, and soon their Jesuit colleagues, then carried the Christian faith into the areas now called New Mexico and southern California. At the opposite end of the North American continent, in Nova Scotia and along the north shore of the St Lawrence River, French Jesuits and Franciscan Recollets in the early decades of the seventeenth century participated in the establishment of Christian settlements.

Chaplains aboard the fishing vessels off the North American coast were the first missionaries to bring the Christian gospel to the Amerindians. These clergy were mostly members of religious orders who were authorized by the Holy See to carry out apostolic enterprises.[1] The first missionary to land with the French colonizers in Acadia was the diocesan priest L'abbé Jessé Fléché. He was brought here to convert the Mi'kmaws in 1610 by Jean de Biencourt, sieur de Poutrincourt. Within the year he baptized one hundred and forty converts including Chief Memberton and his family. The next year two Jesuits, Pierre Biard and Énemond Massé, landed at Port Royal to follow up on the work of Fléché. They soon discovered that the Mi'kmaw neophytes were not instructed in the faith. The truth was that Fléché did not know Mi'kmaw; hence the icons of the Catholic faith, the Apostles' Creed, the Lord's

Prayer, and the Ten Commandments, were not translated for the first Amerindian Christians. The Jesuits immediately learned Mi'kmaw, translated these Christian icons, and taught catechism to the Mi'kmaws. But this idyllic scene of missionary activity did not last long. It was interrupted in 1613 by an English Protestant force from Virginia. Samuel Argall from the ship *Treasurer* led a raid on the colony, burning the habitation and pillaging its grain supplies. The Virginians were angry at the French intrusion in Acadia on what they claimed was English territory. This action all but ended the first French effort to colonize and evangelize Acadia.[2]

The highly motivated Samuel de Champlain chose the strategic location of Quebec as the centre for the commercial, political, and religious conquest of Canada. In 1608 he planted the *fleur-de-lis* to initiate French civilization and evangelization among the Amerindians. Catholic religious and lay missionaries began evangelizing the native people. By contrast, the Huguenot trading companies of New France were not much concerned with evangelization during the first two decades of the seventeenth century but were principally interested in doing business with the Amerindians. Under pressure from the French Crown, trading companies invited the Recollet Fathers to come to Canada to minister to the colonists and Amerindians.[3]

Four Recollets arrived in 1615 to evangelize the French and Amerindians, spread along the river systems from Tadoussac upstream to Quebec and to Georgian Bay. Father Denis Jamet, the Recollet superior, constructed the mission house of Notre-Dame-des-Anges near Quebec in 1621. Father Jean Dolbeau was appointed to the Montagnais mission at Tadoussac, and in 1620 it was he who blessed the cornerstone of the first Canadian seminary for French and Amerindian boys. They planned first to make Frenchmen of the Amerindians to prepare them for Christianization. Father Joseph Le Caron located himself in Huronia at Carhagouha where Samuel de Champlain resided in 1615[4] and began the first mission among the Hurons. He compiled Huron, Algonkian, and Montagnais dictionaries. Brother Pacifique Duplessis was sent to Trois-Rivières to preach the gospel, care for the sick, and teach the children. He is credited with being the first schoolteacher in New France.[5] The Recollets, following their Mexican successes in the conversion of native people, as James Axtell recounts, "set about trying to squeeze the local [Canadian] natives into a European mould." They failed to appreciate the uniqueness of the Laurentian Amerindians and the strength of their religious beliefs.[6] It can be argued that the four Recollets covered an immense expanse of territory but, since the Amerindians firmly resisted their efforts, failed to show significant results.

Meanwhile, the papal Curia in Rome withdrew the responsibility of evangelizing mission countries from the Crown heads of Europe, a task the royals had exercised for one hundred and twenty-five years, and began directing missions in America, Asia, and Africa. The Congregatio de Propaganda Fide (Congregation for the Propagation of the Faith) was founded in 1622 to direct the future development of world missions. It undertook the delicate task in New France of the directing church activities without offending the traditional prerogatives of the French Crown and the French bishops.[7] The Catholic church in New France was unique in that it was never entirely subjected to the state as were the churches of England or France. Cornelius Jaenen explains the anomaly this way: "The church in New France was the creation of the metropolitan Gallican Church, but never became its creature."[8] The driving force of the missionary church was propelled by the dynamic post-Tridentine spirituality,[9] whereas financial and logistical support came from the Crown and private sources.

Three years after the founding of Propaganda Fide, Fathers Charles Lalemant,[10] Jean de Brébeuf,[11] and Énemond Massé[12] of the Society of Jesus, along with Brothers François Charton and Gilbert Burel, landed at Quebec to assist the Recollets and to give new crusading energy to the evangelization of the Amerindians. Charles Lalemant was made superior, and three more Jesuits arrived the following year. Despite the difficulty of having his supply lines for the next four years raided at sea by both French and the English antagonists, Lalemant continued staunchly to guide the mission. Brébeuf was sent to winter with the Montagnais in 1625 to learn their language and customs. The following year he was sent to a different language and culture group, the Hurons. Énemond Massé lived with the Recollets and saw to the completion of the residence and seminary of Notre-Dame-des-Anges. The Jesuits, unlike the Recollets, accepted the sincere conversion of the Montagnais nomadic hunters and believed that their transient way of life was compatible with the practice of Christianity. The Jesuits believed it was unnecessary for the hunters and gatherers to enter a reserve village to become Frenchified before they could be baptized. "As long as they carried Christ's message in their hearts, prayed regularly, and honored the seven sacraments when they were available," writes James Axtell, "the Indians of Canada were accounted *bons catholiques*, at least by their Jesuit mentors."[13]

During these centuries of evangelization, the nascent Canadian church and royal government adopted a relationship of cooperation in the common task. The king considered himself the senior partner in this arrangement as he believed that from the earliest times he was king by divine right and had received the crown directly from God without the mediation of the church or the people. To cope with absolute sovereignty, the church coordinated its goals with those of an overbearing state, and the state reciprocated by supplying appropriate legislation and funds to the church.[14] This meant that the French government, along with private benefactors,[15] supplied the funds, settlers, and appurtenances to establish the church in New France. In a coordinated effort, the church staffed the mission stations of New France, the government recruited the settlers, and at the various settlements lay and religious church workers served both the French settlers and the Amerindian communities. The trading companies showed little interest in recruiting settlers as settlements interfered with the fur trade. A second English incursion in 1629, with Huguenot assistance, forced the French companies to withdraw from Canadian shores.[16] Both the Recollets and the Jesuits closed down religious activities in the colony and returned to France.

QUEBEC

The Jesuits in 1632 returned a second time to Canada and founded two principal centres for evangelical activities, one a college in Quebec mainly for the French inhabitants, and the other a mission on Georgian Bay at Sainte-Marie (1639–49) for the Amerindians. As James Axtell points out, the missionaries initiated a "distinctive brand of gunless warfare" to win their own victories in the war for souls.[17]

To renew the Jesuit ministry to evangelize the Amerindians, Paul Le Jeune projected a plan. The first step was mastering the necessary languages for communication with the Laurentian people. Their languages were subtle and complex, and for Jesuits learning them was the priority. The Amerindian custom was that community problems were discussed in assemblies and policies were set accordingly. Thus it was imperative for the missionaries, if they were to lead the chiefs towards Christianity, to address their assemblies in the manner of captains discussing worship and extending the invitation to baptism. Le Jeune's second step was to build seminaries for Amerindian children, to educate them in French culture, and to initiate them into the Christian way of life. Moreover, he believed that the construction and staffing of hospitals would be powerful manifestations of Christian concern for the sick and the aged. Lastly, he thought it better that the Christian Amerindians give up their itinerant life and settle on reserves so that they could form agricultural communities and regular parishes.[18]

Quebec had been founded primarily as a commercial base to exploit the resources of New France. It was reorganized under the Company of One Hundred Associates in 1628 to emphasize religious and agricultural activities. A Jesuit college was founded in 1635 to educate Amerindian and French boys.[19] Five Huron boys enrolled at the school but shortly after vanished into the countryside. It is uncertain whether they were seriously ill and withdrew, or whether they deliberately chose to strike a blow for freedom against the relentless discipline of school. In any case, the boys seized the first canoe they discovered and paddled for the safety of Huronia.[20] This blow to the college ended the Jesuit effort to Frenchify the Amerindians and focused their energies on their own inculturation into native life.

For the education of girls and the care of the sick, the Jesuits sought assistance from religious women. In 1639 two orders of religious women arrived at Quebec, the Ursuline Nuns to educate young women and the Hospitallers of St Augustine to look after the sick. The nuns immediately began providing health care at Sillery and in 1642 attended a hundred Montagnais, Algonkian, Abenaki, and Huron people who were suffering from smallpox. Owing to the Iroquois foray two years later, the nuns withdrew from Sillery to Quebec and established the first Canadian hospital, the Hôtel-Dieu.[21]

Ursuline Sr Marie de l'Incarnation (1599–1672), two of her sisters, a young companion, and Mme de La Peltrie opened a school for girls in 1639. "A mystic imbued with a sense of action," Marie de l'Incarnation believed that she had been inspired by God to join the Ursulines and go to Canada. A good and loving person, she believed that her apostolate was to educate both French and Amerindian girls. She exhorted her sister companions to be endearing in their treatment of their small charges. Agreeing with the Jesuits, Marie realized that it was useless to attempt to Frenchify the Amerindian children in the schools. A capable manager, she cultivated a garden, operated a farm, defied the Iroquois raids, and even sometimes defied the ill will of the colonists. Her spiritual adviser was the Jesuit superior Fr Jérôme Lalemant. He instructed her in the native languages, and she went on to master Algonkin and Iroquois and compose dictionaries for missionaries. With the assistance of Jérôme Lalemant, she formulated the Ursuline Constitutions of 1646 to guide the religious lives of her Canadian community. The magnates of the colony consulted her about many problems, and she wrote voluminously about her feelings, thoughts, and experiences.[22] During these early years the men and women religious leaders offered the French and Amerindians an active and intense religious life, but the focus of the Quebec colony continued to be business and commerce.

HURONIA

Huronia was the second location of Christian evangelization and became a Jesuit centre for inculturation[23] on the south shore of Georgian Bay. Travelling in Huron canoes, Fathers Jean de Brébeuf, Anthony Daniel, and Ambroise Davost paddled up the Ottawa and Mattawa rivers, crossing Lake Nipissing and going down the French River to Georgian Bay, landing at Huronia in 1634.[24] Twenty-five thousand Hurons occupied a land of abundant fish, open fields, broad meadows, mixed forests, and sandy loam soil. The hundred-and-forty-day growing season provided a surplus corn crop to supplement the winter diet of fish and meat.[25]

For the first five years the Jesuits lived in the Amerindian villages, sometimes in their own houses and sometimes in the native long houses that sheltered ten to twenty families. For their survival, the Jesuits quickly acquired the Amerindian ways since no one looked kindly on those who did not know the customs or were slow learners. The Jesuits, initially without the benefit of dictionaries or grammars, picked up the Huron language during the course of everyday life, while paddling canoes, carrying heavy packs over the portages, eating native foods, and sleeping in crowded long houses alongside crying children and barking dogs. The sedentary Recollets avoided this type of inculturation whenever possible.[26] Despite the rigorous demands of Huron etiquette, Jesuits managed to show the required cheerful face and learned not to be irritable.[27]

The Hurons gradually accepted the French priests as partners in their villages but nevertheless had mixed feelings about their presence. In their own environment the Hurons were very confident and knew that the French had much to learn from them. After all, it was they who were in the majority, they who knew the river systems and the arts of hunting and fishing, and it was they who knew the languages and customs of Canada. The Hurons were not altogether pleased with their French allies. They found the appearance of French beards ugly and wondered if French women might be equally unattractive. They thought the Jesuits' celibacy unmanly, the French marriage codes humorous, and child-rearing practices too strict.[28] The Jesuits had some success with converts to Christianity and set up Christian villages to accommodate them. Jan Noel writes, "when the *Jésuites* set up villages for their converts, they tried to persuade wives to be more submissive; they humiliated independent women and condoned men beating disobedient spouses."[29] The Amerindians remained self-confident and believed that the French needed them more than they needed the French.

The Hurons gradually learned to admire the Black Robes because they were not avaricious in pursuit of their "land, women, war, and pelts." Under torture and in the face of death, they showed great personal courage as hardened warriors were expected to do and proved to be "men of uncommon spirit." The immunity of the Jesuits to epidemic diseases, even while working among the sick and the dying, made a strong impression upon observers. Moreover, the Jesuits were able to master native speaking techniques to the point where they could influence the outcome of matters dealt with at public assemblies and defuse explosive situations. By means of a two-hour harangue at Onondaga in 1654, Simon LeMoyne, "speaking slowly and in the tone of a Captain," won a peace council with four Iroquois nations. And the following year Joseph Chaumonot, strutting about in Amerindian style and with "a torrent of forcible words," reaffirmed the treaty. The Jesuits also learned to give gifts to confirm friendships and alliances. Gift giving became an important part of their diplomacy with the Huron and Iroquois people.[30]

The priests brought the gospel to the Amerindians, and part of its message was sin and damnation. The Amerindians had little experience of their own sinfulness and did not necessarily feel the need for French salvation or heaven.[31] Their dreams directed them in spiritual quests, and they questioned the suitability of Christian teaching. The priests administered baptism to dying Amerindians to give them the grace of a happy death. Consequently, many Amerindians feared baptism as it seemed to be the harbinger of sickness, disease, and death. The Jesuits challenged the gods of the Amerindians as St Boniface in the eighth century had challenged Thor of the German tribes by felling his sacred tree. In similar fashion, Jesuits entered into contest with the Amerindian "sorcerers" and "jugglers" to expose their impotence and demonstrate the power of the Christian God.[32]

The Jesuits discovered that Amerindians had a belief system that worked for them, and thus that the Amerindians were not necessarily willing candidates for Christian baptism. The Jesuits conceded that the spirit of God could come through other cultures and that the Huron culture could shed God's light.[33] For those Amerindians who became Christian, the Jesuits admired their singing and discovered that "the Indians have much aptitude and inclination for singing the hymns of the Church, which have been rendered into their language." Elsewhere another Jesuit commented, "Their voices are both mellow and sonorous, and their ear so correct that they do not miss a half-tone in all the church hymns, which they know by heart."[34]

The adjustment that the Jesuits made to Huronian culture was not without difficulty. The new superior, Jérôme Lalemant, determined that for their own well-being a central Jesuit mission station should be built. There the missionaries would live and take spiritual refreshment, and from there they would travel on regular visits to the Huron villages. Sainte-Marie was founded for this purpose in 1639 and by the middle of the 1640s, the Christian centre had grown to include seventy Europeans and hundreds of visiting Hurons. The agricultural methods employed at Sainte-Marie were both Huron and European and provided a bountiful harvest and adequate sustenance for the year. From the centre the missionaries circulated throughout Huronia to teach, baptize, and hold services. Sainte-Marie among the Hurons welcomed travellers and supplied them with food and hospitality. The centre during the seventeenth century became the first site for the inculturation of Europeans into the Amerindian culture and the Christian evangelization within the Amerindian environment.[35] Many Hurons, along with Montagnais, Iroquois, Petun, and Neutrals, were converted to Christianity to establish the beginnings of Canadian Christianity west of Quebec. According to the *Jesuit Relations* more than sixteen thousand Amerindians, or about twice the number of French inhabitants,[36] received baptism between 1632 and 1672.[37] Hurons were among the first Christians in Canada, and in their spirituality, according to Jesuit writings, they could be second to none.[38] Some prominent Amerindian converts were Joseph Chihwatenha, Louis Taondechoren, and Kateri Tekakwitha. The Huron Christmas Carol is an early Christian artefact that dates back to this period.

After prospering for ten years, the destruction of the Huron mission came about this way. Beginning in 1639 the Dutch at Albany, north of New Amsterdam, traded guns to the Iroquois, eager to gain their furs. The French were forced to supply guns but, at Jesuit insistence, only to Christian Amerindians. By 1648 the Iroquois had five hundred guns while the Hurons had only 120. From 1643 the Iroquois in small bands continually roamed the banks of the St Lawrence and Ottawa rivers to intercept the heavily laden Huron trading canoes. For the Iroquois the harvest of furs was rich, but for the Hurons the loss in resources and warriors was devastating. While holding out the hope of peace to divide the Hurons, the Iroquois made periodic assaults on Huron villages. The Hurons, according to Bruce Trigger, now "looked to the Jesuits to use their spiritual and material resources to protect them."[39] By the summers of 1648 and 1649 about one in two Hurons had accepted baptism into the Christian faith.

Huron villages continued to fall to Iroquois attacks, and Father Anthony Daniel was killed in one such raid. The Jesuits, according to Trigger, "failed to provide any military support for the Hurons." Fearing defeat, the Hurons began deserting their settlements and taking refuge among other Amerindian nations on the Canadian Shield. The Iroquois attackers seized the last of the Huron villages, and Jean de Brebeuf and Gabriel Lalemant were put to death on 16 and 17 March 1649 at St Ignace. The remaining Jesuits and Hurons withdrew from Sainte-Marie to Christian Island and the next year, with 300 Hurons, to Quebec. In 1651 an equal number of Hurons arrived at Ile d'Orléans near Quebec. The devastation wrought by the Iroquois on the Hurons thus brought an end to the noble experiment of European inculturation with the Amerindian peoples.[40]

AMERINDIAN CHRISTIANITY

Joseph Chihwatenha (1602?–40) was a Huron of prominence who participated in the fur trade. Trade brought him into close contact with the French, and he was baptized at Ossossanë in 1637. His family were converted shortly afterwards, and initially they were the only Christians in their village. A few people died after baptism, but Joseph recognized that the deaths were coincidental and was not discouraged by them. An honest person, Joseph made a public profession of his faith, assisted the Jesuits in their missionary work in Huronia, defended the Jesuits in tribal councils, and exhorted the Hurons to become Christian. In a visit to Quebec in 1639, he was impressed by French charity and zeal, especially when he saw the convent and hospital. At Sainte-Marie among the Hurons he underwent an eight-day retreat to deepen his understanding of God and Christianity.[41] Bruce Trigger believes his conversion to Catholicism and his friendship with the French may have caused his early death at the hands either of Iroquois raiders or unhappy Hurons.[42] After his death an increasing number of Hurons became Christian, including his brother, Joseph Teondechoren.[43] Other important converts were Thomas Sondakoua, Mathurin Astiskoua, Martin Tehoachiakouan, Paul Atondo, and Jean-Baptiste Aotiokouandoron.[44]

Louis Taondechoren (1600?–77), a Huron chief, was baptized at Sainte-Marie among the Hurons in 1640 and gained the reputation of being an "excellent Christian." At the Huron colony in Quebec he led prayers and watched over the conduct of the Amerindians. He spoke eloquently of Christian truth. On a missionary visit to the Iroquois, he preached Christianity to them. An active Christian, he died at the advanced age of almost eighty years.[45] "The Huron resistance to the gospel, nevertheless, diminished gradually from 1640–1650 to the point that most members of the Huron League adhered to the faith during that period."[46]

Kateri Tekakwitha (1656–80) may be the most famous aboriginal Christian. She was born at Ossernenon near Auriesville, New York, of a

Christian Algonkian mother and non-Christian Mohawk father. During a difficult youth she met a number of visiting Jesuits whose piety and graciousness struck her forcefully. In 1676 she was baptized in her home village by a Jesuit missionary and on this count endured persecution. The following year fled to St Francis Xavier mission at Kahnawake. A friend of her mother's, Anastasie Tegonhatsiongo, acted as her spiritual guide at the mission, and she made rapid progress in the spiritual life. She took a vow of chastity in 1679 and hoped to found a community of Amerindian sisters. She liked to joke and laugh.[47] She had a profound side and a lighter side, and this combination of seriousness and humour attracted many to her circle. In poor health, she died in 1680 at the young age of twenty-four. Although her life was brief, her influence on succeeding generations was great and continues today. She has inspired films, an opera, a play, and a novel about her life, the Ontario Native Kateri Conference, the Companions of Kateri Tekakwitha, and, in the United States, the Tekakwitha Conference. She has been the subject of more than fifty biographies in ten different languages.[48] The Catholic church declared Kateri to be a person blessed by God and honoured her memory in 1980 with the declaration of beatification.

By means of zealous Amerindians, the Jesuits were able to form "cadres of devout, resilient disciples who could withstand the hatred of their unregenerate kinsmen." Prayer captains were selected to lead the prayers and hymns, instruct the neophytes, and carry out pastoral work among the baptized. Hurons spread the faith first among their own families[49] but later among their Iroquois captors.[50] Christian Hurons and Iroquois separated themselves from non-believers and established their own villages and cemeteries.[51] By 1670 there were at least ten Jesuits living among the five Iroquois nations who harboured both pro-Christian and anti-Christian factions.

The Iroquois Garakontie was baptized and became exemplary in his conduct by giving up polygamy, divination through dreams, and non-Christian ceremonies. Over four thousand Iroquois were baptized during these years, and owing to the persecution by non-Christians, Etienne Teganauokoa, Françoise Gonannhatenha, and Marguerite Garongouas shed their blood in defence of their faith. Because of the persecution, many of the Catholic Iroquois felt forced to leave their villages along the Mohawk River and settle in the villages along the St Lawrence River.[52] Indian converts not only left their homelands to embrace Catholicism, but after the fall of New France the vast majority remained in the Faith, at times with no priests to guide them. The Amerindians lived in a sacred universe and were moved by the vividness of Catholic liturgy, hymns, bells, and a flow of words.[53] The sacraments touched them at the major passages of life, birth, puberty, marriage, communion, reconciliation, and death and gave them personal understanding of the creed and the world around them. The witness of the priests and the nuns inspired Amerindians by their celibate spirituality and their freedom to devote themselves to the service of others. In particular the Jesuit receptivity to Amerindian languages and culture allowed them to find the Spirit of God working through native culture and search out a common ground for conversions.[54] A genuine cultural exchange occurred between the Jesuit missionaries learning the native culture and the Maritime and Laurentian Amerindians embracing Christianity.

It must be remembered, however, that at this time the majority of Amerindians did not embrace Christianity. Cornelius Jaenen divides the Amerindian reception of the missionaries into four negative and four positive responses. A revitalized native tradition hoped "to destroy the missionaries or to drive them out" because, it was believed, they were using spells to kill the Amerindians and bringing death and disaster to the people. A second negative response was to reject the missionaries for trying to impose European role models, which would diminish the women's role as educator of children and transmitter of their culture. A third response was passive "disinterest and indifference" to the missionaries and their preaching. The final negative response espoused a dual universe in which one part was for Europeans and their ways and the other was for Amerindians and their culture.[55]

Jaenen's analysis of the four positive responses of Amerindians to the Christian missionaries began with Amerindian "external assent" and positive disposition to the new religion, but with Amerindians always maintaining their own thoughts and convictions. A second response, "dimorphism," posited simultaneous assent by the Amerindians to both the new and the old religion and the embrace of each as needed. Jaenen believes dimorphism was in fact the choice of the greatest number of Amerindians. The third response, today often mistaken as inculturation, was syncretic fusion of the old belief system and the new. The last response was complete religious and cultural conversion to European Christianity and the renunciation of traditional beliefs. Converts often took up residence on Amerindian reserves and acted as a catechists.[56]

VILLE MARIE

In 1642 a third colony was established as a Christian evangelical centre and named Ville Marie (Montreal). Situated 258 kilometres of the St Lawrence River from Quebec at the confluence of the St Lawrence,

Ottawa, and Richelieu rivers, it was ideally located at the crossroads of the fur trade. For two decades, the community of Ville Marie was intentionally apostolic and aimed to establish a self-sustaining Euro-Canadian community.[57] The austere style of religious life it adopted could be described as classically heroic. The French settlers in a challenging environment patiently bore the hardships and shortages involved in establishing a frontier post in the Canadian wilderness as part of the carrying of the cross of Jesus Christ, and from this fragile base, missionaries risked their lives to transmit the Christian gospel to the countryside.

Zealous lay people settled Ville Marie with the singular purpose of evangelizing the Amerindians. The Council of Trent generated a spiritual renaissance among Catholics and inspired a baroque missionary spirit to share the faith. It animated mystical prayer, heroic sacrifice, and energetic action for the love of the gospel. The spirituality of St Francis de Sales, the charitable works of St Vincent de Paul, and the apostolic labours of the Sisters of Charity were well known and imitated by many. Lay Catholics were concerned that thirty years after the founding of New France few colonists had settled and almost nothing was done to evangelize the Amerindians. They demanded action from the Crown and the trading companies. Up to that point, Huguenot trading companies had dominated the colony, failed to attract Catholic settlers, and impeded the work of Catholic missionaries. And in truth during this early period, the citizens of New France were primarily interested in business and private profit.[58]

The youthful Henri de Lévis, duke of Ventadour, wanted to change this ethos and in 1625 purchased the viceroyalty of New France to redirect the commercial atmosphere of the colony. Ventadour was guided by Jesuit spiritual director Philibert Noyrot, the founder of the Seminary of St Sulpice, Jean-Jacques Olier, and the queen mother, Anne of Austria. To establish the religious nature of the colony, settlers were sent to New France, Jesuits made personnel available, and Huguenots were forbidden to take up residence. Ventadour sought more widespread backing for his enormous enterprise by organizing the Compagnie du Saint-Sacrement. A number of aristocrats were recruited to support these good works. The Compagnie became a great clearinghouse through which surplus wealth could be funnelled to charitable causes at home and abroad. The members founded hospitals for the poor and the sick, restored churches and monasteries, and visited the prisons.[59]

The members of the Compagnie de Saint-Sacrement were largely responsible for the founding of Ville Marie. One member, Jérôme le Royer de la Dauversière, sought to form a congregation of religious women in 1635 who would establish a hospital on the island of Montreal. Dauversière met Olier, who was concerned about preparing missionary priests for Montreal. They decided that Olier should ask Pierre Chevrier, Baron de Faucamp, to underwrite the founding of the Société de Notre Dame de Montréal for the conversion of the Amerindians. Other wealthy patrons were also recruited, and together they purchased land on the island of Montreal. They hired thirty-year-old Paul de Chomedey, Sieur de Maisonneuve, a devout Catholic and professional soldier, to lead the expedition. In 1642 at La Rochelle, Dauversière and Faucamp gathered a group committed to settling Montreal. At the last moment Jeanne Mance was added to the group. The original six members of the Société contributed 25,000 to 50,000 crowns, and membership expanded in the year to more than thirty-five "persons of the best rank in France, [both] clergy and laity." The Société recruited settlers and contributed over 200,000 livres yearly.[60] Six out of nine members of the Société de Notre Dame de Montréal were also members of the Compagnie de Saint-Sacrement. The wealth and secrecy of the Compagnie was soon to generate opposition from French bureaucrats and Gallican clergy.[61]

Maisonneuve and Jeanne Mance began to implant the Christian faith at Ville Marie.[62] Thirty-five year-old Jeanne Mance (1606–1673), from a middle-class family, had practised nursing in France. Discerning that God's will was calling her to go to Canada, she volunteered to join Maisonneuve's expedition. The group arrived at Montreal in 1642. With the financial help of a wealthy benefactor, Angélique de Bullion, Mance began caring for the sick in makeshift facilities. In 1645 she opened the hospital that became Montreal's Hôtel-Dieu when it was taken over in 1659 by the Hospitallers of St Joseph.[63] Undeterred by funding problems and Iroquois attacks, Mance, an excellent manager and fundraiser, never lost her courage and strengthened the resolve of Maisonneuve when Ville Marie seemed in danger of collapse.[64] The nursing care the Amerindians received in the Catholic hospitals became a powerful weapon for their eventual conversion.[65]

Thirty-two-year-old Marguerite Bourgeoys (1620–1700), from a comfortable family like Jean Mance, volunteered after prayer and reflection to accompany Maisonneuve to New France as a committed lay person.[66] Also like Mance, she defied the French tradition – which required that single women live within their family home or be protected by a cloister wall – to travel freely in France and Canada. She arrived at Quebec in 1653 and inspired the construction of Montreal's first stone church, Notre-Dame-de-Bon-Secours. She brought four more colleagues from France in 1658 to open a school in a former stable[67] and to accept the risks of the Montreal mission. Patricia Simpson describes the period:

Marguerite Bourgeoys, Engraving by Massard after an engraving by Charles-Louis Simonneau, Paris, 1722, supposedly based on a miniature sent from Montreal. Courtesy Archives CND, Montreal

"They were years of extreme danger and hardship, yet in her later life she was to bring them to mind again and again as representing better and happier days in her Congregation, when life had been shared with the ordinary people of Montreal with an intimacy and a generosity lost in a more secure and prosperous era."[68]

With the additional help of three nieces, she opened in 1676 a boarding-school and day-school for girls. The members of her community were called sisters, not nuns. They were distinguished from contemplative nuns, such as Ursulines, who remained within the convent cloister. In 1689 Marguerite Bourgeoys and her sisters accepted the responsibility bestowed on them by the general hospital in Quebec City to care for the aged. Even though she was under constant pressure from ecclesial authorities to accept the pre-packaged rule of a cloistered order or to merge with the Ursulines, Marguerite resisted firmly and kept her members engaged actively in the vicinity of Montreal ministering the corporal works of mercy – feeding the hungry, burying the dead, visiting prisoners, caring for the sick, and so on. Ahead of her time, she rejected the notion that the only safe place for women was in cloister, and she insisted that her members remain fully active in the life of the Church in the world.[69] In 1982 the Catholic church listed her in the canon of the saints.

During their first forty-two years in Canada, the sisters grew to more than forty in number and served the youth, infirm, and aged. Finally in 1698, the second bishop of Quebec, J.-B. de Saint-Vallier, allowed them to take the simple vows of religious. It took years of active ministry and much patience on the part of the sisters to convince the leaders of the Canadian church to accept the Congrégation de Notre-Dame (CND) as an active religious community, a valid expression of religious life outside the cloister walls. The CND as an active congregation was a new idea both in France and Canada.[70] The sisters of the CND endured through the difficult years of the founding of Montreal and went on to become trendsetters in education in Quebec, the rest of Canada, and the United States.

French support for the evangelical outpost of Montreal waned through the "terrible years" of the Iroquoian raids from 1657 to 1666.[71] It is conjectured that the heyday of the Montreal settlement ended in 1659 at the time of Dauversière's death. Finances were in disarray, and with the advent of Louis XIV in 1661, the Compagnie du Saint-Sacrement and Société de Notre Dame de Montréal were viewed with suspicion by a Gallican government for their ultramontane beliefs.

Four members of the Society of St Sulpice led by Gabriel de Queylus arrived at Montreal in 1657 to provide spiritual leadership, and when New France became a royal colony in 1663, the order was the obvious choice to take responsibility for the outpost's dishevelled finances and then to reignite the lofty goals of the colony. Along with a large debt, the Sulpicians accepted the seigneurial title in 1663 and at the same time opened a seminary to educate clergy.[72] The Jesuits opened a men's college in the 1680s.[73] With firm resolution, the Sulpicians endured the hardships of frontier war and supplied new personnel and additional funding to bolster Montreal's threatened existence.[74]

Although the Jesuits and the Ursulines earlier in the century had stopped trying to frenchify the Amerindians as a condition for baptism, de Queylus and the Sulpician Fathers, as a favour to the Crown, resurrected the defunct Recollet policy.[75] By 1665 the Sulpicians had edged Maisonneuve away from the direction of the Montreal settlement, while the Jesuits withdrew silently to Quebec. The takeover of Montreal by the Suplicians and royal officials ended the noble experiment of the lay-staffed and privately funded church mission. In spite of the Gallican theology still embedded in the loyalists of Quebec, the nascent ultramontane spirituality of the laity and Sulpicians in Montreal was to be the guiding force of the church in the nineteenth century.[76]

ACADIA

The Recollet Fathers landed with royal officials to establish the colony at Louisbourg in 1713 and soon became the mainstay of the spiritual ministry in Acadia. Five years later, the first secular priest from the diocese of Quebec arrived for a visit. While the diocesan clergy remained in the wings, it was the Recollets in season and out of season who ministered to the administrators, soldiers, sailors, and the outlying communities.[77] The Brothers of Charity of St John of God arrived in 1716 to accept responsibility for health care in the colony. Marguerite Roy of the Congrégation de Notre-Dame opened a school in 1727 to teach the girls. During the first half of the eighteenth century Louisbourg was the centre of French maritime commerce on the Atlantic coast. As a port it was the fourth largest in colonial America. Its fishery generated "enormous wealth," and it welcomed over a hundred ships yearly from Caribbean and Atlantic ports.[78] In its final years before the conquest, it numbered ten thousand French colonials.[79] Most Acadians lived there.

In their recent studies of Louisbourg, Terry Crowley and A.J.B. Johnston present pictures of the life of the colony.[80] The Recollets of Paris and Brittany supplied missionaries to Acadia but did not have the resources to cover the needs of Louisbourg and the outlying communities on Ile Saint Jean (Prince Edward Island) and Ile Royale (Cape Breton). Three Recollets were preoccupied with ministerial duties in Louisbourg and other friars circulated among the ports and fishing stations. The friars, not known for their theological acuity or disciplined behaviour, upset the traditionalist and rigorist bishop of Quebec, Saint-Vallier. In 1726 the bishop felt compelled to dismiss the Recollet pastor Benigne Benz for boisterous conduct and canonical irregularities. "The Quebec episcopacy," writes Crowley, "felt that the Louisbourg mission was in a pitiful state in 1731 and it was hoped that the coadjutor [bishop] might visit it to settle disputes and directly instruct Recollets."[81] A secular priest from Quebec was sent to replace the Recollet pastor.

The vicar-general of Quebec, resident in Paris, wrote to Bishop Pontbriand in 1753 to criticize the Recollet handling of the mission. At Quebec discussion centred on how the secular clergy would replace the Recollets. It became increasingly obvious that the severe climate, inadequate funding, poor food, and lack of fresh meat made Quebec a difficult mission for any clergy to endure. Pierre Maillard, a diocesan priest who was very successful with the Mi'kmaws, was appointed vicar-general for the colony. But he proved to be authoritarian and demonstrated few personal skills with which he might deal with the clergy and laity of the colony. An ecclesial compromise saved this untenable situation by retaining Maillard as vicar-general but easing the stress by appointing the

Recollet superior as a second vicar-general. The two vicars were to share responsibilities, and the second vicar directed the work of the Recollets. Yet clergy relations remained strained and under a cloud.[81]

The sisters of the Congrégation de Notre-Dame at Louisbourg gained high praise for educating the girls and young women of the mission, caring for the sick under difficult circumstances, and taking in orphans. The village was an administrative centre for officers, clerks, and merchants who were educated and who valued education for their children. As teachers the sisters offered reading, writing, needlework, and domestic skills and inculcated moral discipline in their students. During that period, a relatively large number of girls attended school for short periods of a few months or years. Progress in the education of women could be seen in the fact that fifty-eight percent of brides, more than the average, signed their own wedding certificates. Despite lack of funding from the Crown, the sisters managed to keep the cost flexible for students of different means and generally low for all. The CND school was the only school in Louisbourg to remain in continual service during the life of the colony.[83]

The Ministry of Marine wanted a hospital constructed at Louisbourg and asked the Brothers of Charity of Saint John of God to take responsibility for it. They had resources and numbers, and in the later year of 1789 355 brothers operated thirty-nine hospitals in France and the colonies, which meant about 5000 beds. The brothers began by operating an older hospital on the north shore of the harbour, and then, when the hundred-bed Hôpital du Roi was completed, they supervised the new facility. Funded by the Crown, the hospital was subject to royal inspectors. The treatment of the time was primitive: "bleedings, enemas, infusions, sweating, and starving."[84] The Crown continually complained that military personnel were not receiving adequate care and that the cost of patient care was excessive. Although other hospital congregations such as the Grey Nuns were considered to replace the Brothers, nothing happened in the end. Hospital care was generally regarded as adequate for the time.[85]

The Canadien traditions of the seventeenth century greatly influenced the eighteenth-century Acadians. Like the Canadiens, the Acadians were parsimonious with their church, enjoyed dancing, drinking, and gambling, worked on Sunday, performed their own baptisms and marriages, and sought a more secularized society. They were interested in enjoying the prosperity of this busy port and were naturally more sympathetic to Gallican rights than ultramontane spirituality. Although the church was an important institution among them, it was less influential in the eighteenth century that it had been in the seventeenth.[86]

Bishop François de Laval, First Bishop of Quebec (1658–87). Archives Nationales du Québec (ANQ P266, S4, P48)

CHURCH CONSOLIDATION

Following the mission period of New France, the second stage of the evangelization process was the consolidation of the mission into traditional church structures. Forty years after the arrival of the missionaries, Bishop François de Laval landed at Quebec in 1659 to lead the diocesan clergy and give direction to the formation of parishes, schools, and hospitals. Rome appointed the well-born Jesuit-educated thirty-five-year-old Laval to be the first bishop for the mission of Canada. Rome, Versailles, and the Jesuits of New France chose him before other possible candidates. Before his arrival, the Jesuits directed the religious activities of the colony. "The male clergy in Quebec," according to Terry Crowley, "consisted of only twenty-one priests belonging to religious orders ... and six lay brothers and secular priests."[87] Laval, the scion of one of the oldest noble families in France, traced his lineage back to Clovis. He had freely chosen to serve the church, whether in France or in a foreign mission, and, ignoring the courtly life, devoted his time to the sick and the needy. He was devout, intelligent, politically neutral, and able to command. From the seminary he built in Quebec, he directed the diocesan clergy as a mobile team to minister to the Canadiens and ceded the Amerindian missions to the Jesuits.[88]

Laval was ordained in Paris as the apostolic vicar of New France on the feast of the Immaculate Conception 1658. The power of bishop was bestowed upon him but the title was denied. This artifice was employed to appease the archbishop of Rouen, who claimed Canada as his jurisdiction and sought the appointment of the Sulpician Gabriel de Queylus. The appointment placed Laval and the embryonic Canadian church under the guidance of Rome and not Rouen. Laval was given the title in 1674 when he was appointed the first bishop of Quebec and remained the ordinary of the diocese until his resignation in 1687. Supported by Propaganda Fide, the French Crown, and the Jesuits, Bishop Laval established his residence at Quebec in 1659 and from there directed the consolidation of the Canadian church. He formed the inhabitants into a closely knit community centred on the seminary that he founded in 1663 and gave the church the appearance of being well supervised. Under pressure from Crown officials, he encouraged six Huron students to enter the junior seminary along with seven Canadians, but this second experiment with frenchification only lasted a few years.[89]

Bishop Laval arrived poor, lived poor, and, in his last twenty-one years after retirement, gave away the possessions he had accumulated to the poor.[90] To New France, he personified Catholic baroque spirituality, which included a mystical and arduous commitment in the face of a challenging environment and the strong defence of bishops' rights in the face of an absolutist royal government.[91]

One of Laval's first actions was to take the place of the Jesuit superior at the colonial council. When the royal decree of 1663 created the Sovereign Council of Quebec, Bishop Laval was named a member along with the governor, intendant, and five other colonists. The Sovereign Council met periodically to implement the political, economic, social, and religious policies of New France.[92] The council dramatized the radical change in New France from a colony operated by trading companies and private philanthropists to a royal colony directed by the king's ministers. At council meetings, the bishop of Quebec sided traditionally with church causes and the spiritual well-being of the faithful, the governor sided with the political interests of the Crown, and the intendant with the economic well-being of the inhabitants. Thus, the stage was set for a monumental struggle among these titans who were yoked together in the leadership of New France.[93]

The sale of alcohol to the Amerindians became a contentious issue between the bishop and the governor. The bishop demanded that the sale of intoxicating spirits be stopped because of its proven ill effect on the Amerindians. The Christians in the village of Sault Saint-Louis successfully resisted the attraction of French brandy, but other Amerindians displayed "a seemingly unquenchable thirst" and became destructive under its influence. The devastating effects of alcohol put a severe strain on families and marriages and prevented the evangelization of many

Amerindians. The Jesuits discovered that the best defence was to move the Amerindian villages away from the French communities and whiskey traders.[94] The governor and the intendant, taking the side of commerce, argued that the brandy trade was necessary if the French were to coax the Amerindians into exchanging their furs at Quebec and not Albany.[95] A compromise solution, whereby the flow of alcohol would be restricted until Amerindians learned to drink moderately and avoid the social disruption of their communities, never materialized.[96]

The bishop was concerned about the indulgent ways of the French inhabitants and criticized them for their delight in luxury and indecent dress, drama, cards, horseracing, and dancing, and their propensity for wasting time during the winter. He expected them to live virtuous lives in and out of season. Laval wished to impose the regular devotions of the French church upon the inhabitants, but he did not always admit to himself that he was pastor of a mission church with few regular parishes and few diocesan clergy.[97] Instead of having resident pastors in thinly populated and sprawling parishes, he instituted the seminary system, sending clergy out to minister to parishioners living on strip farms along the rivers. Most priests lived at the seminary in Quebec and at regular intervals travelled to visit their parishioners and administer the sacraments. The habitant paid tithes to the seminary, which took care of the needs of the clergy, and the remainder was shared with the parishes according to their needs.[98] At the seminary Laval emulated the early church in which believers "kept all things in common." At the same time, this centralized structure provided the sacraments on a regular basis to a lightly settled and extremely large territory.[99] Laval supervised the parishes and the innovative seminary system for twenty-nine years in the diocese of Quebec until 1687. The Sulpician secular clergy later found it useful to install a similar structure in Montreal.

Laval's successor, Jean-Baptiste de la Croix de Chevrières de Saint-Vallier broke up the seminary system. Like Laval, Saint-Vallier came from a distinguished and noble family and was a former student of Jesuit and Sulpician schools. At an early age he was appointed court chaplain to King Louis XIV in 1676. Five years later at the age of twenty-seven, he was ordained to the priesthood. Avoiding the high fashion of the royal court, he wore the soutane, visited hospitals and prisons, and lived an ascetic life. In 1687 at the age of thirty-three, he was appointed bishop of Quebec against the protests of Laval and the Canadien clergy. In the following year he arrived in Canada to oversee the ministry of one hundred zealous priests and the same number of women religious. Energetic, headstrong, and demanding, Saint-Vallier was determined to take command of his immense diocese, which stretched from the Atlantic to the Gulf of Mexico. His ambition to do great things, however, promised not tranquillity for the church in New France but turmoil.

The new bishop soon quarrelled with the diocesan clergy and the community of the Séminaire des Missions Étrangères. In the early years of his ministry Saint-Vallier alienated the governor of New France, the governor of Montreal, the cathedral chapter, the Recollets, the Jesuits, Congregation of Notre Dame, and Hôtel-Dieu. Louis xiv, who kept informed about the running of the church in the New World, ordered Saint-Vallier back to France explain his conduct in person and twice urged him to resign his see. Saint-Vallier twice refused to resign. Repenting the disruption he had caused, Saint-Vallier begged to return to New France, promising prudence in future decisions. Once in Canada, to appease the seminary priests of the Missions Étrangères in Quebec, he drove the Jesuits from the missions that he had previously assigned to them in the Ohio country and Louisiana and handed them to the seminary priests. He also gave the seminary personnel parish work in Acadia.[100]

This young energetic bishop perceived Laval's seminary system as having outlived its usefulness. He saw the need to create new parishes and parish boundaries, and to regularize the practices of the diocese of Quebec. He reorganized the diocese of Quebec along the lines of the dioceses of Enlightenment France. He passed new legislation to clarify the discipline of resident pastors now living in parishes among the people. During his tenure, which lasted until 1727, he doubled the number of residential parishes from forty in 1685 to more than eighty by 1721.[101]

Reinforcing the bishop's leadership and teaching were the popular devotions of New France, where habitants and Amerindians alike manifested a strong belief in miracles, shrines, pilgrimages, novenas, relics, and patron saints. Favourite sites for miraculous happenings were l'Hôpital-General de Québec, Saint-Anne-du-Petit-Cap, Notre-Dame-des-Anges, Notre-Dame-de-Foy, and Notre-Dame-de-Lorette. The laity were enthusiastic initiators of devotions, but the clergy were ever vigilant to see that they respected church norms. This meant that the faithful were properly instructed so that God was seen as the author of favours, the saints as the mediators, and the holy objects as the means of the devotion. The many devotions and reported miracles of New France were carefully framed within the traditional piety of the Catholic church.[102]

To defend his upsetting conduct before Louis xiv, Saint-Vallier took ship for France in 1700 and argued his case at Versailles. While in France from 1702 to 1703, he published *Ritual* and *Catechism*. Jesuit theologians deemed both volumes morally rigorous and Jansenist in tone. In 1704, while sailing back to New France when France and England were at war, Bishop Saint-Vallier received an unexpected respite from the many quarrels he was returning to: the Royal Navy diverted his ship to England and held him under house arrest.[103] Five years later he was returned to France, where Louis XIV kept him for another four years. During that time, Laval, "le monsieur ancient," filled in for the absent bishop until his death in 1708.

In 1713, a chastened Saint-Vallier finally sailed for New France. During his thirteen-year absence from the diocese, he had undergone a sea change and was transformed. He had been aged by his long confinement in England and was now in his sixtieth year. Moving out of the episcopal palace he had earlier built, he took a simple room in the Hôpital-Général, fasted rigorously, tended the sick, and buried the dead. He reconciled with the Jesuits, Sulpicians, and Recollets, as well as with the nuns and sisters he had alienated along with the rest. Yet controversy with the seminary priests and the governor remained to be resolved. Saint-Vallier spent his last years living austerely in isolation.[104] But during his forty-year rule as the second bishop of Quebec, Saint-Vallier regularized the diocese by giving it a definitive organization and adapted it more closely to the pattern in France.[105]

For almost seventy years, the first two bishops of Quebec proved themselves worthy protagonists in the struggle for the leadership of New France. They defended the rights of the Church against the power of the monarch with his belief in the divine right of Kings. The three bishops who followed Saint-Vallier opened a power vacuum as Louis-François de Mornay, who held the post from 1727 to 1733, never sailed for New France. Pierre-Herman Dosquet (1733–1739) took up residence for only two years at his seigneury near Trois-Rivières and directed the church from there rather than from Quebec. The youthful François de Lauberivière spent only twelve days in the colony before his tragic death in 1740 from the plague. This ecclesial interregnum, along with the prolonged absences of Laval and Saint-Vallier, permitted the power of the Crown in the eighteenth century to gain the upper hand in this symbiotic struggle.[106]

One bright spot during this period was the founding of the Grey Nuns. By 1747 the widowed Marguerite d'Youville had overcome her personal and financial woes and was able to accept responsibility for the Montreal hospice which had fallen into disarray. She also founded a religious congregation to care for the sick of the hospice. In 1753 the Crown recognized the new Canadian congregation as the Soeurs de la Charité de l'Hôpital-Géneral de Montréal. The sisters afterwards became popularly known as the Grey Nuns.[107]

The bishops who followed the Conquest of 1763 were cut from much the same cloth as Laval and Saint-Vallier and did much to restore the prestige of the office. They were men of command with long terms in office. After the English victory on the Plains of Abraham, Henri-Marie Dubreil de Pontbriand was the transitional bishop, holding the position from 1741 to 1760. He initiated the policy of cooperation with and submission to the English Crown. Bishop Jean-Olivier Briand (1766–1784) continued this policy of submissive cooperation during the occupation but discovered with the absence of the French Crown new freedom under the English. In the long term, the soft-spoken ecclesial diplomacy which was learned during the military occupation worked successfully for the church. Apart from the interregnum mentioned above, Laval, Saint-Vallier, and Pontbriand transformed the missionary beachhead of New France during their lengthy terms of office into a well-established church that fostered the solid and organic growth of Quebec.

CONCLUSION

At the beginning of the seventeenth century, the first missionaries sailed with the fishing and trading companies to Canada to minister to the fishers and to spread the gospel to the Amerindians. The Recollets and the Jesuits established missionary stations to seek out the Amerindians and share the Christian gospel with them. Amerindians were in command of the environment and learned to adjust to the influx of French culture, using it for their own purposes. They accepted the missionary offerings in small enough portions to protect their own cultural identity. The Jesuits and the Ursulines soon learned not to try to frenchify the Amerindians and instead offered them Christian initiation and baptism in their own culture. By the middle decades of the seventeenth century, the Amerindians formed a significant community of practising Catholics in New France. "The best missionaries, therefore," according to James Axtell, "were at once the best students of Indian culture and the best teachers of the Christian alternative."[107]

Fifty years after the arrival of French Catholicism, and during the one hundred years that followed, the time seemed right to establish the traditional structures of the Church – diocese, parish, school, and hospital. The early Canadian bishops organized the colonial faithful into a number of geographically extensive parishes that were guided by mobile clergy from the seminary. The clergy defended the rights of the church against the encroachments of the state. They established a mystical and austere spirituality that became the norm of French Catholicism. The laity accepted the church/state symbiosis but did not always embrace its idealistic spirituality. Laval's successor, Bishop Saint-Vallier, abandoned the seminary-centred community, reorganized the diocese of Quebec as a unit in the contemporary enlightenment church, and gave it a definitive structure similar to a French diocese. During the British occupation, the Canadian church probed British tolerance with subtlety, tact, and diplomacy. Catholics survived subjection to the Protestant Crown and strengthened their bonds with Rome. Through the last part of the seventeenth and the first half of the eighteenth centuries, the Canadian Catholic church devised its institutional structures, giving the church a permanent stake in Canadian society.

By 1754 these structures revealed an established diocese of 55,000 Canadien inhabitants and missions consisting of at least an equal number of Amerindians. In fact the church in New France in the eighteenth century relied upon the French Crown for funding (forty per cent),[109] on clergy for shaping the diocesan structure, and on the religious orders for missionaries. The seigneur's land, private donations, royal funding, and the inhabitants' tithe provided for the needs of the churches dotting the banks of the St Lawrence and its tributaries. The parishes were supervised by the *fabrique* of elected officials with a militia captain in charge. By the eighteenth century the zeal of the inhabitants was wearing thin, and, with the shortage of clergy, creeping secularism, and the pursuit of worldly pleasures, their religious fervour cooled.[110] As the period of New France came to a close by the late 1750s, the fragile Canadian Catholic church continued to look to Paris for financial support and to Rome for spiritual direction.

2 The Church after the Conquest

Resplendent in their red uniforms, the British forces rejoiced in victory and took up their places in the streets of Quebec and Montreal to the beat of the drums and the squeal of the pipes. With heads bowed the blue-and-white forces of France boarded naval vessels and sailed silently back to France. But the French-speaking inhabitants remained stolidly behind to face the British conqueror and, as French Catholics, felt helpless before the overwhelming power of English Protestants. Since the Reformation, the penal laws in England condemned Catholics and Catholic practices and terrorized them by hanging, drawing, and quartering their leaders.[1] As the British ensign was unfurled over Quebec, Bishop Henri-Marie Dubreil de Pontbriand prepared his clergy and faithful for submission to the powerful occupation force in their midst and then, at the end of the first week of June 1760, gave up the ghost.[2] The seven vicars general (at Quebec, Montreal, Trois-Rivières, Acadia, Illinois, Louisiana and Mississippi, and Paris), 138 priests, 118 parishes, and seventy thousand parishioners grieved the bishop's demise. During this interlude the church was leaderless. Doom and gloom were all that could be predicted for the future of the Canadiens who remained behind. Only five years previously the same British army had rounded up the hapless Acadians and in a most brutal fashion shipped them south to the English colonies along the Atlantic coast and to England and France. The English colonies to the south were unprepared for Acadian refugees and made little effort to welcome or care for them. The English colonial governments, moreover, took little comfort in the "new inhabitants of the Crown" since they were French

Catholics in a Protestant colony. Their presence was marginal as the English penal laws barred them from holding public office, serving as military officers, attending university, or being useful subjects.[3]

MILITARY OCCUPATION

At the very moment when the British forces were on the verge of complete triumph in North America, British control of the English colonies to the south was challenged by the prosperous American colonists. The British commander in Quebec, General James Murray, sensing the danger from the thirteen colonies, prized the Canadiens as guerrilla fighters and planned to use them as a counterbalance. He knew the American colonists feared the lightninglike attacks of the Canadiens on their isolated communities, especially in the deep snows of midwinter. In the event of hostilities with the English colonies, Murray needed a secure bastion in the North and chose to cultivate the Canadiens by allowing them the free practice of the "Romish religion" as far as the "Laws of Great Britain permit." These laws of course "prohibit[ed] absolutely all Popish Hierarchy ... and ... only admit[ed] of a Toleration of the Exercise of that Religion."[4]

For strategic reasons Murray decided that the inhabitants in Canada were not to suffer the woeful fate of the Acadians. The Canadiens were left in their homes, allowed to practise their religion, and guaranteed access to fur trapping territories stretching to the far west. Sensing a softening in the Draconian occupation, Bishop Pontbriand demanded, in a circular letter of 1759, that his clergy and their faithful greet the English as "courteously as possible" and give full obedience to their new ruler, the victorious king of England.[5] Despite these initial concessions, the long-term goal of the English government remained firm: the transformation of French Catholics into English Protestants, "that the said Inhabitants may by Degrees be induced to embrace the Protestant Religion, and their Children be brought up in the Principles of it."[6] The English government was genuinely concerned that, in granting the exercise of Catholicism, it might be seen as a benevolent conqueror.[7] The government also wished to protect the habitants from the ideology of American republicanism.[8]

At the untimely death of Bishop Pontbriand, the Quebec cathedral chapter acted to replace him, believing that London would prefer a locally elected bishop to one appointed by Rome. They elected a Sulpician priest of obvious talent, Étienne Montgolfier. General Murray quickly rejected the election because he wished for an episcopal replacement who would be less prominent, less ambitious, and less French than Montgolfier.[9] The cathedral chapter then chose the self-effacing Jean-Olivier Briand (1766–84), secretary of twenty years to the former bishop and the first vicar general of Quebec. Pontbriand had previously recommended him to Murray and assured Murray that Briand's views coincided with his own and that Briand would seek reconciliation with the government.[10]

Governor Murray judged Briand to be sufficiently pliable to work with his new masters. He sent him in 1766 to England with a letter of recommendation to pass administrative inspection before taking office. Once the approval was given, the British government, unwilling to involve itself in Briand's ordination, encouraged him to seek the laying on of hands elsewhere. As an excuse to go to France, Briand visited his family in the North and was consecrated by three French bishops in a private ceremony at Suresnes. The British government then recognized him as the "superintendant of the Romish Church."[11] His choice of pastors was severely restricted and the rights and privileges of an established religion were not granted. Briand had merely received approval to supervise "the free exercise of the Romish Religion."[12]

THE NEW BISHOP

The new bishop's amiability and "immense warmth and generosity" had allowed him to pass all the social and political requirements of the English. He was also "a stubborn and vigorous fighter," but always without malice. When embroiled in controversy he exerted a boundless and spontaneous affection laced with humour, which he extended to his enemies.[13] The government believed that by allowing Briand to be ordained as bishop he would be more independent of Rome and more open to British directives. Briand shrewdly accepted government intervention about non-essentials, such as when prayers at Mass were requested for the youthful King George III. Gladly he received a government stipend of two hundred pounds to relieve his financial embarrassment,[14] but he was firm in retaining the church's autonomy in the fundamentals of the faith. In the process he gained more freedom for the Catholic bishops than Anglican bishops enjoyed. He chuckled at his success in conciliating British officials, "for here I am with four bishops [bishop, coadjutor, and two vicars general] in Canada, where it was not possible, they said, to have any."[15]

The British welcomed the new bishop back to Quebec with warmth, and the Canadiens with great joy. Briand had the knack of attracting the friendship of British governors. He thus handled all the business of church and state directly with the governor and avoided confrontations caused by misunderstanding. He took the interest of the government to heart and professed his loyalty and that of his clergy. He accepted Murray's initial interference in the life of the church, hoping to interest him in church activities and thus avoid the governor feeling Catholic pressure to put the church under government tutelage. He altered parish appointments to please Murray and consulted him when it was appropriate to do so. Thus Murray became accustomed to making decisions in religious matters only after first consulting Briand. The bishop at the same time educated the government to respect their separate jurisdictions so that they would not meddle in each other's affairs.[16]

On returning to Quebec, Briand was faced with various problems: a shortage of clergy, fewer revenues, devastated churches, and parish disputes. The number of priests had dropped from 180 in 1758 to 138 during Briand's early years. His cathedral in Quebec was run as a parish, and the trustees (*la fabrique*) claimed control over its use. Twenty-two percent of Quebec churches were in ruins thanks to the Conquest. Poor parishes were no longer being subsidized by the French government, and communities of religious women now encountered debts in their apostolates without the advantage of their pre-war revenues. Without private or royal funds, the new Canadien church was severely impoverished. Uppity parishioners challenged their pastors over church tithes, the site of churches and rectories, and the direction of the ministry. It took the new bishop's considerable personal resources to gain administrative control of the parish trustees and to win the good will of the habitants. To renew parish life, he charmed, cautioned, and excommunicated dissidents but then quickly sought reconciliation.[17]

One celebrated incident of internecine conflict revolved around the question who controlled the ruins of the cathedral parish of Notre Dame in Quebec. The pastor, Jean-Félix Récher, and his churchwardens proposed to rebuild the church, which had been destroyed during the bombardment, on the condition that they would control its use as their parish church. Briand, on the other hand, wanted to use the church as the cathedral of the diocese, a custom established by his predecessors. After restoration began in 1767 and Father Récher died, the seminary and Briand renounced their rightful claim to ownership of the church as a gesture of good will. As work on Notre Dame neared completion in 1771, the churchwardens continued staunchly to defend their claim to the property. The bishop let it be known that as long as his rights were not acknowledged he would not preside over ceremonies in the new church and would continue to celebrate mass in the seminary chapel. The lieutenant governor, Hector Theophilus Cramahé, mediated a compromise whereby the restored structure was designated as both cathedral and parish church. In 1774, to universal cheers, Bishop Briand entered his cathedral for the first time to celebrate restored harmony and to enjoy the peaceful victory.[18]

To regain the allegiance of his clergy, who had survived a long war under difficult circumstances, Briand once more adroitly employed his personal skills. He exhorted his priests to gentleness with their parishioners and moderation in dealing with them. While acknowledging the existence of licentiousness in Quebec society, he urged preachers to take a positive tack, to speak more "of virtue than of the ugliness of vice." He asked the clergy not to accuse their parishioners of sinfulness but to let them discover their transgressions for themselves. Dealing with the reconstruction of churches in the postwar period, he believed that church members should not be forced to donate to construction but that donations should be considered a free "religious act."[19] The Canadien clergy, as the only élite to survive the Conquest intact, as Michel Brunet points out, undertook responsibility for the social, political, and economic welfare of the Canadien people. The bonds thus formed between the Canadiens and the church became "*un véritable pacte d'alliance.*"[20]

OPPRESSION OF THE CHURCH

The British government allowed the Church to exist as it had promised at the peace treaty but cropped back the church services to the least number necessary for survival. Five congregations of religious women were permitted to teach, nurse, and take in novices. The English government wanted the religious women to maintain the lower schools, hospitals, and homes for the aged and to provide basic social services for the colony. At the same time, the government forbade the Jesuits and Recollets to take novices into their communities and thus ensured the demise in Canada of the two orders.[21] Those teachers had operated schools that had shaped the future leaders of Quebec, and their missionaries influenced the native people in major mission ventures. The good works of the orders were to be allowed to die by attrition.[22] In 1800 the last living Canadian Jesuit, Fr Jean-Joseph Casot, gave away the remaining possessions of the Canadian Jesuits to the bishop, the seminary, the Hôtel-Dieu, and the needy. Casot died shortly after this disposition, and soon after the government stepped in and seized the Jesuit estates.[23] The last member of the Recollets disappeared from Canada thirteen years later. By contrast, the Sulpician seminaries in Montreal and Quebec survived to educate parish clergy under the guiding hand of the governor.[24] They were forced, however, to cut their ties with the Society of Saint-Sulpice in France.[25] The military governors reasoned that temperate measures and the moderate imposition of English law would gain the favour of the inhabitants and anticipated that they would then accept English customs and become members of the Church of England. Quebec clergy who married were to be given parishes,[26] but not one Canadien pastor accepted the invitation. The church in Quebec became the principal vehicle for the transmission of French Canadian identity, language, and way of life.[27]

In 1764 the British government hoped to begin the integration of Canadiens into the administration of the colony and introduced for Canadien officials the oath of allegiance and the Declaration of Abjuration.[28] This meant that before taking public office, Canadien officials had to become Protestant by renouncing the basic Catholic beliefs of papal primacy, transubstantiation, the cult of the saints, and the right of Catholic heirs to the English Crown. The inhabitants, did not submit to British pressure any more than their pastors. The British governors, James Murray, Jeffrey Amherst, and Guy Carleton, realizing that government without Canadien representatives was impossible, overlooked this requirement and kept the colony cooperative in the face of the disturbances erupting to the south. After 1769 five Canadiens were sought to fill seats on the fifteen-person council.[29]

EPISCOPAL SUCCESSION

Descended from prominent families on both his father and his mother's side and with the strong recommendation of Governor Guy Carleton, the first Canadian-born bishop, Louis-Philippe Mariauchau d'Esgly (1710–88),[30] was ordained in 1772 as the coadjutor bishop of Quebec with right of succession. His episcopal ordination was the first to take place in North America.[31] The English had reasoned that it was important to cultivate the good will of the Canadiens by permitting them a *de facto* bishop so that "some person here [in Quebec] exercising Episcopal Functions, and the Allowance of a Coadjutor, will prevent the Bishop's being obliged to cross the Seas for Consecration and holding Personal Communication with those, who may not possess the most friendly Dispositions for the British Interests."[32] A contented parish priest, five years older than Briand, partially deaf, and not a seeker of high office, d'Esgly became the coadjutor bishop. Carleton had preferred him to Bishop Briand's choice of the perpetual contender, Sulpician superior and vicar general for Montreal Étienne Montgolfier.[33] Through this period the British government, by denying the existence of Catholic bishops, believed it had successfully subjected the "superintendant of the Romish Church" to the colonial administration.

From his parish rectory at Saint-Pierre on Île d'Orléans, d'Esgly visited the parishes on the island and urged inhabitants to live an honest and good life. When d'Esgly's health showed signs of weakening, Bishop Briand quickly resigned in 1784 to perpetuate Catholic episcopal succession under British rule. D'Esgly was quickly installed as the second bishop under British rule and remained at the parish of Saint-Pierre. Preferring his pastoral role, he deliberately avoided moving into the quarters vacated for him at the Séminaire de Québec. In the administration of the diocese, he delegated jurisdiction to his vicars general. He solicited Irish priests for Canada and appointed James Jones in Halifax as the superior of the mission for Nova Scotia.[34] After four uneventful years as bishop, d'Esgly died in 1788 and was succeeded by his coadjutor, Jean-François Hubert, who was bishop from 1788 to 1797. Briand died six years after d'Esgly in 1794, the episcopal succession assured.[35] Following the devastation of the seven Years' War between England and France, at a difficult juncture for the Catholic church in Canada, Bishop Briand through his personal warmth, diplomatic skills, and humble poverty re-established the church and became recognized as its "second founder."[36]

CANADIANIZATION OF THE CATHOLIC CHURCH

Civil rule for the colony was long overdue. The British Parliament passed the Quebec Act in 1774 to end military rule and move towards peacetime government. The civil and religious rights of Canadiens were reinstated, the "Laws of Canada" re-established, borders restored, and the church allowed tithing.[37] The Oath of Loyalty, which replaced the Oath of Renunciation, demanded only that the Canadiens pledge allegiance to the Crown and acknowledge the right of the Protestant bishop of Quebec. Still the inhabitants declined to take the simplified oath, and Governor Carleton, anxious to get on with peacetime government, accepted their decision to resist and included them in the new civilian government.

Secret instructions accompanying the Quebec Act made it clear that Catholicism was to be tolerated only temporarily. The original goal of the British government for Canada remained the establishment of English culture and the Church of England. The continual pressure of restrictions, it was hoped, would lead the Canadiens into the Anglican fold. Correspondence by Canadien clergy with Rome was forbidden, pastors were to be approved for a limited time only, and the government was to supervise the seminaries. Carleton sensibly overlooked these secret instructions because he understood the importance of winning the cooperation of the Canadiens for the good order of Quebec and the control of North America. He was not disappointed. In May 1775, after the first battles broke out between Massachusetts colonists and the British troops at Lexington and Concord, Bishop Briand published a *mandement* asking Canadiens to defend the English king and country.[38] Having suffered through several imperial wars, Canadiens looked upon the struggle in the thirteen colonies as an English war and kept their heads low and their loyalties to themselves.[39]

Gilles Chaussé asserts that Briand at this point lost the political leadership of the Canadien people by his ostentatious loyalty to England and his repeated condemnations of the American democracy.[40] Briand insisted that Canadiens who fought for the Americans were to be excommunicated and not to be admitted back into communion unless they repented and made public restitution.[41] He condemned those who sympathized with the Americans in a letter of 1776: "What an abyss of sin you have plunged into ... How many sins have you committed before God! ... [You] have fallen into schism and separated ... [yourselves] from the Church."[42] Briand placed the church firmly on the side of the British imperial government and alienated many Canadiens who sympathized with the French Enlightenment ideals emerging within the American democracy.

Briand and his episcopal successors were obsessed with the hierarchical spirituality of the divine right of kings, which saw legitimate order and government coming from God through the church to the king, and from the king to the people. God's blessings flowed from this order and ruled out rebellion of any kind. Rebellion against legitimate authority employed violence against the social community and thus was an abomination and work of the devil. The king ruled by God's blessing, and defying a king was defying God, and such actions were sinful. In the view of the bishops, Canadiens could not take up arms against their legitimate monarch in favour of an unholy and untried system of government. Any attempt to do so would defy the sacred order of God, the Scriptures, and the church and was gravely sinful.[43]

The Acadians returning to the Maritime provinces remained firmly attached to the Catholic faith despite lack of clergy. Missionary Bailly de Messein, who arrived in Acadia in 1768, was warmly received but returned to Quebec in 1772 because of formidable Protestant opposition. He was replaced the same year by James Macdonald on Prince Edward Island and Joseph-Mathurin Bourg at Tracadièche (Carleton in the Gaspé). Thomas-François Leroux was appointed the first resident pastor to Memramcook in 1781. Putting up with the mistrust from the British population, the Catholic missionaries baptized children, married adults, and found their services very much sought after.

The British government during this time sent Huguenot pastors to proselytize and anglicize the Acadians.[44]

The bishops of Quebec made occasional visits to the Acadians to sustain their faith in these difficult times. Émigré missionary Father Jean-Mandé Sigogne arrived from France at the turn of the nineteenth century and ministered to the Acadians in Nova Scotia, New Brunswick, and Prince Edward Island. For the Acadians, the creation of the dioceses of Halifax and Charlottetown with Irish and Scottish bishops at the end of the 1820s, hailed by the Irish and the Scots, meant they were further cut off from the French-speaking diocese of Quebec. Both they and the bishops of Quebec sought to rectify their abandonment to the hands of Irish and the Scottish bishops.[45]

Feeling equally abandoned were the French, Scots, and Métis at the forks of the Red and the Assiniboine rivers in the Canadian West. Following the conflict between fur traders of the Hudson's Bay Company and the North West Company, Governor Miles Macdonell called for Catholic missionaries to bring peace to the settlement. In 1818 Bishop Plessis sent Father Joseph-Norbert Provencher, along with Father Sévère Dumoulin and seminarian Guillaume Edge, to establish a mission at the Red River. Lord Selkirk provided a grant of twenty square miles on the east side of the river for this enterprise. Provencher was named auxiliary bishop for the Canadian North West in 1820. He followed Bishop Plessis's directions about cultivating the good offices of the Hudson's Bay Company, which responded in 1825 by granting the mission fifty pounds yearly and increasing the annual grant. He and his missionaries opened boys' and girls' schools, regularized marriages, and dealt with alcohol abuse. Through these years, thirteen diocesan missionaries assisted the work of the bishop until the arrival of the Oblate Fathers in 1845.[46]

The close British supervision of Canadien religion had the ironic effect of intensifying the indigenization of the Catholic church in Quebec. The French government and other private sources in France no longer provided financing for the church. Canadien Catholics had to recruit and train clergy and supply funding. The secular and religious clergy by 1764 were fifty-six percent Canadian-born and on average forty-six years of age.[47] Natural increase maintained the clergy for a time, and by 1774 there were 25 new parishes and about the same number of new priests. Over the next fifteen years, numbers decreased and sixty-five parishes were left without a priest.[48] After 1790 the British government permitted more than fifty émigrés priests to come from France. These products of the Gallican church took leadership roles as professors, chaplains, and parish priests, and they inspired the Canadian clergy by their commitment and visionary zeal. They believed strongly in the divine right of kings, union of church and state, and a strong national church. In dramatic and exuberant sermons, the new arrivals reinforced a determined Catholicism in Canada.[49] Despite its subjection to a conquering power, the Canadien church between 1775 and 1817 established its own identity, discovered its own resources, and forged firmer bonds with Rome.[50]

Some Canadiens totally rejected the clergy's cooperation with the British government. Impressed by the principles of democracy disseminated by the American and French revolutions, the merchants and professionals denounced the backward-looking pact forged by the cross with the Crown. They saw the church as the hand of the past cooperating with the British government in the suppression of genuine Canadien aspirations. One critic from the Canadian nobility was Michel Chartier de Lotbinière who had already been deprived of his land and public office by the British government. He joined the dissident minority and criticized the church for its "servility and opportunism in appropriating a political role that was not properly theirs."[51] A minority worked for popular elections to select a government that would be responsible to the people.

The native people and Métis asked the government for Catholic priests and remained committed to the practice of Catholicism. They successfully resisted Protestant attempts to proselytize and extended Catholicism to native people on the prairies and along the Pacific coast. Bishop Hubert in 1794 spoke highly of native Catholics: "They are intelligent, obedient, respectful towards their priests, and good Catholics. They pray often, eagerly listen to the word, and display tender and loving devotion." Some years later, Bishop Plessis in 1816 affirmed this view: "Here we generally find that their morals are more pure than the Europeans.'" In native settlements the missionaries did not have enough personnel to regulate the routine of the villages. The native people thus regulated their own devotions and practice. The missionaries printed songbooks and prayer books in the native languages, which they had mastered. Alcohol remained a problem that was best resolved by curtailing the supply. The "benign paternalism" of the missionaries envisioned the settlement of native people on farms and their gradual acculturation to the Euro-Canadian way of life.[52]

THE CANADIAN CONSTITUTION OF 1791

Between 1759 and 1791 the Canadien population doubled from 70,000 to 140,000.[53] At the same time, the British government wished to accommodate the thousands of Protestant Loyalists pouring in from the former American colonies. The English immigrants did not wish to live in French Catholic communities, so the British Parliament passed the Canadian Constitution of 1791, which provided for separate political and cultural environments for Catholics and Protestants. The Canadian constitution allowed for two different geographical provinces, political governments, and religions for Upper Canada and Lower Canada. The Loyalists demanding an English style of government laid the groundwork in Upper Canada for their own legal and parliamentary traditions. The Canadiens were granted Lower Canada within which they forged their own distinct religious and political identity.[54] In Upper Canada an English government consolidated a province based on Protestant politics, while in Lower Canada a French government consolidated a province based on Catholic politics.

Bishop Hubert enjoyed the many privileges that the Canadiens received as they formed a majority government. He had apprehensions, however, about the enthusiasm of some Canadiens for the American Declaration of Independence and the civil liberties it proclaimed, and he was anxious about the direction the elected legislature of Lower Canada might follow. He was appalled to discover that the Canadian elites were reading Voltaire, Montesquieu, Diderot, and Rousseau, whose works were easily available in public libraries. Ignoring the devotion of church confraternities, discussion groups were founded to explore the thinking of the philosophes and the ideals of the French Revolution. The Quebec and Montreal *Gazettes* extolled the benefits of liberalism, democracy, and independence. The Montreal newspaper described the Church as oppressive and the seigneurs as opposed to the formation of a legislative assembly. Its editorials called for a social revolution in Lower Canada. However, the war between the British and French empires that began in 1793 put an end to any further publication of pro-French communiqués in Canada.[55]

Many Canadiens continued to sympathize with the French Revolution and hoped for a French victory in the field. Citizen Genet exhorted Canadiens to free themselves from British slavery. The rumour that French troops were hovering off the east coast aboard the ships of a French naval squadron added to the hope of deliverance. As Briand had spoken earlier, Bishop Hubert in 1793 and Bishop Denaut in 1796 reminded Canadiens that the tie with France was irrevocably broken and exhorted their loyalty for Britain.[56]

Protestant proselytising left the majority of Canadiens unmoved and unreceptive to either secular or religious overtures. This did not mean, however, that their regular practice was above reproach. Bishop Hubert in 1787 enumerated to Propaganda Fide the Canadien weaknesses in the practice of their faith. Mixed marriages led to indifference, he wrote, immoral books were destructive of faith and encouraged licentiousness, some business deals involved dishonesty, usury was common, and the payment of church tithes was avoided. He added that the Sunday respite became for some an opportunity for laziness, dancing, and feasting. In addition, the legislative assembly became a rallying place for middle-class professionals who were pursuing democratic ideals. While the clergy preserved their "sobriety, dignity, and selflessness," the bishop continued, many Canadiens sought only freedom. Few considered serving the community by entering the priesthood or religious life. From this period to 1840 the liberal bourgeois gathered together in the Parti canadien, alienating themselves from clergy and church. The church leaders, as Gilles Chaussé has clearly established, experienced a fifty-year "period of hibernation" from the faithful from 1791 until 1840.[57]

Certainly it was true that after the conclusion of the Napoleonic Wars in 1815, a lay élite in the legislative assembly challenged the clerical leadership of the province. The Parti canadien, with *Le Canadien* as its mouthpiece, demanded an elected legislature, responsible government, and careful scrutiny of wasteful government expenses. Bishop Plessis was shocked at these proposals and feared that the newspaper would "destroy every principle of subordination and set the province ablaze." Many of his clergy came from ordinary families, however, and were sympathetic towards the struggle of their compatriots against a British oligarchy. Some clergy read *Le Canadien* and supported the Parti canadien directly.[58]

The Canadien split was healed temporarily by a British parliamentary act of 1822 that purposed to unify Upper and Lower Canada. The Canadien liberal bourgeoisie and the higher clergy united against such an abomination. Bishop Jean-Jacques Lartigue protested: "Besides the harm in the civil domain that this proposed bill would cause us as Canadiens, it would oppress us even more as Catholics by a clause [clause 25] that establishes the spiritual supremacy of the king over our Church, and that would have the appointment of all parish priests in Canada depend on the favour or whim of a Protestant governor."[59] Both the clergy and the Canadien bourgeois joined together in a petition asking that the proposal be withdrawn. This was one of the few times that the church left its position of political neutrality to choose political sides on the issue.

GALLICAN SPIRITUALITY EXTENDED

Joseph-Octave Plessis was a bishop with vision for the reorganization and expansion of the Canadian church. In 1806 the Montreal-born priest was appointed the fifth "Superintendant of the Romish

Church," a position he retained until 1825. At the Séminaire de Québec he had excelled in his studies and was a strong leader, and during those impressionable years he was introduced to Gallican pastoral and ascetical theology. He was confirmed in the practice of this theological tradition when he was chosen to be the secretary of Bishop Briand. He served Briand in this post, along with his episcopal successors, d'Esgly, Hubert, and Denaut. Jean-François Hubert, bishop from 1788 to 1797, recognized Plessis's capacity for work and appointed him the parish priest of Notre Dame in Quebec. There he became involved in the working-class suburbs of Saint-Roch and Saint-Jean and had to deal with grinding poverty and rampant illiteracy. His natural vigour and bright disposition served him well as he worked 16-hour days, building schools, organizing food support, and forming spiritual confraternities.[60]

As secretary, Plessis became a spokesperson for Bishop Hubert. On the bishop's behalf, Plessis cultivated working relationships with influential colonial leaders such as the Anglican bishop Jacob Mountain, Lieutenant-governor Robert Shore Milnes, Solicitor General Jonathan Sewell, and Attorney General Herman Witsius Ryland. Milnes and his government were determined to re-establish control over the Catholic church.[61] Plessis disarmed them with his, outspoken expressions of loyalty to the British political system during the turmoil of the French Revolution and gained the government's favour. Because of his high profile he was taken as the power behind Hubert. When Hubert resigned in favour of his coadjutor, Pierre Denaut (1797–1806), Plessis was then named to be coadjutor bishop with the right of succession. Bishop Denaut preferred to reside at Longueuil and leave his coadjutor in Quebec City to govern, just as d'Esgly in the 1780s had favoured living at Île d'Orléans and allowed his vicars general to govern in Quebec City. The difficulty of communication with Longueuil, forced Plessis, in Quebec, to take charge and make significant decisions on his own.[62]

His influence as the coadjutor bishop grew. On his periodic tours he got to know the clergy and gained extensive experience in governing the diocese. He had a way about him, and he "regaled clerical gatherings with expertly told stories" drawn from his wide reading and from an endless stream of humorous incidents he experienced between 1819 and 1820 during diocesan visits and his voyage to Europe. He welcomed chats with his clergy, who could depend upon his answers to their letters and his support when they needed him. Other events also enhanced his leadership at the turn of the nineteenth century. Plessis succeeded Denaut as "superintendant" in 1806. The fact that Pope Pius VII was held in French captivity from 1809 to 1814 and could not advise Plessis on the governance of the Canadian church permitted him to make necessary decisions on his own. Lastly, the suppression of religious orders left him the undisputed spiritual leader of the church in Canada. Self-assured and decisive, Plessis ruled the Canadian church with quick wit and steadfast authority.[63]

His leadership of the Catholic community, however, was not uncontested. The rising professional classes, which included many members of the nationalist Parti canadien, wished to share in the romantic ideals of the French Enlightenment. They inspired democratic hopes and embraced secularizing tendencies that anticipated the establishment of civil liberties in Canadien society. One particularly contentions issue was the problem of usury. The legal fraternity, for example, was alienated by the church's outdated interdiction against money lending for profit. The prohibition was enforced through drastic penalties such as excommunication, and an austere and rigorous Gallican spirituality hung oppressively over the province. Yet Plessis continued to serve as a bridge between the Canadien liberal bourgeoisie, who advocated resistence to English hegemony, and the government, which demanded absolute loyalty. Though some craved greater freedom, many Canadiens voted with their feet, betraying a taste for the traditional practices of Catholic piety. The popularity of religious books demonstrated the popularity of Catholic devotions. Canadien newspapers continued to be respectful of the idea of the Church's assuming a major role in Quebec society. The new auxiliary bishop of Montreal, Jean-Jacques Lartigue, assured Plessis in 1821 that "the people of the middle class are the most submissive and the most attached to religion and to their ecclesiastical superiors."[64] Disputes that arose among the faithful dealt more with practical matters than theological issues. Squabbles arose, for instance over the distribution of pews, the location of churches, new parishes, and the extent of pastoral powers.[65] Resolving such practical problems did not demand theological reflection.

Plessis gave moral leadership to his clergy and insisted, as he had done in the parish of Notre Dame in Quebec, that they be solicitous of the needs of their parishioners. In agricultural and urban crises, he believed the pastors should experience the parishioners' desperate needs and employ the skills of parish confraternities to work out solutions. Only when the pastors could no longer cope with extraordinary problems would they seek government help. For Plessis, the Church had to demonstrate solidarity with those in need and have the resources to meet those needs.[66]

Anglican and Methodist proselytizing prompted an immediate response from Plessis and his clergy. The principal response was the pursuit of primary education for Catholics. Plessis sought legislation to provide funding to the parish *fabrique,* but legislation failed to materialize. Offered a seat on the secular board of trustees of the Protestant-front Royal Institution for the Advancement of Learning, Plessis declined membership. Rather, he determined that every Catholic parish should have a primary school and exhorted his pastors to provide them. The younger clergy, whom he helped to educate during their seminary years, recognized the urgency of his plan and built schools. Many clergy, nevertheless, were lackadaisical and preferred to decorate their churches.[67] The Anglicans, encountering little success in their proselytizing, discontinued the services of the Huguenot pastors and suspended missionary work among Canadiens. The Methodists, along with other evangelical groups from New England, continued to send evangelists.[68]

Plessis remained positive about the political environment for the Canadiens as he wrote to a pastor, "We are … in a country … where there is more faith, and where the ecclesiastical offices are exposed to fewer difficulties" than anywhere in the world. Enjoying good relations with governors of Lower Canada, Sir George Prevost and Sir John Coape Sherbrooke, Plessis initiated a petition in 1812 for the official recognition of his office and that of his coadjutor. He could point out the orderliness of Canadien society and its obedience to the Crown. While no immediate response was forthcoming to this petition, the bishop's salary was increased to one thousand pounds sterling the following year.[69] It was also noteworthy that during the War of 1812 Canadiens demonstrated their loyalty to Britain at Chateauguay and elsewhere. Lord Bathurst encouraged Sherbrooke to name Plessis to the legislative council. This appointment for the first time gave personal recognition to Plessis as the bishop of Quebec, but it did not extend the honour to his successors.[70] Nevertheless, the significance of the event, according to James Lambert, was "the triumph of a decade of diplomacy by Plessis."[71] After sixty years the government had legally recognized the Church of the Lower Canadian majority.

Since his accession to the episcopate in 1806, Bishop Plessis had made a number of attempts to subdivide the enormous geography of his diocese. To govern a church of five hundred thousand Catholics, Plessis needed to expand the ecclesial structure. He proposed a plan to London and Rome in 1817 whereby five bishops would be appointed to Nova Scotia (which had 10,000 Catholics), Montreal (200,000), Upper Canada (15,000), Prince Edward Island, New Brunswick, and Cape Breton (a total of 15,000), and the Red River country (3,000). For Quebec (200,000) he proposed an archbishop and ecclesial province to unite the five suffragan sees. In the meantime, a missionary vicar apostolic under the Holy See had already been created for Nova Scotia. Propaganda Fide in Rome understood the importance of Plessis's plan, adopted it, and appointed Plessis archbishop with associate bishops serving in Upper Canada and Prince Edward Island. When Plessis brought this elaborate scheme to London, Lord Bathurst balked and scaled it back, replacing the bishops with auxiliaries to the bishop of Quebec. Rome fell into line with London's limited version of the plan and named auxiliary bishops of Quebec rather than bishops of their own sees: Mcdonell at Kingston, MacEachern at Charlottetown, Lartigue at Montreal, and Provencher in the North west. Halifax had already received its own vicar apostolic appointed by Rome.[72]

Plessis, while on the same visit to London, was joined by Lartigue. They wished to address the pending seizure of the Sulpician estates by the colonial government. In Canada, the Civil Secretary, Herman Ryland, remarked cynically on Plessis and Lartigue's visit to the British government: "The Sulpicians were aware of the advantage they will derive from the presence of this Personage [Plessis] in England, where he will possess the means of making a splendid appearance, and they flatter themselves, with reason, that his subtlety and Talents, and sanctimonious Professions of Loyalty which have already contributed so much to their advantage on this side … cannot fail on the other."[73] Ryland was right that Plessis would be successful in delaying the seizure of the Sulpician estates. Of interest here is that this was the first time in fifty-three years, since Briand went to England and France in 1766, that the bishop of Quebec had been allowed to travel in Europe.[76]

On his return visit to Rome to gain approval for the London strictures and to secure Roman diplomatic backing in Britain for the archepiscopal status of Quebec, Plessis was impressed by the city's monumental buildings and beautiful art. However, his firmly rooted Gallican spirituality remained untouched by the romance of the ultramontane spirituality arising in Rome. He held steadfastly to the Gallican beliefs of his seminary years, which had been reinforced by the émigré clergy in Canada during Hubert's episcopacy. Gallican spirituality animated a strong church buttressed by a powerful Crown imposing peace, order, and good government. Plessis believed firmly in the hierarchical political structure for both church and state. Forthright with Vatican functionaries, he was struck by the competence and directness of the secretary of state, Cardinal Ercole Consalvi. Quebec's Roman agent and rector of the English College, Robert Gradwell, impressed by Plessis's round of diplomatic encounters, asserted that "there was not in Rome one bishop who stands higher in general estimation."[75]

Plessis returned via Paris, London, and New York to a grand welcome in Quebec in August 1820. He carried with him papal bulls appointing Lartigue auxiliary bishop in Montreal and Provencher auxiliary bishop in the North-West. At the legislative council in Quebec, Plessis steered a neutral course between the parti Canadien and the colonial government. He voted with the parti Canadien against approval of the outrageous entrenchment of expenses on the civil list. His long-term political instincts, however, remained with the government. He considered the views of both Louis-Joseph Papineau in favour of a democratic assembly and the colonial government's retention of autocratic control of the budget too extreme.

This stocky, assertive, energetic, and charming bishop of Quebec, because of his deteriorating health, moved his quarters in 1810 from the seminary to the Hôpital Général. From 1816 on, Plessis endured daily discomfort, fevers, rheumatism, and phlebitis in his legs, spending increasing amounts of time in the hospital. His succession was assured in 1825 when the Canadian government approved Pierre-Flavien Turgeon as his coadjutor. Soon afterward, his health deteriorated, and while engaged in conversation with his physician, he peacefully slipped away. Greatly loved and respected, he was buried solemnly with all the pomp and circumstance of an Anglican bishop.[76] His many sorties against the formidable forces of the colonial government and Canadien liberalism won him considerable success. He built a number of schools, animated a slight increase in vocations, and re-established the see of Quebec with four auxiliary bishops and one vicar apostolic.[77]

LARTIGUE AND ULTRAMONTANE SPIRITUALITY

Plessis's brilliant appointment of the Sulpician Lartigue to be auxiliary bishop in Montreal edged the religious culture away from Sulpician dominance. As auxiliary bishop Lartigue embarked upon construction of the cathedral church of Saint-Jacques and drew away leadership of the Montreal Catholic community from the Sulpician pastors of Notre Dame.[78] He also built schools and expanded hospitals and orphanages. Provincial legislation in 1824 provided funds for parish schools and further encouraged rural pastors to provide schools for the children of their parishioners. By 1830 the number of schools had doubled. A similar expansion occurred in the hospital system under Lartigue's direction. In addition to the traditional religious congregations of the Ursulines, the hospitallers, and the Grey Nuns, new institutes of committed religious were initiated by the Sisters of Providence and Sisters of Mercy. Committed lay women formed the Dames-de-charité to collect funds for the poor, visit the homes of the needy, run soup kitchens, and establish orphanages.[79]

Since 1820 Lartigue had been greatly inspired by the ultramontane spirit of Joseph de Maistre and Abbé Félicité de Lamennais. Like them, he believed in papal primacy and papal infallibility. Like them, he believed that the Canadian church should look to Rome for leadership and abandon close collaboration with royal governments. Papal primacy defined the right of the See of Peter to jurisdiction over the other episcopal sees of the world. Papal infallibility meant that when the pope was speaking *ex cathedra* on faith and morals, his statements – with or without the college of bishops – were infallible. In his loyalty to the Holy See, Lartigue sought to transform almost two centuries of Gallican spirituality in Canada. At the Collège de Saint-Hyacinthe, Mennaisianne theology and spirituality were taught to the seminarians, and the seeds of a new Canadian spirituality were planted.[80]

The gallican Plessis saw the Catholic church and the British state necessarily yoked together for the good of society, but at the same time he defended the pre-eminence of episcopal leadership in the Canadian community. For the clergy and faithful, he promoted an ardent and austere spirituality and loyalty to both church and state. The London government in 1844, acknowledging after several decades of delay the continued loyalty of the Canadiens, recognized the see of Quebec as a metropolitan province.[81] This full acceptance of the church was due mainly to the persistent pressure of Bishops Plessis, Lartigue, and Bourget. With the death of Plessis in Quebec and the inspired leadership of Lartigue and Bourget in Montreal, the torch of the Canadian Catholic church for the next half century passed from the heights of Quebec to the crossroads of Montreal.

CONCLUSION

The threat of revolution from the South impelled the British government to make concessions to the Canadiens, who thus escaped the fate of the Acadians.[82] The Quebecois were thus allowed to farm their own lands, speak their own language, follow their own laws, and practise their own religion. When Bishop Pontbriand died in 1760, his successors were at best tolerated by the English government as leaders of an outlawed religion. The government offered inducements for Catholic clergy to defect to the Church of England and marked male religious communities for extinction. The return of peace in Quebec brought Canadien leaders into the colonial government, and with this, Catholic church services were restored at the minimal level. The Gallican clergy accepted the political changes, believed they should serve the government in power, and encouraged loyalty to the English Crown. In their zeal for order and legitimacy, the clergy opened up a gulf in Canadien society between the liberal bourgeois and the Canadien loyalists that was not resolved until the 1840s.

After the formation of Lower and Upper Canada in 1791, diocesan structures were fortified and the number of parishes, schools, and hospitals were increased. We have seen how in the first decades of the nineteenth century the bishop of Quebec, through adroit diplomacy, exacted auxiliary bishops from the Protestant Crown to accommodate the rapid growth of Catholicism. Yet new forces soon shattered the subdued victory of Gallican spirituality. The ethnic forces of the Scots and Irish eventually overturned the Canadien monopoly of the Catholic church, and the love affair with ultramontane spirituality replaced the lean austerity of the past two centuries. The impact of the Scots and the Irish on the Canadian church will be considered in the next chapter. The shift of the dynamic centre of the church from Quebec to Montreal and from Gallican spirituality to ultramontane spirituality will be discussed in chapter 4.

3 Maritime and Central Canadian Catholicism

The Quebec church, which survived the rigours of seventeenth-century missions, the oppression of the Conquest, and the threat of the British-American war, continued by its muscular Gallican spirituality to stir the seat of deeply rooted Canadien Catholicism. A new challenge from the East now threatened Gallic control of the Catholic church in British North America. Landing on the beaches to the east of Lower Canada were the Scots and the Irish. The Irish arrived in the middle of the eighteenth century as summer workers for the Newfoundland fishery and, after some decades, began to settle there permanently. Some of the Irish workers moved westward to Nova Scotia and New Brunswick where they became involved almost immediately in a struggle for basic rights against the remnants of the Penal Laws that were still in effect in British North America. During the last decades of the eighteenth century and the first decades of the nineteenth Scottish Highlanders reached the shores of eastern Nova Scotia, Cape Breton, and Prince Edward Island and landed in Upper Canada. Gaelic speaking, they were both Protestant and Catholic. The Scottish Catholics sought their own clergy to administer the sacraments and to open schools.[1] Scottish and Irish Catholics fought to achieve the civil and religious rights they had hoped to find in their new homeland. The Roman Congregation de Propaganda Fide, puzzled by the ethnic mix emerging among Canadian Catholics, drew up a strategic plan for the pastoral care of the new Canadians.

ROMAN PLAN FOR NORTH AMERICA

The arrival of Scottish and Irish Catholics in Canada from 1720 to
1850 ended the exclusive franchise of the Canadien clergy in the Canadian church. If the British Conquest had failed to weaken French
control over church and society, the influx of Scottish and Irish Catholics heralded the beginning of the cultural devolution of the Catholic
church that was to continue throughout the nineteenth century. The
time was quickly arriving for the Canadian Catholic church to devise a
plan from within to weave together the native, Canadien, Scottish, and
Irish branches that were rooted in Canadian soil during the century.[2]

Through the Quebec vicar general dwelling in Paris, Propaganda
Fide in Rome guided the Canadien higher clergy and the direction
to be taken by the Canadian Catholic church. There was a steady
stream of communication from Quebec through Paris to Rome, and
back again through Paris to Quebec until the middle 1780s. With the
outbreak of revolution, correspondence was redirected from Upper
Canada, the Maritime colonies, and Quebec through London and
Dublin to Rome. The French-speaking church, coping with the British occupation, focused its efforts on survival. Its strategy in dealing
with the occupying forces was threefold: cooperation, compromise,
and non-confrontation. What this meant in fact was avoiding quarrels
with the colonial office, adjusting to the demands of British rule, securing the free exercise of the Catholic religion, supporting the
Crown, and recruiting suitable clergy. The Quebec Act of 1774 initiated toleration of Catholics in Canada and its influence had extended eastward to Nova Scotia and Newfoundland by 1783–84.[3]

Paris and Rome, observing the immigration of Scots and Irish Catholics to the Maritime colonies, mistakenly sought French clergy to minister to the new settlers. Luca Codignola comments that the cardinals
of Propaganda Fide were slow to appreciate the cultural differences in
Canada among the Scots, the Irish, and the French. They were slow to
respond to the cry of the Scots for Gaelic-speaking priests and the Irish
for English-speaking priests. The Irish congregation of Halifax, feeling
spiritually neglected, invited an Irish Capuchin, Father James Jones, to
Nova Scotia in 1784,[4] and the same year the Irish congregation of
St John's invited James O'Donel to Newfoundland.[5] In 1790 Father
Angus Bernard MacEachern was welcomed to Prince Edward Island by
Scottish immigrants,[6] and in 1804 Father Alexander Mcdonell accompanied Scottish settlers to Upper Canada.[7] The Scottish and Irish settlers revealed their pioneering initiative by importing their own clergy
to supplement the pastoral care provided by the bishop of Quebec.

Catholic lay people in the Maritime provinces, as in New France in the early years of the seventeenth century, showed their enterprise by attracting professional clergy to become a spiritual leaven for their community.

Canadian communications with Rome were abruptly interrupted by the destruction of the French church during the Revolution. Canadian ecclesial correspondence was no longer routed through Paris. Canadian communications to Propaganda Fide collapsed entirely during the Napoleonic era and then passed through Ireland, Scotland, Britain, or through the papal port of Leghorn. The Scottish and Irish settlers preferred to correspond directly with Rome because they felt that Quebec was not adequately concerned with their outlying communities and perhaps even delayed the appointment of the bishops they requested. Fathers Edmund Burke of Halifax, Angus B. MacEachern of Prince Edward Island, and Alexander Macdonell of Upper Canada circumvented the jurisdiction of the bishop of Quebec and sought direct help from Rome to establish episcopal sees in their communities. Yet Bishop Plessis of Quebec, despite suspicions to the contrary, did not block their plans but desired what the Irish and Scottish leaders desired, the subdivision of the huge diocese of Quebec and the appointment of Irish and Scottish bishops over its more peripheral regions.[8]

The Roman bureaucracy, recovering from the ravages of the French Revolution and the Napoleonic Wars, was slow to re-establish links with North America. When it did, Propaganda Fide developed a strategy to exercise spiritual control over the vast regions of North America via Quebec and Baltimore. The plan called for the orderly development of the North American church under the guidance of the two sees. In fact, however, the awakening Roman sensitivities to the individual needs of the local churches rendered the plan inoperable. Rome listened to the petitions of the communities in Nova Scotia and Upper Canada for the appointment of bishops who were culturally sympathetic to them. Thus, in 1817 the Irish priest Edmund Burke, after much personal lobbying, was appointed by Rome the vicar apostolic of Halifax. This meant that his jurisdiction was rooted in the Holy See rather than in Quebec. In 1819 the bishop of Quebec named two Scottish priests, Angus B. MacEachern and Alexander Macdonell, as auxiliary bishops, MacEachern for Prince Edward Island and New Brunswick and Alexander Mcdonell for Upper Canada. In 1820 the Canadien priests Jean-Jacques Lartigue and Joseph-Norbert Provencher were named auxiliary bishops for Montreal and the Canadian Northwest.

This attention to the particular linguistic and cultural needs of Catholics in the Atlantic region, Lower and Upper Canada, and the western prairies produced a fragmented ecclesial pattern that contrasted with the episcopal supervision planned by the see of Quebec. In the United States, John Carroll was appointed archbishop of Baltimore in 1809, and other bishops were then named to the suffragan sees of Boston, New York, Philadelphia, and Bardstown, Kentucky.[9] These appointments resulted for a time in further ecclesial devolution, and they ended the Roman plan for the orderly development of the North American churches under the metropolitan sees of French-speaking Quebec and English-speaking Baltimore.

The first six auxiliaries of Canada soon became bishops of their dioceses. And from these six a second generation of dioceses was created: Toronto (1841), Saint John (1842), Arichat (1844), Victoria (1846), Ottawa (1847), Saint Hyacinthe (1852), Grand Falls, Hamilton and London (1856), and the archdiocese of Halifax (1852).[10] Sympathetic to the requests of ethnic communities, Propaganda Fide demonstrated its flexibility by adjusting to the needs of the various groups.[11] The Canadian church in this early stage of its development was genuinely multicultural. The Scots and the Irish were the harbingers of other ethnic groups that would challenge the Gallic-Celtic symbiosis at the end of the nineteenth century.

THE IRISH IN NEWFOUNDLAND, 1720–1850

Waterford, Wexford, and other ports of southeastern Ireland supplied many workers to the Newfoundland fisheries from 1720 to 1750. These workers brought their priests to Newfoundland, but the Penal Laws of the mid-1750s made them feel the fear persecution. As Raymond J. Lahey observes, "For allowing Mass to be said, Catholics in the Conception Bay area had their houses and stores burned, and for their participation faced fines and even deportation; the priest was hunted by the authorities, although without success."[12] Repression by British authorities, however, proved to be irregular and of short duration, and Irish immigrants, undeterred by adverse reports, sailed to Newfoundland in increasing numbers. By the British relief acts of 1783, Catholics were permitted to practise law, lease land, invite resident priests, and construct chapels and schools.[13]

The following year the Holy See responded to the petitions of Newfoundlanders and designated the island a mission territory under the jurisdiction of Propaganda Fide. An ecclesial superior was appointed as pastoral guide to Newfoundland Catholics with responsibility for disciplining "vagabond" clergy and ending associated scandals.[14] An Irish Franciscan, James Louis O'Donel, OFM, was appointed the first apostolic prefect in 1784. He had been a popular preacher in Waterford and because of his fluent Irish was able to bond with the Newfoundlanders.[15]

His staunch conservatism and loyalty to the Crown won him the confidence of the colonial government. Governor John Campbell conceded discretionary power to O'Donel and his associate priests, which included the right to perform marriages.[16] By 1790 the three priests working with O'Donel made converts, expanded the number of the faithful, and built chapels at Placentia, Harbour Grace, and Ferryland.[17] In 1796 O'Donel's ecclesial power was affirmed when he was ordained the vicar apostolic of Newfoundland (1795–1806). Not only was he the ecclesial superior of Newfoundland but he was also an auxiliary bishop directly under Rome.[18]

The collaboration between the English Crown and the Catholic Church proved useful to both institutions. With Jansensist asceticism, O'Donel welcomed the support of the colonial government to provide backup on ecclesial problems, including the handling of troublesome clergy.[19] For instance, a troublesome priest, Father Patrick Power, resided for a number of years at Ferryland. But facing disapproval from the two jurisdictions of cross and Crown, Power finally caved in to the concerted pressure and in 1792 returned willingly to Ireland. Much preferring the peace and order implanted by the British government to the dangers of republican liberties, O'Donel preferred the sight of Irish troops marching to Catholic chapel under Protestant officers to the sight of French prisoners arriving at church in their revolutionary uniforms. The insignia of the French Revolution on their uniform hats spoke to him of "infidelity and rebellion" and annoyed him greatly.[20]

In April 1800 the United Irishmen at St John's organized cells among the townsfolk and members of the Newfoundland Regiment of Fencibles to overthrow the colonial government. The revolutionary literature of Tom Paine and other radicals was in the hands of the new immigrants. When O'Donel discovered the brooding conspiracy, he alerted the commanding officer of the Fencibles, John Skerrett. The conspirators were quickly rounded up and some were executed. The bishop condemned the "revolutionary tendencies of the plotters" because they were deceiving the people in using religion for their own political goals.[21] Although many of the Irish obviously would not have agreed with him, he nevertheless calmed the troubled waters of Newfoundland and won appreciation of the government and the merchants.[22] To demonstrate further the loyalty of the Catholics, O'Donel asked the parishes to pray for King George III and the royal family and requested that the clergy exhort their parishioners to be obedient to the laws of England. Acknowledging this service, the Crown paid the vicar apostolic an annual stipend of fifty pounds beginning in 1814.[23] The colonial government further accommodated the Catholics by allowing the clergy the right to bury the dead (1811) and to marry the engaged (1824). The Irish Benevolent Society, which welcomed members of different denominations, was founded in 1806 to provide assistance to needy individuals and families. In Newfoundland the collaboration between church and state stabilized the civil and religious affairs of the colony.

O'Donel's four successors were also Franciscans with a strong tinge of Jansenism. Patrick Lambert, OSF (1807–16), was appointed coadjutor with right of succession in 1806, and at the beginning of the next year, succeeded O'Donel who retired to Ireland. The general prosperity of Newfoundland at the end of the Napoleonic Wars between 1811 and 1816 provoked the rapid increase of immigration from Ireland. The Irish influx doubled the population of Newfoundland, and conversions to Catholicism continued by "the thousands along the coast." This boom time collapsed, and several years in a row, house fires in St John's burned down the village, causing great hardship for the needy and unemployed. Disorders arose. The government, however, felt confident it could rely on the loyalty of the bishop and his five pastors to keep order among the faithful. It thus granted the bishop a stipend of seventy-five pounds, made ministry concessions, and in 1811 conceded to Catholics the use of their own cemeteries.[24]

Thomas Scallan, OSF (1816–30), became bishop at a time when wartime prosperity had ended, and many of his parishioners were out of work. Scallan fed ten people daily at his table, and under such stressful poverty he and the clergy struggled to assist the poor and preserve law and order. Many of the Irish made their way in desperation to Halifax, Charlottetown, Saint John, Quebec, and New England in pursuit of work.[25] As his predecessors had done, Scallan maintained a close relationship with Bishop Plessis in Quebec, and each named the other his vicar general. By their own cooperative agreement and also with papal approval in 1820, Plessis handed over jurisdiction of Labrador and Anticosti Island to Scallan so that ecclesial boundaries would respect political boundaries. The most outstanding of Scallan's achievements was the harmony he established with Protestants in Newfoundland. He enjoyed good relations with Protestant clergy and attended services at the Anglican church on various occasions. The conversion of numerous English settlers to Catholicism continued uninterrupted under the third bishop. In 1830 Anglican and Methodist clergy joined Catholic priests and seven thousand mourners to grieve at Scallan's funeral.[26]

The cooperation between Catholic church and British Crown did not always hold. For instance, the annual stipend that was given to the first two vicars apostolic and that was still paid to the Anglican archdeacon was discontinued under the third Catholic bishop. Scallan applied in 1819 and 1823 to regain the stipend, but the government in London, despite the warm recommendation of the governor, chose to ignore his requests. The schools of some religious denominations were supported by the government, but a subsidy was refused to the orphan asylum, which was effectively a school for poor Catholics. Scallan, forbidding Catholics to attend Bible society schools, sought funding for Catholic schools. In 1825 the Benevolent Irish Society offered to contribute one hundred pounds sterling for the school and appealed to the governor to do the same. The Colonial Office would not approve this added expense. St Patrick's Free School at Harbour Grace suffered a similar rejection.[27] Events such as these caused friction in the normally smooth relationship between cross and crown.

When Bishop Plessis was appointed to the executive council of Quebec in 1817, the question was raised in Newfoundland why a Catholic could not sit on the council. Following this precedent, Governor Thomas Cochrane attempted in 1825 to appoint an interim council that included three Catholics: the military commander of Newfoundland, Lieutenant-Colonel Thomas Burke, a merchant, Patrick Morris, and the third vicar apostolic, Thomas Scallan. After due consideration, the Colonial Office ruled that in the absence of oaths of allegiance and supremacy, such appointments could not be presented to the king for approval, and he rejected them accordingly. Four years later in 1829, the British Parliament passed the celebrated Catholic Emancipation. Newfoundland Catholics marked this event with a day of public thanksgiving, including Mass, parades, and bands.[28]

British North American governments abolished the remaining vestiges of the penal laws and extended the rights of British subjects to Catholics. Unfortunately, the government in Newfoundland made the excuse that a legislative assembly did not exist to implement Catholic emancipation, and nothing could be done until the Colonial Office took action. Relief from civil disabilities was to come a few years later. In 1832 the governor's commission provided the legal frame for a Newfoundland House of Assembly. An election followed, and the newly elected representatives proceeded to implement Catholic emancipation. The election of the first House of Assembly was a giant step forward, though it was attended by the emergence of religious sectarianism in Newfoundland. In future this meant that many voters in Newfoundland strictly followed their religious interests during elections: "denominational ties and church influence henceforth became matters of great importance."[29]

After a century of civil disabilities, it became clear to Catholic voters, who were a majority, that Catholic political solidarity was absolutely essential. Uppermost in Catholic minds was the blatant discrimination they faced: "government support of the Newfoundland [Protestant] School Society, the financial subsidies to the Church of England, the marriage question, the exclusion of Roman Catholics from the council, and Catholic emancipation." Such grievances begged to be resolved by the new legislature and provoked further division between Protestant and Catholic denominations. These issues forced Newfoundlanders to implement denominational proportionalism to guarantee each religious group its due.[30] Funds, benefits, and jobs in Newfoundland were henceforth proportional to the voting strength of each religious group.

SCOTTISH SETTLERS, 1770–1840

Catholics in Scotland were impoverished by a series of wars with England from 1560 to 1745, by the anti-Catholic penal laws from 1559 to 1829, and by the rocky soil and harsh climate of the Highlands. After the middle of the sixteenth century the English Crown enjoyed a succession of victories over the Catholic Highlanders. It then penalized them by imposing civil disabilities and criminal punishments and in the process reduced them to poverty and ignorance. Following the Scottish defeat at Culloden in 1746, the English acted quickly by disarming the clans, seizing Catholic estates, suppressing Highland culture, and burning Catholic homes and chapels. By 1793 a *détente* had been struck between the Scottish clans and the British government. In exchange for the loyalty of Catholic clans and Highland regiments, the government promised to support Catholic clergy and schools. The Catholic clergy were very much part of the cohesiveness of the clan system in the Highlands. Yet full restoration of Catholic rights had to await the Catholic Emancipation in 1829.[31]

Scottish Catholics seeking a better life migrated to Canada in two phases. From 1770 to 1815, the "relatively well-off Gaelic-speaking tenants" arrived from the Highlands in Prince Edward Island, eastern Nova Scotia, and eastern Ontario. Between 1815 and 1840, the more impoverished Gaelic speakers left Scotland under pressure from their landlords and settled in eastern Canada. The Scottish immigrants were different from the Irish in several ways. Arriving earlier, they came with large extended families. The Scots were politically traditional and more interested in raising livestock than in farming. The Irish arrived some years after the Scots, usually without families, were politically liberal, and preferred farming. Although both immigrant groups had more personal and financial resources compared to those they left behind, both arrived in the Maritimes poor and needy.[32] The Irish Catholics "settled overwhelmingly in rural areas and ... their most frequent occupation was farming."[33]

The Scottish Catholics informed the bishop of Quebec that they needed their own clergy, churches, and schools, but owing to lack of resources and perception of the problem, the response was painfully slow. Not having Gaelic-speaking priests available, the bishop tried to recruit Irish seminarians who spoke Gaelic, but the manner and accent of the Irish was not acceptable to the Scots. Some Scottish seminarians were sent to Quebec for training returned home for lack of funds or preparation. In general, Scottish Catholics in Canada were impoverished and forced to maintain their Catholicism with great simplicity. The sight of Scottish priests administering the sacraments with little ceremony and without the benefit of religious furnishings shocked the visiting Quebec vicars general. The Quebec clergy ministering to French and native people were understaffed and overwhelmed with the extent of the demands put on them. Thus it was that they were largely unfamiliar with the existence of other cultural expressions of Catholicism as those of the Scots and the Irish.[34]

According to J.M. Bumsted, the emergence of a Canadian Scottish hierarchy brought an end to the unilingual French-speaking Catholic church. Of the six bishops in Canada by 1830, three were Scottish and three were French. Impressive as these numbers were, the realities were something else. Robert Choquette demonstrates how the infrastructure of the early nineteenth century Catholic church depended very greatly upon the resources and stability of the Quebec church.[35]

The Scottish priests, Alexander Mcdonell and Angus Bernard MacEachern, were serving their parishioners respectively in Upper Canada and Prince Edward Island/New Brunswick. Before the War of 1812, Macdonell had raised a Glengarry regiment for service under General Brock. This loyalty was not forgotten by the British government, and after the war in the autumn of 1816 Macdonell embarked for London and Rome as the spokesperson for Bishop Plessis to secure the approval of the restructuring of the huge diocese of Quebec. He proposed a number of apostolic vicariates that, he explained, would curry loyalty for the British government. Names of the new vicars were also included in the proposal, which the British government approved and passed onto the Holy See. In 1819 Mcdonell was named vicar general "with episcopal character" for Upper Canada, and at the same time, his colleague MacEachern was appointed vicar general with episcopal character for Prince Edward Island/New Brunswick.[36] In 1826 Kingston was created a diocese with Macdonell as its bishop; Charlottetown became a diocese in 1829 with MacEachern as its bishop.

While Mcdonell received the episcopal powers to govern, he lacked the necessary funds, schools, clergy, and churches. He quickly discovered that he was dependent on Bishop Plessis in Quebec for these resources. This was not the reality for which he had hoped when he was freed from the centralizing tendencies of Quebec. He sought to encourage and lead the Scottish church in Upper Canada. Persistent points of contention between the Scots and the Canadiens manifested themselves in terms of clerical dress, church design, and cultural conformity.

The Canadien bishops who visited the Scots in Upper Canada or the Maritime colonies were shocked to find that their clergy did not dress in the priestly soutane while doing their priestly rounds. The emphasis that Bishop Plessis placed on clerical decorum was lost on the Scots, who had never seen clergy dressed like the Canadien clergy, in cassocks. While admiring the staunch and lively faith of the Scots, Plessis was puzzled by "the cassockless missionaries" also failed to see the importance of suitable clerical dress. Plessis wished that the Scottish clergy, like the Canadiens, could be identified as proper Catholic clergy and not be confused with Protestants. He hoped to impose Quebec standards on the Scots, which he believed would unify the external appearance of Catholics throughout Canada.[37]

The Catholic and Presbyterian Scots, in contrast, shared a common culture, language, and resistance to English and French domination. Whereas Protestant and Catholic Quebecers lived in separate communities, the Catholic and Presbyterian Scots felt no need to follow suit. Catholic and Protestant Scots were even buried in the same graveyards. One Canadien priest complained, "faithful and infidels, Protestants and Catholics, circumcized and uncircumcized [sic] are buried one beside the other by their respective ministers, or by other persons who, without being such, perform the functions of them, in a wood open in all directions."[38] To underwrite the cost of church construction, Plessis permitted Catholics to receive Protestant donations but forbade Catholics to donate to Protestant churches. For the bishop, Catholic sacraments, such as Mass and baptisms, were to be conducted not in the homes of the faithful but in a Catholic church. In the eyes of Canadien clergy, priests landing from abroad often brought with them various heterodox customs that shattered the clear and consistent directions established in Quebec. All Canadian churches, it was hoped, would be properly decorated with altar linens, chalices, and furnishings worthy of the service of God.[39]

Quebec by 1815 welcomed fifteen Scottish seminarians to the seminaries at Quebec, Montreal, and Nicolet so that they might be properly trained. The diocese of Quebec and the Sulpicians of Montreal underwrote the cost of this priestly education. With the limited education provided in Upper Canada, the seminarians from this province encountered difficulty in coping with the overwhelming environment of both the French language and Canadien culture. Macdonell had hoped to gain Colonial Office support to educate the youth in the Scottish language and replicate the Gaelic culture in Upper Canada as a way of insulating them against the American republican culture. "Thus secured by the double barrier of their language and religion they might for a long time stand proof against the contagious politics of their democratical [sic] neighbours." Using his own and government funds, he succeeded in bringing to Upper Canada thirty-four clergy and opening a number of schools.[40] Macdonell wanted to establish a fully functioning diocese, but lack of resources prevented him from achieving his goal. He sought a suitable coadjutor bishop from Lower Canada and was turned down three times before receiving in 1833 a positive reply from Rémi Gaulin.[41]

In addition to Bishop Macdonell in Upper Canada and Bishop MacEachern in Prince Edward Island/New Brunswick, a third Scot was appointed to succeed Burke in Nova Scotia. William Fraser was appointed the vicar apostolic of Nova Scotia "with episcopal powers" in 1826 and the first bishop of Halifax in 1842. When a coadjutor bishop was named for his diocese in 1842, Fraser remained in eastern Nova Scotia among the Scots. From Antigonish, he educated young men for the service of the church and sent his future successor, the young Colin F. MacKinnon, to the Urban College in Rome. A pastor rather than an administrator, Fraser was "essentially a missionary priest" and played "a minimal role in founding institutions of higher learning."[42] The Scottish bishops in Canada aligned themselves easily with Canadian administrators and merchants, many of whom were also Scottish. Along with their Canadien episcopal brethren, moreover, the Highland bishops allied themselves firmly with the British government. The second quarter of the nineteenth century was truly the heyday of the Scottish Catholic hierarchy in Canada.[43]

EPISCOPAL CONFLICT IN NOVA SCOTIA

Although the Scottish bishops dominated the non-French-speaking church in the Maritime provinces during the second quarter of the nineteenth century, the Irish were never far away. The Irish arrived in Nova Scotia in three periods: the first up to 1815, the second from 1825 to 1845, and the third after 1845.[44] They arrived at the Newfoundland fishing ports in the middle of the eighteenth century, and thereafter many Irish moved to the mainland ports of Halifax, Sydney, and Saint John.[45] During the middle phase, almost 500,000 Irish immigrants arrived in British North America. The Irish who came during these years were both Protestant and Catholic, and many passed on to the ports of Quebec, Montreal, and Toronto. Most were single and spoke English, and forty percent of this number were women. More Irish immigrated to British North America before the famine than during and after the famine. In the twenty years after the famine, the Irish immigrated less to British North America and more to the United States. Nevertheless, an impressive number of 400,000 Irish immigrated to British North America after 1845, the majority of them women. The Irish who came to North America were inclined to be ambitious and adaptable emigrants from a country that had been beggared by the penal laws for more than two hundred years.[46]

In the late eighteenth century the Irish Catholics in Halifax, who were without the benefit of resident clergy, set up their own parishes and constructed their own churches following the new world practice of lay trustees.[47] They sought out the Capuchin James Jones of Cork to come to Nova Scotia to minister to their spiritual needs. Securing his agreement to come, they went through the ecclesial channels of Bishop D'Esgly of Quebec and Bishop Butler of Cork to gain Jones's appointment to Halifax. After his arrival he was approved by the vicar general of the Maritime colonies, Joseph-Mathurin Bourg, and was appointed superior of the missions. His office as superior was an atypical appointment for a local diocese to make and would normally have been made only by Rome. Jones encountered numerous problems in Nova Scotia, such as low personal income, recalcitrant clergy, and the control of church property by lay trustees. The arrival of émigré clergy from France helped to resolve these problems. Jones found it necessary to dismiss an Irish priest, William Phelan, whose carping against both Jones and the parishioners caused trouble. In August 1800, after fifteen years as superior of the mission, Jones left his charge in the hands of Edmund Burke, OP, and retired to Ireland.[48]

During the periods of uncertainty and clerical interregnum, the founders and benefactors of the Halifax church claimed a decisive role in the appointment of priests, control of churches, and implementation of church standards. Throughout Jones's tenure, the lay trustees challenged the wisdom of their pastor about finances, who might be appointed assistant pastor, and who might be buried in the Catholic cemetery. During the year that the first Edmund Burke was superior of the mission, the parishioners split into factions, the wealthy minority on one side and the ordinary majority on the other. The minority wished to impose compulsory church fees on parishioners for membership and for burial in the churchyard. The majority opposed these impositions and proposed a voluntary system of church support, parishioner voting in parish elections, and the allocation of a larger portion of parish revenues for poor relief. The dispute was referred to Bishop Denaut in Quebec, and he appointed a new pastor, vicar general, and mission superior, another Edmond Burke. For the second Burke, it was a horizontal move from vicar general and superior in Upper Canada to the

Maritime colonies, and he was well prepared for conflict with the trustees. When he settled in Halifax, he restricted parish business to meetings held in his presence. The elections of the wardens were henceforth
limited to a committee that met under his supervision. All future measures to be passed were first subject to his approval. Burke asserted firm
episcopal control over Halifax church life.[49]

While he was vicar general of the missions of Upper Canada near
Detroit, Burke became convinced of the need to break up the huge diocese of Quebec into more manageable sections. He suggested the
creation of a diocese at Montreal and an apostolic vicariate in Upper
Canada. Encouraging Catholics to be loyal to the Crown, serve in the
militia, and withhold liquor from the Indians gave him success with the
authorities but also generated opposition among some gun-slinging
westerners. Armed guards accompanied his movements day and night,
and he complained that some of his parishioners were "wicked men
given to every vice, but especially to drunkenness and sins against nature. Scarcely can you find a girl of ten years that has not suffered
violence."[50]

Later in Nova Scotia he wanted to establish a college-seminary as
part of the infrastructure for the future diocese of Halifax. Opposition
from the governor and the Anglican bishop ended the project quickly.
Burke engaged in verbal battles with his assailants but remained on
cordial terms with them.[51] While in Europe for his health in 1815, he
travelled to Rome to propose the appointment of a vicar apostolic for
Nova Scotia. His request was received by Propaganda Fide, and two
years later he was named the first missionary bishop of this extensive
territory. Bishop Plessis of Quebec learned of the purpose of Burke's
trip to Rome only when he received news from Rome of the dismem-
berment of his diocese. Plessis would have preferred a suffragan status
for Halifax so that Quebec might continue to assist in the foundation
of the new jurisdiction.[52] Accepting a jurisdiction without resources,
Burke passed away three years later in late November 1820 without
leaving a coadjutor bishop in his place.

It was a while before a successor was appointed. In the interim, the
lay trustees sprang to life to fill the gap in episcopal control. Burke's
newly ordained nephew, John Carroll, filled the post as parish priest
but was no match for the long-serving trustees. They directed the parish and asserted their control. In 1826 William Fraser from the Scottish Highlands was appointed vicar apostolic to replace the second
Burke. He had first arrived in Nova Scotia in 1822 and was assigned by
Bishop MacEachern to the mission at Antigonish. Fraser was recognized as a committed and competent priest and a possible successor to

the deceased Edmund Burke. When there were no Irish priests on the horizon, Fraser was consecrated in 1827 as missionary bishop of Nova Scotia at St Ninian's Church in Antigonish. His flock included the Scots of eastern Nova Scotia, the Acadians of the Southwest, and the Irish of Halifax. Fraser estimated in 1831 that of his fifty thousand Catholics, more than half were Scottish and only one-tenth were Irish. Thus, he seldom left eastern Nova Scotia and felt justified in remaining at Antigonish to minister to the Scots.[53]

Bishop Fraser sent Irishman Father John Loughnan to Halifax to be his vicar general and to minister to the Irish. Rigorous in his demands, Loughnan believed it was his duty to prohibit mixed Catholic-Protestant marriages, and by doing so he alienated the middle-class merchants who were amenable to the possibility of marrying their youngsters to the children of Protestant colleagues. In a short time, he stirred up urban parishioners against him.[54] The Halifax Irish were not consoled by an absentee bishop living incommunicado at Antigonish and looked for an episcopal leader for Halifax. They sought to recruit Irish clergy. Archbishop Daniel Murray of Dublin, with the approval of Bishop Fraser, sent two popular Irish priests, Lawrence Dease and Richard O'Brien, to Halifax. Rallying the Catholic community by Roman devotions, confraternities, and the founding St Mary's College, the two priests stimulated Catholic self-confidence and led a popular movement. After a time, the movement was thought to be undercutting the authority of Vicar General Loughnan and Bishop Fraser. The bishop refused to appoint Dease as the second pastor in Halifax. It was clear that the Dease's enthusiastic ministry was being rejected by an absentee bishop, and the priest's return to Ireland in 1841 caused more upset. An American bishop assessed the turmoil in Halifax and reported to Archbishop Murray, who recommended to Rome that an Irish coadjutor bishop with right of succession be appointed in Halifax to assist Fraser.[55]

Propaganda Fide responded by appointing an accomplished Irish ecclesiastic, William Walsh, as coadjutor bishop to Fraser and by changing Halifax from a missionary to an episcopal diocese. Walsh was urbane and witty, an able speaker and forceful writer.[56] A.A. Johnston explains that Rome had neglected to consult Bishop Fraser about the coadjutor's appointment to Fraser's see. At his rustic retreat in Antigonish, having read about the appointment of his coadjutor in the newspaper and in Walsh's letter of introduction, Fraser was too bewildered and hurt to respond.[57] The Nova Scotian episcopal drama became more strident as the Scottish bishop in Antigonish who did not want episcopal jurisdiction over the Irish Canadians stood firm against the Irish coadjutor and the Irish bishop at Halifax who was not adequately received was not able to exercise jurisdiction.

At Rome's insistence Walsh, accompanied by his Capuchin private secretary, Father Thomas L. Connolly, sailed straight to Halifax in October 1842 and into a morass of explosive feelings. He and his secretary established their residence, and Walsh appointed a new sacristan for St Mary's Cathedral. The vicar general, John Loughnan, rejected this appointment and took the opportunity to exercise the jurisdiction of Bishop Fraser and deny the sacristan's authority. Bishop Fraser affirmed his vicar general's action. Walsh was clearly caught between the Scottish bishop, who did not want him, and the Halifax Irish, who demanded he be their bishop. As a remedial measure, Walsh in 1844 asked Rome for a temporary division of the Nova Scotian diocese between Fraser and himself.[58]

In response to Rome's query, Fraser asked for a permanent split by dividing two-thirds of the diocese to form the diocese of Arichat (Antigonish) under himself, leaving the remainder for the diocese of Halifax. He demanded Walsh's resignation and the election of a new bishop by the priests of the diocese of Halifax. Father Colin MacKinnon, the friend of both bishops and Fraser's secretary, acted as a go-between. MacKinnon felt that Fraser, through his unrelenting support of John Loughnan, was bringing himself "into disgrace in the sight of the Apostolic See." When consulted by the Holy See, MacKinnon recommended that the diocese of Nova Scotia be divided and Loughnan be removed from Halifax. From the distance of Quebec City, Bishop Joseph Signay dispassionately observed that one bishop was enough for Nova Scotia.[59]

In 1844 Propaganda Fide divided the Halifax diocese according to the recommendation of Bishop Fraser that the three eastern counties and Cape Breton Island should remain with him as he became bishop of Arichat. Bishop William Walsh was made the administrator of the diocese of Halifax, then bishop two years later and archbishop in 1852. Walsh's appointment to Halifax was clearly a victory for the lay activists who sought their own bishop. At the same time, capitalizing on their support, Walsh centralized ownership of the parishes and St Mary's College into an episcopal corporation. An enthusiasm for ultramontane restructuring called for the formation of episcopal corporations, which were first initiated in Baltimore in 1833. This move ended the democratic involvement of lay trustees in Saint John, New Brunswick, in 1846 and in Halifax in 1849. Thus Walsh's episcopal leadership decisively ended a brief experiment in democratic Catholicism in Halifax, restored ecclesial stability to the community, and assumed direction of the devotional community.[60] When the tranquillity was restored to Halifax, Fraser's vicar general, Father John Loughnan, and the prominent pro-Walsh activist Father Richard B. O'Brien were quietly asked to leave Halifax. The former went to Arichat and the latter to Ireland. The Scottish-Irish episcopal conflict had been defused.[61]

FOUNDING CATHOLIC COLLEGES

In 1852 Colin F. MacKinnon succeeded William Fraser to the see of Arichat. MacKinnon founded the college at Arichat in 1853, moved it two years later into a new building at Antigonish, and named it St Francis Xavier College. It then became the first, and remains today one of the few, free-standing Catholic universities in Canada. In the diocese MacKinnon made regular parish visits, built churches, increased the number of clergy fivefold from nine to forty-seven priests, and improved its administration. It was Bishop MacKinnon who established the institutions of the diocese of Arichat and expanded them into permanent structures.[62] He was a builder-bishop who constructed churches and schools, an educator who saw to it that boys, girls, and university students were given educational opportunities, a peacemaker who promoted communication between Bishops Fraser and Walsh, and a leader who persuaded Nova Scotian Catholics of the importance of supporting Canadian confederation.

Dr John Cameron succeeded MacKinnon in 1877 as bishop of Antigonish (1877–1910). In three years the energetic young bishop paid down the large debts on St Ninian's Cathedral and the Catholic schools and began a campaign to renew the enrolment and academic programs of St Francis Xavier College. Cameron invited the Congrégation-de-Notre-Dame to open a convent school for girls in 1883 and then a college in 1894 in conjunction with St Francis Xavier.[63] To the impoverished Scottish immigrants, the colleges offered the hope of an education for their children and a higher standard of living for themselves. Its classical curriculum provided students with both university education and character formation, and many of its graduates joined the professions.[64]

A voting franchise for the Catholics of Prince Edward Island was rejected by its government in 1827 because it believed that Catholics were not adequately educated for the responsibility. Despite this setback and in order for Charlottetown to become a diocese, it was felt that a seminary-college would provide educated leaders of the church. St Andrew's College was founded in 1831 to educate the future clergy of the diocese. The college closed its doors after thirteen years; but its successor, St Dunstan's College, rose on a site closer to Charlottetown in 1855. Much to the distress of the diocese, the government never extended the fifty-pound subsidy from St Andrew's College to St Dunstan's, so funding became a major preoccupation of the college administration. Peter McIntyre, "one of his diocese's greatest bishops," offered the Tory party Catholic support for the election and Canadian confederation in exchange for the funding of Catholic schools and St Dunstan's.[65] But much to the disappointment of Catholics, once the Tories were in power they failed to act. McIntrye was bitterly disillusioned by the Tory failure to keep what he believed was a campaign promise. Funding continued to be the main issue for the survival of St Dunstan's College.[66]

Catholic laity in Halifax organized financing in 1838 to establish St Mary's College, for which professors were sought from the archdiocese of Dublin. With the arrival of Fathers Richard O'Brien and Lawrence Dease at Halifax, St Mary's College commenced classes in January 1840. Michael Hannan (1877–82), the future archbishop, W. Iver, and E.J. Gleason were also part of the original staff on Grafton Street. Father Thomas L. Connolly joined the staff and became the president in 1850. Government grants, which increased from £250 to £440 pounds yearly went a long way to maintaining the sound financial footing of the college.[67]

In 1881 the Nova Scotian government threatened to cut off funding to religious colleges if they did not surrender their degree-granting powers to the secular University of Halifax. As the threat was not carried out, partial funding of denominational colleges continued.[68] Anticipating the financial shortfall at St Mary's, the new archbishop of Halifax, Michael Hannan, laid out in 1877 a futuristic plan for the federation of Catholic colleges in the Maritime provinces. The federation was to include St Francis Xavier of Antigonish, St Mary's College of Halifax, and St Dunstan's College of Charlottetown. Its site would be relocated at a newly constructed convent at Pictou, considered to be equidistant from the three constituencies by water transport.[69]

It was hoped that the cash-strapped small colleges could reduce costs by combining the administration and faculty at one central location. Université Laval, it was hoped, would contribute faculty and students to the federated college. Questions remained for the Pictou college: could the Scots and the Irish share their different cultural heritages in this common academic enterprise? Would the Province of Nova Scotia fund such a creative plan? Michael Hannan's enterprising idea collapsed because it included too many problems, and no subsequent formula was found to save the proposed Catholic university. The private benefactors of individual colleges, in fact, kept the colleges divided rather than uniting them in a common cause. Irish and Scottish Catholics, however, did share their meagre resources at the three separate campuses, but these resources remained far from adequate.[70]

CONCLUSION

Ethnic groups and regional requirements undermined the initial hope of Propaganda Fide for the uniform religious development of Canada. The arrival of each new group of Catholic settlers on Canadian shores strengthened the variegated missionary roots of the Canadian church. The Irish and Scottish Catholics arrived with their own linguistic and cultural needs and thus prolonged the missionary mandate of the Canadian church. Canadien missionaries ministered to the inhabitants and native people alike. But the Scots and the Irish quickly challenged the Canadien monopoly over the church in Canada. The two Celtic groups desired their own churches, schools, and colleges, and they needed their own bishops and priests to accomplish this. The Canadien clergy acted as substitutes until suitable Irish and Scottish clergy could be found.

The struggle for Catholic schools in Newfoundland led to religious sectarianism, which in turn led to the evolution of denominational proportionalism. Denominational proportionalism permitted an equitable distribution of provincial jobs, resources, and schools and restored to Newfoundland political and religious peace. The Canadien, native, Irish, and Scottish members of the church learned with difficulty to collaborate with one another – especially when they disagreed sharply on cultural and linguistic matters. It must be pointed out that the Scottish bishops in the second quarter of the nineteenth century played a significant role in the life of the Canadian church, and that their influence continued into the next century. To deal with Canadian cultural diversity, Rome approved piecemeal the establishment of new church institutions. The rapid and dynamic growth of Roman spirituality during the nineteenth century countered ethnic fragmentation and became a powerful unifying force within the Canadian church. The Holy See succeeded during this time in centralizing governing and devotional structures throughout the western world and inspired an explosion of ultramontane spirituality.

PART TWO

Romanism

4 Ultramontane Catholicism

The origin of ultramontane spirituality can be found in seventeenth-century France. Religious orders such as the Jesuits and the Dominicans opposed the four Gallican articles upgrading French autonomy and episcopal powers and downgrading Roman primacy and political leadership. At the beginning of the nineteenth century, after the devastation wrought on Catholicism by the French Revolution, neo-ultramontanes encouraged loyalty to the spiritual and political leadership of the Holy See as the best way to reconstruct Catholic life, worship, and culture. Catholics in France and other European countries sought a new spirituality beyond the rationalism of the French Enlightenment. Like an Old Testament prophet rising up after the Babylonian captivity, Joseph de Maistre sought the symbiotic restoration of Catholicism and the monarchy under the leadership the Holy See. His thought inspired the democratic Félicité Lamennais to offer a second brand of ultramontanism for liberal Catholics. Accepting the reality of the French Revolution, these Catholics, under the spiritual guidance of the Roman pontiff, sought reforms adopting the best of the Enlightenment. They believed that by encasing the ancient wisdom of Christianity in the contemporary format of Enlightenment, the Catholic church would inspire the development of the modern world.

On the western side of the Atlantic, the Canadians welcomed the warmth of this new spiritual movement. Within a few decades at the middle of the nineteenth century, the crusading bishops of Quebec had changed the spiritual landscape of the province. In Newfoundland

and central Canada, the Irish and the Scots entered into the trades, professions, and various levels of Canadian society. They renewed their commitment to Catholic devotional life and fought for Catholic schools. Further to the west during this same period, the Oblate Fathers, Grey Nuns, and Sisters of St Anne moved speedily to evangelize native and Euro-Canadian communities on the Canadian Prairies.

ULTRAMONTANE VIEWS IN PARIS

Count Joseph de Maistre, in desiring the reunion of cross and crown spoke for traditional Catholics. In 1797 Maistre's *Considérations sur la France* described the French Revolution as "providential." Condemning the anti-religious tone of the Enlightenment, he saw the redemptive value of the suffering forced on the church by the Revolution. Violently purged of extreme Gallican nationalism, the church was now ready to shed its pretensions of limiting papal power. In Maistre's view the constitutions composed by the French and American revolutionaries were not of divine origin but mere scraps of paper signifying nothing. The renewed French church had to accept the mission of spreading its own constitution of divine origin under an infallible papacy.

The most important of Maistre's writings was *Du Pape*, published in 1819. He exhorted Catholics to abandon Gallican liberties and to embrace the spiritual leadership of the pope. As Gallicans considered the council more powerful than the pope, Maistre challenged them by diminishing the power of the French church and the church council and amplifying the monarchical and aristocratic nature of the papacy.[1] He saw the pope as divinely designated to lead the Christian world. He rejected the translation theory, passed down from Aquinas to Bellarmine and Suarez, which saw the power of God as handed down to the people to be delegated to a particular leader. Maistre believed, rather, that God by his paternal authority mystically inspired designated individuals to govern others. By the same token, subjects would discover religious truth in their faithful obedience to this designated individual, such as a pope or a monarch.

Maistre predicted that it would take twenty-five years before the message of *Du Pape* would be fully appreciated. Historian G.P. Gooch ranked this volume "among the classics of political and social philosophy with those of Burke and Locke, Rousseau and Marx, all of which were designed to change the outlook of Europe and have deeply influenced the course of history."[2] Forty editions of *Du Pape* were published during the nineteenth century in French, German, Spanish, and English.

Inspired by *Du Pape*, l'abbe Félicité de Lamennais sought to bind together the twin pillars of Christian society and the new liberal politics,
to yoke democracy with Catholicism, human liberty with papal leadership, and religious tradition with the secular state. The church should
abandon its dependency on the monarchy, Lamennais believed, and
rely upon its own spiritual resources. As the spiritual leader of the
people the pope should forego aristocratic privilege, and the Church
should relinquish the patronage of the civil governments and the diplomatic leverage of concordats. The Word of God reveals itself in the
people, and the future church will be found in the popular will. Because of the crusading ultramontane spirituality of his book, *l'Essai sur
l'Indifférence*, Lamennais was received by the conservative Pope Leo XII
in Rome in 1824.[3]

In 1830 and 1831, with the help of Count Charles de Montalembert
and l'Abbé Henri Lacordaire, Lamennais published the daily newspaper *L'Avenir*. The paper, whose motto was "God and Liberty," rejected
the divine right of kings to which many bishops firmly clung and
wanted to replace the royal church with the papal church. Church and
state should be separated and clerical salaries suppressed. It was believed by the reformers that it was preferable for the clergy to trust in
God and live poor rather than be silenced as state employees of an unjust regime. The Gallican bishops were looked upon as being blind,
worldly, and unsympathetic to ultramontane spirituality. The sovereignty of the people, by contrast, was believed to be the wave of the future for civil society, and the church should recognize and adjust to
the new state of affairs. This would mean respecting freedom of conscience, speech, press, and association.[4]

L'Avenir championed these liberal attitudes throughout France. Yet
many French Catholics united themselves with the pope, who ruled by
divine right and was bound by his office to his brother monarchs. This
daily newspaper on behalf of people's sovereignty, pleaded with a hierarchical church preoccupied with legitimacy and order. Leo XII and
Gregory XVI sided with their fellow monarchs in the suppression of Polish Catholics by the Orthodox tsar, Italian Catholics by the French and
Austrian armies, Belgian Catholics by the Protestant king of Holland,
and Irish Catholics (O'Connellites) by the Protestant king of England.
On all these occasions, the papacy had stressed that loyal obedience to
the legitimate kings suppressing the religious and political freedom of
Catholics was the moral imperative. To offer disobedience to the divinely anointed monarch was to offer disobedience to God.

Lamennais went so far as to criticize the non-believing bourgeois
king Louis-Philippe for the royal privileges he enjoyed in appointing
bishops, censoring communiques from Rome, and approving Catholic

religious orders and educational institutions. Cardinal de Rohan and many French bishops allied with Louis-Philippe to denounce Lamennais to Rome. For fear of being outmanoeuvred, Lamennais, Lacordaire, and Montalembert made a personal pilgrimage to Rome in November 1831 to seek papal support. In the name of obedience and proper order, the newly elected Gregory XVI had endorsed the imperial oppression of Catholic republicans struggling for basic rights. Lacordaire, having received no answer from the papal office after months of waiting, intuited a negative reply and returned to France, leaving Montalembert and Lamennais to drift off to Munich in August 1832. Attending a banquet there in their honour, the three met again. The newly printed papal letter *Mirari Vos* was handed to Lamennais who read it and whispered to Lacordaire, "I have just received an encyclical of the pope against us; we must not hesitate to make our submission."[5]

Gregory condemned the ultramontane-liberal synthesis of Lamennais, Lacordaire, and Montalembert. He condemned freedom of conscience, liberty of the press, and separation of church and state. He would not allow Catholics to embrace the liberal ideas of the Irish, Polish, Belgian, or Italian republicans. Philippe Buchez summed up the papal letter thus: "In vain does one search in the overblown and trite Italian prose for a Christian thought. It can only repeat the phrases of backward minds against freedom, the press, and revolutions … Not a word of encouragement, not a word of pity for those who suffer; no solicitude except for princes and powers, as if Jesus Christ died to confirm the right to use force on the part of the patricians who condemned him."[6]

Despite the difficulty of accepting such a document, which might have been written by the Austrian chancellor Metternich, Lacordaire broke with Lamennais's critical attitude towards Rome, submitted to the *Mirari Vos*, and became a popular preacher at Notre Dame in Paris. He joined the Dominicans, became a superior, restored the Order of Preachers in France, and avoided political life. Montalembert with some difficulty also submitted to the document. Lamennais at first submitted but later published *Paroles d'un Croyant* in 1834, predicting the victory of the people over the corrupt political and ecclesial leaders who oppressed them. God, he believed, would act directly through the democratic actions of the people. The pope condemned Lamennais's latest utterance as "immense in perversity." When the unreconciled Lamennais lay dying in 1857, a great crowd from the slums mourned his loss. He was buried, as he wished to be, with the poor.[7] A sombre ending to so promising a life, Montalembert struggled on alone through the middle of the nineteenth century as the champion of liberal Catholics.

The editor of the popular Catholic newspaper *L'Univers*, Louis Veuillot, assumed leadership of the French militant ultramontanes in the early 1860s and crusaded against what he considered to be Protestant parliamentary government, scientific progress, and religious indifference. Piously he stressed that "the word liberty is not used in Christian countries."[8]

Opportunity came for Montalembert when the Belgian Catholics sponsored a universal congress at Malines in 1863. Cardinal Sterckx invited Montalembert, who was received with "an explosion of applause the likes of which I never heard before."[9] Montalembert proclaimed that democracy was a permanent fixture in modern governments, ending the old alliance of cross and crown. The key blocks in the future of Christianity, in his view, were universal suffrage, equality, and the freedom of association, the press, and conscience, as well as the freedom to teach. Of these Montalembert knew that freedom of conscience was paramount. The old system of coercion had left Italy, Spain, and Portugal in a deplorable state. At the end of Montalembert's address Cardinal Sterckx warmly congratulated him. The papal office reacted to the Malines congress by immediately condemning liberalism and reprimanding Montalembert. The following year the Holy See's full answer to liberalism was published in the encyclical *Quanta Cura (How Much Care)*, containing the "Syllabus of Errors." It condemned the slogans of the italian republicans mustering menacingly outside the gates of Rome and their doctrines of religions freedom, progress, and liberalism. Six years later that condemnation was followed by the proclamation of papal infallibility at the First Vatican Council, and it was intended that liberal Catholicism would be crushed once and for all. Yet Catholic liberalism was kept alive by such outstanding leaders as Lord Acton, Ludwig Windthorst, Don Luigi Sturzo, Marc Sangnier, and Jacques Maritain until its embodiment, following the Second World War, in Christian Democratic political parties.[10]

CRUSADING ULTRAMONTANES IN MONTREAL

An ardent advocate of Mennaisienne thought in Canada and at the Collège de Saint-Hyacinthe was the first bishop of Montreal, Jean-Jacques Lartigue (1821–40).[11] While in Europe with Bishop Plessis in 1819–20, Lartigue read Lamennais's *l'Essai sur l'Indifférence* (1817). The engagingly written two-volume essay extolled religion as necessary if society were to teach people to subsume their own self-interest in the service of the common good. Religion was the inner life of every society known to history. Thus, it was important that Christians rally around their chief pastor in his effort to lead the church away from the bondage of the secular state.[12] Lamennais taught in *L'Avenir* that when a state based its activities on Christian principle, the union of cross and crown made sense, but now that national states were religiously neutral it made no sense to have non-believing officials choosing bishops, approving of religious orders, and directing Catholic schools.[13] Lartigue, a keen reader of *L'Avenir,* perceived that by submitting to the British government the Canadian church was "held in slavery under the guise of protection." He experienced less freedom to act as a pastor than the bishop of Bardstown, Kentucky; hence he advocated radically changing the policy of his predecessors, Plessis, Panet, and Signay, in favour of the separation of church and state in Canada.[14]

The Parti Canadien challenged Lartigue's spiritual and political leadership. By means of the Lower Canadian legislative assembly, the liberal bourgeois hoped to take direction of the schools, hospitals, and parish councils from the Catholic clergy. They forced passage of the schools act of 1829 and the parish *fabriques* bill of 1831. The effect of this legislation was to create provincial schools that paralleled the Catholic schools. The running of these public schools was placed in the hands of elected trustees in each parish, and the legislation tripled the number of provincial schools within a few years.[15] Control of education was slipping from the hands of the church.

The emergence of representative institutions in Canada, Lartigue believed, meant the church did not have to remain in symbiotic relationship with the government but should respond more creatively. In short, the church had influence over the faithful who would be elected in the assemblies and thus could form the future Canadian state. Lartigue thus reasoned that he no longer needed permission from the Colonial Office in the exercise of church affairs. He found that asking both London and Rome for the building of a Montreal parish put any legitimate proposal in double jeopardy from endless delays. Consequently, without government permission or consultation, Lartigue determined to forward to Rome the petition of the Montreal clergy to establish Montreal as an episcopal see. This request was granted by Propaganda Fide and the diocese was erected in 1836. Lartigue, suffering from poor health, asked the following year that Rome appoint Father Ignace Bourget his coadjutor. *Ex post facto*, the British government, after dragging its feet for a time, approved the appointment of the coadjutor. Once again, a church appointment was achieved without consulting the colonial government. Thus it was that Lartigue asserted church independence from the British government and ended further subservience.[16]

Bishop Ignace Bourget of Montreal (1840–76).
(Archives Archevêché de Montréal [AAM])

At the same time Lartigue cautioned the Patriote leaders in 1837 against civil rebellion. Some of the liberals were his cousins, especially Louis-Joseph Papineau and Denis-Benjamin Viger. He warned them against such action and divorced the church from the Patriote cause. In October 1837, protesting his indifference to their cause, more than twelve hundred Patriotes paraded past the new Montreal Cathedral of Saint-Jacques.[17] The movement collapsed, however, when the Patriotes were defeated at Saint-Charles-sur-Richelieu and Saint-Eustache and the leaders were sent into exile. With the republicans defeated, humiliated, and dispersed, Lartigue, once more unopposed, assumed the mantle of leadership. He signed the priests' petition advocating the rights of Canadiens and, along with Bourget, he demonstrated compassion in assisting and seeking the release of prisoners. When Lord Durham's report surfaced with its plan to unify the legislatures of Upper and Lower Canada and establish non-denominational schools, Lartigue encouraged the signing of a petition of protest to the queen, House of Lords, and Commons. Through the insightful and resolute actions of Lartigue, the Canadien church regained the moral and political leadership that had been lost to the liberal bourgeoisie since the beginning of elected institutions in 1791.[18]

Canadian and American clergy travelling to Europe and Rome were inspired by the power of the ultramontane spirituality they encountered. Canadian clergy like Bishops Bourget and Laflèche chose to follow the more conservative French ultramontane thinkers such as Joseph de Maistre, René-François Rohrbacher, and Louis Veuillot.

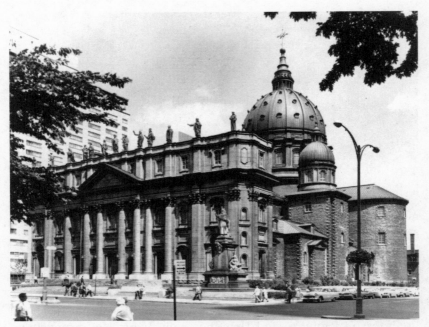

Cathedral of Saint-Jacques, 1870; symbol of French-Canadian ultramontane spirituality (AAM)

Montreal now emerged as a centre of ultramontane thought. In 1840 the new bishop of Montreal, Ignace Bourget (1840–76), invited the famous French orator, Bishop Forbin-Janson, to visit Quebec to renew the religious spirit in the province. Forbin-Janson visited sixty cities and villages where he preached parish retreats. These events might last as long as a month, such as one retreat he preached in Montreal. He spoke about confession, the last things of death, judgment, sin, and hell, the passion of Jesus, Christ's divinity, the Blessed Eucharist, and divine mercy. To some he seemed like Jesus preaching the good news, and at the end of his address, he walked in procession with as many as ten thousand people to erect a mission cross. The strength of his personality and eloquent preaching had a dynamic effect on the renewal of religion in Quebec.[19]

Meanwhile, Bishop Bourget travelled to France and Rome in 1841 and was inspired by his meetings with the leading spokespersons of ultramontane spirituality. He was impressed by Abbé Desgenettes of Notre-Dame-des-Victoires, Théodore de Ratisbonne who was a Jewish convert and founder of the Daughters of Sion, Jean-Marie de Lamennais who founded the Brothers of the Christian Schools, Cardinal Louis-Edouard Pie of Poitiers, Archbishop Charles Joseph de Mazenod of Marseilles and founder of the Missionary Oblates of Immaculate Mary, and Louis Veuillot, editor of *L'Univers*. In Rome the Jesuit general superior, John Roothaan, directed Bourget through an eight-day retreat, after which he had lengthy discussions with Pope Gregory XVI.[20] Bourget returned to Canada fully inspired by and immersed in ultramontane spirituality.

For the good running of society, Bourget became convinced that the church must direct the civil government in regard to religion, education, and censorship. He was impressed with the importance of confraternities, sodalities, and other religious societies in maintaining the fervour of Catholic devotional life and providing moral leadership for Canadiens. The Jesuit sodalities of Our Lady, Carmelite confraternities of the Holy Scapular, and similar organizations strengthened their members to do good works, live good lives, and prepare themselves for a happy death. Learning to master these organizations and observe their devotions fostered the development of a parish elite that set the pace for others.[21]

The relics of the saints, crucifixes, medals, scapulars, banners, statues, holy water, and other material aids to spirituality were greatly sought after. The filtered light of stained glass in gothic churches became an important part of vertical spirituality. Bourget knew he needed the zeal of the French religious congregations to guide Catholic revival and to establish educational and health care organizations. He returned to Canada with the expectation that Oblates, Jesuits, and Redemptorists would preach parish missions during Advent and Lent to make the last things, heaven and hell, fire and brimstone, vivid in the minds of the parishioners.[22] Retreats through the year would also keep the reforming tradition alive for the Canadiens. Bourget invited the Sisters of the Sacred Heart and the Good Shepherd to open schools and orphanages to care for and educate young women in the truths of the faith, so that the young women could in turn educate their children. Filled with the zeal of ultramontane spirituality, Bourget also helped found a number of religious congregations in Montreal and established the St Vincent de Paul Society there.[23]

As the second bishop of Montreal, Ignace Bourget was the driving force behind ultramontane spirituality. He inspired the devotional life of the Canadiens with a love of the Church and its visible head in Rome. To him the soul was the life-giving principle of the human body, and in a similar fashion, religion was the life-giving principle of the state. Thus, in his view, it was the ultramontane clergy who would heal the breach between cross and crown and restore this historical unity.[24] Louis Veuillot also had a strong influence on the Canadiens in this regard.[25]

Bourget strove to convert Montreal into a "petite Rome,"[26] to which end he constructed the second cathedral of St James, which was identical in design to St Peter's Basilica in Rome but respectfully one fifth its size. The Montreal diocese and its seminary formed the nucleus of staunch Canadien fidelity to the Roman tradition.[27] The bishop desired that Catholic teaching be uniform throughout Canada. At the first provincial council of Quebec in 1851, he supported the adoption of an updated version of the Plessis catechism of 1815. He believed that teaching should be rooted in the Council of Trent and the Roman catechism. For the Canadiens he wanted a contemporary version of the Plessis catechism and for the English-speaking Canadians the Butler Catechism approved by the Irish hierarchy. He hoped that the two publications would provide Catholic doctrine as unified and solid throughout the land.[28]

Conformity to the Roman practices was expected of the laity in their annual observance of confession and communion as well as the days of fast and abstinence. Bourget restored the devotion of Our Lady to the month of May and of St Joseph to March. The regular reception of Holy Communion was encouraged on Sundays and feast days. Novenas were instituted for the principal passages of life, and indulgences were available to emphasize the importance of those occasions. Processions and gatherings on feast days became a communal demonstration of the Canadien Catholic will and revealed preference for Catholic pomp and Roman ritual.[29]

Pilgrimages were another group activity that communicated the love of Catholic values and God's benefits. Pilgrims launched out on a trek in the hope of touching the divine and being cured of their afflictions. This ancient Christian custom put pilgrims in touch with their spiritual and historical roots and nourished the participant. Pilgrimages to the ancient holy sites of Notre-Dame-des-Victoires in Quebec, Notre-Dame-de-Bonsecours in Montreal, or Sainte-Anne-de-Beaupré north of Quebec offered seekers the hope of inner conversion, physical healing, and confidence that God has understood their anxiety. As a demonstration of Catholic faith and heritage, pilgrimages were approved and encouraged by the bishops.[30]

Out of loyalty to the Holy See, a unit of 135 volunteer papal zouaves were sent from Montreal in March 1868 to defend Rome from republican military aggression. The Canadiens were part of an international brigade of 4,592 volunteers who arrived to protect the Patrimony of Peter and preserve its separateness during the struggle for Italian unification. They sought to bolster the papal army in its defence against the forces of Piedmont and Sardinia, which wanted to seize Rome and make it the capital of a unified Italy.[31] On 20 September 1870, after an hour-long bombardment, the Italian armies breached the Porta Pia and seized Rome. The papal forces capitulated. The Canadien zouaves spent a short time in squalid and hungry imprisonment before returning home to Montreal and a hero's welcome.

Religious congregations such as the Oblates, Jesuits, Redemptorists, Sisters of the Sacred Heart, and the Good Shepherd were the vanguard for the evangelization of the Canadiens and the proselytization of the northerners and westerners.[32] They supplemented the apostolic work of the Sulpicians who survived in Canada during the Conquest and its aftermath. These Catholic religious followed up on Monsignor de Forbin-Janson's mission crusade awakening the Canadiens to their spiritual responsibilities. The first six Missionary Oblates of Mary Immaculate arrived in Montreal in 1841. Bourget assigned them Saint-Hilaire Parish on the Richelieu River as a centre from which they could fan out to preach missions. During their parish missions they founded temperance societies and Marian confraternities to continue the reform. Seven years after their arrival, Bourget, obviously pleased with their zeal, entrusted them with a second parish in the heart of Montreal, Saint-Pierre-Apôtre. Their mission work spread quickly to northern Quebec, Labrador, the Northwest, the Pacific, and the Arctic.[33] They were to become the most successful religious congregation in Canada and operated an extensive network of schools, colleges, parishes, bishoprics, missions, and residential schools from sea to sea.

At the request of Bishops Bourget and Power, the Jesuit Pierre Chazelle and eight companions arrived at Montreal in 1842. Two years later Dominique du Ranquet, Joseph Jennesseaux, and Jean-Pierre Choné travelled to the native missions in Canada West at Walpole Island, near Windsor, and Wikwemikong on Manitoulin Island. Other Jesuits remained in Montreal to open Collège Sainte-Marie in 1848. Over the next forty-five years one hundred and nine Jesuit priests and brothers from ten nations sailed to Canada to spread the gospel message. Many were former French seminary instructors who were fluent in Latin and Greek, German and French, and who believed they were called by God to do mission work. They joined the Jesuits to serve on the Canadian missions. They arrived in Canada in their late thirties with excellent educations and well-developed language skills. Among these French-speaking clergy were thirty-two anglophone brothers and five priests from Ireland and the United States. Many travelled to the interior of the country building churches, schools, hospitals, and rectories to instruct, baptize, and bless the marriages of settlers and native people.[34]

Other male religious travelled to Canada to support the energetic evangelization inspired by Bourget and the bishop of Toronto,

Armand de Charbonnel (1850–60). The Redemptorists in 1833,[35] the Brothers of the Christian Schools in 1837, the Congregation of the Holy Cross in 1837, the Clercs de Saint-Viateur in 1847, Basilians in 1852, and the Resurrectionists in 1857 arrived to educate the youth and to evangelize the adults.[36]

Many women's congregations survived the British Conquest, among them the Ursulines (who arrived in Canada in 1639), the Hospitalers of St Augustine (1639), the Congregation of Notre Dame (1653), the Hospitalers of St Joseph (1659), and the Grey Nuns (1737). In addition to these existing congregations, the Sisters of the Presentation arrived in Canada from Ireland in 1833 to teach school, operate orphanages, and build hospitals, and the Lorettos followed them in 1847. The foundation of religious congregations in Canada strengthened Catholic involvement in social programs. The Grey Nuns of Montreal gave birth to other Canadian branches following their rule: the Sisters of Charity of Québec, Saint-Hyacinthe (1840), and Ottawa. The Grey Nuns of Ottawa then saw the founding of the Grey Sisters of the Immaculate Conception of Pembroke. The sisters, both Canadien and from France, strove to care for the young, sick, aged, and abandoned. Rosalie Jetté founded the Misericordia Sisters in Montreal in 1848 to provide unmarried women with maternity and infant care. The Sisters of Providence and the Sisters of the Holy Names of Jesus and Mary were established at Montreal in 1843 to serve the poor and needy. The Sisters of St Anne were founded in 1850 to educate the young.[37]

Bourget saw that Catholic newspapers were needed to spread information about church activities at home and abroad. His newspapers, *Les Mélanges Religieux* and *The True Witness*, carried the latest information to Catholics on church festivities, the lives of the saints, parish activities, and secular news, and they did battle with the anti-Catholic propaganda of the *Montreal Witness* and the Toronto *Globe*.[38] The journalistic effort by Catholics helped to change "the antagonistic tone of the non-Catholic press to one of tolerance and respect for Catholic rights."[39]

The Montreal diocese grasped the Roman *Syllabus of Errors* in 1864 as an occasion to join Pius IX in condemning the atheistic slogans of liberalism, progress, and modern civilization. Catholic journalists loyal to these pronouncements launched the *programme catholique* in 1871 to demand that Catholic politicians follow the teaching of the Holy See. The following year, they drew first blood with the defeat of the popular government leader in Montreal East, George-Étienne Cartier.[40] This manifesto, Roberto Perin concludes, "specifically denounced laws on marriage, education, civil registers, and parishes that the Conservatives had passed or refused to amend."[41] Bourget and his colleague from Trois-Rivières, Louis-François Laflèche, encouraged those who implemented the program. Members of the program supported politicians who endorsed conservative principles and condemned those who promoted liberal politics. Bourget promoted composition by the Quebec hierarchy of a pastoral letter condemning Catholic liberalism. Two years later, he wrote a pastoral letter to this effect advocating the use of the pulpit and the confessional to extirpate liberalism from the Catholic fold.

Through mobilizing direct political pressure in the Quebec assembly, the bishops gained the passage of the education act of 1875 and control of the Catholic school system. In future, religious orders directed primary and secondary education. Regretting the extent to which the church was exorcizing influence in politics, the archbishop of Quebec, Elzéar Taschereau (1870–96), published a letter in 1876 urging priests not to indulge in blind partisanship.[42] To quell the widening episcopal rift over the extent of clerical involvement in politics, apostolic delegate George Conroy was sent by Rome to engineer a joint pastoral letter in October 1877 directing Catholics away from political partisanship. Taschereau and Laflèche crafted the joint pastoral incorporating key sentences from the Roman directives. It exonerated liberal supporters and forbade the use of the pulpit and confessional to direct or punish voters. The Congregation of Faith recommended that Quebec bishops should halt their polemics and remain silent on political issues.[43] The joint pastoral was not welcomed in Montreal where the retired Bishop Bourget continued to hold sway over the diocesan clergy.[44] The militant ultramontane zeal of the Montreal diocese through those years reflected what Jay Dolan describes as the profound but "narrow papalism of the nineteenth century."[45]

The intense nature of this spirituality provoked strong opposition, which was centred at the Institute canadien in Montreal and in the newspapers *l'Avenir* and *Moniteur canadien*. The Catholic opposition advocated the democratic reforms of liberty, progress, separation of church and state, and a possible rapprochement with the United States. Their leader was Louis-Antoine Dessaulles whose advocacy of democratic reforms greatly irritated Bourget.[46] The bishop, originally a patron of the Institute Canadien, withdrew his support and in a series of letters in 1862 condemned those who borrowed its books, read the newspaper *Le Pays*, or attended its seminars and lectures. *Le Pays* enthusiastically advocated the Italian Risorgimento, which to Bourget was an arrow aimed directly at the heart of the Holy Father and the Catholic church.[47]

IRISH CULTURE IN ST JOHN'S

Denominational proportionalism provided a made-in-Newfoundland mechanism to keep the peace between the different sectarian groups. A new political and religious consensus emerged in Newfoundland, providing a stable platform on which Catholics and Protestants could establish their institutions. Following the irenic Vicar Apostolic Scallan, his crusading replacement Michael A. Fleming stepped forward to establish new episcopal structures and to Romanize the Newfoundland Catholic community. He was a pivotal figure in the Newfoundland church and radically different from his three predecessors. Where Scallan fostered tranquillity and harmony among Christian denominations, Fleming was feisty with those who did not walk with him but accomplished enormous fetes for the Catholic community. Fleming and Scallan for a number of years worked zealously together and learned to accept each other's "repeated differences." Once in office Fleming refused, as Scallan and his predecessors had done, to continue handing over to the Anglican rector marriage and burial fees.[48] When travelling abroad, Fleming sought funds for church and school buildings, recruited clergy and religious from Ireland, and defended his political activities before the courts of Rome and London. Fleming was not intimidated by the Protestant government and did not hesitate to let the real needs of Newfoundland Catholics be known both at home and abroad. He maintained close friendships with Roman officials and dismissed his opponents in Newfoundland as Catholic "liberals." He knew Daniel O'Connell and considered him a colleague in the struggle for the underprivileged against the establishment. Having little time for episcopal chats with other North American bishops, Fleming preferred visiting the villages and outports of his diocese.[49]

When Fleming became bishop, he readied the diocese for action. He sold the episcopal carriage, let Scallan's manservant go, ended the practice of holding sumptuous dinners for the élite, emptied the wine cellar, and used all available monies to build schools and buy "vestments and Mass books ... Altar furniture and Chalices."[50] The first opposition to his reforms came from his own flock. A Waterford reformer, he disbanded the Orphans Asylum Committee, which consisted of Wexford old élites that had raised funds and supervised the school for Catholic boys, and ran it himself so that Catholic instruction and practices might be inserted into the curriculum. From Ireland he invited the Sisters of the Presentation of the Blessed Virgin Mary and the Sisters of Mercy to teach the young women of St John's. Through an array of academic courses, he wanted the sisters to nurture young women in Catholic truth so that they could in turn nurture an educated Catholic middle class. Besides the scholastic courses, the sisters also offered their students music and foreign languages.[51] Fleming rallied the new families of Waterford to side with him in carrying out these reforms. The Waterford wheybellies displaced the Wexford yellowbellies by initiating new and disciplined ultramontane spirituality.[52]

Like Burke in Halifax thirty years earlier, Fleming challenged the ingratiating attitude of the wealthy Catholics towards the Protestant élites. In his view they sought secular leadership but without the corresponding sense of responsibility. He beckoned them to be more sensitive to the needs of their fellow Catholics for poor relief and Catholic schools, and to take seriously the Real Presence and Catholic devotions. As a strong and determined leader, Fleming seized the leadership from his opponents and gained the support of the majority of Catholics. Using this advantage, he rallied Catholics to the full support of their community.[53]

Fleming's movement generated powerful opposition, particularly in response to Father Edward Troy whom Fleming left in charge when he was away. In the Chapel, Troy managed to insult a number of the Wexford families and refused the sacraments to twenty-eight other "Liberal Catholics." Petitions, letters, and clippings of protest were sent to the governor, who forwarded them to the Colonial Office. The message was that Bishop Fleming had gone beyond his spiritual competence and was now aspiring to political influence in the colony. The Colonial Office sent four appeals to Rome to have Fleming removed from his see. But Fleming, defending himself ably, protested his loyalty to British Empire and papal office alike and remained unassailable to the Wexford yellowbellies.[54] Rome transformed the vicarate into the diocese of Newfoundland in 1847.

Gaining the high ground at St John's, Fleming constructed a powerful monument to Newfoundland Catholicism, the large Cathedral of St John the Baptist. Fleming had first dismissed the Chapel Committee so that he might make plans more efficiently without disputatious factionalism. Then he inveigled the British government and its governor, Sir Thomas Cochrane, to give up a nine-acre former garrison site following "a long and acrimonious relationship concerning the land."[55] Fleming recruited volunteers in 1839 to dig the foundation, sought workers to cut stone on Kelly's Island and shipowners to haul stone to St John's, and then recruited even more volunteers to draw it uphill to the site. Working at the site much of the time, Fleming guided this herculean effort to construct the massive Roman structure.[56] The cathedral followed the plan of a classical basilica with a cruciform nave and transept. The interior walls were faced with cut limestone and granite from Ireland. He triumphantly celebrated Mass in the unfinished cathedral on 6 January 1850, the feast of the Epiphany. In July, in his fifty-eighth year, having named Father John T. Mullock as his successor, Fleming died exhausted by his physical and spiritual labours.[57] Fleming left the fourteen thousand members of the Catholic community of St John's permanently established and well accepted among a population of nineteen thousand inhabitants.

The last of the Franciscan bishops, John Thomas Mullock (1850–69) was youthful, well educated, and ready to expand Fleming's legacy. Mullock asked Rome to restructure Newfoundland, and in 1856 two episcopal sees were created, St John's and Harbour Grace (Grand Falls). From the beginning, the Irish-born Mullock considered himself a Newfoundlander and encouraged his relatives to move to St John's. He sought native-born vocations to the clergy and the sisters and opened an orphanage and a college. Taking interest in the civil progress of the colony, he sought the improvement of road, ship, and telegraph communications.[58]

A skilled politician, he associated the Catholic clergy and parishioners with the Liberal party. He advocated responsible government, which happened to be a diplomatic way to displace the Protestant ascendancy. He mobilized the priests in the parishes to act "as election managers for the Liberal party" and his diocesan newspaper, the *Pilot*, indicated how the laity should inform their consciences to avoid sin from unwise political choices. In 1855 Newfoundland attained responsible government and, after a Liberal election victory, Catholics for the first time received their share of the patronage. In future the Liberal leader turned to the Catholic bishop when he needed support, such as when the proposed fisheries convention with Great Britain was defeated in 1857. Mullock wrote "a long and eloquent letter" that provoked a "monster meeting" in St John's that led to the defeat of the proposal.[59]

The Conservatives regained power in 1861, although Mullock denounced them for being self-serving. After an outbreak of political violence at Cat's Cove the following year, Mullock put the area under ecclesial interdict, forbidding the administration of the sacraments for one full year. But this time the politician-bishop had overextended his moral credibility. With his political influence in decline, many ignored his political guidance. Seeking to lose his image as "a firebrand and disturber of the peace," he focused more properly on the spiritual leadership of Catholics. At his funeral in 1869, he was greatly praised for "his amiable and kindly disposition." Despite his brash foray into politics in his early years, Mullock's sincere interest in Newfoundland endeared him to the community and enhanced the stature and acceptance of Catholics on the island.[60] The five Franciscan bishops established religious, educational, and social institutions that gave the Irish the inner discipline and the external skills to compete in the English colony. The bishops were unsympathetic to Irish republicanism and exhorted Catholics to remain staunchly loyal to both London and Rome.

SCHOOLS IN CENTRAL CANADA

Central to the flow of central Canadian political tides was editor and politician Thomas D'Arcy McGee. Born in Ireland, McGee lived and worked first in his native land and then migrated to the United States. Beginning his political career as a revolutionary republican and migrating to the new world, McGee gradually moved into the camp of conservative politics. Once opposed to the British Empire, during his mature years he advocated English colonial rule in Canada. This Gallican anti-clerical transformed himself into a Catholic ultramontane.[61]

The Montreal Irish made up twenty percent of the city's population and needed a newspaper to promote their political agenda – especially separate schools for Canada West. The Irish were unhappy with the city's sole English-language Catholic newspaper, *True Witness*, which was edited by an aristocratic Scot, George Edward Clerk. They saw his newspaper as an instrument of the militant ultramontane spirituality of Bishop Bourget, who was considered no friend of Irish national aspirations. He believed the Irish should adjust to Québécois culture and accept Québécois Catholicism. The Irish felt that the high-born Clerk was a convert who did not understand the republican struggles. His *Witness* editorials alienated the Irish Protestants and ended the hope of establishing a united Irish brotherhood that included both faiths. To remedy the desire for a central Canadian newspaper that could speak for the Catholic and Protestant Irish, the Irish Canadians raised two thousand dollars. To lead this new publication they invited D'Arcy McGee, now a seasoned journalist in the United States, to Montreal in 1857 to found an Irish newspaper, *The New Era*. As a gift to his new city, McGee contributed to Montreal's coat of arms the shamrock and the motto, *Concordia Salus*.[62]

The following year McGee was asked to run in the federal election with A.A. Dorion and Luther Holton. They ran as Liberals, captured the Irish vote, and defeated Tories Georges-Etienne Cartier and Henry Starnes. For McGee the choice to run for the Liberals was easy given that the Tories were associated with the Orange Lodge and the Liberals with reform and labour. McGee went on to expand his influence to Canada West by gaining the support of the St Patrick societies and the Toronto-based *Canadian Freeman*, edited by James G. Moylan. He organized committees in Prescott, Coburg, Kingston, Toronto, and London.[63]

When George Brown and A.A. Dorion formed the government of the Canadas from 1858 to 1861, McGee campaigned in a Toronto by-election on behalf of Brown's Reform party. He encouraged the Irish to vote Reform and promised them that the Brown-Dorion government would prepare legislation for a separate school system modelled on the modified National School System of Ireland. McGee's support of the Reform party drew a negative response from conservative Catholics who looked to the Tories to support their agenda.[64]

Journalist George E. Clerk criticized McGee for supporting "rep by pop" (representation by population) and submerging Catholic support in the Protestant majority of the legislature. Clerk attacked McGee for being a traitor to his religion. The Canadian bishops backed these criticisms of the *True Witness* and condemned representation by population, voluntary church support, and politicians who stir up racial feelings. McGee was willing to accept these episcopal condemnations but took exception to the outright censure of "rep by pop." To McGee's mind, representation by population was basic democracy when accompanied by suitable guarantees for minority rights.[65]

Although D'Arcy McGee had political opponents among Catholics, he also had his many supporters, some in unusual places. Bishop Charbonnel of Toronto was among them. At a banquet in Toronto in 1859, the bishop praised the Irish politician and agreed with him on the principles of representation by population and voluntary church support. In the election of 1861 McGee brought out the Irish vote and won re-election.[66]

A separate school bill was introduced into the Canadian assembly in 1861. McGee tried to rally the Reform party to support it, but George Brown and the Toronto *Globe* demanded that the party oppose it. In contrast, Toronto's Bishop John J. Lynch (1860–88) and James Moylan of *Canadian Freeman*, a Kingston diocesan weekly, looked to the Tories to pass the separate school bill.[67] The Reform party formed the government in 1862 under John Sandfield MacDonald, and McGee became an important member. The separate school bill was introduced again, and with George Brown on the sidelines, it looked as if it would pass. After a by-election George Brown unexpectedly returned to the assembly, and at the last minute the separate school bill was scuttled. Brown triumphed, and McGee withdrew from government. McGee became disillusioned with the Reform party, and offered himself as an independent candidate in the 1863 election. In reality he campaigned along with George-Étienne Cartier and John Rose. The elec-

Funeral Procession of Hon. Thomas D'Arcy McGee in Montreal on
13 April 1868. National Archives of Canada (NA, c83423)

tion brought to power John A. Macdonald's government, and McGee
gained a cabinet post. As part of the Great Coalition, he attended the
Charlottetown (September 1864) and Quebec (October 1864) conferences on Confederation. At Quebec he proposed that the rights of
religious minorities should be respected in the education system, a
proposal that was written into the British North America Act.[68]

From his experience of politics in three countries, McGee wanted
Irish Canadians to focus their energies on Canadian political questions
and not on the Irish question. McGee himself avoided discussing Irish
national problems and dissociated himself from the Irish struggle. After
the Fenian invasions of 1866,[69] he went so far as to demand the death
penalty for Fenian prisoners. This forthright stance triggered McGee's
political downfall. In the election for president of the St Patrick's Society in Montreal, lawyer Barney Devlin manoeuvered his defeat. McGee
countered by charging that Devlin had allowed the St Patrick Society
to be infiltrated by Fenian sympathizers. In the House of Commons

election of 1867, McGee, with partial help from the Irish constituency, only just managed to defeat Barney Devlin. The Devlin supporters then proceeded to sack McGee's campaign headquarters.

John A. Macdonald did not include McGee in his first government. McGee became the target for the frustrated national goals of Ireland in North America. One of Barney Devlin's supporters, James Patrick Whelan, shot McGee on 7 April 1868 in Ottawa. It was an Irish Canadian hand that effectively ended McGee's life, and after a glorious funeral, his sudden death "left a vacuum within the Irish Catholic secular leadership."[69] Irish Canadians no longer voted as a bloc, nor would they be controlled by politician or party. For a time Thomas D'Arcy McGee had united the Protestant and Catholic Irish. He placed section 93 in the British North America Act to protect the schools of minorities in Ontario and Quebec. McGee began his charismatic career as a visionary Irish republican and ended it as a Canadian Tory.[70]

IRISH CULTURE IN TORONTO

Catholic clergy and laity were concerned not only with the education of youngsters in Upper Canada but also with the religious and social welfare of new Canadians in Toronto. Great energy was expended to solidify religious devotion and fraternal organization among the Irish Catholics.

The first bishop of Toronto was the son of William Power, an Irish sea captain who immigrated with his wife, Mary Roach, to Halifax, Nova Scotia, where Michael Power was born. The future bishop was prepared for ordination to the priesthood in the Quebec seminary and soon became vicar general of the diocese of Montreal under the ultramontane bishop, Jean-Jacques Lartigue. The thirty-six-year-old Power was recommended to lead Ontario's second diocese because he was both Canadian-born and English-speaking. The Bishop of Kingston, Rémi Gaulin, wrote of him: "This gentleman is sufficiently Irish to be well thought of here and sufficiently Canadian to live up to all we might expect of him." He was ordained the bishop of Toronto in 1842 by Bishops Gaulin, Bourget, and Turgeon. Bishop Power (1841–47) was an energetic spiritual leader who visited many of his 50,000 Catholics, and he convoked the first diocesan synod to implant Roman standards among his fledgling community. Pastors were to dwell in their parishes and wear suitable dress; the Roman missal and breviary were to be used and records kept; fees were not to be charged for the administration of sacraments, and baptismal fonts and confession boxes were to be installed in churches. Power was a solicitous pastor. While tending the immigrant victims of typhus among his flock, he contracted the disease and died in 1847. Michael Power was recognized as the founder of a flourishing diocese.[71]

Church historian Brian Clarke, writing a recent history on the Irish-Catholic community in Toronto during the second half of the nineteenth century, raised the question whether the Catholic laity in Toronto were as involved in the "devotional revolution" as the clergy were. Clarke contends that the devotional revolution, which occurred among the Toronto Irish between 1850 and 1895, stimulated among them an energetic piety and lay leadership. He argues that devotional organizations were guided by both the laity and by the clergy, and together by 1870 they had inspired regular church attendance among Catholics. He also asserts that the laity as well as the clergy demonstrated public leadership qualities in forming fraternal organizations. They organized parades, fed the hungry, protected Catholic rights, provided recreational activities, and saw to the burial of the dead. Clarke concludes that the laity were not simply passive participants in the ultramontane devotional revolution but active participants in its successful outcome. The devotional revolution in Toronto revived English-speaking Catholic piety and put it on par with spirituality in Rome, Dublin, New York, Quebec, and the rest of Canada.[72]

Clarke points out that many Irish who came to Canada before the famine were agriculturalists and landowners of modest means.[73] After the mid-1840s, the Irish came to escape the famine and reinforced the numbers of the Irish Canadians in the Maritimes and Canada. He notes that the second bishop of Toronto, the French ultramontane Armand de Charbonnel (1850–60), sparked a twofold revival of Catholicism in Toronto during the 1850s. First, his presence "set the stage for the emergence of a wide variety of church-based voluntary associations, marking the effective beginning of renewal in the Catholic Church." Irish nationalism at the time inspired voluntary benevolent organizations, which provided recreational activities, insurance policies, and assistance to widows for burials. These organizations included the St Vincent de Paul Society (1850), the Young Men's Saint Patrick's Association (1855), and Hibernian Benevolent Society (1858). The voluntary nationalist organizations peaked between 1850 and 1895 and were then replaced by church-affiliated organizations.[74]

The second revival Bishop Charbonnel sparked was a revolution in the devotional life in the parish. He established fraternities, sodalities, and societies that encouraged the traditional Tridentine devotions. These organizations were parish based and stressed the recitation of the rosary, devotion to Our Lady, the stations of the cross, weekly benediction, annual forty hours, yearly missions, holy week services, jubilees, and pilgrimages. These spiritual activities increased the regular attendance at Sunday Mass.[75] More clergy were available to lead an increased number of devotions, and churches were constructed to provide a suitable environment for liturgical and devotional services. During Charbonnel's episcopacy, the first generation of churches in downtown Toronto was completed: St Michael's Cathedral (1848), St Mary's (1852), St Basil's (1855), and St Patrick's (1858). In addition, Toronto's first church, St Paul's (1822), was enlarged and redecorated.[75]

The parishes became the centre of Catholic devotional life. The neo-Romanesque and neo-gothic churches were the houses of God, centres for worship, and sanctuary of God's benediction. The saints of the New Testament were displayed on side altars, and the prophets of the Old Testament arrayed in stained glass windows above. The stations of the cross portrayed the sufferings of Jesus. The images of the Sacred Heart and the crucified Jesus dramatized God's love for humanity. In the tranquil setting of tastefully decorated churches, the faithful enjoyed the music of the pipe organ and small orchestras that pervaded the churches and turned the Sunday Mass into a memorable experience. The effect of the devotional revolution in Toronto was to provide a harmonious environment that encouraged reflective prayer and contemplative quiet in the house of God.[77]

The third bishop of Toronto, John J. Lynch, inherited a religious community that was well organized and expanding rapidly. He was an articulate spokesman for the Irish Catholic community, and in his popular Sunday lectures at St Michael's Cathedral, did not hesitate to attack the Orange Order, vilify Henry VIII and Thomas Cranmer, and blame the British landlords for Irish ills.[78] During his twenty-eight-year administration, he ordained 70 priests, built 40 churches, 30 presbyteries, and seven convents, enlarged the House of Providence, constructed orphanages, and established a boarding-home for women students and working girls. He convoked diocesan synods to set norms for clergy and laity and passed decrees regulating devotions, parish administration, and finances.[79]

Bishop Lynch, however, was less aggressive in his demands for separate schools than his predecessor. He recognized the limits of working-class ratepayers to support separate schools and also feared the backlash of the Protestant majority, who might renege on political concessions made to the separate schools. His episcopal colleagues from Kingston and London called for a firmer stand to gain additional concessions for Catholic schools. In 1876 dissatisfaction with his lacklustre leadership caused the "lay party" of the Toronto Separate School Board and Patrick Boyle of the *Irish Canadian* to call for an accounting of his stewardship. During the next decade, to thwart his iron-fisted control of the board, the battle shifted to the implementation of a secret ballot in separate school board elections. Lynch saw such opposition as corrosive liberalism, serving only to split Catholic political solidarity. In 1862, for Lynch's continued loyalty to the Holy See, Pius IX appointed him prelate assistant to the papal throne, and in 1870, during the First Vatican Council, he was appointed archbishop when Toronto became a metropolitan province.[80]

By the 1870s the Irish Canadians responded fully to Catholic devotions and seventy percent regularly attended Sunday Mass. The devotions replicated Roman spirituality and underlined Petrine authority. They also demonstrated the high level of lay and clerical involvement in public prayer. Devout Toronto parishioners prayed in uniformity with the Church, its bishops, and its supreme head in Rome.[81]

OBLATE MISSIONS AND NATIVE SCHOOLS

As we have seen, the nineteenth-century Catholic revival and expansion in Canada took many forms, especially in the area of missions and educating Catholic youth. Diocesan priests were the pathfinders for the Catholic proselytization of the Canadian Northwest. Yet it was the three hundred Missionary Oblates of Mary Immaculate who provided the main force of missionaries among the native people in the Canadian Northwest. The Oblates also took care of the spiritual needs of the Irish and French workers on the Canadian Pacific Railway. They visited native settlements, dispensing the sacraments, building churches, keeping records, and operating schools. Oblate Fathers and Brothers were the pioneers in the evangelization of western Canadians.

The territory that the Oblates opened up was enormous, as Robert Choquette points out, "nearly seventeen times the size of France, six times that of Ontario, and four times that of Quebec." The Oblates were "the quintessential product of a new mood in Catholicism, a new militancy, a new urge to conquer the world for Christ and his Church." They focused "almost exclusively on matters such as papal infallibility, Catholic hierarchy, and the magisterium of the Church." The Oblates, Choquette continues, "were among the first ultramontane Catholic clergy."[82]

The formal Catholic involvement in the Canadian Northwest began in 1820 when Joseph Provencher was appointed the vicar general of Quebec for the Northwest mission (1820–53). Based at Red River in the Hudson's Bay Territory, Provencher established the parish of Saint-Boniface with a church and rectory and from there sent out diocesan priests, Modest Demers, Jean-Baptiste Thibault, and Louis LaFlèche, to the Métis and native settlements. In the middle 1840s, Provencher

Bishop Alexandre Taché, OMI, of Saint-Boniface (1853–94), photo from the 1860s–1870s. (Archives Deschâteles [AD])

was able to attract the Grey Nuns and the Oblate Fathers to Saint-Boniface.[83] In 1845 the twenty-one-year-old Oblate subdeacon, Alexandre-Antonin Taché, with Pierre Aubert, paddled fourteen hundred miles by canoe to Saint-Boniface to begin a methodical evangelization of the Northwest. When the aged Provencher laid eyes on the youthful colleagues, he was said to have remarked of Taché, "They send me children! But it is men we need." Provencher revised his hasty judgment once Taché was ordained to succeed him.[84] The Sisters of Charity of Montreal (Grey Nuns) had arrived the previous year to share in the great evangelical undertaking. They constructed a convent and opened boys' and girls' schools in the parish of Saint-Boniface.[85]

Other church institutions emerged: Saint-François-Xavier Parish five miles west of Saint-Boniface (1824), Saint-Norbert Parish south of Saint-Boniface, Saint-Charles Parish to the west on the Assiniboine (1854), Sainte-Anne Parish at Pointe-de-Chênes (1860s), Collège Saint-Boniface (1881), and, across the Red River from Saint-Boniface at Winnipeg, St Mary's Church (1874) and a convent for the Sisters of the Holy Names of Jesus and Mary (1881). The settlement of the prairies was difficult and slow until the Canadian Pacific Railway (CPR) reached Winnipeg in 1885. With the CPR came the railway workers, one-third Canadien and two-thirds Irish, English, Scottish, Icelandic, and Danish. Of this group fifty percent were Catholic. The Oblates opened a parish in 1868 at the settlement of Qu'Appelle (Saskatchewan). They also operated a native residential school, which by 1898 enrolled 238 students. The school was staffed by eighteen religious and lay persons.[86]

When Provencher died in June 1853, his thirty-year-old coadjutor with right of succession and the superior of the Oblates in the Northwest since 1851, Alexandre-Antonin Taché, became the bishop of Saint-Boniface. In Quebec, France, and Rome, Taché incessantly begged necessities for the western church and distributed them to the missions around Saint-Boniface and throughout the Northwest. In December 1869 he sought and was promised by John A. MacDonald an unconditional amnesty for Louis Riel's provisional government in Manitoba.

Taché had hoped that Manitoba could be brought into the Canadian confederation in a peaceful fashion, but at the same time as the amnesty was promised, Ottawa troops were sent to Manitoba to put down the provisional government. The bishop was instrumental in establishing the new Manitoba government and influencing the bill, passed unanimously in 1871, that set up the system of Catholic and Protestant public schools that Manitoban law enshrined in 1871.[87] He continued to plead before the House of Commons committee the importance of an unconditional amnesty for the Métis leaders and wrote several pamphlets to that effect. In 1873 the Manitoba government arrested Ambroise Lepine for the murder of Thomas Scott, forcing other Métis leaders to flee for their lives. Taché now admitted that he had been "used" by the government's promise of amnesty to keep the Métis quiet.[88]

Supporting the founding of the Société de Colonisation de Manitoba in 1874, Taché sent Fathers Lacombe and Doucet to Quebec and the United States to promote French-speaking settlers to the Canadian West. The effort was not successful and English-speaking settlers swamped French-speaking settlers on the Canadian prairies.

When the Métis rose at Batoche in 1885, Taché asked the federal government to assure them "justice and clemency," but once again, the government chose violence and ignored his plea for political settlement.[89] In 1891 he led the fight by Canadian bishops to have the Manitoba school legislation eliminating French schools disallowed. After almost forty years of labour to secure Catholic schools for Manitoba, Taché had to accept defeat at the time of his death in 1894. He was a much-loved and tragic figure who pursued the goals of Québécois ultramontane Catholicism in the Canadian Northwest with great energy. But his hope for a bilingual, bicultural, and bireligious Manitoba was defeated by Anglo-Protestant immigration and the Canadian government.[90]

The Oblate coadjutor bishop of Saint-Boniface, Vital Grandin, organized mission activity in the 1860s in the area of Lac Sainte-Anne and was placed in charge of the Alberta region. He had learned native languages and spent most of his time in native settlements such as Fort Chipewyan and Ile-à-la-Crosse, or touring outlying settlements. In 1868 Grandin took up residence at Saint-Albert and three years later was appointed its bishop (1871–1902). Reputedly a humble and saintly man, Grandin enjoyed warm friendships with Archbishop Taché and Father Albert Lacombe.

Grandin ran into sharp conflict over the Lac-La-Biche mission with Henri Faraud, vicar apostolic of Athabasca-Mackenzie. Archbishop Taché asked Grandin to cede the mission temporarily to the vicariate because it acted as a supply station for Faraud. With the change of Hudson's Bay Company supply routes in 1873, Grandin asked that the Lac-La-Biche mission be returned to the diocese of St Albert so that he could look after the spiritual needs of its inhabitants. For a long time Bishop Faraud refused to return La Biche, a refusal Grandin deemed unjustified. Shortly before Faraud's death, and after twenty years of strife, the mission was finally returned to Grandin's care.[91]

Albert Lacombe served as a roving missionary throughout the Canadian Northwest. Welcomed and trusted by most, he was a missionary at Lac-Sainte-Anne (1853–63) and to the Blackfoot and Cree (1865–72) at Saint-Paul-des-Cris (today northern Alberta). As the immigration agent for the bishop of Regina, he had brought French Canadians to the West. He became the first pastor of St Mary's Church in Winnipeg (1874–80) and then missionary to the railway gangs in Kenora (1880–82).[92] In the mid 1880s Oblate priests undertook missionary visits to the tiny Catholic community in Calgary, and the Faithful Companions of Jesus opened a girls' school there in 1885.[93]

The territory on the Pacific coast was waiting to be proselytized. The French Canadian priest Modeste Demers, an excellent linguist in European and native languages,[94] was consecrated bishop of Victoria (1846–71) and vigorously pursued his ministry on Vancouver Island despite a lack resources. Discouraged at his failure to recruit clergy, he was pleasantly surprised when the Oblate Fathers and the Sisters of St Anne arrived at Victoria in 1847 and gratuitously offered their services. The Sisters of Providence and the Holy Names of Jesus and Mary soon followed them to the Pacific coast.[95] The Oblates focused their missionary work on the mainland and opened native missions at Lake Okanagan (1859), New Westminster (1860), and St Mary's (1863). The Oblate Superior, Louis D'Herbomez was based at New Westminster. Appointed the vicar apostolic of the British Columbia mainland in 1863, he proceeded in the following years to open fifty-five chapels in Indian villages.

He regularly visited these missions on pastoral tours.[96] After his death in 1890, he was succeeded in 1890 by another Oblate, Paul Durieu, who became the first bishop of New Westminster (1890–99).[97]

CONCLUSION

Ultramontane spirituality imbued the faithful with a renewed reverence for the Chair of Peter and respect for its spiritual leadership. On a practical level, it promoted pilgrimages to the crypt of St Peter in the Holy City, uniformity of Roman devotions in Catholic parishes and missions, and the practice of sending bright seminarians from Catholic countries to be educated in Rome and embrace the *Romanità*. Ultramontane spirituality moulded Canadian institutions to reflect the triumphal piety of the restored papacy. It demanded that the liturgical and devotional life of individual parishes reflect the papal devotions of Holy Eucharist, Sacred Heart, Corpus Christi, Forty Hours, and Our Lady. Schools, educating Canadians and new Canadians in both Catholic knowledge and competitive skills, were encouraged to inspire their students with the love of the Holy Father.[98] Canadian neo-ultramontane spirituality transmitted a warm, social, and religious commitment to the Roman tradition.

Bishop Bourget in Montreal exerted political pressure on the government to place schools, hospitals, and social structures under church direction. In Quebec, piety, nationalism, and social services were yoked together in an explosive brew. Recognizing the sharp division between Tory and Liberal policies, Rome advised the clergy to bridge the gap and adopt a policy of moderation and harmony. The Holy See demonstrated its impartiality by appointing the Liberal Elzéar Taschereau as archbishop of Quebec and the ultramontane George Conroy as the apostolic delegate to Canada. Frustrated by Rome's demands that he finance the Montreal branch of Laval University, Bourget resigned his see in 1876. His resignation left the militant ultramontane Canadiens without a champion – except of the brilliant LaFlèche who was left to languish in the ecclesial doldrums. By default Canadian leadership passed to the moderate Taschereau.[99]

The Franciscan bishops in Newfoundland expanded their influence in St John's, kept the Irish submissive to London, and enlarged their credibility in the outports. In central Canada D'Arcy McGee fought for separate schools and enjoyed the success of seeing his work guaranteeing education rights to minorities in central Canada enshrined in the British North America Act. The separate schools and the devotional revolution changed Catholics in the provinces, and both the laity and clergy animated these religious activities.

Diocesan clergy were the pathfinders of the church in the Canadian Northwest, but it was the zealous Oblates and the women religious who swept through the territory establishing Catholic institutions. Ultramontane spirituality of the nineteenth century guided the missions, missionaries, and schools, and for their own reasons the native people proved receptive to this message. Our attention shifts from the Canadian Northwest to the schools in the Maritime provinces and central Canada, which now became the battlefields between ultramontane Catholics and Canadian secularists.

5 Ultramontanes and Catholic Schools

Education in the Maritime provinces and central Canada became the symbol for Catholics of the spiritual struggle waged between the religious and secular worlds. Educational institutions formed young Catholics for competition in the marketplace, but more importantly, they moulded future leaders in Roman devotions, spirituality, and loyalty. The religious sisters in the Maritimes and central Canada built primary and secondary schools to offer Catholics basic education and promote Christian knowledge, and diocesan communities constructed similar institutions to provide university education and skilled professional workers. To further these educational goals, Catholics prepared themselves to support Confederation in the hope of getting government funding for separate schools in the Maritime provinces and central Canada. The Canadian church, under pressure from both conservative and liberal Catholics, was forced to deal with the future. The founding of liberal arts colleges for men and women was a significant step in adapting ultramontane spirituality to Canadian ways.

SCOTS OF EASTERN NOVA SCOTIA

St Francis Xavier College was established in Antigonish to provide Scottish Catholics with the education necessary for their social advancement and cultural integration into Canadian society. Its founder, Bishop Colin F. MacKinnon, believed in the importance of educating youth to become both clerical and lay leaders in society.[1] The Catholic Highlanders, argues historian James D. Cameron, came to Canada with high hopes of

The first four women to graduate with BAs from St Francis Xavier University, 1897:
Florence Macdonald, Mary Bissett, Margaret MacDougall, and Lillian Macdonald. (SFXUA)

a better future. In a rural Nova Scotia, some were content to be subsistence farmers and eke out a meagre existence for their families.[2] Others,
hoping for larger farms, a better standard of living, and more substantial
homes, had to tame the Nova Scotian landscape with roads, towns, mills,
and schools while at the same time providing their families with the necessities of life. Mixed employment in farming, fishing, manufacturing,
mining, shipbuilding, export trade, and civil service generated prosperity for many. Together the subsistence and market farmers struggled to
open up this new country.[3]

Key to the future for most farmers was a good education for their
young. The founding of St Francis Xavier College was part of this dream.
The liberal arts curriculum was to be taught in English, not Gaelic, and
gradually law, medicine, and theology were to be introduced. In the
nineteenth-century tradition, great emphasis was placed on academic
discipline and character formation. This formula worked for St Francis
Xavier students, many of whom later became professionals not only in
Nova Scotia but also across Canada and the United States.[4]

Bishop John Cameron of Antigonish (1877–1910) with his diocesan priests, ca. 1895: Back Row: Frs possibly Michael Laffin, Colin F. MacKinnon, Michael Mackenzie, Roderick MacInnis, Alexander F. MacGillivray, Archibald J. Chisholm, James Quinan, VG, possibly Dr Alexander Chisholm, possibly Alexander L. MacDonald, unidentified, Duncan Paul MacDonald; Front Row: Dr Daniel MacGregor, Bishop John Cameron, Daniel J. MacIntosh. St Francis Xavier University Archives (SFXUA)

The third bishop of Antigonish, John R. Cameron (1877–1910), was energetic and political, and he exuded the *Romanità*.[5] He wielded great influence at home, and his advice was sought by Rome, Quebec, and Ottawa. Soon after becoming bishop, he stabilized the finances of St Francis Xavier, revitalized the faculty, and expanded its facilities. The renewed college was in the forefront of education for women and produced its first four women graduates in 1897.[6] The Alumni Association, formed in 1893, gained importance within the college and throughout the Maritime provinces. With two of its members on the St Francis Xavier board of governors, it played an advisory role in the educational policy of the college. The alumni executive was outstanding enough to attract to its ranks people of provincial prominence.[7]

The college celebrated its golden jubilee in 1905. In his address to alumni and students, President Alexander Thompson proclaimed that St Francis Xavier had helped Highlanders overcome a "legacy of poverty, oppression, and inferiority."[8] Ultramontane Catholicism moulded the Nova Scotian university youth in a tradition of discipline and morality. Their families were strengthened and devotional practice was enriched, but the necessity for financial stringency did not entirely leave Nova Scotian life. A good number of those with poor holdings were forced to migrate to New England, Ontario, and western Canada. The Scots paid a heavy price for their assimilation to Canadian ways. Over the century they prospered in Canada but lost their Gaelic language, Highland traditions, and much of their Scottish identity.[9] The college revealed the herculean effort of the Catholic Scots to enhance their social standing and to assist their cultural integration in Canada.

WOMEN'S EDUCATION IN CENTRAL NOVA SCOTIA

The goal of the Sisters of Charity of Halifax was the education of Irish youth in central Nova Scotia just as the goal of St F.X. was the education of Scottish youth in eastern Nova Scotia. Catholic education in Nova Scotia preceded provincial legislation creating the public schools. The Sisters of Charity originated from Emmitsburg, Maryland. It was there that they adapted the seventeenth-century rule of St Vincent de Paul to the contingencies of North American life. Founding Catholic schools throughout the United States, they quickly became professionals in teaching and administration. Their schools became axiomatic for disciplined teaching and operated in the principal cities such as Boston, New York, and Philadelphia. Bishop William Walsh, a great friend of the ultramontanist archbishop of Dublin, Paul Cullen,[10] requested in 1849 that the Sisters of Charity in New York come to Halifax to open a school and, if possible, a hospital and orphanage. Responding within the year to his request, Sister Mary Basilia McCann came with four sisters from New York City to Halifax. They opened a school, and by the end of its first school year it had enrolled over four hundred students.[11]

Attracting several recruits, the Sisters of Charity set up an independent Motherhouse at Halifax in 1856. They started with five sisters. Two years later, the fourteen-member community was legally incorporated in the province of Nova Scotia. The Halifax-born Mary Josephine Carroll was appointed mother superior and supervised their three schools and orphanage. In 1860 the sisters added houses at Bathurst, New Brunswick, and western Nova Scotia, and in 1866 they volunteered to care for cholera victims on McNab Island. The Mount St Vincent Motherhouse was opened on Bedford Basin in 1873.[12] Adapting the spiritual tradition of St Vincent de Paul to Nova Scotia, the Sisters of Charity in a very short time inculturated their religious community into the needs of the Halifax environment.

When the Conservative government of Charles Tupper came to power in 1863, he had two major goals. First, he was committed to bringing Nova Scotia into the Canadian confederation, and second, he was determined to establish free schools throughout the province. In the school act of 1864 he established county boards of commissioners and local school districts under elected trustees and offered trustees funds to build free schools. Subsequent acts over the next two years imposed a compulsory tax assessment to provide regular funding and a universal system of common schools. Premier Tupper assured Archbishop Thomas Connolly of Halifax (1859–76) that Catholic rights would always be protected by local arrangements. Bishop Colin MacKinnon of Antigonish accepted the same assurances. By a gentlemen's agreement schools would be provided to parishes for public instruction and for religious instruction after hours. The working out of this gentlemen's agreement was problematic in that Halifax and Sydney were well provided for, but Dartmouth and other Catholic communities did not have schools. Cape Breton became "a bewildering patchwork of arrangements."[13] Catholic institutions under these haphazard agreements had to shift for themselves and provide schools where financially possible. Committed religious sisters were the mainstay of a system that provided high-quality education at modest cost.

The Sisters of Charity of Halifax governed themselves under the direction of a mother superior and her elected council. A local priest appointed by the archbishop was their superior general and spiritual adviser. The unhappy division of authority between the mother superior and the superior general was a source of continual conflict. Controversy erupted in 1876 after the death of Mount St Vincent's champion, Archbishop Connolly. His successor, the Irish-born Michael Hannan (1877–82), did not like the independent style of the sisters and thought that they lacked discipline. Hannan, who had been influential with the government of Charles Tupper, was an active member of the Halifax Board of School Commissioners from 1865 to 1874. In negotiating Catholic school matters, Tupper preferred Hannan to the more explosive Connolly.[14] Hannan had good relations in Rome, and the apostolic delegate, George Conroy, consecrated him the archbishop of Halifax in 1877 at St Mary's Cathedral.

Hannan's distrust of the sisters dated back to before his consecration when he was superior general of the congregation. He was an acknowledged expert on Canadian education and ecumenism. According to historian Marianna O'Gallagher, he "attempted to force his own views onto the Sisters and was callous in badgering the young members into supporting him against the Mother Superior, to whom they had also vowed obedience."[15] Archbishop Connolly, when he understood how the priest had manipulated the young sisters, removed Father Hannan in 1859 from his position as superior general to the sisters.

Eighteen years later Father Michael Hannan succeeded Connolly as archbishop of Halifax. He was industrious in the construction of schools and consolidating the "gentlemen's agreement" between the province and the church.[16] Nevertheless, his pettiness in dealing with the Sisters of Charity remained, and his episcopate became euphemistically known to the sisters as "the Time of the Troubles."[17] As O'Gallagher puts it, "He [had] interfered in school board appointments, attempted to prevent public attendance at Mount St Vincent closing exercises, and caused other difficulties."[18] In the face of episcopal harassment, Mother Mary Francis Maguire (1876–81) refused to back down and continued to direct affairs within the congregation. She corrected any irregularities and brushed aside abuse from the archbishop's office. Acting on the advice of their lawyer, John Sparrow David Thompson, the future prime minister of Canada, the sisters prepared a report and sent it to the cardinal prefect of Sacred Congregation of Propaganda in Rome.[19] The struggle caused a rift among the Halifax sisters between those who took the side of Archbishop Michael Hannan and those who stood by Mother Mary Francis. Strong feelings erupted, and thirteen sisters left the congregation. To resolve the conflict, the Holy See called upon Bishop John Cameron of Arichat (Antigonish) to prepare a report. His account criticized Hannan for mismanaging the archdiocese as well as for his pettiness towards the Sisters of Charity.[20]

The matter was resolved in 1880 when Pope Leo XIII, in a highly irregular procedure, changed the ecclesial jurisdiction of the Sisters of Charity of Halifax, taking it from the archbishop of Halifax and placing it under Bishop Cameron of Antigonish.[21] As part of Rome's policy of increasing involvement in local church affairs, the Holy See had shown itself willing to take a direct interest in the plight of the sisters and intervene on their behalf. The sisters in Halifax were grateful to the Holy See for this timely action.[22] Mother Mary Francis, worn-out mentally and physically, resigned to allow for the election of a new superior.

Life improved for the sisters when a new archbishop was ordained in 1883 to replace the deceased Michael Hannan. Prince Edward Island-born Cornelius O'Brien was the first Canadian-born archbishop of Halifax (1882–1906). After obtaining doctorates in divinity and phi-

losophy from the Urban College in Rome, he lived an idyllic life as a
Prince Edward Island country pastor, writing poetry and philosophy.
Partly because of his scholarship and deep spirituality and partly because he was innocent in the ways of archdiocesan politics, the youthful priest was appointed to the Halifax see.

In the archdiocese he fostered the creation of a network of Catholic
social and educational institutions and prevented the legal takeover in
1892 of the diocesan-built Russell Street school by the Board of School
Commissioners, which funded it. He reopened St Mary's College in
1903 and supported the establishment of the Acadian Collège Sainte-
Anne at Church Point. As president of the Royal Society of Canada in
1896–97, he brought prestige to the Catholic community.[23] When it
was clear to the new archbishop that a Catholic hospital was necessary
for Halifax, he called upon the Sisters of Charity in 1886 to open the
Halifax Infirmary.[24] This collaboration closed the breach of the
Hannan years and restored the friendship between the archdiocese of
Halifax and the Sisters of Charity.

One great twentieth-century mother superior of the Halifax Charities was Mary Berchmans Walsh. From 1901 to 1926, she led the congregation during a period of expansion and consolidation. She
obtained a college charter for Mount St Vincent in 1925 and pushed
for the college's right to award graduate degrees.[25] That goal was
finally met in 1966, when the Nova Scotia legislature granted Mount
St Vincent a university charter.[26]

Since the time when Bishop John Cameron was appointed by the
pope to be superior general of the Charities, the Spiritual Exercises of
St Ignatius were key to the spirituality of the sisters. When she became
superior in 1901, Mother Berchmans renewed the emphasis on Igna-
tian spirituality and made spiritual growth the first priority of the congregation. She emphasized the importance of an uninterrupted two-
year novitiate education in the spiritual life rather than two years of
on-the-job training. Each sister in the community was to make an annual eight-day retreat preached by a retreat director of the Society of
Jesus. Retreat masters periodically exhorted the sisters on different aspects of the Jesuit spirituality of "action in contemplation."[27]

The diocesan priest Edward J. McCarthy served Mount St Vincent
on a regular basis over many years. He was an influential member of
the archdiocese and its archbishop from 1906 to 1931. Appointed the
superior general of the congregation in 1906, Father McCarthy encouraged the sisters to seek papal approval for their institute. When
they gained this approval, the Charities would no longer need a priest
superior general and the mother superior would automatically become the mother general. Completing the five-year trial period for

approval, the Sisters of Charity of Halifax became a Pontifical Institute in 1913. Papal approval meant that the religious congregation was trans-diocesan, had direct communication with Roman congregations, and gave its obedience to the Holy See. During those years Mother Berchmans opened houses and initiated new apostolates, and the number of sisters in the congregation increased from 190 to 678.[28]

Her successor, Mother Mary Louise Meahan, expanded the existing institutions and kept pace with the increasing demand for new apostolates and more workers. Between 1926 and 1944 she renovated Mount St Vincent to provide adequate facilities for novitiate, college, and offices. She rebuilt the Halifax Infirmary and made it a public institution. She opened catechetical and social centres and a Native residential school at Shubenacadie, Nova Scotia.[29]

A number of commanding and capable mother superiors directed the apostolates of the Sisters of Charity of Halifax and enabled them to become leaders in the operation of Catholic schools. They embraced the ultramontane spirituality of their Canadian and American associates and adapted it to the unpredictable dictates of the gentlemen's agreement. They deepened their identity as Canadian church women by adopting Jesuit spirituality and embracing its great love for service in the Nova Scotian community. Firmly anchored in their mission, they were able to open schools, win autonomy, gain a university charter, and remain staunchly committed. In all their endeavours the Sisters of Charity revealed their love of the Christian church and of the Catholic culture working its way into the life of Nova Scotia.

WOMEN'S EDUCATION IN NEW BRUNSWICK

A similar expression of Catholic religious culture was established in New Brunswick. As in Nova Scotia, Catholic schools were established in the province before public schools. Bishop Thomas Connolly of Saint John (1852–59) founded the Sisters of Charity for the Diocese of Saint John to educate poor immigrant Irish girls in religion and life skills and to assist in the cholera epidemics of the early 1850s. In 1854 four Sisters of Charity from New York City who were still novices volunteered for service in New Brunswick. Sister Honoria Conway led the small band to Saint John and became the founder and first mistress of novices. In October 1854 Bishop Connolly received the religious vows of the first four and adapted their constitutions to the needs of New Brunswick Sisters of Charity. The community rapidly took root and within ten years the sisters had thirty-five members in two communities at Saint John and Fredericton. In 1857 the first French-speaking community was opened at Sainte-Basile de Madawaska. In Saint John, Connolly also established the Religious of the Sacred Heart to educate daughters of middle-class Catholics.[30] Not to be outdone, the New Brunswick legislature passed legislation in 1858 providing generous grants to parish schools in an effort to make schools more accessible, especially in rural areas. Catholic schools among others were the recipients of those grants.[31]

The leadership of the Sisters of Charity rotated for the first twenty years and encouraged participation of the sisters in the governance of their communities. Beginning in 1874 to 1897, Mother Augustine O'Toole became the first long-serving mother superior. In full control of the congregation, she began a policy of expansion. She opened a high school for girls in Saint John and allowed the sisters to be involved in social work. She founded St Patrick's Industrial Home in 1880 for orphan boys and a nursing home for the elderly in 1888. With both English-speaking and French-speaking sisters in the congregation, the membership settled at about two-thirds Irish and one-third Acadian. A French-speaking novitiate was opened at Buctouche in 1881. At the close of Mother O'Toole's term of office, the congregation numbered ninety-five members who spoke either French or English, but the administration and customs remained English.[32]

Rapidly increasing in numbers and exercising their ministry beyond the boundaries of the Saint John diocese, the sisters recognized that it was time to seek an international charter from Rome. New Brunswick-born Mother Thomas O'Brien (1903–18) followed the route of the Sisters of Charity of Halifax and submitted the rules to the Holy See for approval. The Holy See made the Sisters of Charity of the Immaculate Conception a Papal Institute in 1914. The congregation was then free to govern itself and to expand outside the diocese to western Canada.[33]

The expansion to other Canadian provinces meant that the English-speaking Charities accepted leadership roles across the country. The Acadians recognized that the expanded number of Canadian communities threatened their existence and preferred to give more attention to the needs of Acadians in New Brunswick. In 1914 the French-speaking sisters asked to leave the English-speaking congregation and to reopen the Buctouche house, which had been closed in 1890 as a French-speaking novitiate. Permission was not immediately given, and by 1923, more than two hundred and twenty sisters carried out the mission of the congregation.[34]

Doubling the number of houses and ministries, Mother Alphonsus Carney (1918–30) enlarged both English-speaking and French-speaking services. For the English speakers, the congregation opened schools, orphanages, homes for the aged, hospitals, and industrial homes for boys both in New Brunswick and Saskatchewan. For the Acadians, the congregation opened houses in Memramcook, Shediac, Buctouche, and Moncton. In 1924, despite some attempt at accommodation, fifty-three Acadian sisters elected to separate from the other two hundred and thirty sisters to serve the Acadian community exclusively. They named their new congregation Les Religieuses de Notre Dame du Sacré-Coeur. After the separation the Sisters of Charity erected new houses in Alberta and British Columbia. Novices from the western provinces broadened the ethnic composition by adding English, Scottish, German, and eastern European names to their ranks. Yet the Irish Canadians continued to administer the Sisters of Charity.[35]

During the thirty years prior to the Second Vatican Council, the sisters enjoyed a period of stability. More emphasis was placed on educating and professionalizing the sisters than on their fulfilment of charitable needs. During the 1920s and afterward, young women who entered the congregation arrived with university degrees in arts, nursing, and teaching. In the spirit of the time, they entered the church for careers of service.[36]

The professionalization of teaching, nursing, administration, and social work placed new significance on degrees and specialized training. It was now important for young sisters to complete professional programs in religious life and to specialize in areas of need. In the 1930s sisters began degree programs at Catholic institutions such as Mount St Vincent and St Francis Xavier, the Catholic University of America, and St Louis and Fordham universities. At the same time the congregation extended its ministry beyond the prairies to British Columbia, opening five houses, including a hospital, in Vancouver.[37]

Historian Elizabeth McGahan has established that life in the convent during the interwar period, rather than imposing restrictions, offered "more potential opportunities for professional self-fulfilment than the secular workplace." That generation, she states, was "ahead of the secular world by providing such opportunities, especially for talented women coming from the working classes."[38] In the postwar period, sisters enhanced their skills by attending secular universities in New Brunswick, Ontario, Alberta, and the United States.[38]

During the administration of Mother Joan Kane (1948–60), the congregation arrived at the highpoint of its membership and the numerical growth of its apostolic houses. The number of sisters reached more than three hundred and seventy-five. The interwar experience of continual growth moulded the attitude of superiors and the congregation. As she completed major projects in New Brunswick and western Canada, Kane became known as a builder. As these institutions were being erected vocations to the sisterhood began to decline, signalling that fewer people would be available in future to staff the expansion projects. Bishops and Catholic communities continued to demand more schools and more hospitals, placing a heavy burden on staff. It became apparent from the struggles of the 1950s that expansion had peaked and that no new work could be undertaken.[39]

The community's expansionary phase reached a plateau by the middle 1960s at about four hundred members. During this period, government regulation and financing brought about the gradual secularization of religious institutions operated by the Charities. Job requirements were raised and salaries were increased, while employment opportunities for women improved. The influence of the congregation waned as fewer sisters worked on staff and in administration. Church people and religious sisters struggled on the governing boards to maintain some guidance and control of educational and medical policies.[40] The loss of personnel and the professionalization of the staff reduced the responsibilities of these sister volunteers who operated an extensive social network at modest expense.

WOMEN'S EDUCATION IN QUEBEC

The warm embrace of French Canadian culture deterred the Irish Catholics from leaving *la belle province* and focused the attention of French and English speakers alike on the values of religion, family, and education.[41] While the education of young men was considered crucial and followed the well-established program of the *collège classique*, the education of young women was considered less necessary. In fact, the ultramontane church in Quebec, as in Ontario and the United States,[42] was reluctant to allow women's colleges to open. It feared that such a move might encourage the spirit of modernity, a movement condemned by the church. Following the Conquest of 1763 and the Quebec Act of 1774, the church gradually gained control of French- and English-speaking Catholic education from primary to university level. Integrating the values of religion, nation, and family into a Catholic system, the Church in the 1840s and 1850s left a definitive mark on education in Quebec. The downside to this integrated and cohesive society, according to historian Jean Huntley-Maynard, was the church's belief in conformity. It thought that a healthy society must be guided by a firm hand; hence it did not hesitate to influence Quebec newspapers, shun politicians who deviated from ultramontane spirituality, or crush the liberal club *Institut Canadien*.[43]

The Council of Public Instruction was set up by legislation in 1869 to oversee education in Quebec. It consisted of two committees that separately governed the Catholic and Protestant school systems. No education bills passed the assembly without the prior approval of the Catholic and Protestant committees. Further legislation in 1875 guaranteed that the bishops of Quebec would be members of the council and in fact control the majority of votes. The Catholic committee offered the *collège classique* under the direction of religious orders to instruct young men and prepare them for university. The Jesuits and the Presentation Brothers operated colleges for English-speaking Catholic youngsters. Only in 1931 was D'Arcy McGee High School opened as the first Catholic public secondary school in Montreal.[44] The *collège classique* and the *petit seminaire* appeared to be élitist for young men and necessarily excluded females.[45] During these years clerics moulded the school curricula according to the vision of ultramontane theology. This arrangement lasted until the 1960s and the advent of the Quiet Revolution in Quebec.

To receive a secondary school education of quality, Catholic girls had to attend Ville Marie, which was operated by the Congrégation-de-Notre-Dame (CND), or other private schools guided by the Sisters of the Sacred Heart, or the Holy Names of Jesus and Mary. Those who wanted post-secondary education attended secular universities such as McGill or universities in the United States or France. The Canadien leaders disliked having to send their daughters to secular universities, a circumstance of which the church did not approve.[46]

A conservative spirituality circumscribed the ambitions of young women by assigning them the functions of motherhood and homemaker. Women, according to this view, were to preserve the sanctity of the home and educate the children in piety and religion. The church and the Catholic home were united into a firm bulwark against the dangers of secularism and materialism. The Catholic devotional revolution in the 1840s and 1850s fostered the growth of sodalities, devotions, and activities that idealized the role of the Virgin Mary as the model for women. This gentle, pious, and romanticized vision of women was pervasive among the middle and upper classes in the Victorian era.[47]

As an interesting alternative to a life of domesticity, women could join the sisterhood and become members of teaching or hospital congregations of religious women.[48] The teaching or hospital sister had considerable influence in her society. The Congregation of Notre Dame, founded in Quebec in the second half of the seventeenth century by Marguerite Bourgeoys, extended its schools to the Maritime provinces, Ontario, and the New England states and played a pivotal role in women's education. Throughout the nineteenth century the scope of women and religious sisters slowly expanded. Women provided services for children, the aged, the blind, and the deaf, operated shelters, and offered instruction in domestic science. The entry of women into higher studies was still in the future.[49]

Sister Sainte-Anne-Marie (Marie-Aveline Bengle (1861–1937) Photo by Albert Dumas,
courtesy Archives CND, Montreal

Lay women traditionally shared in the charitable and philanthropic
activities of Quebec convents. They became partners in the various
apostolates exercised by the sisters. Women were soon to cross the in-
visible frontier into the educational and cultural life of Quebec. Both
lay and women religious began to work for changes. With an eye to increasing the educational opportunities for women, a Montreal branch
of the National Council of Women was formed in 1893. Prominent
Montrealer Marie Lacoste-Gérin-Lajoie "looked to the Congregation
of Notre Dame to support the cause of education for women and to
plead its case with Archbishop Paul Bruchési."[50]

Bishops such as Bruchési and politicians such as Henri Bourassa were
shocked that Catholic women would publicly plead for educational facilities and were inclined to greet their overtures with ridicule. They argued that women activists were betraying the Catholic values of church,
family, and society. The principal of Mont Ste-Marie, Sr Ste-Anne Marie,
quietly and effectively lobbied the administrators of the Congregation of
Notre Dame to convince them that teaching at the university level was a
suitable apostolate for sisters. She also pointed out that the university
might be a propitious recruiting ground for religious vocations.

In 1904 women were allowed for the first time to audit literature courses at Laval University. Robertine Barry lobbied the congregation, arguing that now was the time to establish a college for women who planned to attend university. Marie Lacoste-Gérin-Lajoie advised the sisters that her daughter Marie would go to university in 1908 – in Montreal if possible, but if not, out of the province.[51]

Sr Ste-Anne Marie beefed up the high school program at Mont Ste-Marie with "philosophy, chemistry and law." The parents of the students pressured the Congregation of Notre Dame to award their daughters academic diplomas that would qualify them for university. The sisters proposed to the Catholic committee of the Department of Public Instruction that they be allowed to teach post-secondary courses. The committee turned them down flat, and the issue was dropped for the moment. To complicate matters, the congregation itself was divided between those who understood the importance of this venture and those who dismissed Sr Ste-Anne Marie's efforts as "modernism." The CND general council reviewed Sr Ste-Anne Marie's proposal and determined it was not urgent.[52]

The breakthrough came in 1908 with the announcement in *La Patrie* of the opening of a non-denominational *lycée* for young women with a curriculum imported from France. This unexpected turn of events caused the CND general council and Archbishop Paul Bruchési (1897–1939) to reverse their positions. They urged Sr Ste-Anne Marie to go ahead with the opening of a classical college for English- and French-speaking women leading to a four-year baccalaureate degree. In September 1908 Laval University became affiliated with Notre Dame Collegiate Institute and École supérieure d'enseignement pour les jeunes filles. Sr Ste-Anne Marie became the director of the school and Sr St Agnes Romaine the dean of the institute. Post-secondary education for women in Quebec had begun.[53] The Catholic School Commission later named Sr Ste-Anne Marie as its first female member. The sisters of the École supérieure were part of the first wave of Quebecoise women seeking educational opportunities and professional career equality.[54]

At the end of the nineteenth century the Quebec church, at the apex of ultramontane spirituality in Canada, was reluctant to encourage the foundation of women's colleges for fear of giving way to modernism.[55] Nevertheless, at Montreal in 1908 a four-year university program was initiated with the approval of the church by the Congregation of Notre Dame. Despite the resistance of some authorities and several newspapers, higher education for women was launched and the seeds of a more open church were spreading.

WOMEN'S EDUCATION IN ONTARIO

In the early 1840s Canada East (Quebec) and Canada West (Ontario) created public and separate schools. Canadian-born Bishop Michael Power of Toronto (1841–47) served as chairman of the public board of education in Toronto from 1845 to 1847 "to associate himself with the new education movement."[56] By contrast, his successor, Bishop Armand de Charbonnel (1850–60), insisted that children in his diocese attend the schools administered by the separate school board. Education remained a priority for Ontario Catholics, and their primary schools were maintained despite shortfalls in government support. Other religious minorities did not open schools at all or were soon discouraged and let their schools go. Catholic interest in separate schools gained momentum and increased steadily through the century. The Catholics considered education a religious issue, so for them elementary education was a first priority.

The British government handed down the Act of Union of 1841 to join the provinces of Upper and Lower Canada into one legislative unit. For administrative purposes Canada was then divided into the jurisdictions of Canada East and Canada West. The Education Acts of 1841 and 1843 instituted in Ontario the tradition of public and separate schools. These acts provided school boards to administer Protestant common schools and other school boards to administer separate schools for religious minorities.[57] The arrangement lasted until Queen Victoria proclaimed Confederation on 1 July 1867 when the funding of Ontario denominational schools was extended into the new era. Catholic schools in Nova Scotia and New Brunswick were not included in the agreement because their schools were not considered to be publicly funded by law at the time of Confederation.

In Canada West funding based on attendance was conceded to the schools of religious minorities, who were in conscience not able to attend the public schools, and this concession included Catholics and dissenting Protestants. Catholics and some other denominations opened separate schools with partial funding from the provincial government. Funding was based on attendance and on the willingness of the separate schools to accept the same provincial examinations and inspections as the public schools. The legislation effectively guaranteed Protestant schools in Canada East and separate schools in Canada West to those who could not in conscience attend the common schools. All religious denominations in Canada West had the opportunity to open separate schools, but only the Catholics demonstrated long-term interest by building schools and maintaining them in spite

Bishop Lynch of Toronto (1860–88) attended the First Vatican Council, and, as the first archbishop, was the ultramontane leader of English-speaking Catholics

of inadequate funding from the province. Catholic schools began modestly and continued to expand alongside the public school system.[58]

In the 1850s the Irish Canadians, unhappy with the stingy sums spent on separate school education, agitated for more adequate funding. To do this they attempted to forge an alliance with the Reform party. Thomas D'Arcy McGee, Canada's most prominent Irish politician in the 1860s, fought arduously for suitable appropriations for separate schools by allying himself first with the Liberals and then with the Tories. Bishop Armand de Charbonnel worked diplomatically for more funding and sought help from George Brown, leader of the Reform party and doubtful friend of Catholics.[59]

Replacing Charbonnel in the Toronto struggle for school funding, Bishop John J. Lynch (1860–88) led Catholics in pursuit of fair treatment for separate schools. He took their cause first to the Reform party of George Brown and then to the Tory party of John A. Macdonald and Georges-Étienne Cartier. To remedy the inequity of partial funding of Catholic schools in nineteenth-century Canada West, the Liberal member of the legislature from Ottawa, Richard W. Scott, introduced legislation in 1861 to provide guaranteed public funding for the separate school system. With support from the Tories, the Scott education bill passed the legislature two years later. Scott unfortunately lost his seat in the next election. The enactment of the bill in 1863 legally guaranteed the existence of Catholic schools in Ontario. This legislation became the basis for section 93 of the British North America Act of 1867 guaranteeing public funding for separate schools in Ontario and Protestant schools in Quebec.[60] Owing to the anti-Catholic political pressure in Ontario during the 1880s and 1890s, both the Liberal and Conservative parties allowed Catholic separate schools to be inadequately funded.

North American universities and colleges began to register women towards the end of the nineteenth century. As we have seen, although the Quebec church was reluctant to allow the opening of women's colleges, Catholic women could receive a college education in Montreal in 1908, and St Francis Xavier College in Antigonish awarded its first four women's baccalaureate degrees in 1897.[61] On the admission of women to university work, however, the Catholic colleges were ten years behind the University of Toronto, which admitted women in 1884, and twenty years behind Canada's pioneer, Mount Allison, in Sackville, New Brunswick.[62] By the beginning of the twentieth century women were visible on both the undergraduate and graduate levels at Canadian universities.

In 1851 Bishop Charbonnel invited the Sisters of St Joseph to Toronto to operate an orphanage. Arriving from Philadelphia, the sisters opened the orphan home and the following year taught in Catholic separate schools. Complying with Charbonnel's request, they opened a boarding and day school on Power Street. The boarding school was named St Joseph's Academy, and its curriculum offered a program similar to that of other private schools in Ontario. While the school stressed the academic, educator Elizabeth Smyth found that it also included in its curriculum fine arts and music. The academy educated lay students as well as members of the St Joseph's religious community.[63]

Founded in France in 1650, the Sisters of St Joseph ran hospitals, visited prisoners and the sick, and instructed young girls. They lived outside the cloister wall, which was mandatory for contemplative nuns, and like the Congregation of Notre Dame, they were active as religious sisters in urban communities. They offered the innovative approach of committed women living outside the convent walls and were thus able to perform useful ministry in cities and the countryside.[64] They were a religious congregation of autonomous communities decentralized under the jurisdiction of the local bishop in various dioceses and countries.[65]

Although it was a private school, St Joseph's Academy found it useful after 1882 to follow the academic curriculum of the province of Ontario. This was necessary because the academy prepared many students to be teachers. The administration realized that the right to issue a

Distinguished St Joseph's graduate Gertrude Lawler, MA (1890), LLD (1927), member
of the Faculty of Education of the University of Toronto, member of the university
senate, and first president of the Catholic Women's League of Toronto. (TF)

certificate of matriculation to successful students was essential for the
future of the institution and its students. To teach school, professional
certificates were becoming more necessary, and to teach in the secondary school a first-class certificate was required. By 1906 the "normal
school" certificate became the standard route to a teaching position,
and St Joseph's offered the necessary certificates. The certificate of matriculation became necessary for gaining access to universities and professional associations.[66]

By establishing in 1890 an annual conference in professional development, the Sisters of St Joseph demonstrated their commitment to
teaching and its methodology. The annual conference made teaching
a special ministry of the congregation and focused on preparing members to undertake this specialty. All teachers in the separate school system were welcome to attend the annual conferences. The Ontario
minister of Education, George W. Ross, addressed the conference in
1895. In between conferences, the academy sponsored other lectures
and events, all with the aim of professionalizing instruction. After 1905
women who wished to enter the Sisters of St Joseph with the intention
of teaching were accepted only when they had completed their own
certificate. St Joseph's Academy produced many outstanding graduates who brought honour to the congregation. One of them was Gertrude Lawler, the Gold Medal winner of 1882, who went on to enjoy "a
brilliant academic career at the University of Toronto."[67]

A high-quality education was the principal concern of the staff of St Joseph's Academy. Affiliation with the wider educational community was imperitive to pursuit of its goal. School instruction in music and art was linked to programs at the University of Toronto music department and the Toronto School of Art. Commercial courses were affiliated with Toronto business schools. Professional certificates and degrees assured graduates future employment and a life of financial independence.[68]

The university division was separated from the academy in 1909 and named St Joseph's College. St Michael's College, in conjunction with the University of Toronto, conferred its first degrees in 1910 and welcomed the participation of the Catholic women's colleges in this university world. St Joseph's and Loretto colleges, through the powers invested in St Michael's, offered their first courses in 1912. Women at the college level registered for arts courses at St Joseph's and Loretto,[69] religion courses at St Michael's, and other university courses at the university proper.[70]

Sisters teaching at universities in the United States visited St Joseph's College and shared teaching materials and curricula, and sisters from the college returned their visits by travelling to American colleges. The Sisters of Charity of Halifax, the Religious of the Sacred Heart, and the Ursulines also visited St Joseph's College to share information on higher education. The sisters prepared their own staff members for university work. Especially successful was Sr Austin Warnock, who in 1909 won the Edward Blake Scholarship for modern authors. The following year she won the George Brown Prize and the Italian Prize, both for academic achievement.[71]

With the support of the Sisters of St Joseph, lay women founded the Catholic Women's Club at the University of Toronto in 1908 to provide a forum within which Catholic undergraduates could socialize. The club's first meetings were convened at St Joseph's Convent so that the members of different faculties and departments of the university could become acquainted with one another. The Sisters took an active interest in the success of the club.[72]

As Elizabeth Smyth has observed, historians have generally trivialized or overlooked the outstanding achievement of Catholic sisterhoods.[73] The Sisters of St Joseph are a case in Point. Sixty years of educational endeavour "hurled" the sisters, ready or not, into the twentieth century. In that short period, they opened schools on the primary, secondary, and university levels. They initiated a teacher certification program and a preparatory program for university. They founded St Joseph's College to teach university courses in conjunction with other institutions at the University of Toronto. The congregation

Six women graduated with BAs from St Joseph's College, Toronto, 1918: Kathleen Gilmour, Edna Madden, Mary Hodgins, Madaline Murray, Geraldine Kormann, and Florence Quinlan in front. (TF)

made the necessary adjustments and changes in plant, personnel, and ideas to ensure that the new college was thoroughly modern.[74] The founding of St Joseph's College and the establishment of its university program opened up professional careers for sisters, women, and church members.

The students responded well to the personal and academic attention they received from their teachers. On provincial examinations they achieved much success. St Joseph's College was a training ground for the leadership of both Catholic women and religious sisters. Several graduates achieved public prominence: Florence Quinlan lectured in physics at the university; Gertrude Lawler was a teacher, scholar, administrator and university senator; Teresa Korman Small functioned as a prominent community volunteer. St Joseph's College was distinguished by its links to secular institutions and by the variety of careers its graduates pursued in the public sector. Graduates maintained close ties with the sisters and a small number joined the sisterhood.[75] The college had a liberalizing effect on both the teachers and the students. Through their teaching skills, Catholic graduates played a significant role in expanding the separate school system in the face of limited funds and a provincial monopoly.

MEN'S EDUCATION IN ONTARIO

In Waterloo County to the west of Toronto, German-speaking Catholics numbered twelve thousand in the 1850. John Holzer, sj, writing to his brother in Austria from Guelph, described the need for German and Austrian clergy to come and open schools: "What are so many able and learned men doing there with you in your universities, when here so many souls are lost ... Before all else we must establish Catholic schools else we shall lose the Catholic youth."[76] In fact, only eight priests ministered to an extensive area containing a total of twenty-eight thousand Catholics in the recently erected diocese of Hamilton. While on a visit to Rome, Bishop Charbonnel asked the Resurrectionist Fathers to send some of their members to his diocese.

The Polish-speaking fathers of the Resurrection, according to James A. Wahl, sent their one German-speaking priest to the new Hamilton diocese. Father Eugene Funcken arrived in 1858 at St Agatha, Waterloo County. Seeing the desperate need for sacramental ministry and Christian schools in this area, Father Eugene in 1862 returned to Europe to attend the ordination of his brother Louis and to recruit him for German Canadians in Ontario. The two Funcken brothers returned to St Agatha in September 1864.[77]

Father Louis Funcken shared his brother's firm belief in the importance of education to offset the lack of Catholic leadership in the agricultural community. Louis opened St Jerome's College in January 1865 in a rented log cabin, and in October 1866 he moved it to Berlin (Kitchener). A true educator in the liberal arts tradition, Louis believed that a familial spirit in the school would win from students an obedient heart and obviate the need for confinement or caning. For a curriculum he improvised a program of Christian classics. Good as the idea was, the students found his Christian classics "laughable" and "dry as straw." Becoming more familiar with Canadian academic requirements, Louis revised the curriculum according to the requirements of the University of Toronto and Laval. Commercial courses were also added to the program.[78]

St Jerome's goal, as defined by Louis, was to educate honest people and intelligent Christian leaders. The director of the school, he believed, "ought to love his students ... be concerned with their entire being and future." For Father Louis, "the cardinal point of discipline is charity, fraternal concern and mutual respect."[79] Given this emphasis on familial love, Louis thought that a little disorder was better than too many rules, a view that pleased the students. Although St Jerome's curriculum was aligned with the Ontario curriculum, Father Louis was still determined to maintain a strong German presence at the college. Students had to learn both German and English. Only in 1878 did English become the primary language of instruction owing to pressure for change from the Irish. Meanwhile, clerical critics, claiming that Louis's academic philosophy lacked rigour and that the school needed discipline, denounced Louis to Rome.[79]

During the last half of the nineteenth century St Jerome's College obtained some instructors from its own graduates. Resurrectionists Theobald Spetz and William Kloepfer returned in 1878 and 1879 respectively to teach on the college staff. In the same decade, the Resurrectionist Fathers in Poland adopted a new rule handed down by the visionary, Mother Marcelline Darowska. In the spirit of a medieval penitential order, the rule stressed "self-denial, renunciation, and mortification."[80] Strict observance became an end itself. Its adoption by the Congregation of the Resurrection emphasized "a less active and more contemplative" lifestyle and endangered the very existence of St Jerome's. Moreover, a new father general was elected in 1874 to redirect the focus of the congregation and emphasize Polish missions at the expense of the community's work in North America. Were it not for the intense campaign of Fathers Louis and Eugene Funcken in close collaboration with sympathetic colleagues in Rome, St Jerome's College would have been closed. In contrast to this threat, the arrival of Spetz and Kloepher signalled an important victory for the continuance of the college in Canada.[81]

Father Louis was very proud of his alumni and enjoyed documenting their successes. He estimated that over a hundred graduates from the bilingual college were ordained to the priesthood, and five taught at St Jerome's. Other alumni, inspired by Father Louis's Christian humanism, became medical doctors, barristers, editors, teachers, and school inspectors. Wahl concedes that together the alumni were a peaceful, liberal, and ecumenical influence on Waterloo County. Father Louis set an example by welcoming not only Catholics to the college but also Lutherans, Anglicans, and Mennonites. Protestants as well as Catholics were officers in the alumni association and shared in its beneficial influence upon the community. For his loving attitude Father Louis was highly regarded.[82] He and his students left a legacy of liberal Christianity throughout Waterloo County, the diocese of Hamilton, and beyond. St Jerome's College seemed to be a happy exception to ultramontane zeal manifested elsewhere in Canada.

St Jerome's College was a good omen on the Catholic horizon. Many ultramontane Catholics unnecessarily feared the modern world and republican institutions as an oppressive rather than enlightened force in society. To the open minded, ultramontane Catholics seemed obsessed with the dangers of secular education, especially the mixing of the sexes. They believed secular education would lead to religious indifference, and that God spoke only through the voice of the Church.[83] Ultramontane spirituality, liberal Catholics feared, failed to respect the freedom of the individual and lacked adequate compromise with the realities of life. St Jerome's College under the direction of Louis Funcken embraced the liberal arts tradition and believed in forming students in a spirit of mutual respect and familial love. The college, for liberal Catholics, was a bright light in the sombre sky of ultramontane loyalism hovering over Canada.

CONCLUSION

The founders of Catholic schools and colleges formed institutions that energized the Catholic cultural and devotional revolution. In their schools and colleges, Catholic instructors emphasized academic and moral discipline to inculcate in youth a love of the Catholic church and Canada. The educators guiding these schools insisted on the harmony of Catholic principles and adjusted them to the exigencies of the Canadian environment. Catholic graduates marched from their colleges into the future, giving their spiritual and intellectual skills to the Catholic community and the Canadian nation.

The admission of women to colleges in Antigonish, Montreal, Toronto, and, slightly later, at Brescia College in London (1919) was a bright light for many Catholics and demonstrated that their church was able to go beyond the modernist scare and prepare women for professional careers in the contemporary world. Bright and well-educated women came into the service of the church and began the transformation of the church's traditional image of women. Catholic women made their contribution in the secular world and religious life, but they were largely ignored by church leaders. For it was only after the Second Vatican Council that the Canadian church underwent a radical change and welcomed women into its administration.

6 Church, Politics, and a New Canada

Confederation did not resolve the school issue, but it provoked Catholics to press more resolutely for separate schools in a Protestant state. Faced with rapid population increases, church people in Quebec and Ontario worked for the extension of their Catholic schools, but controversies erupting in New Brunswick and Manitoba over schools punctured Catholic hopes for federal intervention to save their schools. As a result, considerable planning was needed to maintain and expand the Catholic educational system to keep pace with the growing population.

After the forced union of 1841, the two central Canadian provinces fell into a political and economic stalemate. A double majority of French- and English-speaking legislators was needed to move bills through the legislature and political deadlock was common.[1] To go beyond the standoff, Canada East and Canada West groped their way towards unity by persuading the sceptical Maritime provinces that Confederation would be a positive step towards resolving their mutual problems. The successful conclusion of the American Civil War and the Russian-American negotiations for the purchase of Alaska revealed the expansionist mood of an ebullient United States.[2] Under the threat of encirclement, the vulnerable British North American provinces needed political stability to defend their vast interior. But the political cohesion necessary to initiate such a strategy was lacking. As we shall see, Catholics in Nova Scotia, New Brunswick, and the two Canadas had reason to fear a unitary Canadian state imposing Protestant culture on them.

NOVA SCOTIAN CATHOLICS
AND CONFEDERATION

Catholic attitudes in Nova Scotia towards Confederation in the early 1860s were hardly different from the attitude of most other Nova Scotians. Regional prosperity was high. Its ships plied the oceans and enjoyed free trade with the United States, Great Britain, and the West Indies. As historian David B. Flemming demonstrates, the province was not greatly interested in Central Canadian railways, tariffs, and high taxes. Catholics, like other Nova Scotians, feared Canadian interference in the Maritime provinces.[3]

Yet because of the anti-Catholic attitude of political reformer Joseph Howe and a number of anti-Catholic incidents, Nova Scotian Catholics began to drift away from the Liberal party. Moreover, in 1857 ten assemblymen representing Catholic constituencies defected from the Liberals to the Conservatives over the defeat of the education bill. The then bishop of Saint John, Thomas Connolly, soured by the attitudes of Liberals, actively encouraged defections from the party. In the election of 1859 Catholic constituencies voted Conservative, while Protestants supported the Liberals, widening the political rift.[4]

In 1864 Archbishop Connolly of Halifax embraced the Tory strategy of Confederation. He wanted to halt accusations that Irish Catholics supported either the Fenians or annexation to the United States. In March 1865 Connolly demonstrated this change of heart by writing to Bishop John Sweeney of Saint John (1859–1901), who opposed Confederation, that "Confederation is thoroughly sound in almost every point of view."[5] Connolly also disagreed sharply with Timothy Anglin, the editor of the Saint John *Freeman,* and "a running debate" ensued. Bishops Colin MacKinnon of Arichat and James Rogers of Chatham joined Connolly in supporting a pro-Confederation policy.[6] Some years after Confederation had become reality in the four provinces, Peter McIntyre (1860–91), bishop of Prince Edward Island before its admission, supported the Tory pro-Confederationist government in the hope of winning separate schools to Confederation. However, the Tory government showed little interest in Catholic concerns, and McIntyre redirected his support to the Liberals and their anti-Confederation policy.[7]

Connolly's about-face on the Confederation issue was conditioned by his demand that the new Canada guarantee separate schools in the Maritime provinces in the same way they were guaranteed them in Canada East and Canada West. In 1866 the charming and intelligent Connolly,[8] with the support of his suffragans, sailed to London to lobby for a legislative provision that would recognize separate schools in

Maritime provinces. He attempted to persuade delegates Hector Langevin of Canada East and William McDougall of Canada West, both then in London, to support such a provision in a new constitution. They declined, saying that any initiative on separate schools would have to come from Maritime delegates, none of whom were Catholic. In the final version of the British North America Act of 1867, much to Connolly's frustration, Catholic schools although protected in Ontario and Quebec, were left unprotected in the Maritime provinces.[9]

Undeterred by this defeat, Connolly asked Catholic legislators in the Nova Scotian assembly to prepare separate school legislation.Charles Tupper, the government leader, refused to introduce the bill because he said it was certain to cause discord and would be defeated. Catholics thus had to be satisfied with something less than a constitutional guarantee and accept "a gentlemen's agreement" as a negotiated settlement. The settlement would tolerate only those Catholic schools that were controlled and operated by a secular school board. Despite this disappointment, Archbishop Connolly and Halifax Catholics remained steadfastly and diplomatically committed to Confederation. They came to believe that Confederation would be the best defender of the rights of the Canadian provinces and the strongest guardian of toleration for religious minorities. They also prayed that Confederation would bring industrial and economic advantages to the Maritime provinces.[10]

NEW BRUNSWICK CATHOLICS AND CONFEDERATION

The New Brunswick Catholics, like Nova Scotians, were originally opposed to Confederation. In this and other political matters they tended to follow the opinions of Timothy Warren Anglin, editor of the Saint John *Freeman* from 1849 until 1883. An articulate citizen and energetic politician, he put himself forward as the unofficial spokesperson for Catholics in New Brunswick. He tirelessly explained to his readers a Catholic viewpoint on numerous issues, which for him included not supporting the Tory-driven confederation. As a close friend of Bishop Sweeney of Saint John and Archbishop Lynch of Toronto, his newspaper became the unofficial voice of these Catholic prelates. He was a committed Liberal who felt that a stand against Confederation was a suitable way to oppose Tory anti-Catholicism. He had sharp political disagreements with bishops Connolly of Halifax, Rogers of Chatham (New Brunswick), and MacKinnon of Arichat (Nova Scotia). Yet while crusading for Catholic separate schools and other religious causes, he gained the entire support of the Catholic bishops.[11]

Remarkably, Anglin maintained an amicable relationship with Rogers and MacKinnon in the pages of the *Freeman* despite their opposing views on Confederation. He belittled MacKinnon's open letter to eastern Nova Scotian Catholics in favour of Confederation and dismissed Rogers's open letters on the same topic, claiming that his arguments were superficial. Harsh words were exchanged between the two.[12] In 1866 Rogers and Connolly challenged Anglin's leadership of New Brunswick Catholics and during the provincial election helped turn the tide in favour of the pro-Confederation Samuel Tilley.[13] Yet through it all, Rogers and Anglin remained friends and colleagues. In the election of 1872, Rogers supported Anglin, wishing him "success and benediction."[14]

Anglin reported in his paper about a Wesleyan Methodist judge, Lemuel A. Wilmot, who told an outrageous story to the Bible Society of Saint John. Wilmot's tale illustrated the prevalence of anti-Catholic prejudice in New Brunswick in the mid-nineteenth century. The story was about a Catholic boy from the Miramichi who loved to read the Bible but whose father forbade him to do so. The father called in a priest to convince the boy. Failing in this task, the priest tied the boy to a tree and whipped him until he was too exhausted to continue. The boy, however, refused to relent. The priest gave up, according to Wilmot, and said, "It was mighty difficult to beat the Protestant out of him." The boy then became a Methodist and told his story to the judge, who repeated it to the Bible Society.

A priest from the Miramichi challenged the veracity of the story. He asked Judge Wilmot to give specific names, dates, and other pertinent details. Six months later, at another meeting of the Bible Society, Wilmot refused to supply the information or to substantiate the story. Anglin pointed out that the judge "did not dare to assert that the story was true, or to attempt to prove it true by giving what any one would receive as proof." Anglin concluded that the story was just a story, but that it revealed the latent anti-Catholicism in the province that he was determined to fight. The incident also showed the confidence that the Catholic bishops placed in Timothy Anglin as a defender of the church, clergy, and Catholicism.[15]

Anglin was an outstanding spokesperson on the New Brunswick school question. He claimed that education was not solely the preserve of the province but also "the concern of the parents and the church."[16] For this reason, he argued, denominational schools were necessary for the province. The New Brunswick education bill of 1858 allowed grants to hundreds of Catholic schools, and Anglin concluded that this informal arrangement implied in law a special status for Catholic schools.[17] However, the political establishment in the province viewed support for Catholic schools in a different light. Premier Samuel Leonard Tilley's contended that "denominational schools could only be established in New Brunswick and Nova Scotia by the vote of the Local Legislature," and his reasoning prevailed among the legislators of New Brunswick.[18] Anglin continued to make the case for separate schools and expressed deep regret that Catholics in the Maritime provinces were not treated as fairly as Protestants in Quebec.

In 1871 the New Brunswick Act established common schools and completely ignored Catholic efforts to establish a separate school system. It forced Catholics in general and Acadians in particular to pay taxes to a system they had no desire to support. Between the 1850s and 1870s the Congrégation-Notre-Dame and the Hospitalières-de-Saint-Joseph opened schools throughout the province to fill the gap in Catholic education for Acadian children.[19] In addition to these remedial efforts on the part of both Irish and Acadian Catholics, Catholic politicians continued to seek justice before the New Brunswick legislature.

In Ottawa parliamentarians Auguste Renaud and John Costigan sought federal disallowance of the New Brunswick legislation. Anglin, now a member of Parliament, also argued that the act of 1871 was "unjust and oppressive and insulting."[20] He suggested that Catholics in New Brunswick should not pay the school taxes. Some Catholics who withheld their taxes had their property confiscated; others were arrested.[21] Anglin's vigorous support of separate schools in his home province dissipated in 1873 when Alexander MacKenzie and the Liberals took power. Anglin became the speaker of the House, and as such was neutral in all political matters. During his term no single legislative act or court decision was passed in favour of separate schools. In fact, concessions won for Catholic schools in New Brunswick were obtained not by Ottawa's intercession but by negotiations at the local level.[22]

Anglin also espoused the right of Catholic and Protestant clergy to be involved in political events when those events clearly had a bearing on religion and education. When the clergy were speaking on political matters, the laity had the right to disagree. "The Catholic," he wrote, "is quite as free to think and judge for himself as others are."[23]

Anglin's open-handed support for Catholic causes was not without its price. In 1873 his unflinching criticism during the New Brunswick schools question cost him a ministerial position in Alexander Mackenzie's government. Anglin's pro-Catholic *Freeman* lost readers in a predominantly Protestant province. His pen was so sharp that he was not always the ideal Catholic spokesperson. Yet in his favour it might be pointed out that Anglin was intelligent, forthright, and in touch with the Catholic bishops, to whom he gave an indirect voice in New Brunswick's public life.[24] Diplomacy was not one of Anglin's virtues, but he never let his anger get out of hand. He was able to maintain good relations with both clergy and politicians and bridge the gap between his personal religious convictions and the events of public life. Anglin was not successful in his struggle to gain separate schools in New Brunswick, but he was an influential publicist and politician and helped gain the acceptability of Catholics in a Protestant society.

QUEBEC BISHOPS AND CONFEDERATION

Three difficult choices faced the Quebec bishops in the 1860s: whether to lead their people towards legislative union with the other provinces, towards confederation, or towards annexation with the United States. Suspicious of the intentions of an English-speaking federal government and silenced by such uncertainty, the bishops refrained from urging Canadiens in any of these directions. Why their uncertainty? They firmly believed in the advantage of retaining the British connection for the preservation of the Catholic faith and abhorred any thought of annexation to the United States. As a body, the bishops still viewed the framing of Confederation as a political issue but with an important impact on the social fabric of Quebec. Their silence on the issue before Confederation spelled out their toleration of the legislation. It was only after the passage of the British North America Act by the British Parliament and its proclamation by the Crown that the Quebec bishops published their approval of Confederation and asked the faithful to accept it. On this matter the bishops seemed content to acquiesce in the political *fait accompli.* Walter Ullmann contends that the Québécois bishops did not have sufficient reason to oppose Confederation, or sufficient reason to promote it.[25]

Louis-François Laflèche, the vicar general and later bishop of Trois-Rivières (1870–98), rejected the continued union of Canada East and West as tantamount to the destruction of the Canadiens. He also rejected union with the United States as being out of the question for Canada. He believed that the Quebec Resolutions, providing for a federal rather than unitary government, offered an honourable way to end the legislative stalemate and would at the same time preserve both Catholicism and French Canadian culture. He believed that a diplomatic solution was the only way to restore political trust between French- and English-speaking Canadians. In his view, the British North America Act was a legislative compromise that overcame the political paralysis of Canada East and West, provided Quebec with enough autonomy, and restored a workable government to Canada.[26]

Bishop Ignace Bourget of Montreal, the leading force in Canadian ultramontane spirituality, was at best lukewarm about Confederation and maintained an icy silence on the subject. Several Quebec newspapers, along with the intervention of Bishop Laroque of St Hyacinthe, failed to get Bourget to make a statement about Confederation. George-Etienne Cartier, Quebec leader for the federal Tories and lawyer for the Sulpicians, sent him a draft of the British North America Act, but Cartier could not get a statement from Bourget either, only a receipt for the document. It was after royal assent in March 1867 that the Montreal Catholic newspapers, *L'Ordre* and *True Witness*, altered their attitude to speak favourably of Confederation. In the process of explaining the acceptance of this new political reality, both newspapers revealed Bourget's earlier misgivings.[27]

As soon as Confederation was proclaimed on 1 July 1867, the Quebec bishops wrote letters to their parishioners asking them to accept the new political reality. LaFlèche and Laroque were the most enthusiastic of the bishops, but they still had some reservations. Bishop Langevin of Rimouski and Vicar General Baillargeon of Quebec quietly acquiesced in Confederation. Langevin wrote to his parishioners, "*Vous la respecterez donc, Nos Chers Frères, cette nouvelle Constitution, qui vous est donné, comme expression de la volonté suprême du Législateur, de l'autorité légitime, et par conséquent, par celle de Dieu même*" ("You must respect, my dear friends, this new Constitution, which is given to you, as an expression of the supreme will of the Legislator, of legitimate authority, and in consequence, of God himself"). Meanwhile, Bishop Bourget steeled himself to accept God's will through prayer and self-discipline.[28]

With hearts and a sense of loyalty, the Quebec bishops approached Confederation in much the same way their episcopal predecessors had looked upon the Conquest, the Quebec Act, and the Act of Union. They revealed little of their personal attitudes to the legislation and prepared themselves and their people for the worst. In the world of compromise, they preferred confederation to a unitary government and to political and economic stalemate. In any event, they favoured the British political connection over the American. Since the arrival of the British military governors, the Quebec bishops had learned the art of quiet diplomacy and cooperation with the colonial authorities, all the while continuing to press for church control of schools, hospitals, and social services.

SEPARATE SCHOOLS IN ONTARIO

Queen Victoria's proclamation of 1867 extended government funding of Ontario denominational schools into Confederation. Ontario Catholics made education a religious issue, something worth fighting for; hence elementary education became the primary goal of the community. Yet owing to anti-Catholic public pressure in Ontario during the 1880s and 1890s, both the Liberals and Conservatives tolerated inadequate funding for the Catholic separate schools. As the nineteenth century drew to a close, both political parties recognized that the Catholic minority was not a threat at the polls. But this indifference was not to last long. The influx of Catholics from the Ukraine, Germany, Poland, Italy, and other nations both before and after the Great War quickly multiplied the number of Catholic voters.

During the 1880s and 1890s the political pressure generated by the anti-Catholic campaigns of the Equal Rights Association, Protestant Protective Association, and Patrons of Industry convinced the Ontario government to be even more parsimonious in its funding of separate schools. These anti-Catholic campaigns stirred Protestant anger against not only Ontario separate schools but also against both the Jesuit Estates Act (1888) and the Manitoba Schools Issue (1891). However, an informal concordat between the premier of Ontario, Oliver Mowat (1872–96), and Archbishop Lynch succeeded in restricting the damage of Protestant political pressure and permitted modest gains for separate schools. The Mowat government increased tax assessments and provided Catholic inspectors for separate schools.[27]

After the turn of the twentieth century Ontario's Department of Education began to impose professional standards on separate schools. It demanded that religious teachers have certification. Up until then, religious teachers taught because of personal commitment to serving the community. Their academic competence and pedagogical method were left to their own cognizance and the supervision of their religious congregation. The Education Act of 1907 demanded certification but failed to provide the necessary funds to attain the qualifications. Separate schools and their Catholic teachers were put in a terrible financial bind, and professionalization caught up with volunteer educators.

SEPARATE SCHOOLS IN NEW BRUNSWICK

Section 93 of the BNA Act turned out to be a most contentious part of Canadian constitutional history. In New Brunswick it had particular relevance in the years immediately after Confederation. Following passage by the assembly of the Parish Schools Act of 1858, religious denominations operated their own schools. At the London Conference in December 1866, which drafted the final frame of the Dominion of Canada, Archbishop Thomas Connolly of Halifax lobbied for inclusion of the denominational schools of New Brunswick and Nova Scotia, like those in Quebec and Ontario, in the new Canadian constitution. He proposed two educational systems in New Brunswick and Nova Scotia, one for Catholics and the other for Protestants, both to be paid for by the school taxes of their respective denominations. This dual school system would be operated by the federal government and enshrined in the British North America Act.[30]

The first blow to Connolly's proposal was delivered by the Canadien delegates at the London conference, Hector Langevin and Etienne Cartier. They objected to any federal system of schools which would override provincial control of education. Connolly's proposal was subsequently scaled down by D'Arcy McGee to what eventually became section 93. It protected provincial autonomy over education by promising not federal denominational schools but merely federal intervention in cases where a province infringed the rights of denominational schools. In fact the legislation referred only to denominational schools in Ontario and Quebec. The courts later judged that denominational schools in New Brunswick and Nova Scotia had not legally been established prior to Confederation and therefore that section 93 of the BNA Act did not protect them.[31]

Another crushing blow to the separate school system in New Brunswick followed on the heels of the 1870 provincial election. The New Brunswick government passed the Common Schools Act of 1871, which established free and compulsory education for all children. The act prescribed that only non-denominational schools be funded by compulsory school taxes. This legislation spelled the end of separate schools and excluded any chance of school funding by Catholic ratepayers.[32]

New Brunswick MP, John Costigan, with the encouragement of Prime Minister John A. Macdonald, made a first effort to restore the loss of these schools. He put an amendment before the House of Commons in 1872, calling for extension of the practice of separate schools from central Canada to the Maritime provinces. The leader of the New Brunswick Tories, Sir Samuel Tilley, felt undermined by such an amendment and threatened to resign from Macdonald's government. Costigan's proposal was quickly watered down to an expression of regret over the elimination of New Brunswick's hoped-for separate schools. The amendment of regret passed, and the separate school proposal died.[33]

Costigan tried a second time to restore separate schools. He tabled a motion in the House of Commons asking that the government disallow the New Brunswick Common Schools Act of 1871 because it violated the rights of the Catholic minority. Some federal Conservatives, especially Canadiens, voted with the Liberal opposition to pass this motion. The Quebec hierarchy thought it was important to speak out in favour of Catholic schools and issued a statement calling upon the federal government to disallow the New Brunswick Schools Act. Yet any serious threat of federal intervention in New Brunswick threatened to divide the federal Tories and bring down the government of Sir John A. Macdonald.

Macdonald's reaction to this threat was to refuse to carry out the disallowance. The House was in turmoil. John Costigan and Timothy Anglin drafted a motion of non-confidence in the government, but at the last moment the Quebec bishops withdrew their support and advised against allowing the Macdonald's government to fall. Quebec remained firmly committed to the Tory government and the principle of provincial control over education.[34] Thus, for the second time in less than seven years cooperation between the Quebec church and the Macdonald government "defeated the aspirations of the Catholic minorities of the Maritimes."[35] Twice the Quebec members of Parliament failed to intervene on behalf of New Brunswick Catholics. The first time was at the London Conference of 1866, and the second during the disallowance motion of 1873.

In general Quebec newspapers allotted little space to the New Brunswick School Act of 1871, and Canadiens were hardly aware of that controversial issue.[36] When Canadiens became aware several years later that the Acadians were losing out on Catholic schools they expressed their sympathy, but for them it was a religious issue, not a linguistic or cultural issue.[37] The Quebec Tory leader, George-Etienne Cartier, agreed in the Commons with Macdonald's view that section 93 of the BNA Act was not intended to apply to the New Brunswick School Act. The Tories believed that disallowing the act would go against the will of the majority of New Brunswickers and provoke an undesirable backlash against Catholics. In fact despite this repressive measure against Acadians, only a minority of Canadiens opposed the Schools Act of 1871 and insisted it should be disallowed.[38] The dispute rose through the courts to the Privy Council in London, which sided with the government's school act.[39]

The Canadien vision and its role *vis-à-vis* minorities widened between 1874 and 1875. A series of events alerted Canadiens to the threat they were facing from English cultural imperialism. Ambroise Lépine was arrested in 1874 at Red River and tried for the murder of

Thomas Scott. Canadien pressure demanded an amnesty for him, and the governor general commuted the capital sentence. In New Brunswick Acadians and other Catholics were arrested, for refusing to pay compulsory school taxes.[40] Finally, the Caraquet Riots broke out in 1875 in an effort to maintain control of Acadian Catholic schools. These events alerted Canadiens to the pervasive hostility towards both Catholicism and French culture. As *Le Canadien* put it: "One is tempted to believe that there is an immense conspiracy against the French race in the dominion. Trampled underfoot in Manitoba, crushed in New Brunswick, we are threatened with annihilation."[41] A mission arose among the Canadiens of Quebec to protect Canadien minorities outside the province as well as within.[42]

The Catholic defeat in the school question spurred further intolerance towards Catholics in New Brunswick and quickened Acadian nationalism. In the 1870s there was already considerable intolerance in the wake of the First Vatican Council and the definition of papal infallibility. Religious tensions intensified considerably when the government determined to impose a school tax on the centre of Acadian Catholic culture, Caraquet. This move resulted in an English minority seizing the French Catholic school, which in turn provoked the Caraquet Riots of 1875 and the rise of Acadian patriotism.[43] Strong feelings boiled over, and an Acadian candidate rose up in 1878 to contest Timothy Anglin's seat. The challenge was unsuccessful at the time,[44] but two years later a nationalist organization sprang up. John A. Macdonald, however, would still not disallow the provincial Schools Act of 1871. He assured Quebec that control of education was sacred in any province, and that minority rights must consequently be overlooked.[45]

The federal government's unwillingness to embrace the educational needs of religious and linguistic minorities revealed to Acadian and Irish Catholics that any resolution of their school problems would have to come from them. Understanding this, they invited religious congregations from Quebec and elsewhere to operate and staff the schools funded through their own initiatives. A compromise was reached in 1875 by which Catholic students were grouped in the same schools, Catholic religious were allowed to teach in religious garb, textbooks were agreed upon before use, and Catholic schools would be rented by the province for this purpose.[46] Yet the success of the new arrangement depended greatly on the ability of the bishops and pastors to negotiate at the local level for adequate funds and classroom space. The system worked well for ninety years, dispensing equal benefits in supplies, services, and salaries to both secular and religious. The breakup of the system only began in 1967 with the introduction of regional school boards. The boards closed smaller schools and grouped students and teachers of different denominations together in larger regional schools. At the same time Catholics failed to construct schools for the new suburban subdivisions. Older buildings in Saint John were closed and their students and teachers sent to the newer Catholic schools which made religious instruction onerous and a Catholic environment difficult to create.[47] In the long run, the existence of alternative schools in New Brunswick and Nova Scotia proved to have a strengthening and liberalizing effect on education.

The federal government could have supported the cause of New Brunswick Catholic schools, but Quebec Catholics did not want federal intervention. Canadiens reasoned that it was more important to defend provincial rights than to support the rights of New Brunswick Catholics. Canadiens imagined the problem as a religious and not a cultural issue, and believed, as did the Acadians, that it was a battle between the English Protestants and the Irish Catholics for control of the schools. Until 1875 the anglophone Protestant government in New Brunswick showed little tolerance for either French- or English-speaking Catholics when the Compromise of 1875 arranged for Catholic children to be grouped in the same schools. After 1891, in a similar way, the English Protestant government in Manitoba lost tolerance of the French schools of the minority. The New Brunswick school question, as historians George Stanley and Peter Toner point out, was more about religion than language, since in the end both French- and English-language groups were deprived of Catholic schools.[48] In Manitoba, by contrast, the issue was about language, and as a result Quebec nationalists more readily interceded to demand federal intervention.

SEPARATE SCHOOLS LOST IN MANITOBA

Manitoba was admitted to Confederation by the Manitoba Act of July 1870, which guaranteed to the French-speaking majority and the English-speaking minority the same rights for bilingual and denominational education provided in Ontario and Quebec.[49] English-speaking settlers to Manitoba over the next twenty years increased so rapidly that the number of French-speaking inhabitants decreased to only 7.3 percent of the provincial population.[50] This radical reversal of the demographic balance in such a short time had profound political ramifications. The majority of Manitobans and their legislators saw no reason to continue with a policy of bilingualism for a dwindling French-speaking minority. In 1890 English members passed legislation ending "the official use of the French language in the Legislative Assembly, the civil service, government publications, and the provincial courts."

Then another bill in the same spirit ended public support for French schools.[51] As Manitoban legislators disregarded constitutional rights, the French-speaking minority could appeal for protection to section 93 of the British North America Act. The provision offered the federal government the option of remedial action to alleviate discrimination. Both federal parties allowed the problem to end up in the judicial system, hoping that it could be resolved peacefully. The Canadian Supreme Court authorized the federal government to take remedial action, but the Privy Council in London ruled that only a minimal response was necessary under the law. No practical solution emerged and the Tories continued to hope for remedial legislation to remedy the injustice. The Liberals, for their part, offered the promise of the "sunny ways" of Wilfrid Laurier.[52]

It was during the federal election of 1896 that the resolution to the Manitoba school problem was hammered out. Sir Charles Tupper, the Tory leader, offered an ambiguous solution of federal intervention. To French speakers he indicated that there would be French schools in the future, but to the English speakers he implied that the separate school system would not be restored. With such assurances, for instance, he tried to gain the political support of Hugh John Macdonald, the popular son of the deceased prime minister, who lived in Winnipeg and never supported the restoration of the French schools in Manitoba.[53]

Liberals were just as capable as the Tories of disseminating elusive information on the school issue. Wilfrid Laurier attacked the dilatory nature of the Tory solution while proposing an equally ambivalent resolution. He promised the French-speaking minority justice on the school issue without specifying what he meant. At the same time, he promised a solution that would come about without prejudice to the English-speaking majority.[54] In this way Laurier was able to gain Ontario's support, including that of the premier, Oliver Mowat, who was considered the champion of separate schools in the province.[55]

As the electioneering intensified, many Quebec bishops felt the need to publish a joint *mandement* in May 1896 to give encouragement to the electorate. Two factions existed among the bishops. The first, which included Bishops Langevin, Laflèche, and Labrecque, wished to instruct the faithful to vote for politicians who backed remedial legislation and to reject those who did not. The other faction, which included Bishops Emard of Valleyfield and Fabre of Montreal, believed the less said the better about how to vote and preferred only a positive instruction on electoral honesty.[56]

A month before the election, Archbishop Bégin was able to bring the two factions together in Montreal to discuss a joint letter. To Bégin's surprise, the bishops selected the Langevin draft over his own,

and Fabre and Emard cooperated to revise it. John Cameron of Antigonish wanted the draft to be more forceful. It was intended to be read
from the pulpit without comment. The letter instructed voters that
a decisive vote was necessary and ambivalence was not permitted
for Catholics by separating their private from their public thoughts.
Rather, it said that Catholics must vote for whichever candidates were
committed to accommodate the school rights of the minority in Manitoba, regardless of party. As historian Paul Crunican has observed, the
circumspect manner in which the *mandement* was prepared and its
moderate tone demonstrated that the bishops were not, as some historians and newspapers have claimed, trying to manipulate the outcome
of the election of 1896.[57]

The bishop's *mandement* was read from the pulpit on Sunday, 17 May
1896, five weeks prior to the election. The Conservative and Liberal
newspapers described it as "a very mild sort of document" giving
"sound advice" and revealing the neutrality of the clergy. It was only
with the radical interpretation of Bishop Laflèche that the letter
caused any stir.[58] Crunican describes the scene: "At High Mass on May
17 in the cathedral of Trois-Rivières, the seventy-eight-year-old prelate
appeared in the pulpit with the *mandement* in one hand and a copy of
Hansard in the other." He denounced Laurier's brand of liberalism as
the kind condemned by the Church. As far as Laflèche was concerned,
"Catholics, under pain of grave sin, could not vote for Laurier or his
followers until they had publicly disavowed this position" of moderation on the Manitoba schools and unless they promised a remedial law
approved by the bishops. Laflèche's pronouncement polarized the
clergy into conservative and liberal camps.[59]

The Laurier Liberals won a splendid electoral victory in the June
election. Laurier took 118 seats across Canada, leaving only eighty-
eight for the Tories and 7 for other candidates. In Quebec he
managed to turn the tide against the Tory majority by taking forty-nine
of sixty-five seats.[60] After the election, the Liberals complained to
Rome about the extreme attitudes of Bishops Laflèche, Labrecque,
Cameron, Blais, and Gravel. Bégin cautioned all his colleagues that
prudent wisdom demanded the bishops support whichever party supported remedial legislation since the Church was not a one-issue institution.[61] Crunican contends that when all the evidence was reviewed,
Quebec clergy remained neutral during the election, and that identifying anything like an "anti-liberal clerical crusade in Quebec in 1896
represents a popular misreading of the event."[62]

Langevin discovered the neutrality of the Canadian bishops when he
paid a call on Archbishop John Walsh in Toronto in April 1896 to line
up support. Ontario bishops would not even sign the *mandement*. The

Catholic Register also disagreed with Laflèche's extreme interpretation of the letter. The Sisters of Loretto in Toronto were reported to be more sympathetic to Laurier than to Tupper. Crunican concludes that, French speaking or otherwise, there was little unanimity among Catholic voters during the election of 1896. Although some Quebec newspapers picked up the radical line of Laflèche, his attitude was not characteristic of the other bishops. In fact, Canadien voters seemed willing enough to follow the direction of the *mandement* because of its bipartisan tenor.[63] The Liberals delighted in the magnitude of the vote – especially in ridings where Laflèche and Blais governed the Church.

What conclusions can be drawn from the Quebec bishops speaking about the election of 1896? First, the decisive Liberal victory in Quebec showed that Canadiens would not necessarily choose French ethnicity over their religious commitment. If we look more closely, we find that Laurier was a charismatic politician whose party waged a well-organized campaign. Since the execution of Louis Riel in 1885, the Conservatives had lost direction and were slowly disintegrating, and they fought a poorly organized campaign in the spring of 1896. In the long run, it proved easier for the Liberals to attack than for the Conservatives to defend. The Quebec clergy proved to be flexible and the Quebec voters proved to be more sophisticated than anticipated. The strong Liberal victory in Quebec upset the Conservative party and pushed it into political collapse.

Was the Liberal electoral victory of 1896 a bad omen in terms of the Manitoba schools issue? As it turned out, not at all. The Liberal victory in Ottawa along with the federal Conservative victory in Manitoba augured positively for a resolution of the dispute. Manitoba Liberal Clifford Sifton was brought into the Laurier cabinet to resolve the issue. By November after the election, the Laurier-Greenway settlement had been reached. With compromises on both sides, the agreement allowed instruction for ten or more students of other languages, which included after-hours religious instruction.[64] It allowed Catholic schools to exist in French but did not meet the minimum requirement as laid down by the second Privy Council decision. Within the same month five bishops, including Bégin, Laflèche, Labrecque, Blais, and Gravel, published a pastoral letter condemning the blatant shortcomings of the agreement.[65]

The feeling of frustration and injustice intensified Protestant-Catholic tensions in Canada. Crunican conjectures that it was unlikely that remedial legislation could have been imposed on the strong Manitoba opposition. Canadiens had opted not to migrate to the Canadian West but to remain in Quebec or go south to New England. These French-speaking immigrants were forever lost to Manitoba and the western prairies. In the New Brunswick and Manitoba school questions the national government would not intervene and proved that section 93 of the British North America Act was dead letter. Canadiens who contributed to the Laurier victory had simply chosen to vote for one of their own.[66]

CONCLUSION

Catholics in the 1860s abandoned the Liberal party, believing that it was more useful to support the Tory-led confederation movement. They hoped that they would be rewarded with separate schools. Archbishop Connolly and Catholic Liberals in Nova Scotia and New Brunswick moved to the Conservative camp expecting that Catholic schools would be established. Tory promises, however, did not translate into federal or provincial legislation and separate schools eluded Maritime Catholics. Timothy Anglin and his followers, in contrast, continued to trust that the Liberal party would guarantee separate schools. Neither political party, as it turned out, represented the political support required to gain the passage of legislation for separate schools in the Maritime provinces.

Despite the conservative nature of the Catholic church throughout the nineteenth century, the *fin de siècle* in Canada brought surprises. To protect their culture and schools, Quebec bishops opted for the new federal framework, which promised a brighter future. Openness to Canadian life sprouted from the soil of church membership. Cardinal Taschereau and the professors of Laval University steered the Canadian church away from extreme ultramontanism. The *mandement* of the Quebec bishops before the election of 1896 proved to be moderate and not provocative. The Catholics of Quebec voted for Wilfrid Laurier and the Liberal party, hoping that Laurier could resolve the dicey Manitoba schools issue and English-French tension. Pope Leo XIII advised the Quebec hierarchy to cooperate with the new prime minister in his handling of the Manitoba question.[67]

Catholic political thought adjusted itself to the view that Confederation was a defender of the rights of religious minorities, a promoter of tolerance for Catholics in a Protestant society, and a political framework that would end the stalemate in Ottawa. The Catholic vote at the time of Confederation and for two decades afterwards remained that of a minority and tended to lean towards the Conservative party. Catholic voters would change their loyalties towards the end of the century and return to the Liberals. While encouraged by the establishment of separate schools in Ontario, Catholics remained disillusioned at the closing of their schools in New Brunswick and Manitoba.

7 Church and Society

The wars of religion in Europe were long over, and the political and economic barriers between Christian denominations were coming down. The legal framework employed by the British government for the repression of Catholic minorities remained in place. From the time of British supremacy in North America starting with the Conquest in 1763 until the Catholic Emancipation Act of 1829, government suppression of Catholics continued from Newfoundland through to Ontario. When the legal barriers disappeared in the nineteenth century, voluntary fulminations of religious anti-Catholicism replaced them for one hundred years. English cultural imperialism in the twentieth century replaced religious condemnation as the way to keep Catholics confined and socially in their place.

When asked by Pope Leo XIII in 1900 to report on Protestant inroads among Canadian Catholics, the Catholic bishops were able to give a fairly positive report indicating fair exchanges enjoyed by Catholics with Protestants and civil governments. Because legislation provided a level playing field and Protestant proselytizing of Catholics was not happening, Catholics were able through the nineteenth century to extend medical care, hospitals, and schools across the nation.[1] Canadian clergy and laity collaborated with business and government to support the Canadian economic take-off at the turn of the twentieth century.

CATHOLIC-PROTESTANT RELATIONS

From the reign of Edward VI and Elizabeth I, England considered itself a Protestant nation and imposed its beliefs on its subjects with fire and sword. These strong Protestant convictions towards the end of the eighteenth century were softened by England's union with Scotland, which brought Highland Catholics into the kingdom, and its union with Ireland in 1800, which weakened anti-Catholicism still further. In Canada the English conquest followed by the Treaty of Paris in 1763 planted the British flag over seventy thousand Catholic subjects. General James Murray, the first commander of the army of occupation, granted the Canadiens the practice of the Catholic religion. The Quebec Act of 1774 tolerated Canadien law, religion, and the tithe.[2] The Canadian constitution of 1791 confirmed concessions to Catholics and provided land and a legislative base for their expansion.[3] In the words of John Moir, the English government used the toleration model for dealing with Catholics until the 1840s.[4]

Although anti-Catholicism did not take root in the Canadian constitutional tradition, many provinces, in a fashion similar to the mother country, restricted Catholics during the early years through legislation and the penal laws. From 1760 to 1832 the Atlantic provinces dismantled their restrictive legislation against Catholics, allowing them to vote, own land, and practise their religion under the guidance of clergy.[5] Historian J.R. Miller contends that religious anti-Catholicism in Canada during the 1830s replaced the institutional restrictions of an earlier period. Instead of the anti-Catholic legislation of the past, ministers and divines now initiated verbal assaults on Catholics based on biblical and reform theology. They filled their pamphlets, journals, and pulpits with diatribes and attacked the customary irritants of idolatry, saints, papal power, Catholic schools, clerical celibacy, and indulgences.

Nova Scotia became a seedbed for anti-Catholicism during the 1840s and 1850s. Nova Scotian Protestants came to fear Catholicism as a "system of beliefs promoting disloyalty and oppression and leading to moral, economic, and social backwardness."[6] The English Protestant fear of Catholicism was assimilated in a unique way by Nova Scotians, who were reacting to the large Irish Catholic immigration in the first half of the nineteenth century, which overwhelmed the native population. By 1851 one out of every three Haligonians was Catholic. Catholics made Halifax their own, founded St Mary's College in 1840, formed a diocese in 1842, initiated six Catholic organizations, received two congregations of sisters, and became a metropolitan see and archbishopric in 1852.[7]

Halifax in the 1850s became the centre of Protestant reaction, which led to interdenominational alliances for purposes of anti-Catholic agitation. The Free Church of Scotland and the Presbyterian church of Nova Scotia founded the Protestant Alliance in 1858, hoping to unite all Protestant denominations against Catholics. A new lecture series centred on the vilification of an Anglican clergyman who defected to Rome. The lectures were well attended, and copies of the talks soon disappeared. Newspapers and pamphlets in "strident tone" supported this anti-Catholic barrage. They complained that Catholics were running Nova Scotia through their control of the Liberal party. They grumbled about papal aggression and repeated accusations of the former priest and apostate Alexandro Gavazzi and the American Know-Nothings.[8] They gratuitously associated Catholic popery with violence, lawlessness, and the Dark Ages.[9]

Catholics struck back in their weekly, the *Cross*, by condemning the "soul-destroying doctrines ... of the traitorous and bloody Knox, as well as the bloody, suicidal tenets of the faggot-lighting, hypocritical monster, Jack Calvin, the Robespierre of Geneva."[10] The editors summed up Catholic feelings about these public attacks by stating that "Protestantism is based on falsehood, its essence is deception, its food is calumny."[11] The Liberal party, having been associated with Catholicism, joined the anti-Catholic attacks to extricate itself. This action forced eight Catholic members along with two Protestants from Catholic ridings to cross the floor of the Nova Scotian assembly in 1857 to sit with the Tories.

This action brought the Liberal government down. The ensuing election was fought over the issue of Protestant versus Catholic ascendancy in Nova Scotia. The Liberals were returned to power in an anti-Catholic victory. As the decade spent itself tensions eased because most of the Irish immigrants had been absorbed and the internal weaknesses of the Orange Lodge. These decades of religious discontent, historian A.J.B. Johnston contends, were rooted in decades of economic uncertainty in Nova Scotia. Britain was dismantling its navigation system and no longer giving preference to maritime goods, and Nova Scotia had not yet replaced this lost trade with a reciprocity agreement with the United States. Johnston argues that economic uncertainty provoked Protestant fears, which were expressed in the 1840s and 1850s by making Catholics the scapegoats of these anxieties.[12]

Events in New Brunswick developed in a similar nativist pattern. The Loyal Orange Association landed during the early part of the nineteenth century with the British garrisons, especially those coming from Ireland. In his recent study *Riots in New Brunswick*, Scott W. See analyses the impact of the Protestant Orange Lodges on Irish Catholics in New Brunswick. The arrival of Irish immigrants both before and during the famine played into the job competition during a slack economy. The Orange resentment of needy immigrants was taken out on Irish Catholics, whom the Orangemen saw as advance Vatican battalions sent to romanize Loyalist New Brunswick. The Irish Catholics were seen as a worldwide conspiracy that had to be stopped at all costs.[13] The lodges, convinced that they were the ones protecting the law and order of the British Empire, carried weapons, marched on the public streets, and resorted to vigilante tactics to intimidate Irish Catholics. Their belligerent methods provoked Catholics in the late 1840s to defend their neighbourhoods against the intruders. Riots broke out in Woodstock, Fredericton, Saint John, and Portland. Unprepared to cope with social disorder, the government allied itself with the marching Orangemen, using their militancy to impose order on the disenfranchised. The vigilantism of the lodges, far from resolving the problem, provoked bloody conflicts and pitched battles with Catholics.[14] The aggressive militarism of the Orangemen became a "midwife for social violence."[15] The courts extended a prejudicial system by playing their part in finding Irish Catholics guilty and punishing them, while Orangemen were exonerated and praised.[16] Even during the third quarter of the nineteenth century, as if Catholic Emancipation had not happened, Irish Catholics were deliberately excluded from positions of responsibility in public life.[17] The success of the Orange Lodges in fusing the different levels of authority in New Brunswick in exclusion of Irish Catholics, See concludes, ratified the "success of vigilante behaviour and institutionalized nativism."[18]

The Protestant Protective Association protested papal aggression[19] and, long after the famine, the influx of Irish Catholics.[20] The association confused distressed refugees from the famine with Irish Catholics who were well established in Canadian society, and the Protestant Protective Association saw Catholics as a threat to a well-ordered Protestant society. Former priest Charles Chiniquy preached in Quebec and Ontario, against Catholic decadence and the heady stories of sex and religion by Maria Monk were used to verify his contentions.[21] George Brown of the Reform party protested against legislation for separate schools and took issue in the *Globe* with Catholic advocates.[22] The confrontational model during the 1840s replaced tolerance and persisted until the exigencies of the Great War in the twentieth century.

Catholics were perceived to be against Canadian confederation because of the ambivalence of the Quebec hierarchy on the issue and the number of high-profile anti-confederationists, such as Timothy Anglin of New Brunswick and Bishop Terence Sweeney of Saint John's. Canadian Catholics were forced to use political pressure and the election campaign to encourage members of the legislature to be more receptive to their needs. Their political activity produced some tangible results, such as when Sir John A. Macdonald, the central player in the Confederation struggle, abandoned his initial preference for a Protestant-dominated unitary government in favour of a genuine confederation of provinces to accommodate Canadian Catholics.[23] After the passage of Confederation, the attention of Canadians shifted to the issues that were thrown up as Catholics and Protestants adjusted to each other. These cultural problems included the Catholic take-over of Quebec education in 1875, Protestant jubilee riots in Toronto the same year,[24] Jesuit Estates of 1888, growth of French-language instruction in eastern Ontario, French-speaking settlements spreading across the Canadian prairies, and the rebellions in support of Louis Riel.[25]

The Riel rebellion exploded like a bomb, shattering the fragile relations between English and French. When the Métis of Red River were confronted by Canadian surveys of lands they had always worked, Louis Riel formed a provisional government in Manitoba to ensure that the Métis were not dispossessed of what they thought of as their land. The military forces of Colonel Garnet Wolseley approached, and Riel fled to the United States. He was elected in 1874 to the House of Commons, and the next year the Canadian government granted him an amnesty, once he had accepted a sentence of banishment for five years. The Métis of Batoche, fearing the loss of their lands in 1884, asked Riel to return to the Canadian prairies to lead them against those who would confiscate their homes. The North West Rebellion commenced in March 1885, and after the arrival of Canadian troops, the Métis were forced to surrender in May. The government seized Riel and hanged him in November.[26] Louis Riel became an instant hero for Canadiens, and his execution became an analogy of the Canadian mistreatment of Canadiens.

In the last decade of the nineteenth century and into the twentieth, anti-Catholicism reshaped itself into the driving force of English cultural imperialism. It saw medieval Catholic culture as the hand of the past and a threat to the growth, freedom, and light of Canada. D'Alton McCarthy led the anti-Catholic movement in Ontario and Manitoba and protested against French-speaking Catholic schools as being unsuitable for a English nation. Historian J.R. Miller describes this force in positive terminology as "more a matter of coercive nationalism than religious bigotry." Protestant mission schools spread across the North and the West in a concerted effort to anglicize the inhabitants and combat the network of Catholic schools.[27]

The papal decree *Ne Temere*, published in 1908, made it clear to Catholics that a marriage between two Catholics, or between a Catholic and a Protestant, must be witnessed by a Catholic pastor and two lay persons. This decree was intended to protect Christian women from private marriages of convenience that could afterward be repudiated. Although aimed at Catholics, its implications caused great anger, fear, and frustration among Protestants in the United Kingdom and Canada. They saw the Roman letter as overthrowing Canadian marriage law and Catholic-Protestant marriages. This was just the opposite of what progressive Canadians had hoped for: they believed that mixed marriages would be a natural institution through which Canadians could assimilate the various ethnic groups. The Holy See had not anticipated the strong Protestant reaction.[28]

In 1911 the Methodist *Christian Guardian* recounted the story of a Presbyterian woman in Belfast whose Catholic husband deserted her and kidnapped their two children when she refused to have their marriage blessed in the Catholic church. The magazine condemned the inhumanity of the proceedings and cried out that "the church ... has no right to counsel him to break the solemn and binding vow which held him to his wife." What was wrong, the *Guardian* declared, was that the Roman church was declaring the marriages officiated by non-Roman clergy as invalid. Such teaching applied in Canada would invalidate Canadian marriage law.[29]

This fear came to pass in Quebec when the marriage by a Methodist minister of two Catholics, Eugéne Hébert and E. Cloutre, was annulled by Archbishop Bruchèsi in 1909. The annulment was then confirmed by the Quebec Superior Court in 1911. The *Presbyterian* explained, "The civil law [in Quebec] follows the law of the Church, so that the marriage of two Roman Catholics is not considered valid unless performed by a priest of their own Church." The publication went on to urge that Quebec law be changed so that weddings performed by validly ordained clergy be always valid; spouses would thus be encouraged to remain faithful to each other.[30]

The *Canadian Congregationalist* reacted strongly, telling off the pope: "This self-constituted autocrat at Rome, kindly mind your own business and allow us to mind ours." Roman interference to invalidate Canadian marriages should be seen as "high treason and punished accordingly."[31] Anglican Bishop John Cragg Farthing, upset with the annulment, asked that the Hébert case be appealed to the Privy Council. The *Guardian* supported the bishop's proposal.

Protestant church councils met quickly to deprecate *Ne Temere* and to ask for suitable legal action. The Methodist church's general conference decried "the right of any church ... to declare invalid or cast doubt upon the validity of any marriage solemnized according to the law of any of the provinces of Canada." It believed that each religious denomination should have equal rights in every one of the Canadian provinces. The Congregational Union at its annual general meeting sought cooperation with other religious bodies for effective action to correct the situation in Quebec, protect the sanctity of the home, and guarantee the rights of all denominations. The Presbyterian church's general assembly called on the provincial legislatures to erase "all ambiguities in the law affecting the validity of marriages" and "to provide that the legal hindrances to marriage should be defined by the Civil Law, and not by any Church or other religious body whose rules do not apply to the whole community." The general assembly cautioned members against entering into mixed marriages, under the circumstances, with Catholics. The Anglican church demanded legislation to end this "serious interference" with Canadian marriages. The Evangelical Alliance moulded interdenomination cooperation to insist on the amendment of Quebec's civil code and an end to the coercion of Catholics in the matter of marriage.[32]

Interest in these decisions lingered in the Protestant magazines, and the Evangelical Alliance collected almost 300,000 signatures on a petition against the acceptance of *Ne Temere*. A second Quebec Superior Court decision in February 1912 appeared to settle the issue, stating that the papal decree had "no civil effect on said marriage" and that the archbishop's pronouncement had "no judicial effect in said case."[33] Thus the validity of the marriage of a Catholic couple before the Methodist minister was upheld in Quebec law. The Supreme Count also declared in favour of mixed marriages performed by Protestant ministers in Quebec.

A second case of a Protestant minister marrying Catholics in Quebec went through the courts to the Privy Council, and in 1921 the Privy Council upheld the legality of the marriage. Quebec Protestants thought they had won the issue once and for all. Yet Superior Court judge Alfred Forest granted annulments when requested, certain that he was not bound by these civil precedents. The issue of the validity of mixed marriages dragged on until finally, in 1940, three Catholic and two Protestant judges of the Quebec Court of Appeals ruled unanimously in a third case for the validity of marriages in Quebec presided over by Protestant ministers.[34]

During the Great War and into the depression, the sharp edges that divided Catholic from Protestant wore smooth, and anti-Catholicism waned. The common bond needed to win the war inspired camaraderie among the two groups.[35] A typical example of the new Christian spirit that was being worked out, suggests Mark McGowan, was "the joint Protestant-Catholic effort to raise funds for the Knights of Columbus Catholic Army Huts programme in Europe."[36] And during the hard times of the 1930s, a common commitment to the social gospel aroused Catholics and Protestants to work together to solve economic problems, house the homeless, and feed the needy. Communist success in the Soviet Union challenged Christians to cooperate in the service of the poor or face a soviet-style revolution. Christian theologians working to resolve mutual problems around the world developed a theology of peace and harmony among the Christian faiths. In the early 1960s the Second Vatican Council, in describing interfaith relationships, was moved to go beyond the model of Catholic and Protestant solitudes and introduce a spirit of cooperation and reconciliation.[37] Fellow Christians sensed common bonds linking them together to face the powerful force of secularism that was threatening western Christian society.[38]

RETHINKING CATHOLIC-PROTESTANT RELATIONS

Reports submitted by twenty-five Canadian bishops to the Holy See on Protestant proselytism in Canada reveal further evidence of a changing climate in Catholic-Protestant relations at the turn of the twentieth century. The Holy See asked the bishops whether the Catholic minority in the dominion felt itself oppressed by Protestant evangelization. Rome called on the bishops to respond to three questions on Catholic-Protestant relations in Canada. The bishops were first asked to describe the extent of direct Protestant proselytism in their dioceses. Second, they were asked to assess the state of both clerical and lay piety. Third, they were invited to estimate the extent of indirect proselytization in Canada and to make suggestions about how to strengthen the faith.[39]

In an appraisal of the bishops who created the reports of 1900–01, historian Mark McGowan discovered that they were native-born, well-educated, younger than sixty-five years, and had only held office for five years or less. The exceptions were the French-born Oblate prelates from the missions of western Canada.

Archbishop Cornelius O'Brien of Halifax reported that Maritime Protestants had not engaged in proselytizing to entice Catholics away from the faith. Bishop John Cameron of Antigonish pointed to Protestant proselytism in the late 1850s and early 1860s in Nova Scotia but conceded that since that time respectable Protestants had not taken part in such activities. Prince Edward Island and New Brunswick reported a general harmony between faiths, except for some ineffective efforts at sheep stealing by Protestant ministers among the Acadians. Schools were a concern in the Maritime provinces as Catholic education was not regularly funded by the government. Catholic parents were caught in a dilemma. Those who sent their children to the neutral public schools feared the children would be harassed by unscrupulous Protestant teachers. Other parents who sent their children to Catholic schools were penalized into paying both school taxes and school tuition.[40]

In eastern Ontario, Bishops Richard O'Connor, Alexander Macdonell, and Charles Gauthier dismissed fears of proselytism. Nor, they added, would public opinion tolerate Protestant solicitation of Catholics by the enticements of food, clothing, and other gifts. They acknowledged Ontario's fairness in funding separate schools for the education of Catholic children. Mark McGowan sums up the eastern Ontario bishops' report by concluding that "Catholics were [not] threatened institutionally or publicly by Protestants."[41]

Southwestern Ontario was another story. Its small number of Catholics was divided among French, Irish, and Germans who were surrounded by a sea of militants, that is, the Protestant Protective Association and Equal Rights Association. The bishops admitted that the indirect propaganda of the Methodist Sunday schools, the distribution of Protestant tracts, public lectures promoting "heresy," sewing circles, and Bible societies had led to some defections. They believed that Catholics in Ontario hospitals and prisons were exposed to the work of Protestant chaplains. Yet overall, the bishops conceded that civil ministries were fair, even if they were dominated by Protestants.[42]

In Quebec, where Catholics constituted ninety percent of the population, Protestant proselytizing was not seen as a threat to the majority. The relationships between church and government, laity and clergy, were positive and peaceful. The bishops reported that they had perceived little organized Protestant proselytizing, although Protestants had sometimes sown dissension when conflict arose between Catholic pastors and parishioners. One such occasion was the relocation of the church at Maskinongé, where seventeen families left their parish to form a Protestant congregation. Despite incidents such as this, the bishops reported that the Canadiens successfully resisted Protestant overtures and remained fervent Catholics.[43]

The French-born missionary bishops of the Canadian Northwest were highly sensitive to living in a Protestant nation and reported that they saw well-organized Protestant missions targeting native people and Ukrainian Canadians. They saw Methodists and Anglicans, financially supported by Protestant Bible societies, central Canadian congregations, the Methodist Bureau, and the Anglican Church Missionary Society, offering native people food, clothing, and schooling for their children. The Department of Indian Affairs hired few Catholics as Indian agents and reserve employees. Nor did Catholic schools receive a fair share of corporate tax revenues. The missionaries witnessed the Presbyterians training Ukrainian ministers to penetrate the Greek-Catholic communities on the Prairies. Archbishop Adélard Langevin, not to be outdone, recruited Redemptorist clergy to serve Eastern Rite Ukrainians and Polish Catholics and funded the publication of the Ukrainian newspaper in Winnipeg. The Ukrainian population grew rapidly and the shortage of clergy was a nagging problem, but it was handled by the appointment in 1912 of the first Ukrainian bishop, Nykyta Budka of Lwow.[44]

Overall the bishops reported to Rome that there was little or no organized Protestant proselytizing, that governments were generally impartial in dealing with religious groups, and that Catholic-Protestant harmony was typical of the Canadian religious environment. The Catholic clergy were zealous, and both Euro-Canadians and the native people resisted Protestant advances and remained staunch Catholics. They continued to worry about the fraternization, however, that occurred in mixed marriages, neighbourhoods, businesses, recreations, schools, and libraries. Mixed marriages occurred seldom in the Maritimes and Quebec, with their large Catholic populations, and even when they did take place, the non-Catholic party after the usual preparation often became a Catholic. In Ontario and western Canada where the Catholic population lived among many Protestants, mixed marriages were more common, and if the dispensation was refused, marriages were often solemnized outside the Church.[45]

The bishops were concerned not over direct Protestant proselytizing but over the indirect proselytizing where Catholics were in the minority and lacked schools and religious organizations. To remedy this, they suggested to the Holy See more clergy, schools, newspapers, social organizations, and institutions of higher learning. Mark McGowan believes that the disparate nature of the information collected from coast to coast points to the complexity of Canadian life and to the "limited identities" of Canadians.[46] Catholics from all ethnic groups settled in every province. They were ethnically and culturally diverse, French and English, Scots and Irish, German and Hungarian, Ukrainian and Polish. Canadian Catholics have learned to live in comfort with Protestant and other neighbours. The presumptions of a Catholic monolith or Protestant-Catholic strife was far from Canadian reality. These reports at the turn of the century reveal interfaith forbearance rather than institutional squabbles. Protestant-Catholic communities enjoyed a mutual tolerance and shared in the growth of a common language. Both sides had learned in the multicultural weave of Canada to live with each other and enjoy these advantages.[47]

CATHOLIC HOSPITAL CARE

Catholic hospital care in Canada has an extensive and rich heritage. Care for the sick, elderly, homeless, and marginalized has always been a Christian concern. The first hospitals in western history were founded by Catholic religious orders in thirteenth-century Europe to look after the wounded and the suffering who could not care for themselves. In a period before the knowledge of bacteria and viruses, antiseptics and anaesthesia, modern surgery and drugs, caring for the sick was an unglamorous undertaking only for the brave of heart who often gave their lives for the wounded and the plague stricken.

Canadian health care began in the seventeenth century with the arrival of the Hospitallers of St Augustine and the Hospitallers of St Joseph. A century later Marguerite d'Youville accepted responsibility for the Montreal hospice. Since that time, her spiritual daughters, the Grey Nuns, have opened hospitals throughout Quebec, and also in Ottawa, Winnipeg, Regina, the Canadian Northwest, and the United States.[48] Meanwhile, as noted earlier, the Sisters of Charity of Halifax opened the Halifax Infirmary in 1886.[49] The Congregation of St Martha opened eleven hospitals in the Maritimes and western Canada and operated four schools of nursing.[50] These religious enterprises represent a part of the Catholic hospital interests and investments. But let us examine one particular hospital in depth.

In Toronto St Michael's Hospital was founded to help deal with the annual outbreaks of typhoid, diphtheria, and scarlet fever during the last decade of the nineteenth century. Dr Norman Allen, a Toronto health officer, sought three volunteers from the Sisters of St Joseph to nurse plague victims. They were to take charge of the old Isolation Hospital located on the site of Riverdale Hospital behind the Don Jail. Impressed by the commitment of the sisters in caring for the afflicted, Dr Allen proposed that they open a general hospital. Notre Dame des Anges, a girls boardinghouse on Bond Street, was renovated for the purpose, and the fledgling hospital received its first three patients on 1 July 1892. Among other ailments patients were admitted for tuberculosis, venereal disease, typhoid, and Bright's disease. The early records show that few patients arrived with heart disease or cancer. The new hospital included 26 beds and the first Catholic school of nursing in Canada. In addition to the begging of the sisters and benefactions from generous citizens, the province paid the hospital a maximum of 30 cents a day for the indigent sick. The Hugh Ryan wing was opened in 1895, providing the hospital with 110 beds and making it the second largest of the city's twenty-eight hospitals, after the Toronto General.[51]

In its second year of operation, St Michael's became affiliated with the school of medicine at the University of Toronto and began an unbroken and mutually beneficial relationship with the university. Toronto newspaper listings in 1906 showed "St Michael's with eleven physicians, seven of whom held appointments at the university, and six of whom were also on the staff at the [Toronto] General; fifteen surgeons, twelve of whom held appointments at the university and ten of whom were also at the General; two specialists in eye, one in nose and throat, and one in obstetrics, all of whom had university appointments."[52] Medical students from the university regularly came to St Michael's for clinical experience. To supervise the school of nursing, Miss Harrison, a graduate from the Bellevue Hospital in New York City, was hired to implant the Florence Nightingale principle of character formation at St Michael's nursing school. In 1894 the two-year program was extended to three years and followed an apprentice system. Applications for admission arrived from such distant locations as Halifax and Chicago, Buffalo and Texas. At the opening of the Hugh Ryan wing, Archbishop John Walsh (1889–98) articulated an early mission statement for St Michael's Hospital. He stated that the institution should be competitive only in doing good for the sick, in welcoming every race and religion, and in respecting the religious convictions of all patients. Clergy of other denominations should be welcome to attend to the spiritual needs of the sick.[53]

In 1912 St Michael's D Wing was opened, housing large hospital wards of twelve to sixteen beds. This raised the number of beds to 350. A seven-storey residence was completed in 1921 to board 150 nurses. In 1913 Archbishop Neil McNeil enhanced the power of the hospital board by giving it executive powers dealing with the university, expenditure of donations, appointment of an auditor, and examination of plans and contracts for new construction. The hospital was thus run by a troika consisting of the hospital's board of governors, administration, and medical advisory board. The hospital board was heavily involved with external matters, the superior and her council guided the internal management of the hospital, and the medical board was instrumental in policy making and devising new initiatives in patient care. Hospital cooperation was further enhanced by the amalgamation of the Catholic Hospital Associations of the United States and Canada. The editor of the *St Michael's Hospital Medical Bulletin* reflected that "incorporation in the Catholic Hospital Association ... in 1918 ... more than any other single factor has stimulated progress."[54]

The well-developed Catholic health care practice in Canada was throw into panic in 1942 by the threat of national health care insurance. Catholic hospitals were a very large enterprise in Canada, accounting for thirty-four percent of the hospital beds and forty-two percent of the nursing schools. Father Émile Bouvier, SJ, prepared a report warning against socialized medicine and expressing the fear that the government might take control over Catholic hospitals and usurp the Church's traditional role as defender of the poor. In response to this perceived threat, Catholic hospital administrators quickly formed the Catholic Hospital Council of Canada in November 1942, which included 206 hospitals. The Canadian bishops, forming their own conference in 1943, set up a permanent commission on Catholic hospitals. During the 1940s and 1950s Catholics remained unhappy with the idea of Canadian health insurance. In 1954 the Catholic Hospital Council of Canada struck a new constitution and in 1954 renamed itself the Catholic Hospital Association of Canada (CHAC). The CHAC was now composed of eight regional conferences and claimed 220 hospital members. They believed that the uniqueness of the Catholic hospital stemmed from a human approach in which compassion and competence were fused together. For twenty years an average of three thousand nursing sisters joined the ranks of Catholic hospitals every five years, but between 1960 and 1965 the number was halved to fifteen hundred a year as other jobs opportunities arouse.[55] By the 1960s the bishops saw the advantage of giving the laity a larger role in Catholic health care and accepting national health insurance, which became law for all Canadians in 1965. The bishops encouraged the CHAC to support these new considerations.[56] As Archbishop Maurice Roy put it, "The awakening of the laity to its responsibilities within the Church is fortuitous and will allow religious communities to devote themselves to an apostolate that is more in keeping with their religious character."[57]

During the period of secularization following the Second Vatican Council, the Catholic health establishment went through a profound crisis. Between 1970 and 1975, the CHAC executive director, Father Norman Andries reported in the *Catholic Hospital* that the number of Catholic hospitals declined from 264 to 151.[58] The CHAC, which began as a Catholic organization of mostly men and women religious, became a Catholic organization of health care workers with ecumenical linkages. To reflect these changes, the name was changed in 1976 to the Catholic Health Association of Canada. Father Everett MacNeil was selected as executive director from 1978 to1989, and he revitalized the CHAC with extensive colloquia and broad networks of national and international relations.[59]

CHURCH INITIATIVES FOR ECONOMIC GROWTH IN QUEBEC

The magic touch of Wilfrid Laurier proved to be economic as well as political. His government launched Canada into its economic "take-off" period (1896–1914). Quebec participated fully in Canadian pros-

perity, and its industrial production during this period increased by
74.9 percent, or 5.7 percent per annum. Some historians, such as
Michel Brunet and A.R.M. Lower, accused the Catholic church of im-
peding the economic expansion of Quebec. They contended that the
clergy directed Canadiens towards agriculture and away from industry.
William F. Ryan shatters this contention with his research into the Quebec economy.[60]

Ryan conducted an intensive study of the economic history of two
Quebec regions, St Maurice River Valley and Saguenay-Lake St John,
during the period of economic take-off. The St Maurice River Valley
experienced economic growth and soon became a large supplier of
newsprint, aluminum, and chemicals. The ultramontane bishop, Louis
Laflèche of Trois-Rivières, welcomed industry to the region and
blessed the first pulp mill in 1887. Ryan discovered that *curés* of the
region sought to improve education, culture, and prosperity for their
parishioners. To that end, they brought in settlers, sought government
help, and organized the building of schools, roads, and public facilities. They worked to upgrade agriculture and were instrumental in introducing the new dairy industry. The pages of the Trois-Rivières
diocesan newspaper were full of promotional information on industry,
agriculture, and education.[61]

In the Saguenay-Lake St John region, the bishops sought good relationships with the railway owners to assure adequate facilities for their
towns. The *curés* in the parishes promoted railways, industry, and electrification. Some rectories acted as hubs for business people, local
industrialists, and the exchange of ideas on regional progress. In Chicoutimi a business course was added to the commercial program of the
school. The city's big pulp mill was the darling of the clergy. The manager, M. Dubuc, was knighted by the pope in 1904, and the president,
N. Garneau, received a warm message from the bishop. Ryan argues
that the Quebec clergy in these regions were the friends of progress
and sought to promote the "kingdom" of the Saguenay.[62]

A more general review of the province reveals that *curés* often over-
saw the construction of secondary roads, culverts, and bridges. In
projects to upgrade the region, government reports listed forty priests
as "overseers, contractors etc." *Curés* promoted railways and scientific
agriculture and were officers of agricultural clubs. Other reports reveal
that *curés* petitioned the government for settlers, industries, pulp mills,
sawmills, flour mills, woollen and cotton mills, clothing factories,
foundries, tanneries, brickyards, cheese and butter factories, and food
preserving industries. The *curés* were clearly not indifferent to the
founding of industries and the creation of jobs in their parishes.[63] We
can see from Ryan's research that the smaller urban centres sought out

industry to bring jobs to their parishioners who might otherwise seek work in Montreal, New England, or the Canadian West.

Ryan surveyed ninety-five parish histories, which showed *curés* promoting communications, railways, roads, the new dairy industry, the *caisse*, utilities, telephones, education, and the improvement of the waterworks. In Montreal, Archbishop Paul Bruchési (1897–1939) was active in settling strikes and disputes, promoting the economy and the work ethic, and encouraging temperance and education.[64]

Ryan concludes that the Catholic church was deeply involved in Quebec society on every level, especially in the promotion of business and industry. The clergy involved themselves in the cultural, linguistic, and national interests of the province so that the Québécois could reap the benefits of modern enterprise and would not need to migrate to the United States and lose their French Catholic identity. Challenged by the Canadian economic take-off, the church adjusted to accept trade unionism and cooperative economic associations. While preferring industries that were controlled by Québécois, *curés* learned to be open to business and often acted as intermediaries with the Anglo-Saxon business community.[65]

Ryan discovered that the clergy who were professors and writers, in contrast to the *curés*, tended to be more theoretical in their analyses of the economy of Quebec and less in touch with local businesses. As a result, their academic and popular publications were less representative of business and commerce than practical perceptions of the parish clergy. Monsignor Laflamme, for example, promoted the ideals of scientific forestry and the conservation of forest lands and waterpower. Monsignor Lapointe laboured to expand the "kingdom" of the Saguenay. And Abbé Baillargé wrote the first Canadian economic textbook. The Trappist monks at Oka, meanwhile, operated a college for scientific agriculture and published research.

There were also a few decidedly false prophets. They included agriculturalists, nationalists, journalists, orators, and colonization missionaries. They promised the impossible dream, encouraging Québécois to farm uninhabitable regions, and urging young people to embark on hopeless missions to Christianize the world.[66] The ideals of this group, which have been taken by some as typical, were definitely not typical of Quebec *curés* and their progressive attitude to modern business.

Education in Quebec was updated to accommodate science and technology but within the humanistic framework of the *collège classique*. This advance was fundamental to the curriculum. Unfortunately, however, the church was caught in a paradox of its own making. While it helped to lead Quebec into the modern world, Ryan states, the church built a "Chinese wall" around French Canadians to preserve "their culture, language, and religion."[67] His study shows that the Catholic church was not antithetical to the economic development of Quebec; that Québécois clergy were in fact progressive in their promotion of commerce and industry. But the cost of progress was steep, and it included continued isolation behind a self-imposed cultural wall. Despite vigorous economic activity, general prosperity in the years leading up to the First World War eluded Quebec. It is ironic that credit for the modernizing effort went not to the clergy for its animation of the movement but to the business people who had their hands firmly on the levers of growth.

CONCLUSION

Anti-Catholicism emerged in the mid-nineteenth century and continued through the remaining decades into the first third of the twentieth century. From the institutional nature of colonial anti-Catholicism, hostility shifted during the nineteenth century to ideological denunciations, and then in the twentieth century to coercive English cultural nationalism. At the beginning of the twentieth century Catholic hospitals had considerable influence in Canadian communities as they cared for the sick of all faiths and employed staff from the various religious traditions. Competition among Canadian Christians softened during this time when camaraderie forged by the war, shared good works, and the struggle against communist secularism brought them closer together by the middle of the twentieth century.

If few of the Quebec bishops supported the Liberal government of Wilfred Laurier, many of the *curés* enthusiastically welcomed Laurier's sunny ways. They involved themselves in the business life of the province so that their parishioners could reap the benefits of the economic upswing. The bishops for their part welcomed industrialists, encouraged the workers, and prayed for the success of the new enterprises. The clergy gave their blessing to the new economic order. Openness increased among Catholics who sought professional life and the opportunity for lay leadership in Catholic institutions. As a rapidly changing world teased traditional church institutions at the turn of the century, a tidal wave of immigration crashed against these creaking structures. Ethnic groups and their distinctive cultures challenged the devotional and jurisdictional edifice of the Roman Catholic Church.

PART THREE

Canadianism

8 Two Messianic Groups in Conflict

At the end of the nineteenth century there was a flood of immigrants to Canada. In addition to the country's native peoples, French, Scottish, and Irish habitants who were already well established across Canada were joined by Germans, Ukrainians, Polish, and American Catholics. They settled in northern Ontario, the Prairies, and the West Coast. During the same years Maritimers and Ontarians boarded railway carriages in the East to hurry over the freshly laid steel rails to the west. While English- and French-speaking Canadians skirmished with each other for control of the Maritime and central Canadian church, new Canadians, as we shall see, were asking to be heard, accepted, and counted in the new settlements and parishes of the West.

Quebec clergy recognized the importance of establishing French-speaking institutions to guard the language frontier and protect their culture. The University of Ottawa was one such institution, an outpost on the frontier of Quebec. The clergy were alert to the importance of linking religion and nationalism for the spiritual welfare of the Canadiens. Quebec clergy continued to grieve over French speakers who emigrated to English-speaking communities in New England or the Canadian Prairies. But if for economic reasons Canadiens had to emigrate, the clergy reasoned, it was hoped that they would reinforce francophone enclaves in the Canadian Northwest and be secure in their faith. A.I. Silver articulates the visionary Canadien experience – a French and Catholic nation within a Protestant and English jurisdiction with the mission to maintain French Catholic rights anywhere in Confederation.[1]

Western Settlement

With equal concern about populating the West, the Toronto-based Catholic Church Extension Society was highly enthusiastic about western settlement and sought to extend the English-speaking church into those unsettled regions. Loyal supporters of the Extension Society from Montreal, Toronto, and London espoused the beliefs and progressive values of the British Commonwealth. From their ranks came volunteers to serve in the First World War and affirm their bonds with the English-speaking majority. Thus it will be seen during this period, and especially when the issue of conscription was introduced, that sharp ethno-linguistic cleavages deepened across Canada, pitting French- and English-speaking Catholics against each other. They believed they must secure their cultures and protect the institutions they considered vital for their survival. In messianic fashion both Canadien and Canadian Catholics believed their respective cultures and religious practices were superior, and that only they, with their particular language, culture, and religion, could successfully evangelize westerners.

ENGLISH-FRENCH TENSIONS, 1840–1930

Differences between the two messianic camps were manifested most intensely from 1840 to 1930. French and English Catholics waged a hundred-year war for linguistic, cultural, and religious control over the Canadian church. While the English and French churches manoeuvred for leadership of Canadian Catholicism, the Anglo-Saxon Protestant majority preached their own brand of superiority over the two Catholic groups. Throughout the British Empire and the English-speaking world, the Anglo-Saxon Protestant majority trumpeted the doctrines of political order, economic progress, racial superiority, and a world devoid of "popery." Canadian Catholics, meanwhile, wrestled not only with each other but also with the enthusiastic but oppressive Protestant majority. The internecine Irish-French cultural struggle, as delineated by Robert Choquette, can be traced through the Atlantic provinces to Ontario and the Northwest.[2]

Prior to 1815 the Catholic church in Canada was principally French, with the exception of some scattered Scottish and Irish settlements in the Maritime provinces, southeastern Ontario, and the Northwest. The significant influx of Scottish immigrants to eastern Nova Scotia and Prince Edward Island and of Irish immigrants to Newfoundland, Halifax, and Saint John challenged the French dominance of the church. It was in the Maritime provinces that the irritants first surfaced between English- and French-speaking Catholics.[3]

The French-speaking Catholic Acadians became a minority within a larger ground of coreligionists with the arrival of the Scottish and Irish

Catholics. Scottish-Irish differences diminished during the nineteenth century because both groups accepted anglicization, but differences between French- and English-speaking Catholics in the Maritime provinces intensified. The first field of conflict was ecclesial appointments. The Acadians had been driven to the northern and eastern districts of New Brunswick and to southwestern Nova Scotia by the Loyalists. Despite dislocation and the resultant poverty – which also happened to the Micmacs and the Abenakis – the Acadians held on to their faith, and the visits of the Canadien and French émigré clergy strengthened their religious observance. The Acadians had large families and outnumbered other Catholics three to two in New Brunswick, but they had few resident priests and no bishops.[4] As historian Robert Choquette writes, Acadians had been "held back from advancement in the ranks of the hierarchy not only by their poor education system but also by the influence of the English-speaking clergy in the Maritimes, a group that reflected, somewhat earlier than elsewhere in Canada, the widespread bigotry prevalent in the English-speaking world after the mid-nineteenth century."[5]

One prime example is Thomas L. Connolly, bishop of Saint John (1852–59), and later archbishop of Halifax (1859–76). Although liked by many, according to Choquette, he headed a biased hierarchy that was "detested by the Acadians." Only in the twentieth century were Acadian bishops appointed, first among them Edouard LeBlanc in 1912 as bishop of Saint John and Patrice-Alexandre Chiasson in 1920 as bishop of Chatham.[6] This tardiness in the ecclesial appointments of Acadians left a long-term grievance.

A second field of conflict in the Maritimes was the schools. The Province of New Brunswick eliminated Catholic separate schools by the Common Schools Bill of 1871. Catholics launched a political battle to regain their schools but were unable to form a common front. Anglophone Catholics spoke on behalf of English-speaking Catholic schools and Acadians on behalf of French-speaking Catholic schools. Indeed, Acadians were wary of their Irish coreligionists trying to lure them into English-speaking Catholic schools, just as they were wary of the English Protestants trying to lure them into non-denominational schools. English speakers had shown little sympathy when the Collège Saint-Joseph at Memramcook was threatened by closure in 1862, or for Collège Saint-Louis in 1874.[7]

During the early years of the Catholic church in Ontario, there was little cultural conflict because French and Irish Catholics lived in separated communities. Most of the first bishops ordained for Ontario were of French origin. In 1856 the French-speaking bishops outnumbered English-speaking bishops four to two. Alexander Mcdonnell and

Rémi Gaulin, both trilingual (Gaelic being their third language), were bishops in Kingston. Three other bishops were bilingual: Joseph-Eugène Guigues of Ottawa, who was consecrated in 1847; Armand de Charbonnel of Toronto, consecrated in 1850; and Pierre Pinsoneault of London, consecrated in 1856. The result of these appointments was that the French clergy outnumbered the English clergy and their number was out of proportion to the growing number of English-speaking parishioners.[8]

During the 1870s newly settled francophones began to open French-language schools in eastern, northeastern, and southwestern Ontario. Protestants and English-speaking Catholics feared Ontario was being transformed into a French-speaking appendage of Quebec. Alarmed, Archbishop John J. Lynch of Toronto called for a halt to the influx of French-speaking immigrants. He also wanted to lure the diocese of Ottawa away from the ecclesial province of Quebec and make its bishop a member of the Ontario bishops. Lynch reasoned that all Ontario bishops should be English speaking and allied with the bishop of Toronto. The first bishops of Ottawa, Joseph-Eugène Guigues (1847–74) and Joseph-Thomas Duhamel (1874–1909), aligned themselves with their Quebec colleagues and successively resisted Lynch's overtures. To halt any further annexation attempts, Rome designated Ottawa an archdiocese in 1886. Other public events aggravated a cultural environment that was already rife with misunderstanding. The hanging of Louis Riel in 1885, the Mercier government's compensation of the Jesuits in 1888, D'Alton McCarthy's Equal Rights Association, and the Manitoba Schools Question of 1891 increased tensions immeasurably.[9] In addition, episcopal appointments were enmeshed in the politics of language and the diplomacy of culture. Between 1890 and 1930 controversies erupted over the appointments to the sees of London, Alexandria,[10] Ottawa, and Sault Ste Marie.

The rapid increase in the number of Franco-Ontarians between Confederation and the Second World War led to an explosion in the number of French-language schools. After the restrictive provincial legislation of 1885, the French schools moved away from the direction of the public school boards to separate school boards, where the political climate was warmer – if only slightly. However, contends Choquette, "English-speaking Catholics have proved willing to sacrifice French schools in order to preserve separate schools."[11] Affirming this statement, one might also say that French-speaking Catholics in Manitoba proved equally willing to sacrifice English Catholic schools to preserve the operation of their own. Both messianic language groups seemed at times more interested in promoting their respective language rights than in sharing their common religion.

Student demonstration against Regulation 17 in February 1916. University of Ottawa (UO)

Most regrettable in this conflict was Ontario's education regulation of 1912. Under Regulation 17 the Department of Education forbade the use of French as an instructional language after the second grade. After its implementation, Canadiens "tended to see themselves as victims of an unparalleled provincial tyranny abetted by Irish Catholics."[12] This edict proved to be unenforceable in the long run and was buried in 1927.[13] It nonetheless inflicted great damage on the province's social and religious fabric. In the midst of the prolonged crisis, two bilingual archbishops, Charles Gauthier and Neil McNeil, became the voices of reconciliation, pouring oil on the troubled waters of English-French relations.[14]

The third sphere of conflict was the Canadian Northwest. French-speaking diocesan priests founded missions in the Northwest as early as 1818. The Oblate Fathers arrived in 1844 on the Red River and in 1845 on the North Saskatchewan River to offer Catholic services in the Indian and white settlements across the Northwest. In 1885 English-French conflict arose when the Canadian Pacific Railroad began unloading English-speaking settlers across the West. The railroad interests and the newly elected Liberal government encouraged immigrants from the Canadian provinces and Europe to settle the Prairies. Among them were many Catholics who chose to learn English as a second language and asked for parishes, schools, and clergy. The popularity of

English culture was at its peak and English became the language of communication on the Canadian prairies. English-speaking bishops appointed to Winnipeg, Calgary, Edmonton, Regina, Victoria, and Vancouver changed the face of the church in the Northwest. The battle for English-speaking bishops appointed in Ontario sees had spread to western dioceses.[15] The new immigrants soon learned English, and against concerted Canadien resistance the demand for English-speaking bishops in Edmonton and Regina was recognized in Canada and granted by Rome.[16]

MESSIANIC STRATEGIES PLAYED OUT IN OTTAWA

Ethnic messianism of the two Canadian solitudes, as envisioned by Robert Choquette, united religious and nationalist convictions into English- and French-speaking camps. It combined the powerful ultramontane spirituality with strong nationalistic aspirations.[17] The Canadien messianic myth believed that God chose Catholics over Protestants, and French Canadian Catholics over English-speaking Catholics. The messianism of Irish Catholics, Choquette points out, was formulated in exactly the same way except that, in this case, God chose English speakers to lord it over French speakers.[18] Mark McGowan, on the other hand, having conducted extensive research on Toronto Catholics, writes that by the twentieth century Irish Catholics had jettisoned their extreme nationalism for the more modest posture of being pro-Canadian and anti-American. The Catholic press, schools, and social organizations encouraged loyalty to the Holy See, British Crown, and an autonomous Canada.[19]

These messianic positions were clearly revealed in the struggle for control of the University of Ottawa at the turn of the twentieth century. Bytown College was founded in 1848 as a bilingual institution. In 1866 it became the University of Ottawa. By 1874, owing in part to the changing composition of the student body and the city, it became a unilingual English-speaking university. It remained so until 1896, when the Oblate Michael F. Fallon was appointed vice-rector of the university. Fallon raised ethnic hackles and was considered to be the vanguard of an Irish coup. He was accused of having "ridiculed" the French language to students and, in the university newspaper, of having criticized the Canadien bishops as being too far removed from the people.[20]

Two years later another Oblate, H.A. Constantineau, replaced the rector of the college and reforms began immediately. The English-speaking university "suddenly performed a kind of about-face" and became a French-speaking university, adding a French section to the English section. After some skirmishing with the new administration about this, Fallon was reassigned as the pastor of St Joseph's parish at the edge of the campus. Provocative and articulate, he remained leader of the Irish community and rallied popular opinion in favour of more English-language instruction at the university. Fallon was a thorn in the side of the Canadien community clamouring for more French in Ottawa.[21]

In June 1901 Fallon was removed from St Joseph's parish and exiled to an Oblate parish in Buffalo. The English-speaking community of Ottawa began to agitate to bring him back to the university. With Fallon's distant support the same community made three attempts to gain justice for its cause. The first was a memorial on the situation at the university, copies of which were sent to Archbishop Joseph T. Duhamel, the Superior General of the Oblate Fathers, the Apostolic Delegate, and Propaganda Fide. The "Irish Memorial," as it was known, argued that the university was founded and chartered to serve English-speaking Catholics and that it should preserve this function. In addition to the removal of Father Fallon from the university, it protested the absence of professors whose mother tongue was English. The sum of five thousand dollars was offered to the university if Fallon was appointed rector and English-speaking Catholics were given some control over the institution.[22] Archbishop Duhamel, defending the French-speaking Oblates, sent letters in 1902 to Propaganda in Rome and the apostolic delegate in Ottawa, justifying their work at the university and dismissed the allegations as "exhorbitant claims and unjust accusations of a few Ottawa Irishmen."[23]

A new Oblate rector, Joseph E. Emery, was appointed in the spring of 1902 and tried to remain neutral in the English-French conflict. Having taught in the United States, the Canadien Emery was presumed by the others to be "an apostate French Canadian." In trying to please both sides, the beleaguered rector became a "chameleon" and succeeded only in alienating both sides.[24]

In Rome Propaganda Fide rejected the Irish claim that the university had been established as an English-speaking university and declared that, as a Catholic university, it should serve students of all nationalities. The congregation also confirmed that Father Fallon would not return to Ottawa since Archbishop Duhamel was committed to a bilingual university.[25]

A disastrous fire in December 1903 set the scene for the second attempt by the Irish contingent to restore the English-speaking university. Following the destruction of much of the physical plant, Emery had the arduous task of seeking benefactors to rebuild the institution. A funding-raising banquet and reception in May 1904 attracted Cardinal James Gibbons of Baltimore, Archbishop Charles-Hugues Gauthier of Kingston, the apostolic delegate, Donato Sbarretti, and Archbishop Duhamel of Ottawa. Emery, with the approval of Duhamel and the apostolic delegate, had invited Fallon to give the principal talk. Although on his best behaviour, Fallon raised the hackles of the French-speaking auditors. A few days later, Duhamel called Emery into his office and demanded an explanation. Emery explained how, with the approval of the apostolic delegate, he had tried to bring both sides together at the ceremony and had succeeded in attracting the Ontario bishops. Despite the effort at reconciliation, differences sharpened between Duhamel and Emery, and finally the archbishop asked the Oblates to replace the rector. In September 1905 the vice-rector, Father William Murphy, replaced Emery and temporarily stabilized the volatile English-French atmosphere.[26]

A mysterious pamphlet anonymously published in September 1906 constituted the third attempt by the English-speaking community to expose the oppression it believed it had suffered. *A Searchlight Showing the Need of a University for the English-Speaking Catholics* argued that the university was founded to attract English-speaking Catholics who might otherwise go to secular universities. They believed that French-speakers might go to Université Laval and other Quebec colleges. They felt the Ottawa university had drifted from this original objective of educating English-speakers and should return quickly to this goal. The mysterious authorship of the pamphlet was later attributed to a member of the university staff. An earlier article by Father J.F. Coffey in the London *Catholic Record* established that the University of Ottawa had originally been set up as an English-speaking college, as a complement to the French-speaking Université Laval, and should thus be restored to its original purpose.[27]

In a previous report to Rome Duhamel had refuted what he considered to be false accusations and maintained that he and Bishop Guigues had intended to create a bilingual college to "unite these two peoples." The institution, he affirmed, was meant to provide the French population of central Canada with the advantage of a university education and bilingual professionals to serve a bilingual population.[28] Finally, Choquette concludes, "the university question" in Ottawa, far from uniting the two peoples, sparked "the ethnic awareness of the hierarchy, the clergy, and the Separate School Boards" up the Ottawa Valley and across Canada.[29]

FRENCH STRATEGY FOR THE WEST

The appointment of Olivier-Elzéar Mathieu from Laval University as bishop of Regina in 1911 recognized the importance of the French majority among Saskatchewan Catholics. Mathieu planned to create compact "blocks" of Canadien Catholics. The settlers in western Canada believed they were heirs to the mission of Catholic France from the time of Clovis's conversion in 496. Jesuit zeal in the seventeenth century carried the gospel to New France, and Oblate dynamism in the nineteenth century set up a network of missions, parishes, and schools throughout the Canadian Northwest. Canadien travellers to western Canada believed they were "the source of a revitalised Catholicism to spread across North America and continue the glorious mission of France."[30]

The first diocesan missionaries to the West were replaced by the numberless Oblates who came to the Northwest after 1844.[31] The Sisters of Charity of Montreal (the Grey Nuns) arrived at the gateway to the Canadian West the same year and quickly followed the Oblates into the Northwest.[32] Their communities and those of other congregations performed "functions that were indispensable in a developing society, [and] they did so for little cost in accordance with their vow of poverty."[33] They helped to maintain the French language and culture in the West.

Two priests, Father Jean Gaire from France and Father Moise Blais from Saint-Boniface, hoped to create a triangle of French-speaking settlers in the southeastern corner of Saskatchewan.[34] They met with little success, and a second team of immigration agents, Father Louis Gravel from Quebec and Father A. Royer from Auvergne, were recruited to do better by the archbishop of St Boniface, Adélard Langevin (1895–1915). Many Canadiens working in New England and New York felt culturally and religiously oppressed by Irish clergy and American culture.[35] Father Gravel, who was living in New York City, succeeded in recruiting these French Canadian expatriates. He sent them to the small southern Saskatchewan communities of Gravelbourg, Laflèche, Mazenod, Meyronne, Courvall, Lac Pelletier, Coderre and Les Cyprès. Father Royer founded Ponteix in southern Saskatchewan. Similar colonies at St Hubert de la Rollandrie and Willow Bunch were settled through the initiative of the laity. Despite their efforts, however, the number of French-speaking settlers from Quebec failed to fill out into blocks of settlement, remaining instead as a sparce chain of Canadien homesteads. Other immigrants from England, Germany, Scandinavia, Ukraine, and Hungary filled in the empty lots around them.[36]

Bishop Adélard Langevin of St Boniface (1895–1915) strongly promoted French Catholic schools in Manitoba. He is shown here with Étienne Lamy, member of the French Academy, at the French Language Congress at Université Laval, June 1912. (AD)

In 1911 Father Gravel told Bishop Mathieu that the French communities needed the leadership of Canadiens with professional careers. This meant the recruitment of doctors, lawyers, teachers, priests, and nuns. Mathieu, anxious to deflect the charge that he was not active enough in recruiting French settlers endorsed Gravel's plan and encouraged settlers to come to the Prairies and settle in a "milieu sympathique."[37] In Montreal a *bureau de renseignement* had been opened in 1895 to attract Quebec settlers to the West. In western dioceses, information offices were created to assist the settlers as they arrived on the Prairies.[38]

Anxious that recruitment for Saskatchewan should succeed, Mathieu requested that the federal government appoint Father E. Dubois of the diocese of Mende in France as immigration agent. Dubois offered to recruit francophone settlers from Belgium, France, the United States and Quebec for southwestern Saskatchewan. The Tory government under Robert Borden agreed there was a need for an immigration agent but believed that Gravel excluded himself as Liberal. The government chose in 1912 to disregard the bishop's suggestions and to appoint its own agent. Mathieu's failure to gain his own francophone agent for the diocese of Regina brought the accusation that he was soft on colonization.[39]

Two apparent breakthroughs then occurred. The first took place in 1914 when Bishop Mathieu finally succeeded in having Father Napoleon Poirier from the Saint-Hyacinthe diocese appointed by the federal government as *missionnaire-colonisateur* for the diocese of Regina. Receiving salary and expenses, Poirier brought settlers from the United States and rural Quebec. The second breakthrough happened two years later when Father Arthur Benoit organized the Compagnie Canadienne de Colonisation. Its mission was to raise capital to buy farms for French Catholic parishes out west and then sell the properties to francophones at low interest rates. Despite its great promise, this last venture proved to be unsuccessful, and in fact the Compagnie Canadienne was "accused of charging exorbitant prices for its lands." A year after the return of the Liberals to government in 1921, Father Gravel replaced Poirier. To foster a new generation of French-speaking professionals, the College Mathieu was founded in 1918 at Gravelbourg.[40]

The dream of a Canadien West came to an end when the Orange Lodge and various Protestant denominations put persistent pressure on the federal government to abolish immigration agents, thus ending any further recruitment. Immigration agents were eliminated by the government in 1927.[41] A second event revealed Orange Protestant hostility to Canadien Catholics. The Saskatchewan government, under pressure from these groups, forbade the wearing of religious garb and the use of French in the public schools. The Anderson amendments to the Public School Act in 1930 and 1931 eliminated from the classroom the crucifix, religious garb, and French as a language of instruction. The Liberal government promised to repeal the legislation when it came to power in 1934. Once in power, fearing the strength of militant Protestants, they reneged on their promise. The minister of Education, however, insisted upon enforcing the anti-Catholic legislation on the Prud'homme School District by threatening to withdraw public funding if the amendments were not obeyed. Father Maurice Baudoux, the parish priest, quietly but firmly pursued the matter with the ministry, the government, and the archbishop's office. A negotiated compromise governed the church-state relationship over the next three decades. The sisters modified their dress, the crucifix on the classroom wall was covered by a white cloth, inspectors learned to be more tolerant of Catholic culture, and by 1962 "the issue had withered away!"[42]

The number of French Catholics in the archdiocese of Regina did not rise above six percent of the general population. André Lalonde believes the policy to attract Canadiens to Saskatchewan failed to take off because the settlements lacked a well-educated Canadien élite. We must also remember that French Catholic clergy were not enthusiastic about emigration from Quebec and did not encourage Canadiens to do so. When English-speaking James C. McGuigan replaced Archbishop Mathieu in 1929, recruitment for French speakers ceased. Moreover, Saskatchewan entered into the Great Depression, and a western drought made prairie agriculture a bad investment. Any further strategies of colonizing western Canada dried up. Migration reversed, and able French-speaking settlers returned to Quebec.[43]

ENGLISH STRATEGY FOR THE WEST

The Catholic Church Extension Society (CCES) offered the English-speaking church a strategy to compete with the Canadien settlements on the Prairies for the domination of western church structures. It planned to be the vanguard of the English-speaking Catholic church, which set out to Canadianize the new immigrants of the Northwest. From 1896 to 1914 three million eastern and southern Europeans trekked from their homelands and spilled onto the Canadian prairies. Many of these new Canadians were Catholics who became English speakers, undoing the English-French balance in the West. The English-speaking church needed a vehicle from which to reach out to these new Canadians and their communities. CCES was founded in 1908 to make contact with them, help meet their needs, and anglicize them.[44] The energetic but short-lived archbishop of Toronto Fergus P. McEvay organized the society's board of governors, which included "a who's who of Catholics,"[45] the chief justice of the Supreme Court, Charles Fitzpatrick, distinguished Toronto brewer Eugene O'Keefe, prominent engineers Michael Hanley and Michael Davis, Father Alfred E. Burke of Prince Edward Island, Louis Alexandre Taschereau, the future premier of Quebec, and Judge Nicolas Beck.[46] The controversial cleric Father Burke was appointed president of CCES and editor of its newspaper, The *Catholic Register and Canadian Extension.*

Despite his boundless energy and good will, Burke could not help but reveal himself, especially to the Canadiens, as an "imperialist and English nationalist."[47]

One of the first concerns of the Extension Society, Mark McGowan recounts, was the care of the Ukrainian Catholics, who needed "clergy, chapels, schools and religious items for the celebration of the Mass." The CCES had grandiose plans and pledged itself to fund these works. It founded a missionary college to educate clergy for the Prairies as part of its scheme to create one English-speaking Catholic civilization throughout western Canada.[48]

The CCES under Monsignor Burke was hardly a success. During his tenure, the society collected a meagre three cents per Catholic per year; at the same time, the Canadian Missionary Congress reported collections of $1.19 per Protestant per year. The best annual collection during the Burke years was $17,000. Burke himself was believed the problem. His style of leadership offended both French- and English-speaking Catholics. Even more, his imperialism in personal dealings with others was alarming, and his English nationalism manifested itself in the pages of the *Catholic Register*. For these reasons, the archbishops of Montreal and Ottawa refused to allow Burke to open offices in their archdioceses. A third French-speaking archbishop, Adélard Langevin of St Boniface, was annoyed because he was not consulted about church activities that were being planned for his archdiocese and because future missionaries were not being trained in his seminary. For the Canadian prairies, Langevin advocated an agenda of multilingualism and multiculturalism, as opposed to the unilingualism of the anglicizers.[49]He provided funding for Ukrainian parishes, schools, and newspapers. Canadiens in general looked upon CCES as a front for anglicization.[50]

It must be confessed that Canadien fears about the intentions of CCES were well founded. Reading the *Catholic Register* raised concerns for the future of the French language and culture in the Canadian Northwest. Numerous articles and editorials proclaimed the benefits of the English language as a unifying force for those of different linguistic traditions. In 1909, as if to show his love of Canada's imperial connection, Burke, editor of the *Register*, invited the Catholic duke of Norfolk to help recruit English clergy and laity to settle in the Canadian West. This overture was not well received by Canadiens. Tensions worsened in Montreal during the following year when at the Eucharistic Congress Archbishop Bourne of Westminster exhorted future missionaries to the Canadian West to remember, "It is only by bringing the English tongue ... that Canada can be made a Catholic nation."[51] Canadien anger was ready to explode.

As if the CCES did not have enough of a credibility problem, one of its ardent supporters was Bishop Michael F. Fallon of London. He was well known as the English hierarchy's spokesperson for opposition to bilingual education in Ontario. When he stated privately that bilingual schools were substandard and then advocated their abolition to the Ontario government, the secular newspapers exposed him publicly for his collaboration with the Ontario government. The *Catholic Register*, ignoring the anger this collaboration caused among Canadiens, gave in defence of Bishop Fallon a very negative appreciation of bilingual schools. The insensitivity of the newspaper forced the resignation of the two francophone members of the board of governors, Bishop Joseph Archambault of Joliette and Archbishop Louis Bégin of Quebec. Activist Archbishop McEvay of Toronto, equally insensitive to these complex feelings, exhorted the Canadiens to accept the inevitable anglicization of immigrants for the sake of church unity. Despite the misgivings caused by CCES, many French Canadian dioceses in the West, such as St Albert, Regina, Keewatin, and Prince Albert, were helped by its contributions and enjoyed its support.[52]

The renovation of CCES began in 1912 with the appointment of Neil McNeil as the new archbishop of Toronto. He reviewed the activities of the society, including its alienation of the French-speaking bishops, its independence from the Canadian bishops, its leadership by Monsignor Burke, and its strident publication, the *Catholic Register*. McNeil took the initiative and recommended a monthly magazine to replace the *Catholic Register*. His suggestion caused a split among the board of governors with half of the board supporting McNeil and the other half Burke. Finally in 1915, Monsignor Burke read the handwriting on the wall and resigned to become chaplain in the Canadian Expeditionary Force.[53] McNeil began rebuilding the Catholic Church Extension Society by appointing Father Thomas O'Donnell as president and J.A. Wall the editor of the *Register*. Wall transformed the *Register* into a suitable Catholic newspaper, and O'Donnell expanded the Extension Society throughout English Canada. The Society's revenues began to increase and gradually rose to over $100,000 yearly. Catholic Extension experienced successes such as the establishment of a Ukrainian college in Yorkton, Saskatchewan. Yet despite its generosity to Canadien settlers living on the Prairies, the society failed to move them towards anglicization.[54]

The Canadian Catholic Extension Society desired to be the yeast of Catholic unity in the West, but its goals collapsed, and its activities only intensified the strife between English and French Canadians. Monsignor Burke's leadership was divisive, the training program for mission-

Gustave Lacasse protested against Bishop Fallon's persecution of French Canadians, 12 November 1917. (UO)

aries was too narrow, the appointment of bishops caused dissension, and all these irritants contributed to the deepening rift between French- and English-speaking Catholics.

BISHOP FALLON AND BILINGUAL SCHOOLS

Bishop Michael F. Fallon of London supported arguments against French Canadian church leadership in Ontario and against French as a language of instruction in Ontario schools. An advocate of unilingual schools in Ontario and of Home Rule in Ireland, he favoured extending British civilization around the world. Fluent in French, he saw English as the language of opportunity for Catholic students and argued for the restriction of French-language instruction in the schools.[55]

Fallon had an active mind and an energetic spirit that revealed a lifetime's interest in education and the pursuit of knowledge. As the bishop of London he "had a life-long passion for education," built English-language schools and colleges but never wavered in his opposition to bilingual schools.[56] He believed they were substandard and should be suppressed. He exuded a presence that was larger than life in whatever he was doing – such as when he was editor of the University of Ottawa *Owl*, a member of the university rugby team and later its undefeated coach, Oblate novice at Aachen (Germany), doctoral student at the Gregorian University in Rome, professor and vice-rector at the University of Ottawa from 1896 to 1901, and Oblate superior in

Buffalo from 1901 to 1909.[57] Because his strong views were known by all, the high-profile Father Fallon was relegated to third choice on the second short list for bishop of London when it was sent to Rome. Nevertheless, it was he who was chosen to be ordained the bishop of London in 1909 because he was recognized to be a strong leader and a bilingual speaker.[58]

Fallon's ambivalence towards Irish nationalism and the British Empire was puzzling but it could be explained. He admired the power of the English language, culture, and nation, which, he believed, would lead world nations to international order, peace, and prosperity. He trusted that, like Canada, Ireland would be granted dominion status in the British Commonwealth. He feared the totalitarian nature of the German Empire and preferred the democratic nature of the Commonwealth, which was to him the precursor of the League of Nations. He saw in the revival of Catholicism in England democracy in action.[59]

While admiring the order of British life, Bishop Fallon was greatly annoyed by a particular custom of the royal family. The coronation oath still contained declarations against transubstantiation and Catholic heirs to the throne. Fallon protested that this Whiggish oath was anti-Catholic, and in an address to the University of Ottawa, he claimed that the king should not speak such offensive words regarding his subjects. Resolutions were passed in Ottawa, and the British *Tablet* picked up the campaign. At the ascension of King George v to the throne in 1911, the anti-Catholic phrases were struck from the oath. Bishop Fallon thus influenced the British Commonwealth in this modest way.[60]

As of 1850 the languages of instruction in Ontario were English, French, and German. However, the Department of Education decided in 1885 to enforce a policy of English-only instruction in publicly funded schools. Aware of the new policy, German schools changed to English instruction on their own. French schools, with more at stake, ignored the policy.[61]

Bishop Fallon worked diligently to enhance the quality of Ontario separate schools and strongly objected to the existence of bilingual separate schools. While preparing students in his diocese for confirmation, he discovered that many bilingual students were inadequate in English and French and very few of them qualified in later years to attend high school. For the good of these students, Fallon believed, bilingual teaching should be eliminated in English-speaking provinces so that children graduating from school would be proficient in English and thus well equipped for personal advancement in life. He sought a meeting with the Ontario government in 1910 to express his view. Bishop Fallon's private conversations and correspondence were leaked to the French and English press. Not in the least embarrassed by this revelation, he explained that he held his views because "the alleged bilingual system [in Ontario] ... is utterly hostile to the best interests of the children, both English and French."[62]

That same year the Ontario government appointed a respected official of the Department of Education, Dr F.W. Merchant, to examine the question of bilingual schools. In his report of 1912 he found some difficulties with bilingual education but thought that overall "the quality of the students and teachers compared favourably with their counterparts in the better uni-lingual public schools." He noted that the Ontario bilingual schools shared similar problems with bilingual schools in Wales, Ireland, Scotland, India, and South Africa .[63]

The positive nature of the Merchant Report was ignored by the Ontario government. Regulation 17 was handed down to the schools in June 1912 and imposed the elimination of French as the language of instruction after grade two. After 1913 French instruction ended entirely, and English instruction became the norm.[64] In the years that followed the Ontario government had to face the fact that the law was unenforceable, and it turned to Dr Merchant again in 1927 to study the issue and to communicate his findings. The second Merchant Report recommended, first, that bilingual normal schools be established to insure the quality of French teaching in bilingual schools, and second, that a special committee be established in the Department of Education to oversee bilingual education.[65] Bishop Fallon's views remained unchanged, and he continued his irrevocable opposition to bilingual schools. Why did Fallon remain so staunchly opposed even when the data provided a more positive view of bilingual schools? John Farrell gives two reasons. First, Fallon had been deeply wounded by the French Canadian takeover of the University of Ottawa, an event that shaped his thinking. Moreover, as an Irish Canadian, Fallon believed it was important for all Canadians to learn English as a vehicle for their careers in the new world dawning upon them. He was horrified by what he believed was the disastrous failure rate in bilingual schools.[66] Fallon was an outstanding leader, but he was stubborn to the point of foolishness when he believed himself to be right. Two other outstanding examples of his folly were the pitched battles he fought against the French-speaking parishioners at Ford City, Ontario, over bilingual schools and then later against the Basilians at Windsor for moving their Assumption College to London.[67] Overall, Fallon greatly enhanced the standing of the diocese of London, but his adamantine nature contributed to the destruction of bilingual education in Ontario for a time and heightened tensions between French- and English-speaking Catholics.[68]

IRISH COME TO GRIPS WITH
THE BURDEN OF EMPIRE

During the First World War military recruitment and the threat of conscription replaced bilingualism and western settlement as the major irritants between French- and English-speaking Catholics. The Irish Catholics in Montreal and Toronto responded enthusiastically to the wartime recruitment of the Canadian Expeditionary Force. The Canadien church, meanwhile, had encouraged loyalty in the defence of England, but Canadiens showed themselves reluctant to volunteer for a British imperial war.[69]

The guns of August thundered into action in 1914 and the Great War commenced in Europe. As the fighting intensified, a committee of twelve Irish Canadians met in Montreal to organize an Irish regiment in the Canadian militia. H.J. Trihey, a successful young lawyer, graduate of Loyola College, and former captain of the Montreal Shamrocks, took the initiative to organize the Irish Canadian regiment. He was eagerly supported by C.J. Doherty, the minister of Justice in the Borden government, and Father Gerald McShane, pastor of St Patrick's Church. Trihey was named the commanding officer of the militia regiment, designated "the 55th Regiment, the Irish Canadian Rangers." It was being organized for home defence and consisted of Canadians of Irish descent from both Catholic and Protestant religions. Its members accepted the facts that Irish Home Rule was suspended for the duration of the war and that they should volunteer for service in a just war. In Montreal, "the ranks of the four companies were soon filled and each was drilled on alternative evenings."[70] Lieutenant Colonel Trihey trained at the officer's school in Halifax and his rank was confirmed.

In 1916 at the St Patrick's Day parade, the Irish Canadian Rangers marched and the colour guards included the Union Jack. Officered by a number of Loyola graduates, including Lord Shaughnessy's son, William, the Irish Canadian Rangers offered to raise an overseas battalion. Father William Hingston, SJ, of Loyola was named its chaplain. The ranks were filled with volunteers of Irish descent, many of whom had previous military experience in imperial wars. Joint fund raising gathered donations so that the Orange and Green could march together in defence of democracy.[71]

In Montreal on Easter Monday, 1916, the unsuspecting Irish Canadian Rangers launched a recruiting drive. Then the tragic news from Dublin began to trickle into Montreal of the Easter Rising and the devastating suppression of the Irish republicans by the British army. Across Ireland martial law was quickly imposed, and the English military heartlessly executed the nineteen leaders of the rising. The news crippled recruiting in Montreal, and six months later the Rangers were still trying to complete the overseas battalion – which remained one hundred soldiers short. Recruiting was also undermined by the poor health of many of the applicants and the rising incomes of those who stayed behind. The duchess of Connaught became the royal patron of the regiment in an effort to lift spirits and encourage recruiting.[72]

The Rangers left Halifax for England in late December 1916, and their first assignment was a recruiting tour of Ireland. Once the Irish Rangers were overseas, the British command informed the Canadian government that despite its promise, the battalion would be broken up and fed into the line in France as reinforcements. Trihey, Hingston, and others in command resigned their commissions and returned to Canada. The Irish Canadian enthusiasm for British imperial policy went flat, but it did not reject military service altogether. Trihey was miffed by what he believed was the employment of 150,000 British troops to suppress the Irish people. He wondered why the Canadian government was willing to recruit another 100,000 Canadians when British troops in Ireland would be better employed fighting against the German army. The Ancient Order of Hibernians felt they could no longer tolerate supporting English policy, which saw the partition of Ireland as part of Home Rule. Yet the Montreal Irish continued to vote for their minister of Justice, C.J. Doherty, who supported Canadian conscription for overseas. Doherty was re-elected in 1917 by a large majority. Despite disillusionment with the breakup of the regiment and the feeling of betrayal over Home Rule, the Montreal Irish remained loyal to the Crown and continued to support the Union government. Robin Burns concludes that "the Irish Canadian Rangers were a declaration of that tradition."[73]

Catholics in Toronto, according Mark McGowan, had integrated since 1890 into Ontario society and assimilated the goals of the British Empire. They had won jobs on all levels from labouring and agriculture to business and the professions, and many became Toronto home-owners.[74] No longer interlopers in Ontario society, they had become established members and espoused its goals.[75]

At the advent of the war, the Irish and Scottish Catholics in Toronto, along with French Canadians, Germans, Italians, and new converts, showed their patriotism by accepting the burden of empire. Between 1914 and 1917 thirty-five hundred Toronto Catholics volunteered to serve in the Canadian Expeditionary Force. The majority were Canadian born and had received previous military training in the Canadian militia. They had bonded to the British military tradition. Recruitment numbers remained high, even though in 1915 industrial jobs were readily available and were to continue so throughout the rest of the war.[76] Archbishop Neil McNeil addressed recruiting meetings, stressed the importance of patriotism, and began a Patriotic Fund to aid the war effort. Toronto clergy participated in enlistment drives, supported conscription, and volunteered as chaplains. Parishes opened their facilities for the use of soldiers stationed in the area. The *Catholic Register* (Toronto) and the *Catholic Record* (London) rallied Catholics to acts of patriotism and defence of the British Empire. In the *Register* Henry Somerville backed national registration and conscription. Catholics formed voluntary associations to raise funds and to supply socks for those at the front. Catholic schools held essay and poetry contests and sponsored cadet programs to assist the war effort.[77] Accepting responsibility as members of the British Commonwealth, Catholics enjoyed a new sense of self-identity, belonging, and acceptance. The funding campaigns and the shared religious activities, as McGowan contends, marked the coming of age for Catholics. By their patriotism and sacrifices, they won recognition from the Protestant majority and completed their inculturation into Canadian society.[78]

The fervour of Toronto Catholics for the British war was not especially welcome news to the Canadiens. Canadiens were rankled by Ontario Catholics' negativity towards bilingual schools, Canadien settlement in the West, and Canadien resistance to conscription. To the discomfort of Quebec, the anglophone bishops, including Neil McNeil of Toronto, Michael Fallon of London, James Morrison of Antigonish, and John McNally of Calgary, supported the Union government of Robert Borden. The continuing disagreement between French- and English-speaking Catholics was intensified by the passage of conscription in 1917, which forced McNeil, as McGowan points out, to put himself forward as a moderator between the sides. To explain to Canadiens the position of the English-speaking church, McNeil wrote a series of articles in Montreal's *La Presse* in the spring of the following year. And before Ontario Protestants, McNeil defended papal neutrality in the face of the life-and-death struggle between the British and German empires.[79]

In fact the war pressured Canadian Catholics towards ideological and political collaboration with Protestants. English-speaking Catholics backed the war against German imperialism, and they offered the blood of their children as part of the price to be paid to halt blatant imperialism and to take ownership in Canadian society. A combined effort of the Knights of Columbus, YMCA, Salvation Army, and other voluntary associations collected $200,000 for the Knights-run non-denominational recreation centres for soldiers.[80] The common effort to raise funds for the troops smoothed the rough edges of Catholic-

Protestant tensions and deepened the sense that the anglophone Catholics were part of Canada. Many Old World nationalisms of the Irish, Scots, Germans, and Italians disappeared as Catholics became deeply involved in the preservation of English civilization and identified themselves with Canada. English-speaking Catholics supported national registration and conscription and pursued the British vision of democracy, Christianity, and Canadian autonomy within the British Commonwealth.[81]

CONCLUSION

By the turn of the twentieth century French- and English-speaking protagonists, in striving to assert control over Canadian Catholicism, became highly sensitized to the language issue. The battle for linguistic control of the University of Ottawa became a microcosm of the contest. Language issues spread across Canada, first, with the Canadien missionary efforts throughout the Northwest, and then, with the Catholic Church Extension Society in the urban centres. The overseas service and conscription issues, which intensified the gap between the two Catholic solitudes, began to resolve themselves only when the Great War ended, bilingual schools in Ontario were restored, and the Prairie church was accepted as predominantly anglophone. The conflict between the two messianic language groups resolved itself further during the hardships of the 1930s. Acadians were at last given three more ecclesiastical sees, Moncton in 1936, Edmunston in 1944, and Yarmouth in 1953. After 1929 Franco-Ontarians regained firmer control of their schools, churches, and culture. Anglophone Catholics, as the fruit of their wartime sacrifice, gained new-found recognition and confidence in Canada.

The arrival of new language groups to Canada at the turn of the century helped to make Canadians more cosmopolitan. After this time, Ukrainian, German, and Polish bishops joined the French, Irish, and Scottish at the Canadian episcopal table and shared a broader understanding of the universal Church. The Canadian hierarchy was transformed into a multicultural assembly, and Catholics learned that respect for other cultures was basic to Christian life and should be part of the emerging western Canadian church.[82] The Canadian church and the Ontario government in the 1950s and 1960s moved towards the availability of services in both languages, and Manitoba and Saskatchewan in the next decade dismantled restrictive legislation on French language and culture.

9 Learning Respect
in the Canadian West

Linguistic differences, institutional needs, and world wars shaped the formation of Catholic dioceses in eastern and central Canada. But in western Canada, different ethnic communities formed into separate dioceses. Red River colony, or Winnipeg, became the seedbed of three archdioceses, French, English, and Ukrainian speaking. The French-speaking diocese of St Boniface was established in 1820, and twenty-six years later the diocese of Victoria prepared the foundation for the church on the Pacific Coast. Catholics arriving in the Prairie provinces from the Ukraine at the end of the century formed Canada's first diocese for Eastern Christians. The western settlers, now reinforced by central and eastern Europeans, decisively shifted the language of human exchange to English, and English-speaking bishops replaced French-speaking bishops over a period of twenty years. In Victoria, after a series of principally French-speaking prelates, the seventh bishop was English-speaking. After a hundred years of missionary work in the Canadian Northwest, French-speaking Oblate bishops and school principals perceived that their work often reduced native people to stony silence. They realized that the process of evangelization had not been entirely efficacious. Aboriginal Catholics, in fact, had contributed few vocations, churches, schools, or hospitals. By the 1970s the Oblate Fathers willingly relinquished their schools to the native peoples and looked forward to a native church rising up among First Nations.[1]

UKRAINIANS OF THE EASTERN CHURCH

The completion in 1885 of the Canadian Pacific Railroad brought an influx of new Canadians to agricultural lands in the West. Both French and English settlers were already well established in the West by 1890 when the first Ukrainian immigrants disembarked from the trains at Winnipeg. Most Ukrainian Catholics came from Galicia and Carpatho-Ukraine, and Ukrainian Orthodox came from Bukovina and the eastern Ukraine.[2] The Ukrainians sought inexpensive land on which to settle their families and build their own communities. Eighty per cent of the Ukrainians were Catholics of the Eastern (Byzantine) Rite and had been united with Rome since 1596.[3] The Empress Maria Theresa of Austria in 1774 designated them "Greek Catholics," and over the next century the Ukrainian Uniates produced numerous educated clergy who spearheaded the revival of a vibrant Ukrainian national culture.[4] Those who came to Canada had hoped to prosper in their country of adoption and to preserve their religion and traditional lifestyle. This was made difficult in 1894 when the Holy See forbade married Eastern Rite priests to immigrate to North America. "Since an estimated 97 per cent of the Uniate clergy were married at the time, the 1894 decree had the effect of virtually cutting off all clerical immigration to Canada at a time when Ukrainians were arriving in unprecedented numbers."[5] The absence of priests, Stella Hryniuk asserts, meant the lack of spiritual guidance for their communities and the deprivation of the sacraments. The Ukrainians of Canada, in need of transcendent contact with God amidst so much personal disruption, organized devotions, erected crosses, laid out cemeteries, and constructed eastern-style churches.[6] Without the support of Ukrainian clergy, the new Canadians in their communities sang their songs, said their prayers, and spoke aloud the prayerful readings.[7]

Unfamiliar with the Byzantine traditions of the church, Archbishop Adélard Langevin of St Boniface urged Ukrainians to attend Mass in Franco-Manitoban parishes. To the new Canadians the French language was incomprehensible and the Latin liturgy utterly alien. In 1899 Langevin opposed the formation of the Ukrainian parish of St Nicholas in Winnipeg on the grounds that it was unnecessary.[8] A series of four Ukrainian priests visited their Canadian communities between 1897 and 1900 but, because of the hostility encountered from the Latins, soon left.[9] Three Polish priests tried to fill the breach by transforming the Ukrainians to Latin rite parishioners but succeeded only in renewing Ukrainian determination to remain Byzantine. The Austro-Hungarian ambassador in Rome pleaded with the Holy See to appoint Eastern priests who could be accepted in North America to care for the spiritual needs of the Ukrainians.[10] When the archdiocese of St Boniface tried by legal means to take over the Ukrainian Catholic parish property as was the custom in the Latin church, the Ukrainians wrote to Rome seeking deliverance from such imperialism.[11]

Pressured by open revolt, Langevin reversed his field and, with other Canadian bishops, made overtures to the Ukrainian eparchy of Lviv to send celibate clergy to Canada.[12] Three Ukrainian Basilians and four Sister Servants of Mary Immaculate responded to the call and arrived the Prairie in 1902.[13] Belgian Redemptorists and French Oblates, knowing the deprivation that the Ukrainian communities were going through, began preparing young seminarians to serve in the Eastern church.

A combined effort of the metropolitan of Lviv, Andrii Sheptytsky, Canadian apostolic delegate Donato Sbarretti, the Canadian bishops, and Catholic Church Extension Society convinced the Holy See to appoint an Eastern Ukrainian eparch for western Canada. Sheptytsky chose a theologian and prefect of the Lviv Seminary, Nykyta Budka. When Bishop Budka (1912–28) arrived in western Canada in 1912, he had responsibility for 128,000 Ukrainians spread across Canada from Cape Breton to Vancouver Island and twenty-one priests, eight of whom inculturated from the Latin rite into the Eastern church.[14]

To ease the enormously difficult task that Budka was undertaking, Langevin and the Canadian bishops, now solidly behind the Ukrainian eparch, contributed a church for Basilian monks, schools for the Sister Servants of the Immaculate Conception, an interest-free loan of $26,000, and $10,000 in annual expenses. The bishops supported Ukrainian seminarians at St Boniface and St Albert colleges, and mission stations at Sifton and Yorkton, Saskatchewan, and Brandon, Manitoba. They also underwrote the cost of publishing the *Canadian Ruthenian/Canadian Ukrainian* from 1911 to 1927.[15]

Despite the belated generosity of the Latin church, some Ukrainians complained they were being Latinized. They worried about losing ownership of their churches to the Latin Catholics and complained of the abusive treatment their clergy received at the hands of Latin priests.[16] Nevertheless, Bishop Budka continued to implant the Ukrainian eparchy in Canada. Incorporating its parishes under provincial regulations and its diocese according to federal law, he attained legal status for the Ukrainian church. Some parishioners, fearing loss of property control, resisted this episcopal organization, and in 1918 split off to form the Ukrainian Greek Orthodox Church of Canada. The new church decided to approve of married clergy, who would be selected by their congregations.[17]

Budka sent Catholic seminarians to be educated in Montreal, Toronto, and St Boniface, and after 1913 the Byzantine Redemptorists established themselves at Yorkton and Ituna in Saskatchewan and Komarno in Manitoba.[18] In his newspaper the *Canadian Ruthenian*, Budka preached faithfulness to the Holy See, retention of the purity of the Byzantine Rite, and maintenance of the family custom of daily prayer and regular attendance at church. He exhorted his flock to participate in Canadian society and learn English in addition to the Ukrainian language. He encouraged them to educate themselves to enhance the future of their family and community.[19]

Those who refused to hand over their parishes to the new eparchy became the focus of the opposition to Budka. They, along with the secular intelligentsia who wanted to retain the purity of the Ukrainian culture and have a voice in the education of their youth, founded the first Orthodox churches. The Russian Orthodox Church of the United States and the Presbyterian Church in Canada waited in the wings before the First World War to attract dissident Ukrainian Catholics. At the beginning of the war Budka erred by urging Ukrainians to be loyal to the Austrian Empire, which soon took up arms against the Western allies. Once Britain declared war on Austria, a humiliated Budka was forced to retract his advice. English Canadians were not in a forgiving mood at the time and did not forget what they viewed as Budka's disloyalty. Some younger Ukrainians, humiliated by the breach of loyalty, reacted sharply by changing their names, speaking English, or joining Protestant churches.[20] Jay Dolan points out that in the United States Ukrainians had experienced a similar rejection by the Irish-run church and over 200,000 left to form an American Orthodox Church. Other historians, he points out, conjecture that "as high as 65 percent of the faithful of the Orthodox Church of America are former Uniates who are ethnically Ukrainian-Ruthenians."[21]

Budka had to grapple not only with long distances between parishes and a lack of suitable clergy but also with severe financial constraint. The new Ukrainian Canadians were used to state-supported religion rather than the Canadian system of voluntary church support and, as they struggled to build lives for themselves, were not in a position to contribute substantially to the church. The Canadian Latin church and the Catholic Extension Society provided much of the funding for Budka's eparchy. The archdiocese of St Boniface contributed $180,000, the dioceses of Kingston and Saint John and the archdiocese of Toronto together $140,000, and the Catholic Extension Society $262,302.[22]

Bishop Budka, worn out by hard work and constant travel, wearied by those who opposed his episcopacy, and distressed by the collapse of the newspaper *Kanadyiskyi ukrainets*, went to Rome in 1927 and shortly after resigned his see. He returned to Lviv and was appointed vicar general of that diocese. After the dust of the Second World War had settled in the western Ukraine, the Soviet conquerors sentenced Bishop Budka, along with other Eastern Catholic clergy, to forced labour in Kazakhstan, where he died in 1949.[23]

Hryniuk surmises that Budka's Canadian ministry was a mixture of failure and success. His emphasis on discipline and order alienated the liberal intelligentsia, which she calls "the latently dissatisfied." Perhaps a more outgoing or compromising personality might have been more successful on this difficult mission. On the positive side, Budka recruited forty-seven priests to maintain the Byzantine liturgy in 229 parishes and mission stations. He secured the Catholic Eastern culture in schools and seminaries. In the final assessment, Hryniuk believes that Budka's achievements in Canada were "very considerable."[24] An assessment of Budka's leadership by Mark McGowan states that Budka lacked the confidence of his clergy and the organizational skills to firmly establish an eparchy, and thus, at the end of the war, Ukrainian solidarity crumbled with the rise of Ukrainian nationalism and the emergence of the Ukrainian Orthodox Church.[25] Little thanks to the Latin bishops, Ukrainian Catholics survived in Canada, Roberto Perin contends, because of their steadfast faith.[26] After 1930 the Ukrainian Catholic church saved itself by "developing an indigenous clergy and a solid record of episcopal leadership."[27] Ukrainian Catholics became a third force between the two messianic cultures of Canada and pushed these ethnic groups towards the acceptance of cultural pluralism.[28]

GERMANS, POLISH, AND HUNGARIANS OF THE LATIN CHURCH

In 1867 French and English speakers dominated in Canada, but after Confederation the Germans became the third largest ethnic group in the country."[29] Most of the German-speaking in migrants arrived in Canada from outside the German Empire, from German-speaking settlements in Russia, Poland, Romania, Czechoslovakia, and the United States. The first German speakers to come to Canada were mercenary soldiers who served during the first half of the eighteenth century with the French garrisons at Louisbourg and New France and then, during the second half of the century, with the British regiments in the American War of Independence. German-speaking workers built the fortifications at Halifax in 1750, settled permanently three years later at Lunenburg, and within ten years grew into a community of ten thousand. After the revolutionary war German soldiers settled in small communities north of Lakes Ontario and Erie. Pennsylvania Germans, such as the Amish, Dunkers, Quakers, and Mennonites, settled in Upper Canada at the time. Other Germans constructed Yonge Street from Toronto to Georgian Bay. German Canadians, after French- and English-speaking Canadians, had the skills, numbers, and financial resources to become established members of the dominion.[30]

Before the end of the nineteenth century, a great flood of German speakers sailed to the United States. Forty thousand migrants came in religious groups – Catholics, Lutherans, Baptists, and Mennonites – to Berlin (Kitchener) and to Waterloo County in Ontario. The Germans brought with them their industry, loyalty, rapid development, and religious toleration.[31]

In the early twentieth century Germans chose western Canada in greater numbers. Thousands of German Catholics left the Catholic colony of Josephstal near Odessa on the Black Sea to arrive in Saskatchewan in 1886. This flow of German Catholics was to continue until the outbreak of the First World War. Black Sea Catholics soon became the largest Catholic group in the province. Eight families and a few singles settled at Balgonie, east of Regina. Catholics arrived each spring, increasing their community to over thirty families by 1892. They eschewed the Canadian system of homesteads in favour of "a Dorf in the Russian style," a new Josephstal. They bought enough land for a village site east of Balgonie, calling it St Joseph's Colony, and built a church and their homes around it.[32]

Ten Bavarian families and seven single men from Rastadt and München arrived in 1890 at Balgonie to locate some miles south of the Josephstal group and founded St Peter's Parish. Another forty-three families and some singles from the Dnieper region reached Saskatchewan, and many chose to buy land for a village site, build a church and their homes, and live in community. They founded the rural hamlet of Rastadt and Katharinental. Other arrivals at this time gave birth to similar hamlets geared for agricultural and family life. In 1903 a large church was erected in honour of St Peter to centre their community. Protestants from the Black Sea also chose to settle in this area.[33]

Many Catholics came from Russia and Germany, but the mass of German settlers on the Canadian prairies came from the United States, spoke German and English, and hoped by living in the rural environment to retain their Catholic religion and German culture.[34] They were granted large blocks of land and purchased additional tracts. They laid out St Peter's Colony in central Saskatchewan, St Joseph's Colony in western Saskatchewan, and, Sedley, Grayson, and Claybank in the south. St Peter's Colony encompassed eighteen hundred square miles around Muenster and Humboldt, including the villages of Peterson, Cudworth, St Benedict, Lake Lenore, Watson, and Leroy. The centre of the colony was St Peter's Benedictine abbey whose monks were German Americans from Cluny, Illinois, and St John's Minnesota, who volunterred for service in 1903 at St Peter's.[35] Its abbot was appointed the ecclesial ordinary of the parishes in the area. The number of settlers at

St Peter's Colony increased from six thousand in 1906 to nine thousand in 1920, and to twelve thousand in the 1980s. Many inhabitants of the colony moved elsewhere during the century for personal and business reasons.[36]

Germans who came from the United States were bilingual, worked well with the French-speaking Canadien clergy, and celebrated festivals with sermons in English, German, and French. The German newspaper, *St Peter's Bote,* was initially published in German with an English edition, *St Peter's Messenger.* Still published today, it is widely circulated in western Canada as The *Prairie Messenger.* Catholicism was the most important ingredient of the colony's identity, as the large and well-decorated churches affirm. Social clubs were popular, and cultural gatherings were annual celebrations throughout the West.[37]

Private schools were erected to impart to the students the Catholic religion and bilingual education in German and English. The community magnates were confronted with the necessity of erecting schools – public, separate, or private? The public schools were initially rejected as taking too much time to become operational given the number of regulations involved, especially in regard to teachers. Bilingual teachers were available in the community, but government teaching requirements tended to eliminate them. The separate school option was generally not possible because it too easily became a political football with accompanying delays. Private schools thus became the preferred option. The apex for the construction of private schools was between 1906 and 1909. Parents desired that students learn English well; hence the language of instruction was to be English. Regular instruction in German and Catholicism were part of the curriculum. Teachers who knew both languages were hired at less cost than those with certificates. The private schools were a practical expedient and not planned to be permanent. In numbers public schools eventually dominated.[38]

Polish migrants towards the end of the nineteenth century were pushed off their ancestral lands in Prussia by Bismarck's *Kulturkampf,* which strove to clear the lands and replace them with German farmers. The industrially developing province of Galicia suffered from overpopulation and underdevelopment and the peasants were forced to immigrate. Over three million Poles migrated between 1870 and 1914 to the United States, Germany, Russia, and other European countries. Of this total 200,000 migrated to Canada and the Americas.[39]

During the first wave of Polish immigration before the First World War, 110,000 Poles, most of them Catholic from Galicia, went to Barry's Bay and Wilno in eastern Ontario, to Berlin (Kitchener) in southwestern Ontario, and to western Canada to homestead and establish their own farms.[40] Recruited by agents, they embarked at Danzig

(Gdansk) or Hamburg and disembarked at Halifax or Quebec City for the long train ride to the Canadian prairies. Although the minimum needed to establish a family farm was fifteen hundred dollars, many arrived penniless or with less than five hundred dollars. Like the Ukrainians, the Poles were poor and did the hard work of clearing the land, building cabins, ploughing fields, and maintaining rustic roadways. To be successful at all, they had to learn about agricultural conditions on the Prairies. Many had to hire themselves out as apprentices to generate capital and to learn dry farming techniques on the Canadian prairies. Loneliness for single immigrants could be overwhelming. Women and children often managed the farms while the men were away on work gangs. But gardens, cows, and chickens kept food on the table in lean times and their quality of life gradually improved.[41]

Polish neighbourhoods with churches, boardinghouses, stores, and restaurants emerged in the cities of Montreal, Toronto, Hamilton, and Winnipeg. The camaraderie through the time of hardship eased the pain of living in a foreign language and alien culture. The north end of Winnipeg became the home of seasonal labourers engaged in railway work, bush camps, and the harvest. The women worked as domestics in Euro-Canadian homes. Canadien, Irish, and German clergy directed parish life, and although the liturgy was in the familiar Latin, the Polish workers and their families had a difficult time communicating in other Canadian languages. Spoken German, which reminded them of the *Kulturkampf*, was distasteful to Canadian Polish worshippers. At Holy Ghost parish in Winnipeg, the Polish protested against the German-speaking Oblates. In a more positive vein, the Holy Ghost Fraternal Society of Winnipeg was founded in 1902 to offer Polish members sickness, unemployment, and life insurance benefits.[42]

Polish clergy arrived to serve the Polish-speaking Catholics and, as was their custom, "expected to receive a steady income and to exercise a dominant influence in parish affairs." Religious festivals, feast days, and social events gave the transported Canadians a sense of their Polish identity and an experience of communal cohesiveness. The Polish National Church offered an alternative to dissatisfied Poles who left the Catholic communion.[43] Twenty-five percent of migrants unhappy with the hostile environment in Canada returned to Poland.[44]

Bilingual schools were opened in 1897 in Manitoba and Saskatchewan. During the First World War, however, the Manitoba government imposed English only as the language of instruction, and Polish language instruction was put off until after regular school hours had ended. Polish, Ukrainian, and French speakers in defence of bilingual schools united to justify the practice against Protestant and Orange pro-English imperialists. When the Ukrainians received their own bishop in 1912, Polish

Canadians were hoping that they might receive Polish bishop. This did not come to pass. Two Polish newspapers were founded in Winnipeg, the *Catholic Weekly* and *Czas* (*Time*). The Polish newspapers provided needed intelligence to the new Canadians on how to homestead, become naturalized, find work, and send remittances home.[45]

When the heavy guns in Europe were silenced and business returned to normal, Canadian agriculturalists and industrialists looked for inexpensive European labour to continue the expansion of the economy. In the decade following the war, 52,000 Poles migrated to Canada to join the 145,503 who had made a home in the Canadian provinces. Semi-skilled workers with higher levels of education were now seeking industrial jobs, and the demographic focus of Poles shifted from the agricultural prairies to the eastern manufacturing towns of Toronto, Hamilton, and Montreal. For the first time the Polish government showed interest in the plight of the new Canadians and supported their cultural organizations and newspapers.[46]

By 1929 the Canadian church had established 33 Polish parishes and 157 missions across the country, and the Association of Poles in Canada was formed to coordinate Polish Catholic groups. The Great Depression caused discomfort for many and tragedy for some. Many Polish farmers were able to survive by diversifying their crops and living frugally. In the cities, workers who were laid off and those who were not naturalized could not get relief and were threatened with deportation.[47] "The Polish experience in Canada," Avery and Fedorowicz write, "more closely resembles that of the Ukrainians and Hungarians. These groups met with considerable suspicion and hostility and they looked inward, developing a strong sense of group solidarity and a determination to preserve their ethnic identity. Nonetheless, Poles have assimilated more quickly than their Ukrainian neighbours ..."[48]

Hungarians, according to Carmela Patrias, came to Canada in two waves, the first between 1885 and 1918, and the second between 1918 and 1945. Among Hungarian immigrants Catholics played a major role. The rapidly expanding population in Hungary put great pressure on agrarian workers to subdivide their small holdings into ever smaller parcels of land that could no longer support new families. At the time, the industrial sector in Hungary was not growing fast enough to absorb the surplus of rural workers. By contrast, the Canadian agricultural frontier was opening up in the western prairies and welcoming farm workers.[49]

The first Hungarians trekked from Pennsylvania to Hun's Valley near Minnedosa, Manitoba, in 1885 and to Kaposvar in the North-West Territories (southeastern Saskatchewan) in 1886. Count Paul Esterhazy, an immigration agent in the employ of the Canadian government, recruited Hungarian workers from the Pennsylvania coal fields with the idyllic promise of farm work and a homestead in Canada. Additional immigrants arrived from Hungary and the United States in 1888. The coming of the railway in 1903 saved this settlement, now called Esterhazy in honour of its founder,[50] from isolation and hardship.

Catholics chose to settle at Esterhazy and nearby Stockholm, whereas Protestants chose to go further south at Bekevar. Father Francis Woodcutter, the pastor of Esterhazy, promoted Hungarian Catholic settlement at the Swedish colony of Stockholm to insure Catholic influence in the area. Many second-generation Esterhazians received homesteads in Stockholm. So successful was the settlement that, as Martin Kovacs remarks, "throughout the interwar years, and even later, the Stockholm-Kaposvar district was to be one of the foremost centres of Catholic Hungarian influence not only in Saskatchewan but in the whole of Canada."[51]

Count Esterhazy was highly respected as a leader of the Hungarian community and admired for his command of the English language. Ability to speak English was a high priority among Hungarians and their schools. Their great concern was to found schools and have the Hungarian language and culture stressed but the language of instruction was always English. The schools struggled not only to promote fluency in English and Hungarian but also reconcile traditional Hungarian culture with the Canadian demand for assimilation.[52]

Church, family, and community promoted continuity of the Hungarian culture. Agricultural technology, urbanization, schools, and national organizations cultivated adjustment to Canadian society. The proportion of Hungarian Catholics to Protestants who settled was four to one. According to the 1931 census, Catholics represented 72.5 percent of the population, Calvinists 10.2 percent, and Lutherans 5.3 percent, while the remaining percentages were made up of numbers of the United Church, Ukrainian Catholics, and Jews. Despite the large number of Hungarian parishioners, missions and parishes were slow to develop. Hungarians priests were difficult to find and few communities were affluent enough to support clergy. Canadian clergy doubted the necessity of ethnic parishes and reasoned that Hungarians should attend established Catholic parishes. French-speaking clergy who served Hungarians achieved only a limited command of Hungarian and seldom had the energy to foster Hungarian ethnocultural institutions. Catholic communities, Kovacs points out, were behind Protestant communities in promoting Hungarian cultural activities.[53]

A celebrated controversy arose between the Hungarian community and Adélarde Langevin, the archbishop of St Boniface. A popular but

Numbers of Immigrants Compared

	1921	1971
German	294,635	1,317,200
Ukrainian	106,721	580,660
Polish	53,403	316,430
Hungarian	13,181	82,681

unsanctioned Hungarian priest, Menyhért Érdújhelyi, advocated Hungarian-English private schools and received the support of *Canadai Magyar Farmer*. The archdiocese proposed that the public school was a more suitable vehicle for bilingual education because the government provided most of the funding. Érdújhelyi continued to advocate what he understood to be the "German school" model used by the Benedictines at Muenster. The archbishop demanded Catholic solidarity on public issues in order to deal more effectively with the Canadian government. He felt at the very minimum that Catholics should not support Liberals because of their role in the disastrous Manitoba Catholic Schools issue. The controversy was resolved when the archbishop gained control of the *Canadai Magyar Farmer* and changed its attitude. The Hungarian community received Hungarian priests, however, but not Hungarian teachers.[54] The Great War brought prosperity for the Hungarian settlements but also suspicion and disenfranchisement.[55]

Hungarian settlements were created in the mining regions of Crowsnest Pass, North Sydney, Nova Scotia, and Michael, British Columbia. Workers' communities emerged at Niagara Falls, Windsor, Galt, Welland, Brantford, and Hamilton. Winnipeg became the foremost Canadian centre of Hungarian culture and published *Kanadai Magyar Újság*. In contemporary Canada, the largest centres of Hungarian life remain in the large ethnic parishes at Toronto and Montreal.[56]

ENGLISH-SPEAKING BISHOPS
FOR THE WESTERN CANADIAN CHURCH

During the same period in which Bishop Budka struggled to establish the first Ukrainian diocese, the French- and English-speaking bishops were skirmishing with each other in a prolonged battle to see which side would control the prairie dioceses. Since 1820 French-speaking bishops had guided the development of the western Canadian church. After 1870, however, English-speaking migrants from Ontario and the Maritimes and immigrants from central Europe who would become English-speaking settled in western Canada. By 1906, in step with these

First and last Canadien archbishop of Edmonton, Émile Legal (1902–20), 1910. (AD)

demographic changes, English-speaking Catholics at Winnipeg began to agitate for a bishop, and the apostolic delegate in Ottawa, Monsignor Donato Sbarretti, was sympathetic to their requests. Two years later, two English-speaking parishes were opened in Winnipeg.[57]

A second skirmish concerned the new diocese of Regina. Archbishop Langevin of St Boniface was determined to have a French-speaking prelate appointed and was not beyond seeking support from civil officials. He argued that the French were still the dominant ethnic group. Yet in reaction to his lobbying, the German and Irish communities advanced their own candidates for the office. In 1911 Rome chose O.-E. Mathieu, rector of Laval University, as the first bishop of Regina (1911–29). The *Catholic Register* groaned, as might be expected, that the choice of Mathieu was a terrible setback for anglophones. The next year the ecclesial province of Edmonton was established along with its suffragan diocese, Calgary.[58] Once again a French-speaking prelate, Bishop Émile Legal of St Albert, was selected as the new metropolitan, a religious of "remarkable intellectual and creative talents."[59]

Feeling confident that these procedures were working in their favour, the French-speaking prelates were caught off guard in 1913 by the selection of John T. McNally as the first bishop of Calgary. The appointment, made by Rome without Canadien consultation, added insult to injury. McNally took office and, not one to waste words or be denied, "put the French clergy (80 percent of the clergy) in their place,"[60] immediately removing four French-speaking religious congregations from the diocese. He then demanded that the Oblates hand over St Mary's parish for his new cathedral. A short while later further conflict erupted with the Oblates over a school issue, and McNally ordered them to vacate a second parish in five days.[61]

Archbishop Langevin died in June 1915. With undiplomatic haste Rome within six months announced the creation of the English-speaking archdiocese of Winnipeg facing the Cathedral of St Boniface directly across the Red River. The Canadien bishops continued to argue that the West was multilingual and that French was still the language of choice among settlers. The English-speaking bishops countered that French usage was decreasing and English was the dominant language. The new see of Winnipeg was delineated west of the north-south line of the Red River and Lake Winnipeg, extending to the Saskatchewan border. The French-speaking archdiocese was then confined to the area east of the Red River. The cardinal archbishop of Quebec City, L.-N. Bégin, and the Oblate provincial, Ovide Charlebois, protested that this division was a death sentence for the French Canadians in the West. Arthur Beliveau, Langevin's heir apparent, accepted the episcopal appointment only to change the disagreeable division. Under such pressure, the line between the two archdioceses was redrawn, and the archdiocese of Winnipeg remained west of the Red River but now shifted north of the Assiniboine River. St Boniface extended east to Dryden and then south of the Assiniboine River.[62]

The appointment of Arthur A. Sinnott, secretary to the apostolic delegate, as the archbishop of Winnipeg ignited a further round of strong feelings among the Canadiens. The Canadien bishops protested that the apostolic delegate was promoting the English cause and was an instrument of anglicization. The French Canadian bishops asked Rome to correct this imbalance. They further demanded the division of the diocese of London so that the French majority could have their own diocese at Windsor.[63]

Trying to bridge troubled waters, Pope Benedict xv published *Commissio Divinitus* in which he asked the Canadian bishops to work for an equitable solution to its various problems. The Holy See invited the bishops to send ecclesial difficulties to Rome for resolution, urged the

Catholic press to seek moderation in their reporting, and exhorted the clergy to become bilingual. Benedict pointed out that papal documents taught that both the French and English had the right to suitable instruction in their own language.[64]

When Archbishop Legal of Edmonton died in 1920, Sinnott was already in Rome requesting an English-speaking successor. J.T. McNally of Calgary was also there pleading the same case with Cardinal Sbarretti, the new Roman prefect of the Sacred Congregation. Sinnott and McNally argued that Canadien bishops were preventing the faith from being spread among English-speakers in the Canadian West. French Canadian prelates reacted by arguing to Rome that the French had evangelized the West and deserved the rewards. The following year, H.J. O'Leary was appointed archbishop of Edmonton. His appointment marked the beginning of the end of Canadien influence over episcopal nominations to western dioceses.[65]

Archbishop Mathieu of Regina died in 1929. O'Leary and Bishop J.T. Kidd of Calgary went to Rome to petition for an English-speaking colleague to replace him. On parallel but competing mission, Bishops F.-X. Ross of Gaspé and F.-X. Cloutier of Trois-Rivières travelled to the Holy See to make a case for their own candidates. But it was the apostolic delegate in Ottawa, Archbishop Andrea Cassulo, who chose in 1930 James C. McGuigan of the Edmonton diocese as the successor to Mathieu. As a consolation prize for the Canadiens, the diocese of Gravelbourg was erected south of Regina to provide for the French-speaking communities.[66]

During the depression the government of R.B. Bennett was anxious to seek out the political and social forces that would help him unite the Canadian provinces. To that end Bennett established such national institutions as the Bank of Canada (1934), Canadian Broadcasting Company (1936), and Trans-Canada Airways (1937). He was also determined to have an English-speaking cardinal who could bind Canadian Catholics together in a time of stress. Through intermediaries in Rome, Bennett advised the Holy See that Bishop McNally or Archbishop Sinnott would be excellent choices. Bennett knew McNally was close to Pope Pius XI. In 1933 the Holy See surprised Bennett and the Canadian government by naming the fifty-year-old archbishop of Quebec, J.-M. Villeneuve, as the new Canadian cardinal. Undeterred, Bennett tried to have McNally transferred to the archdiocese of Toronto after the death of Neil McNeil in 1934. Rome again ignored Bennett's overture by appointing Archbishop McGuigan of Regina to Toronto in 1935.[67]

From 1910 to 1930 English-speaking bishops replaced their French-speaking counterparts at the helm of western Catholicism. The loss of episcopal appointments in western Canada weakened French control of the Canadian church and gave the English clergy the important advantage of numbers.[68]

THE DIOCESE OF VICTORIA
IN A FINANCIAL BIND

Another diocese that had originally been under French control but was transferred after the turn of the century to English control was Victoria, British Columbia. Alexander MacDonald, a native of Cape Breton Island, was consecrated in 1909 the bishop of Victoria. He had a formidable reputation as a professor at St Francis Xavier College, vicar general of the diocese of Antigonish, and the author of numerous books and articles. But as Vincent McNally asserts, MacDonald arrived on the scene when the population of Anglicans, Presbyterians, and Methodists was on the rise and the number of the Catholics was falling. In fact, Catholics on Vancouver Island were a minority.[69]

The visionary MacDonald arrived at his diocese during prosperous times. When he began buying property in 1911 and 1912, real estate prices were already at record levels. For a Catholic school and other church projects, MacDonald purchased three properties costing a total of $80,000. By January 1913 the diocesan debt, non-existent on his arrival, had risen to $100,000, on which he paid interest of 6 percent. Most of the diocese was mortgaged for these enterprises. Feeling the financial pinch, MacDonald borrowed an additional $20,000 in December at 6.5 percent from his former Antigonish friend, Neil McNeil, now archbishop of Toronto.[70] But McNeil's help was not enough, and the financial trap was set for the unwary bishop.

Land prices plummeted in 1912 and continued downward for nine years, falling to 11 percent of their former value. The city of Victoria had adopted Henry George's "single tax system," which put the burden of public expenditures on property taxes. Thus, even though the dollar value of real estate decreased precipitously, property taxes decreased only slightly. All property owners, including Bishop Mac-Donald, were caught in the bind.[71]

MacDonald joined forces with the Anglican church and several other denominations in seeking a tax exemption on the property of church buildings – the buildings themselves were tax exempt. In 1911 they petitioned to the Royal Provincial Tax Commission. MacDonald argued that parishioners suffered from a "double tax," one on their own property and a second on their donations to the church. This was not fair to the churches because they promoted "morals and religion" and thus were beneficial to the province. For the same reason religious and private schools should be tax exempt. In a personal note MacDonald pointed out that St Andrew's Cathedral paid $2,800 in taxes from a total annual income of $6,000. Every church that testified before the Royal Tax Commission asked that church sites be tax exempt, and Catholics also asked that schools should be included in the exemption.[72]

In 1912 the British Columbia legislature amended the tax law to exempt not only church buildings but also church sites. But the next year the government removed the word "site" from the act, ending the exemption. The provincial supreme court reversed this, however, by ruling that in regard to the tax exemption, the legislation meant that "the church building" included the church site.[73]

Because public indebtedness was growing, the city of Victoria was reluctant to allow land speculators or large landowners to go untaxed. In a 1914 referendum, the citizens voted overwhelmingly against a tax exemption for churches. Undaunted, MacDonald led a delegation two years later to the municipal committee of the legislature. He argued that a tax exemption was the "economic right" of churches, and that without it the Catholic church would have to sell its properties. His own diocese owned 46 percent of assessed church properties in the city, and without some relief they would have to be sold.[74]

MacDonald then formed a committee of eight to oversee diocesan finances. The fact was that MacDonald needed $25,000 to get through the year 1917. The committee, out of sympathy for the bishop, extended him personal loans amounting to $6,000. They advised the bishop to sell some of the diocesan properties before their value declined even further, but he ignored their recommendations. The committee eventually concluded that MacDonald had vision but little business sense.[75]

During the lengthy dispute, city hall was anxious to collect taxes that were coming due. Early in 1919 it warned Bishop MacDonald that he must either pay $16,000 in back taxes or face the public sale of St Andrew's Cathedral. The date of sale was set for 26 May. For the city this was a test case against the churches. The case went to the British Columbia supreme court, which ruled that the diocese was liable for the taxes. The diocese then appealed. During the litigation, the city ordered that the cathedral be sold to pay the taxes. However, the appeals court ruled in 1920 that the city assessment of church property was "illegal and void." MacDonald then struck back by demanding compensation for taxes paid. The Privy Council the following year affirmed the decision of the appeals court but stated that the Catholic diocese was not entitled to compensation.[76]

Bishop MacDonald had two years to savour his victory before he was summoned to Rome in 1923 to explain the huge diocesan debt.

Although he had advised the Holy See of his predicament, Rome refused help. The Code of Canon Law of 1917 had spelled out the financial responsibilities of bishops. Further financial regulations were imposed in 1922 by the Holy See. "The Vatican," according to American historian Jay Dolan, "had become the nerve center of the church, and the Pope, wrapped in the cloak of infallibility, was restored to a position of power reminiscent of medieval times."[77] Overwhelmed and overreacting to these regulations, MacDonald protested to the apostolic delegate in Ottawa: "My imagination refuses to picture Our Lord and Savior Jesus Christ doling out dispensations and faculties as is done today in Rome." Vincent McNally comments that for MacDonald to be writing this, "given his own vulnerability ... seemed almost career suicide."[78]

In Rome, Bishop MacDonald was threatened with the charge of heresy. Cardinal Caetano de Lai offered to accept MacDonald's resignation as bishop of Victoria. MacDonald asked Pope Pius XI to allow him to return to Victoria to prove his innocence. In a second interview however, de Lai, told him clearly: "You must either resign or go before the Holy Office." MacDonald resigned and the heresy charges were dropped. Nor was he allowed to return to Victoria, teach at St Augustine's Seminary in Toronto, or receive a pension of any sort.[79]

Father Thomas O'Donnell of Toronto was ordained the new bishop of Victoria. He had to face an unhappy city hall, an unpaid defence attorney, and a parish treasurer who sought ten missing bank accounts from the former bishop. Financial help from the Protestant churches that had benefited from the legal victory was not forthcoming – with the exception of the Anglican church. Archbishop McNeil asked for repayment of the $20,000 loan, plus $4,700 interest, but Bishop O'Donnell disposed of the request by replying that in Victoria there was no record of it.[80]

Was MacDonald a victim as he claimed, or was he the cause of his own tragedy? He continued to think of himself as the bishop of Victoria because he believed the pope had no "absolute power in the church" to remove him. Vincent McNally contends that MacDonald was removed because he was a land speculator and an incompetent administrator. Regardless, he was well liked in Victoria. The *Colonist* noted at his departure that he was a "general favourite in the community" and made friends among all denominations. His sincerity and his "fighting gifts endeared him to others."[81] The diocese of Victoria survived the financial crisis to finish out the century as an English-speaking jurisdiction. It might be concluded that the first Maritime bishop of the diocese of Victoria led it onto the rocky shoals of debt from which, only with great difficulty, it extricated itself at a later date.

REDEFINING THE WESTERN CHURCH

While the Bishops MacDonald and O'Donnell were struggling to keep the diocese of Victoria afloat, the Oblates aspired to a mission enterprise that stretched to the far reaches of the Canadian Northwest. Between 1845 and 1945 the Oblates had built an extensive network of missions and schools, orphanages and hospitals. Their preaching made a lasting impression on the native community. The participation of native people in Christian tradition today provides strong evidence that many appropriated Christianity on their own terms and according to their own needs. The First Nations accepted Christian spirituality but resisted the cultural change involved.[82]

The Oblates, according to Raymond Huel, were purveyors of traditional Catholicism and not innovators inculturating Christ into native tradition. Having little empathy with the cultural diversity of the First Nations, the Oblates presumed that the native culture was inferior to that of western civilization. They followed the European canons of Christianity and strove to have them observed. The Oblates inculturated to the extent that they lived in the native settlements and encountered native customs and traditions first hand. They learned native languages and composed native dictionaries and grammars. Their research and publications supported the survival of those languages and cultures.[83]

Contemporary scholars with a profound grasp of native culture and spiritual traditions assert that the government, church, and Canadians sought to assimilate the First Nations, especially through education in the schools. In contrast, the Oblates through their preaching sought the religious inspiration and transformation of the native people but were discouraged by the result. They believed their preaching was too irregular and infrequent to accomplish full native conversion to Christianity. Assimilation, in the Oblate view, was not even a possibility.

The Oblates looked to residential schools to change young native children into Christians who would in turn evangelize the adults in their community. However, the residential schools, which were envisioned as homey extensions of the rectory and the convent, became over time institutionalized and professionalized. The expanded schools, side-tracked from their original goals, no longer operated for the benefit of native youngsters but were forced to satisfy government requirements. The goals thus compromised, the weakened schools gave native people a veneer of Christianity and white civilization. The effort of the schools to educate the young people contributed to the decline of native culture, but the Oblates by themselves, touching less than sixteen percent of the youth, were too few in number to destroy

Catholic mission at Providence, Northwest Territories, 1929. (NA PA 100530)

native culture. The residential schools failed because they gave only enough religion to introduce the native people to Christianity but without the experience of full membership, and only enough educa- tion to assimilate the native people but without full membership in Canadian life.[84]

The Catholic church in North America remained a foreign institu- tion to the native people. It was a replica of the western European church, which had little room for indigenous traditions and aspira- tions. The most embarrassing fact has been the absence of an indige- nous Catholic clergy. The early bishops such as Provencher and Taché, as well as the Oblate Fathers, worried about their non-involvement. Some of the problems blocking the recruitment of a native clergy were celibacy, the great variety of native languages, the unpopularity of the few native clergy among the people, the community's expectation that native clergy would share church goods with the people, and the ab- sence of Roman-style lay leadership in the native community.

It also must be pointed out that the enthusiastic ultramontane spiri- tuality of the Christian missionaries reduced the native people to passive participants in their own communities. During the classical missionary era, conformity to Roman spiritual norms was stressed de- spite the insensitivity of that stance to other cultures.[85]

The period after the Second World War was characterized by sweep- ing changes among the missionaries, native people, and Canadian government. A new flexible spirituality of service directed the activities of the missionaries. At the same time the native people demanded different curricula and better results from native schools as church influence waned and government influence increased. Beginning in 1951, the government was determined to integrate native students into Euro-Canadian provincial schools. The Oblates defended the residential schools as providing a warmer environment and saw the government's policy as an abandonment of native students. By the 1970s the time for change had come, and it was then that the Oblates urged native people to take "control over their own affairs," especially in regard to schools. The native people pressed for an autonomous school system. In light of this demand, the Oblates handed over the Blue Quills residential school to the First Nations in 1970. With this act, the era of the native residential school came to an end.[86] The last residential school closed in the early 1990s.

The following year, the Oblates proposed to the Canadian Conference of Catholic Bishops the establishment of an indigenous native church to develop its own charism according to native customs and social structures. It would be a developing church similar to those of the developing peoples. Resembling the "Third Church" of Africa, Latin America, and Asia, the native church would facilitate the rebirth of Catholicism among First Nations.[87] Euro-Canadian church people must learn the theological benefits of cultural pluralism. A unitary theology has proved itself insensitive and inadequate to the evangelization of other cultures. Learning to allow for theological pluralism, the Oblates were more easily able to understand the Native religious traditions.[88]

The modern missionary does not bring Christ to unbelievers but invites neophytes to uncover Christ in their inner lives and their culture. Religious inculturation "occurs as the Word interacts with the recipient culture to produce a unique response." This unique and indigenous response to the gospel establishes the basis for a local church. The Oblates and the church today are walking with native people and learning native spirituality.[89] The work of inculturation has begun at the Kisemanito Centre in Alberta for the training of native clergy. The eight Oblate bishops in northern Canada are committed to communities directed by native leaders. The bishops hope that these native-led communities will be able to alleviate poverty, seek out the marginalized, minister to native people in the cities, and overcome the traumatic experiences of the residential schools. The school memories of regular discipline and strange food, silence and humiliation, physical and sexual abuse[90] must be resolved by the sharing of the healing circle. Non-native and native Canadians belong to the same family and must express regrets about the past. In future the First Nations are free to accept Christianity on their own terms, and in association with other Christians, create their own indigenous church.[91]

CONCLUSION

During the time when French- and English-speaking Catholics were locked in battle over control of the Church in western Canada, we have seen how eastern European settlers arrived in their midst. They forced French and English Catholics to back away from their internecine strife and address the pressing needs of the Ukrainian, German, Polish, and Hungarian Catholics. The Ukrainians brought with them an eastern European liturgy, language, culture, and custom of married clergy. The Latin church for a decade hoped to assimilate them, but under the leadership of Archbishop Langevin, the apostolic delegate, and the Catholic Extension Society, the Canadian church underwent a heartfelt change. The initial endeavour to integrate Eastern Rite Catholics into the Latin church was dropped and an intensified effort made to provide support for the training of clergy and the construction of churches. It can be said that Bishop Nykyta Budka, along with the Redemptorists and Basilians, established permanently in Canada Eastern Rite church institutions.

The founding of the first Ukrainian eparchy in Canada raised the question of ethnic bishops being appointed for the Germans, Poles, and Hungarians. Although immigrants to western Canada made English the common language of the region, Canadien bishops controlled the dioceses. The last two French-speaking bishops in western Canada were appointed in Regina and Edmonton just before the First World War. After 1920 only English-speaking candidates were elected to episcopal sees. They received the new sees of Calgary and Winnipeg and took over the sees of Edmonton and Regina. By 1930 the English-speaking bishops were firmly in control of Catholicism in western Canada.

On the West Coast the diocese of Victoria slipped into the hands of English-speaking leadership when Alexander MacDonald arrived in 1909. MacDonald took advantage of prosperous times to purchase new properties for future diocesan institutions but was caught in the collapse of property values. He led an interchurch coalition to win a tax exemption for church properties, but the legal battles exhausted both sides, and the diocesan funds drained away. Following the legal victory, the Vatican summoned MacDonald to Rome to explain the debt. He was forced to resign, leaving behind a stricken diocese.

The Oblates accepted the responsibility for Christianization of the Canadian Northwest. They pursued this task in classical nineteenth-century missionary fashion. To bolster the process of evangelization, they established schools, orphanages, and hospitals throughout the missionary territory. The schools were abandoned after a hundred years when they were discovered to be insensitive to native culture and counterproductive to native needs. By the 1970s the Oblates had handed over their schools to native control. The Oblates are presently involved with the First Nations in the formation of native leadership. The future calls for native people, in dialogue with other Christians, to form their own unique First Nations Catholic church.

Western Canadians established permanent institutions by adapting church customs to their needs. By the 1930s the experience of unity in diversity provided both strength and flexibility for Canadian Catholics. This sturdy and multicultural foundation for the Catholic church was important for its survival because it was soon buffeted by the harsh blows of the Great Depression.

10 Catholic Responses
to the Depression

The New York stockmarket crashed on Black Thursday, 24 October 1929, and the dollar, gold, and sterling blocks went into an economic tailspin. Corporations failed, workers were laid off, national economies collapsed, and a trade depression descended upon the world. Many business people lost their fortunes. Some entrepreneurs threw themselves from office towers to their deaths, while others endured impoverishment in forced retirement at home, humbly renewing their personal and family lives. Social networks in most nations hardly existed, and the working and middle classes in most countries suffered greatly and endured the hardship in national and personal isolation.

The economy of the Maritime provinces in Canada was listless during the decade that followed the Great War and into the Depression.[1] In the 1930s, the unemployed in Montreal and Toronto walked the streets looking for work.[2] The editor of the *Catholic Register*, Henry Somerville, went to great lengths during the 1930s to explain Catholic social teaching. On the Prairies, drought intensified the agricultural distress, and many farmers returned to Quebec, Ontario, or the West Coast. The newly founded Cooperative Commonwealth Federation (CCF) showed interest in economic initiatives in rural Nova Scotia, Ontario, and on the Prairies, but many Catholics were ambivalent or even hostile towards the newly founded CCF.

ANTIGONISH MOVEMENT
AND COOPERATIVES

The farmers, fishers, and industrial workers of the Maritimes in the twentieth century received inadequate wages for their work and inadequate prices for their fish and agricultural produce. To counteract the economic ennui, two Catholic priests, Father Jimmy Tompkins and Father Moses Coady, launched an education program for adults and a cooperative movement for the Maritimes. Economic instability continued through the first three decades of the century, but it was at the end of the third decade that the world markets collapsed, triggering a worldwide tragedy in which the Maritime economy slowed to near standstill.[3]

In 1912 Father Jimmy Tompkins attended meetings of British universities in London and became excited when discussion turned to adult education to empower the people. He believed that adult education could stimulate the economic development of a community and improve the lives of the workers. Returning to Nova Scotia, he promoted his new insight and between 1913 and 1915 headed up the Antigonish Forward Movement of adult education. Father Jimmy educated ordinary people, and his students included veterans returning from the Great War, who were awakened to their need for education, and the young between the ages of 16 and 25, who did not have the opportunity of higher education.[4]

In 1920 Father Jimmy published his manifesto, *Knowledge for the People: A Call to St Francis Xavier College.* He analyzed social problems in the Maritime provinces and the economic solutions they demanded. He wrote of the need for better education and health care for the young, and good roads and modern farming techniques for the community. He was impressed by adult education programs sponsored by the Workers' Education Association in England, the Gaelic League in Ireland, workers' groups in Quebec and Saskatchewan, and the University of Wisconsin, which had 43,000 adult learners on its campus. His appeal fell on deaf ears, however, and he took action on his own. Father Jimmy and a cousin of his, Moses M. Coady, were allowed to open the People's School at St Francis Xavier University in 1921. This was the first People's School on a North American campus. Programs ran from January to March, during the farmers and the fishers' off-season. There were no entrance requirements and no fees. The clergy and the laity of the diocese offered their moral support, and the school began to seek out ways to alleviate harsh economic conditions. Sixty participants enrolled during the second year of operation.

Father Jimmy also saw the need for the colleges and universities of Nova Scotia to cooperate to overcome their financial problems. With the encouragement of the Carnegie Foundation, but against the judgment of Bishop Morrison, the Maritime bishops, President MacPherson, and the board of governors of St Francis Xavier, Father Jimmy pressed for the federation of the universities in Halifax around Dalhousie University.[5] Suddenly Father Jimmy was removed from the university campus and appointed the parish priest at Canso. His twelve-year exile in the remote fishing village meant the People's School ceased further operations.[6]

Not overwhelmed, Father Jimmy's creative energies were intensified when he shared the bleak poverty of the hardworking people at Canso. He visited the miserable shacks in which the fisher families lived. During the First World War when fish could not be shipped to Europe, the Nova Scotian fish markets in the Caribbean were lost to competitive Newfoundlanders. Next, a postwar depression engulfed the Maritime provinces. Lotz and Welton describe it thus: "As the Depression deepened, factories shut down or went on short time. Between 1920 and 1926, 42 percent of the manufacturing jobs in the region simply vanished. The steel mills and coal mines in Cape Breton put their workers on reduced work weeks and cut their pay. In 1925, coal miners went on strike, looting and burning down company stores."[7]

Into the 1930s the problems intensified as Montreal and Toronto firms consolidated their factories in central Canada. Freight rates rose, large-beam commercial trawlers scooped up the fish, and the Maritime provinces, declining in population, were allotted fewer members of Parliament. Maritime workers came to be regarded as cheap labour while their wives laboured in fish plants and their gardens and wild berries supplied necessary food.[8] Canso became a laboratory for Father Jimmy to work out his belief that adult education could empower the people. To deal with the hardship and discouragement of life in Canso, he instructed and guided the fishers to set up their own packaging plants in the early 1930s and ship their own products directly to market.[9]

Ted Garland, a member of Parliament for Alberta and Catholic agrarian radical, visited Father Jimmy to learn about his work. Kindred spirits, they exchanged letters and ideas after the visit. In 1932 Father Jimmy supported legislation to launch credit unions in Nova Scotia. A bill provided that any seven citizens living in a particular neighbourhood were entitled to form a credit union. Forty-five credit unions emerged in the province within three years. At the Sisters of St Martha convent, he set up a library and reading room at Canso.[10]

Perhaps the most interesting of all his innovations was the housing cooperative he spearheaded in Reserve Mines when he was appointed

Staff of Extension Division of St Francis Xavier University, including Fr Moses Coady and Sr Irene Doyle, front row. (SFXUA)

the parish priest in 1935. During the summer of 1938 Father Jimmy inspired the construction of nine cooperative houses, which were occupied by working families before the snows came. The project happened because of the cooperative efforts of the Government of Nova Scotia, the miners and their families, and two American women who had built an apartment co-op in New York City. Thus it was that Tompkinsville became a great model of cooperative ingenuity to many in the Maritime provinces, especially to Father Moses Coady of the St Francis Xavier Extension Department.[11]

Moses Coady was a young colleague of Tompkins's from an ambitious farm family. Coady made up for his spotty education with diligent private study. He enrolled at St Francis Xavier College, graduating in 1905, and prepared for ordination to the priesthood by studying at the Urban College in Rome. After his ordination in 1910, he returned to Nova Scotia to teach at St Francis Xavier. He interrupted his teaching to enrol in graduate studies at the Catholic University of America at Washington, DC. When he returned to Antigonish, the young Dr Coady joined forces with Dr Jimmy Tompkins in 1921 to launch the People's School. The two educators were concerned with religious values but they focused primarily on the resolution of economic and social problems.[12]

St Francis Xavier opened its Extension Department in 1930, with Dr Coady as its director.[13] From this position he supervised the growth of the Antigonish Movement, advocating both adult education and the

Student Life at St Francis Xavier University (1944): Front row: Angus MacIntosh, Steven MacLellan, Joseph MacDonald, Dennis Lelièvre, Bernard MacNeil; Back row: Fabian MacDougall, Daniel MacNeil, Leonard MacDonald, Murdock MacLean, Paul Granville. (SFXUA)

introduction of cooperative movements in Nova Scotia and elsewhere. This became his work for the next thirty years, and to spread his ideas he drove himself and others relentlessly, all the while teaching that people had to adjust to changes in the economy.[14]

The staff at the Extension Department included the first secretary, Kay Thompson, and two Sisters of St Martha, Sr Marie Michael Mackinnon and Sr Irene Doyle. They and other staff members were involved with Coady in "writing, speaking, listening, hosting, typing, planning, organizing, critiquing, and generating ideas." From the beginning, women were intentionally included as part of the team to animate working people and give them the tools for survival. By 1940 the staff had expanded to eleven full-time and seven part-time members. By the time Coady retired in 1952, more than fourteen staff members carried out the work of the Extension Department.[15]

Coady taught that cooperatives, not labour unions, were the main pillar of the new social order. Labour unions, he believed, were an appendage of capitalism; they lacked a social philosophy and were afflicted by bad leaders. He argued the need for a new system that went beyond motives of profit and greed. The poverty of the Cape Breton coal miners demonstrated how capitalism and unionism did not work to the benefit of the workers or the community. The workers were paid

90 cents a day, or \$5.40 for a six-day week, \$6.30 for a seven-day week. The workers rented company-owned row houses that were without bathrooms, toilets, or running water. They bought their food from company-owned stores at prices set by the company. Company spies, riot police, and the occasional death of a striker kept dissident workers in line. In response, the United Mine Workers organized strikes in 1909, 1925, and 1930. For all the hardship and lost wages they endured, the miners and their families gained few benefits.[16]

To circumvent this round of futility, Coady turned to *Quadragesimo Anno*, which had been promulgated by Pius XI to celebrate the publication of *Rerum Novarum* forty years earlier. In the original encyclical, Leo XIII tried to meet the challenge of Adam Smith and Karl Marx by basing his arguments on natural law. He stressed the importance of the common good over individual gain, more specifically, the right of workers to form labour unions, take home a just wage, and enjoy decent labour conditions. Leo also supported the right to own private property but always with social considerations, encouraged intervention of the state on certain occasions, and rejected socialism as the answer. He taught not class warfare but the empirical need of the three classes for one another in the pursuit of a better life.[17]

In the anniversary letter of 1931, Pius XI reiterated the earlier teachings of Leo, who advocated the primacy of the common good and rejected the injustice of capitalism and the regimented justice of socialism. The economic system for the average worker, the pope recognized, was "hard, cruel, and relentless." *Quadragesimo Anno* recommended that workers form vocational groups and cooperative organizations. Thus in a peaceful manner like the medieval guilds, vocational groups would gain for their workers a share in the wealth and direction of various industries. They were designated "corporatist" organizations and were to mediate between workers, capital, and the state. The fascist governments of Spain and Portugal employed corporatism with mixed success until in the postwar period corporatism was jettisoned. Functioning differently from corporatism, cooperative organizations initiated "social justice" among the workers and strove to create a new "Christian social order." Although *Quadragesimo Anno* put the church on the side of the suffering poor, it did not speak strongly to the working class. The critics, acknowledging its lofty ideals, responded that the teaching of Pius XI looked back to a former age.[18]

Consequently, cooperative organizations, as mentioned in the encyclical along with adult education, became a main tool of the Antigonish Movement. The Antigonish Movement chose this twofold goal and separated itself from partisan politics. Criticizing this idealism, Gregory Baum doubts the ability of the cooperative way to survive in the free

Left to right: R.J. MacSween, Inspector of Cooperatives Association of Nova Scotia, A.B. MacDonald, National Secretary of the Cooperative Union of Canada, Dr Moses Coady, Director of the Extension Department, and J. Edward O'Meara, Director of Cooperative Statistics and Research, Canadian Department of Agriculture at the Congress of Nova Scotia Cooperatives and Credit Unions held at St Francis Xavier University in July 1951. (SFXUA)

enterprise system. He contends that the movement's failure to support the CCF was misguided, and that a cooperative system could only prosper under a benevolent government, that is, one similar to the CCF. For Baum, the Antigonish Movement offered an "alternative vision of society" and was "the most original and the most daring response of Canadian Catholics to the social injustices during the Depression."[19]

Although primarily committed to Nova Scotians and the Nova Scotian community, Coady and the Antigonish Movement spread to struggling fishing and agricultural communities in Central and South America, Asia, India, and Africa. Jamaica, Puerto Rico, Trinidad, San Domingo, and Dominica among others sent people to study the Antigonish Movement.[20] Coady had the moral courage to involve his university in the economic struggle of the community and to seek justice in economic structures. Many of his ideas were prophetic: environmental conservation, eradication of poverty, economic planning, and use of scientific thinking to further community goals. Although a theological conservative, he was a social radical. He believed Christians should be more concerned with social problems than pious practices. One irony of Coady's life was that he was better known around the world than he was in Canada.[21]

One of the high points of Moses Coady's career was his invitation to speak at United Nations in 1949. There he sought protection for the world's natural resources and their maintenance as a trust for the benefit of all peoples. He also wished to awaken the world body to the importance of the involvement of ordinary people in their own democratic future. He challenged world leaders to provide education for their people so that all nations might be able to embark upon a cooperative way of life. Such cooperation, he asserted, would enrich the spirit of nations as well as their resources.[22]

CATHOLIC SOCIAL ORDER FOR QUEBEC AND THE ALN

In Quebec, investment, urbanization, and industrial production surged during the first decades of the twentieth century to provide an image of steady growth and development. In the period before the First World War Quebec shared in the Canadian economic take-off. One symbol of economic success on the grass-roots level was the *caisse populaires*, a type of credit union that grew quickly during the first decade of the century. The credit unions halted the flow of capital from Quebec and re-employed those funds for regional development. The initiator, Alphonse Desjardins, studied popular banking and credit institutions in Europe and prepared a plan for Quebec. He recognized the parish as the natural base for a credit union because cooperatives must be founded on mutual trust. In the parish environment, he knew people knew and trusted one another.[23]

The *caisse populaire* spread rapidly from parish to parish and was warmly welcomed by the government and the clergy. The financial success of the *caisses* was undeniable, but its goal, according to Desjardins, was also altruistic. He sought to win the participation of the Québécois in the movement and thus to raise the democratic consciousness of participants in their future. The Church, contrary to the Code of Canon Law, overlooked parish priests being involved in the financial operations of the *caisses*.[24]

L'Action sociale, a Catholic publishing company that had published a newspaper of the same name since 1907, was considered the "unofficial spokesman for the Quebec City hierarchy." To its critics, it "seemed clearly inspired by hostility to modern developments." It saw itself as an instrument of education, coordinating diocesan activities and moulding the thought of college students and élites. The newspaper encouraged the growth of the *caisses populaires* and agricultural cooperatives. It regularly attacked the policies of the Liberal party and went after the high-profile Liberal Louis-Alexandre Taschereau.[25]

Vexed by the constant attacks, Tachereau followed Laurier's example and went over the heads of the Canadian hierarchy by writing to Rome in 1912 and, while giving proper assurances, complained of clerical interference in political affairs. While *L'Action sociale* exercised restraint in the interim, the Holy See decided in favour of Cardinal Bégin and the policy of his newspaper. Changed to *l'Action catholique* in 1915, the newspaper sided with the Canadien élites during the First World War, encouraging ordinary Canadiens to support the war effort, enlist, and make sacrifices.[26]

In 1923 Taschereau, having become premier of Quebec was able to intimidate *l'Action catholique* by asking Cardinal Bégin to reign in the newspaper on civil matters such as the Quebec liquor legislation. The following year *L'Action catholique* questioned Tachereau's religious fidelity, and a standoff ensured between the Quebec church and the government. The premier appealed through the speaker of the House of Commons, Rodolphe Lemieux, to the apostolic delegate in Ottawa, who called for a quick remedy to this disruptive affair. The death of Bégin in 1925 and of his protégé, P.-E. Roy, the following year eased tensions, and the appointment of Raymond-Marie Rouleau (1926–31) as the new archbishop of Quebec smoothed the remaining differences.[27]

After 1910, militant Jesuit spirituality spread among eighty thousand Quebec youth in the colleges and the parishes through the Ligue de Sacré-Coeur. The league encouraged the young to go beyond pious practices to become active in the social concerns of the workers and the needy. It aimed to provide amidst changing times a solid bastion of conservative spirituality.[28] After the publication of *Quadragesimo anno* in 1931, a Belgian formula for organizing the youth was carried the following year to Canada. The Young Workers (Jeunesse ouvrière, or JOC), Young Students (Jeunesse étudiente, or JEC), Young Farmers (Jeunesse agricole, or JAC), and Young Independents (Jeunesse indépendante, or the JIC) emerged to organize the youth of Quebec for spiritual goals and social engagement. Magazines were published to inform and bind the members together in the same goals. Parish halls, churches, colleges, and convents became busy with social education to implant the Jocists movement in the soil of Quebec youth. In 1933 women set up their own section, and the movement spread like wildfire to four provinces among the Franco-Americans, and six thousand members were enrolled.[29]

The financial collapse of the Quebec economy after 1929 revealed extensive overproduction and the need for drastic remedies, including cutbacks in labour and production. The École sociale populaire, founded by the Jesuits in 1910, was unhappy with various depression initiatives and proposed a response based on Catholic social thought.

It sponsored Semaines sociales beginning in 1931 to raise awareness on social questions. The activities of the École inspired a generation of Québécois and gave rise to the political movement of radical reform Action libérale nationale (ALN). The movement, writes Gregory Baum, envisioned a future for Quebec in the midst of the world trade depression. It developed this way.

The Cooperative Commonwealth Federation, founded in Calgary in 1932, presented Quebec voters with what they perceived to be the social and political ideals of English Protestant Canadians. The organization of the CCF in Quebec goaded the École sociale populaire to more intense activity to sensitize Catholics to social questions. In 1933 the *École* published its *Programme de restauration sociale*. It contained three separate critiques of the economic system and suggested alternatives.[30]

The Dominican Georges-Henri Lévesque wrote the first essay and repudiated the CCF, judging it to be a communist front organization.[31] In the second essay, Esdras Minville pointed to the abuses of capitalism, such as the exploitation of workers, the concentration of wealth in the hands of a few, and the anarchy of production. He concluded, however, that "capitalism could be made to work again if the law of the market were subordinated to the principles of justice."[32] The last paper, by Jesuit Louis Chagnon, developed a radical thirteen-point program to change the Quebec economy. Chagnon called for the subordination of large corporations to the common good, a just distribution of wealth, protection for workers against accident, sickness, and old age, and farmers' insurance, family wage, and subsidized medical care. He proposed a corporatist society of professional organizations, as advocated by Pius XI, through which farmers, artisans, industrial workers, civil servants, merchants, consumers, financiers, intellectuals could oversee the economy and guide society towards humane capitalism. The initial response from Quebec intellectuals was enthusiastic: social corporatism was seen as a way of liberating the economy from British and American financial control and protecting it from communism. Social corporatism was to be distinguished from state corporatism, which emerged at this time in Italy, Spain, and Portugal.[33] Social corporatism was different from communism, which embraced class war and the destruction of the Christian religion and private property. The Quebec nationalists saw the communists "as trying to take advantage of the Depression to overthrow the social order and inaugurate a reign of paganism, totalitarianism and hate." Condemned by Pius XI, "communism was the supreme enemy," and total war against it was the answer.[34]

The École inspired the left-wing Liberal nationalists, led by Paul Gouin, to hammer out the platform of the Action libérale nationale, adopting many of the ideals of Catholic social thought. These ideas opposed the insensitivity and ineptness of Premier Taschereau's Liberals who were out of touch with reality. Paul Gouin and his colleagues adapted Catholic social thought to the needs of Quebec by replacing Pius XI's social corporatism with Quebec nationalism. They feared the British, Americans, Jews, and Anglo-Canadians who, in their view, owned too many Quebec corporations and also held high positions in Quebec government. They wanted to imitate the success of Franklin Roosevelt's New Deal in regulating such corporations. Large monopolies, such as the financial institutions, electricity trusts, and paper industry, as well as small and medium-sized foreign-owned businesses, controlled much of the Quebec economy and made it virtually impossible for small Quebec-owned companies to compete. Angered by this economic disparity in their own homeland, the ALN leaders wanted the middle class and the workers to buy only goods produced in Quebec, return to small-scale agriculture and rural industry, and sever the secret links between government and corporations. In its zeal, the party continued to remain suspicious of the consultative features of democracy and was remiss to defend civil liberties and minority rights.[35]

In the election of 1935, the ideals of the ALN fascinated the electorate, and the party won twenty-six seats in the legislature, embarrassing the Taschereau government. The Conservatives under Maurice Duplessis won only sixteen seats and were also embarrassed by their poor showing but remained hungry for power. Duplessis invited the ALN to join in "a common front against the common enemy," the Liberals.[36] They would form a new party together, the Union Nationale, and would adopt the ALN platform which included developing small-scale business and agriculture, checking the growth of foreign corporations, and blocking the rise of the CCF in Quebec. Sixty-one former ALN candidates ran in ninety ridings with the remainder contested by Duplessis's former Conservative candidates. They agreed after the election that Gouin would choose the majority of cabinet ministers and Duplessis would be the leader of the party.[37] To the surprise of both Gouin and Duplessis, the "common enemy," Premier Taschereau, resigned as leader before the election. Gouin then determined that the ALN should go into the election alone and announced that the party would support neither Duplessis's candidates nor Taschereau's successor.[38]

The Union Nationale won the 1936 election, taking seventy-six of ninety seats in the legislative assembly. Thirty-nine members were from Conservative ridings and twenty-eight from ALN ridings. Duplessis became the dominant personality and took control of the government. He quickly excluded ALN members from the Union Nationale cabinet.[39] The new party put the promised economic reforms on the back

Maurice Duplessis, Mme and Paul Gouin outside the Quebec assembly, 15 December 1935. (NA PA 74625)

burner, ran the province as a compliant religious society, and attracted "foreign" investors with tax breaks and cheap natural resources. Gregory Baum concludes that the ALN "underestimated the seriousness of the struggle" for social and economic reform and in the process was destroyed by its lack of political savvy.[40] During the next decade, the Bloc populaire canadien resurrected the ALN's ideas and rallied Quebec nationalists to advocate a program of economic cleansing and social reform. In the 1950s, when the rumblings of the Quiet Revolution were first heard, Quebec secular nationalism began to replace Roman Catholicism as the soul of the French Canadian mystique and the glue of its social network.[41]

HENRY SOMERVILLE: SOCIAL ISSUES AND HIGHER EDUCATION

While Quebec had been home to a French Catholic majority for four centuries, Ontario at the start of the twentieth century was home to an English Catholic minority. Largely Irish and Scottish in ethnic origin, Catholics in Ontario suffered the status of a double minority. As English speakers in a Canadian church, they were a minority in a religion dominated by the French-speaking majority. As Catholics in the province of Ontario, they were a minority dominated by the Protestant majority.[42]

English-speaking Catholics responded to this predicament by gathering in parishes to protect their religion and to send their children to Catholic elementary schools. Catholic civil politics in a hostile environment continued to focus single-mindedly on. Always having to look in on government offices from the outside, they pleaded their case with those in power. In late-nineteenth-century Toronto, the episcopacies of John Walsh (1889–98), Fergus McEvay (1908–11), and Neil McNeil (1912–34), as Mark McGowan perceptively points out, offered strong hope to Catholics and painted a new vision for them. They raised their sights from the basic level of primary education for their children to secondary, university, and professional education for their sons and daughters and involvement in Catholic social action for themselves.[43]

One of the leaders in this new approach was Neil McNeil, the archbishop of Vancouver. Appointed archbishop of Toronto in 1912 from Vancouver, he spoke seven languages, earned a doctorate in theology, and was a former rector of St Francis Xavier University. He inspired a new commitment in the Catholic community in Toronto to seek high school education for their young people and to follow it, if possible, by university and graduate studies. He brought Henry Somerville from England to introduce Catholic social teaching to the archdiocese.[44] From 1915 to 1919 Somerville taught seminarians, priests, and lay persons, and introduced them to the ideas of the British Catholic Social Guild and to Catholic social thinking on *Rerum Novarum*.[45]

Somerville was not iconoclastic about pious practices, but like Moses Coady, he stressed the importance of Catholic social action guided by an enlightened conscience. He taught that in a modern industrial society it was important for people to have an adequate wage, property rights, family allowances, low-interest loans, and government-sponsored building projects. Archbishop McNeil, in conjunction with the teaching of Somerville, emphasized the twin need for Catholic higher education and involvement in the social issues.[46]

Somerville sailed back to England during the early 1920s. At a second invitation from the archbishop, he returned to Toronto to become editor of the *Catholic Register*. Guiding its fortunes from 1933 to 1953, he emphasized the necessity of advanced education and Catholic social action. John Webster Grant comments that "only with the appointment of Henry Somerville as editor of the *Catholic Register* in 1933 would the [Catholic] church in Ontario begin to develop a sophisticated social philosophy."[47] The *Register* cautioned its readers to consider thoughtfully the social concerns raised by the CCF's Regina Manifesto of 1933 and advised Archbishop James C. McGuigan of Toronto (1934–71) against condemning the CCF. Somerville believed

Henry Somerville, editor of the *Catholic Register.* Archives of the Roman Catholic
Archdiocese of Toronto

that a spiritually flexible and socially conscious attitude would benefit
Catholics and Canadians.[48]

Somerville's editorial colleague, Murray Ballantyne of the Montreal *Beacon,* gave the same advice to Archbishop Joseph Charbonneau (1940–50). By contrast, his predecessor, Archbishop Georges
Gauthier (1923–39), issued a pastor letter in 1934 with the secret approval of the Quebec bishops, condemning the CCF on the grounds
that it rejected private property, believed in class warfare, and taught
atheistic materialism. Ballantyne felt that church condemnation of a
political party was a "grave matter" and had to be clearly and con-
cretely promulgated or the matter should be dropped. He suggested
to Archbishop McGuigan that a committee should be struck in Montreal to consider the philosophy of the CCF and went on to state that
the CCF platform had many issues in common with Catholic social
teachings. In 1943 at a plenary meeting in Quebec, the bishops Canadianized papal thinking by declaring that "the faithful are free to
support any political party upholding the basic Christian traditions of
Canada, and favouring needed reforms in the social and economic
order which are demanded with such urgency in pontifical documents."[49] Without naming the CCF, this declaration spoke about this
new party as a legitimate Canadian political party for which Catholics
might in good conscience vote. The bishops advocated a more flexible spirituality that included a social conscience that would benefit
all Canadians.

PIONEER WOMEN IN LAY MINISTRY

Two women who manifested strong leadership and Christian compassion after the Great War were Catherine de Hueck in Canada and Dorothy Day in the United States. Both were charismatic women exercising the ministry of the church. Having escaped the communist repression in the Soviet Union, Catherine immigrated to Canada in 1921. Inspired by pre-revolutionary Russian piety, she opened Friendship House in the midst of the Great Depression in downtown Toronto, east of University Avenue. She begged food for the hungry and prepared five meals a day, which according to her, amounted to only about one meal's worth of nourishment. As part of their Spartan routine, she and her co-workers attended the seven o'clock Mass at St Patrick's Church on Dundas Street, or St Mary's Church on Bathurst Avenue. In winter Catherine and her associates begged fuel to heat their several old houses and endured the cold when necessary – as did their neighbours. "We were poorer than the poor," she remarked. When others needed food, furniture, or bed linen, these items were given away, and Catherine recalled that she sometimes slept on the floor covered with a carpet in her overcoat and boots.[50]

To inspire Catherine, Archbishop McNeil gave her a copy of the *Catholic Worker.* The newspaper, published in New York City, sold for twenty-five cents for twelve issues. Its pages introduced Catherine to the ideals of the extraordinary Dorothy Day. McNeil gave Catherine a train ticket to New York to meet the newspaper's originators, Dorothy Day and Peter Maurin. When Catherine arrived at the Catholic Worker House, she found Dorothy working on the soup line, and they immediately struck up a friendship. Dorothy invited Catherine to stay and asked whether she would mind sleeping in the double bed with her in a room filled with cots. When evening came, a woman from the street looking for a place to sleep rapped on the door. She had no nose and suffered from active syphilis. Dorothy welcomed her "like a queen" and told Catherine that she could sleep on a mattress in the bathtub while the woman would sleep in the double bed with Dorothy. Catherine, a nurse, warned Dorothy about the easy communication of the disease. Undeterred, Dorothy replied, "Catherine, you have little faith. This is Christ come to us for a place to sleep. He will take care of me. You have to have faith." Catherine and Dorothy had a strong influence on each other, and their friendship had "profound repercussions on the whole lay apostolate of North America."[51]

During the 1920s Catherine had travelled throughout the United States giving talks on the Chautauqua lecture circuit. She had a knack for cultivating important people. When the liturgists Father Godfrey

Diekmann and Dom Virgil Michel visited Friendship House in Toronto in the 1930s, they were impressed with Catherine and her work and invited her to lecture at St John's College in Minnesota. Other distinguished visitors to Friendship House included the founder of the *Catholic Digest*, Father Gales, and two professors of the Institute of Medieval Studies at St Michael's College, Jacques Maritain and Etienne Gilson.[52] Friendship House attracted the attention of many concerned citizens who were genuinely interested in the charitable works of Catherine and her associates.

Labouring under great stress to support this growing community and to supply the needs of the poor, Catherine provoked stiff opposition from some clergy and laity. She and her associates picketed the Laura Secord Candy Shoppes owned by Senator Frank P. O'Connor "for not paying proper wages to his factory girls." Archbishop McGuigan, upset with this demonstration against a generous benefactor of the archdiocese, called her to the chancery office and, according to Catherine, "wiped the floor with me." She replied by itemizing the injustices existing at Laura Secord and quoted passages to the archbishop from *Quadragesimo Anno*. She concluded to McGuigan, "How would you feel if you were me?" Their friendship survived this altercation.[53]

Some clergy supported Friendship House with food and money. Father Henry Carr of St Michael's College gave Catherine spiritual direction and moral support throughout her struggles. Yet Catherine learned to fear priests who challenged her lay ministry. Parish priests such as Father Campbell W. James of St Mary's Parish and Father Stanley Puchniak of St Stanislaus Parish could not understand how Friendship House fitted into parochial or diocesan structure. Under whose jurisdiction did Catherine operate an apostolate in the name of the Catholic church? Some priests challenged her at lectures, and rumours began to spread among the laity that she was a communist. She was accused of mismanagement and of being cruel to her son. The criticisms caused her much personal pain, and she began to doubt her vocation. Smarting from these rejections, Catherine closed Friendship House at the end of 1936 and travelled again to New York to visit Dorothy Day. She felt crushed that everything she had worked for seemed lost, but her visit with Dorothy was "like a breath of fresh air all around."[54]

Catherine took a break from her labours and worked as a correspondent in Europe, New York, and Chicago. While in New York, she met a famous and lovable newspaper reporter by the name of Eddie Doherty.[55] They married in 1942. Five years later, Catherine and Eddie and her associates took up residence in an old farm house at

Combermere, Ontario. They hoped to create a self-contained Christian community.[56]

At the new community home, soon to be called Madonna House, the day began at 5:30 A.M. Catherine and her spiritual family would start the fires, bake the bread, and walk to the parish church at Combermere for Mass. After a trip to the post office, they visited the neighbours and invited them home for tea. They ran a clothing room for some of the neighbours, who had enough to eat but not enough clothes to cover themselves properly in the cold of winter. Catherine had brought a sewing machine with her, which they used to mend and adjust clothes. In a short time Combermere became a training centre for the lay apostolate and a place of pilgrimage for visitors from near and far.[57]

One of the major exercises of the community was fundraising. Soon after arriving at Combermere, Catherine organized master files of Canadian and American addresses and started the ministry of begging in order to win others to the support of the Combermere community and its various charities. Donations and parcels of clothing and other items began to arrive. Renovations were carried out and ministries expanded.[58]

Catherine was living the Russian spirituality she had learned from her mother and father. The Russians, she would say, liked to contemplate Jesus as a worker-peasant labouring in the homes of working people. Catherine's mother, a noblewoman, would "go out to the people" every summer and work as a maid, teach reading and writing, and nurse the sick. Her father, a doctor, instructed Catherine in medicine and nursing. Her family believed that Christian love demanded that the wealthy make personal contact with ordinary people – that is, get involved with the poor, offer counsel, and show sympathetic interest. Catherine would accompany her mother on lengthy medical pilgrimages to care for the sick, deliver babies, and assist families after the birth. These experiences left an indelible impression on Catherine. Opening Friendship House in Toronto was a consequence of Christian ideals implanted in the former Russian baroness by her parents. From 1947 to her death in 1990, she contemplated Jesus according to the traditions of Russian spirituality as a worker-peasant who loved the poor by living with them.[59]

Charismatic renewal first came to Canada at Combermere in 1968. Nurtured in the spirituality of Eastern Christianity, Catherine sensed in the uniformity of Western Christianity the absence of a deep awareness of the Holy Spirit. She opened contact with charismatic leaders from Duquesne University and Notre Dame and invited them to Combermere during August. The members of the community were coached in welcoming the presence of the Spirit, and as part of the visit they came to a new understanding of the Scriptures, prayed in tongues, appreciated the sacraments more deeply, underwent conversion of life, and rejoiced in the gifts of the Spirit. From that time on, charismatic prayer became an active part of the life of Combermere members.[60]

Despite the opposition of some clergy and lay people, Catherine exercised leadership in some vital ministries of the Catholic church. She and other uncelebrated women like her ministered the healing power of the Church indiscriminately to Catholics and non-Catholics, to Canadians and non-Canadians.

WESTERN CATHOLICS AND THE CCF

Western Catholics, much like those elsewhere in Canada, supported the Liberal party because of its sympathy for separate schools but remained suspicious of the CCF. In Saskatchewan Catholics voted for Jimmy Gardiner and the Liberal party, which defended both French- and English-speaking separate schools. English-speaking Protestants and some Catholics voted for the Tory party, which supported English-only public schools. Most Catholics were not ideological but practical Liberals who dispensed their votes for political advantage. They voted for the political party that promised to protect their rights and offer them some advantages. The Liberal party proved to be more considerate of mainline Catholic interests.[61]

There were some exceptions to this trend, and one in particular was the prominent and ambitious Tory leader in the English-speaking Catholic community, John Joseph Leddy. As a member of the national executive of the Knights of Columbus, he organized the successful Catholic Army Huts project, which provided recreational clubs for Catholic soldiers during the Great War. After serving several terms on the Saskatoon Separate School Board, he redirected his educational interests to improve university education for the English-speaking Catholic community. He guided thinking to the need for educating Catholic young people, especially at the university level, in an atmosphere of faith. Conflict with French-speaking Catholics in the province was inevitable as they moved to found a separate French-speaking university. The Canadiens envisioned different ethnic colleges attached to the one university, including, they hoped, association with an English-speaking college. Leddy and English-speaking Canadians rejected the segregated model the Canadiens offered at Gavelbourg and sought their own college at the University of Saskatchewan, along the lines of St Michael's College at the University of Toronto. With the appointment of Gerald Murray as the bishop of Saskatoon in 1933, the initiative on Catholic colleges passed to the English-speaking hierarchy. Within three years St Thomas More College was established in Saskatoon at the provincial university. An English-speaking college at a central location for Catholic students was a great triumph for J.J. Leddy and Irish Canadians. Leddy and his well-to-do Catholic Tory friends were exceptions to traditional Catholic support for the Liberals.[62]

In 1931, as noted earlier, on the fortieth anniversary of *Rerum Novarum*, Pope Pius XI published *Quadragesimo Anno* in which he praised Catholic social action but warned against mixing it with socialism or nationalism. He believed the root cause of the depression was not capitalism but rather personal greed, materialism, and selfishness. Western Catholics reacted in two different ways to the pope's warning about socialism. Father Athol Murray of Notre Dame School at Wilcox condemned socialism as a blight on the human spirit. He feared the CCF because he believed it would mean the collectivization of prairie farms, the shackling of human freedom, and the denial of God.[63] Two students at Wilcox who were members of the CCF Young People's study group were expelled by Athol Murray. This caused a public incident, and at the request of M.J. Coldwell, Archbishop J.C. McGuigan gave assurances that the church would not interfere in politics. Privately, McGuigan asked Murray in future to say "absolutely nothing" that would make the church seem political.[64]

Other Catholic voices articulated a more favourable image of the CCF. The *Prairie Messenger*, published in Muenster, Saskatchewan, reacted with initial enthusiasm to the concerns of the CCF but later became more cautious in the wake of anti-Catholic statements made by British Columbian CCF radicals. The *Prairie Messenger* expressed its fear of CCF policies by printing Archbishop Gauthier's letter condemning the party and Louis Chagnon's negative analysis of the CCF. At the same time, the newspaper had great praise for the Christian principles and personal sacrifices of J.S. Woodsworth, who was deeply devoted to the welfare of the Canadian people. Henri Bourassa's defence of the CCF in the House of Commons was published by the *Prairie Messenger*.

Archbishop James McGuigan of Regina (1930–34) chose to avoid controversy and issued a neutral message on the CCF. In withholding any negative comments on the federation, McGuigan was following the lead of Archbishops McNeil and Charbonneau.[65]

Many Catholics in Saskatchewan were still convinced that the CCF represented socialism as condemned by papal teaching and preferred to vote for the Liberal party. The *Prairie Messenger*, taking its tone from

Rev Eugene Cullinane, leader of Catholics supporting the CCF in Saskatchewan. Archives of the Basilian Fathers. Morrall Studios, Rochester, N.Y., A quinas Institute Year Book, 1950

the bishops and eastern Catholic newspapers, gradually became more open to the CCF but remained critical of many of the party's radical policies. A coterie of Prairie Catholics supported the CCF for advocating social policies similar to those propounded in the papal encyclicals. Among the supportes were Hector Roberge in Saskatchewan, chief spokesman for Catholic farmers and workers, and Frank Kellerman from Dana. Joseph Burton in 1938 and W.J. Boyle in the 1940s campaigned for the CCF, and both were elected to the Saskatchewan legislature. Ted Garland, member of Parliament from Alberta, campaigned for the CCF in Saskatchewan, reassuring concerned voters by denying that the party was socialist or would nationalize property.[66]

Perhaps the most articulate Catholic spokesman for the CCF philosophy was Basilian Father Eugene Cullinane. He was attracted to the CCF because he believed it was more faithful to Catholic social teachings than either the Liberal or Tory parties. Cullinane's attachment to the CCF platform found its origin in the Catholic social teachings that he learned from his family, studies at Assumption College in Windsor, and such prominent Catholic figures as Jacques Maritain, Dorothy Day, and Catherine de Hueck. As a seminarian he assisted Catherine de Hueck at Friendship House in downtown Toronto and distributed the *Catholic Worker* and *Social Forum*. From 1936 to 1939 he pursued graduate studies in sociology at the Catholic University of America at Washington, D.C., and began a doctoral dissertation on the Catholic priesthood as a basic element in the social order. Before completing this work, Cullinane went to St Thomas More College to teach economics for two years. Serving as a chaplain in the Second World War, he recognized how important it was that Catholics understand more about the social policies of the CCF and how much common ground Catholics and CCF shared. During the war, according to his former student Bernard Daly, Cullinane decided to focus his doctoral work more specifically on Catholics and the CCF and submitted his proposal to the head of the sociology department at the Catholic University of America. He was assured that his thesis would be a bestseller.[67]

Cullinane contended that the CCF was composed of safe (non-revolutionary) socialists, members of the cooperative movement, trade unionists, non-Marxist farmers, and members of the Social Reconstruction party. The CCF, Cullinane assured Catholics, was not against Catholic social teaching, did not advocate the violent overthrow of government, and did not deny the right to own private property.[68] He argued that the CCF combined the Christian cooperative spirit and British parliamentary democracy. From the encyclicals of Leo XIII and Pius XI, he explained how the church rejected both monopoly capitalism and state capitalism. He advocated the building of a cooperative Christian commonwealth where equality was shared by all.[69] From 1945 to 1948 Cullinane worked on the revised dissertation in Saskatoon while teaching at St Thomas More College.

Despite the misgivings of laity, priests, and bishops, Archbishops James C. McGuigan of Toronto, Joseph Charbonneau of Montreal, and Jean-Marie Villeneuve of Quebec City (1931–47)[70] affirmed in 1943 that Catholics in good conscience might vote for CCF candidates. A group that proved enthusiastic in support of CCF candidates were the Protestant clergy.[71] Thus a number of precedents emerged justifying Christian compatibility with the CCF. Unfortunately for Cullinane, Bishop Philip Pocock of Saskatoon (1944–51) did not see the CCF in the same positive light. Cullinane gave a talk to the Newman Club in which he spoke favourably of the CCF. He did the same in Edmonton and North Battleford, Saskatchewan. Word got around that a Catholic priest had joined the CCF. Prominent lay persons protested to the bishop. In 1946, Pocock, while not disagreeing with Cullinane's message, asked him to refrain from public utterances on socialism. Unfortunately at this sensitive time a letter to CCF member H.O. Hansen explaining why he joined the CCF and the shortened revision of a former article were published. Without further ado, Pocock asked Cullinane to leave the diocese in June 1948.[72]

Fr Cullinane had joined the CCF because he believed that heartless capitalism gravely threatened the workers with insecurity, poverty, and hunger. The CCF for Cullinane was another expression of Christian humanism. It pitted itself against the flagrant abuses of both capitalism and communism and advocated the Catholic social goals of justice, freedom, cooperation, and democracy for all.[73] Catholics thus had many common goals with the CCF, and those who were concerned with social justice would support the CCF.

Another priestly colleague who was an articulate spokesperson for the CCF was the Oblate George Walliser, a pastor in Saskatchewan at Wilkie and later Richmound during the 1940s. Because most of his parishioners were Liberals, he had to be careful when he "attended CCF rallies, especially whenever M.J. Coldwell was the speaker." Walliser was convinced that the support "the CCF gave to the Separate High Schools of the province made it amply evident that the CCF party was indeed the only one to help the cause of the Church in Saskatchewan."[74] Other clergy who subsequently supported the CCF were Isidore Gorski, a professor at Campion College of the University of Regina, and Bob Ogle of Saskatoon, who was elected to Parliament for the NDP. Following the Saskatchewan election of 1975, thirteen Catholics were NDP MLAs, and five of these were in Allan Blakeney's 19-member cabinet. "Thus, contrary to the opinion of some historians," Teresita Kambeitz sums up, "the Catholic Church in Saskatchewan at least, never stood in monolithic opposition to the CCF."[75]

CONCLUSION

During the Great Depression, Catholic social policy emerged from the grass roots of the Canadian landscape. There was no attempt to implement Catholic social policy from the ideological centres of Rome, Quebec, or Toronto. In the Maritime provinces, the Antigonish Movement promoted adult education and cooperatives for the outports. The movement encouraged local farmers, fishers, workers, and miners to organize themselves into regional cooperatives. Through the agency of the cooperatives, they learned to sell their products at better prices and buy commercial goods at cheaper cost. The leaders, Jimmy Tompkins and Moses Coady, advocated the cooperative way of sharing benefits and continuing education for ordinary people, the twin pillars of the new Catholic social order. Canadian-born clergy living in these small communities stimulated working-class awareness of participation in education and cooperatives. Coady, along with Henry Somerville, Catherine de Hueck, and Eugene

Cullinane, introduced a new spirituality of cooperation into Canadian Catholicism by advocating lay participation, adult education, and involvement in social problems.

In Quebec the ALN hoped to carry out necessary economic reforms – which the Liberal party did not do. Paul Gouin and associates of the ALN were inspired by Catholic social thought, Roosevelt's New Deal, and French élitism. They gleaned ideas from such programs and integrated them with French Canadian nationalism. They saw the importance of French Canadians being masters of their own economy, agriculture, and industry. In the 1950s, when ultramontane spirituality continued to inspire the Quebec populace, the CCF message appeared to this cohesive society as something hailing from another planet. In the eyes of many Québécois, the CCF paraded itself as a foreign entity – English, Protestant, and secular. The ALN platform proved popular in two Quebec elections, but Maurice Duplessis and his loyalists outsmarted ALN leaders and wrenched their election victory away through political manipulation. It can be seen in the next chapters that the *Bloc populaire canadien* and the Quiet Revolution seized the political legacy of the ALN and brought its labours to fruition in the early 1960s.

After early prohibitions, the Canadian bishops demonstrated their political maturity by admitting that Catholics might vote for valid political parties such as the CCF. Catholics responded to the Canadian depression in a number of different ways, but Catholic social thought, although still under construction, showed its solidarity with the Canadian working and middle classes grappling with economic tragedy.

11 Catholics Caught between Communism and Fascism

Catholics during the depression were forced to go beyond the theory of papal teachings and seek out Canadian solutions to economic and social problems. Clergy and laity implemented adult education and the cooperative movement in the Maritimes and sought a new social order in Quebec and social justice in Ontario. On the Prairies some looked to the CCF for political leadership and social reforms. Yet from Rome came the clear message to Canadian Catholics to condemn communism as the most destructive force in society. The Roman church painfully endured fascism but determined that it was the less noxious of the two totalitarian systems. The Catholic Church remained extremely wary of the fascist regimes in Italy, Spain, Germany, and Vichy France but for survival played a diplomatic game of cat-and-mouse to get as much wiggle room as possible. The fact that the Holy See, although uncomfortable, tolerated the Fascists influenced the Canadian Church and its perception of the world struggle. Both the Communists and Fascists made significant efforts to organize political activities in Canada, and Catholic clergy and laity responded in different ways.

COMMUNISM IN QUEBEC

Following the Bolshevik revolution in 1917, the Communist party sent tentacles throughout the western world and opened its first Canadian branch in 1921. Marxist activities in Canada were carried out in secret because of the watchful eye of the government. Montreal was the centre for Canadian industrialization, and as Gérard Dion tells us, Quebec workers were thought by many to be the most exploited in the world. Recognizing this, the Communist party and the Young Communist League established itself there in 1925. Through these organizations, Fred Rose and Sam Carr diffused Marxist propaganda. It was not until 1940 that Canadian law forbade the existence of Communist organizations because of their subversive nature. The name of the Communist party was therefore changed to the Labour Progressive party, and Young Communist League to the National Federation of Labour Youth.[1]

In Quebec, the Communist party was the seat of activities directed from Moscow. The Communist Party of Canada was a full member of the Communist International, or Comintern, which was controlled by the Communist party in Moscow. To be a member, the Canadian party had to subscribe to Twenty-One Points that included obeying resolutions of the Moscow executive, rendering every possible assistance to the Soviet Union, and being committed to the overthrow of capitalist states. The party in Canada was committed to the class struggle, dictatorship of the proletariat, and nationalization of the economy. To gain the immediate favour of workers, it sought workers' rights, better working conditions, government relief, and public works to create full employment. Moscow's acceptance was needed for new Canadian officers, national conventions, and the approval of the minutes of meetings.[2]

The party expected obedience and imposed what Dion called "une discipline de fer."[3] In Quebec it had its own summer school to train militant leaders in either French or English. Students were to be fully involved in the revolutionary philosophy of Marx and the historical analysis of labour union history in Canada. In later years, veteran militants, such as Emery Samuel, Evariste Dubé, and Henri Gagnon, who at one time had guided the Ligue d'Action Ouvrière but disagreed with the party, were exposed and condemned by the party's *Combat* magazine. They were touted as enemies of the working class and traitors involved in criminal activity against it.

Beginning with the crash in 1929, the depression brought "a widespread intensification of ideological struggles."[4] On the upswing in a world of overwhelming need, the Communist movement seriously challenged the liberal democracies to demonstrate their ability to cope with the human desperation of the depression. The Communist party and the Young Workers League formed cells to indoctrinate their members in world revolution and to penetrate Quebec society. Cell groups successfully infiltrated the artistic, cultural, and athletic associations of new Canadians. Social organizations that were penetrated with some skill included the United Ukrainian Canadian Association, United Jewish People's Order, Polish Democratic Association, Lithuanian Workers, American Literary Association, Federation of German Canadians, Order of Italian Canadians, Finnish Organization of Canadians, Hungarian Democratic Society, National Council of South Slavs, Slovak Benevolent Society, Federation of Russian Canadians, Carpatho-Russian Society, Lamko Organizations for Ukrainians, Russians and Poles, and the Sons' and Daughters' Association for Lithuanians. The Communist party controlled these gatherings, but the name Communist was never used. The leadership was under Communist direction, but the rank and file were not card-carrying members. The leadership provided language instruction, plays, concerts, and evening entertainments in various languages. The new Canadians and their children were exposed to their own culture – along with Marxist teaching – in the hope that they might one day become party militants.[5] Paul-André Linteau and colleagues assert that "left-wing ideas enjoyed a fairly warm reception among lower-class immigrants in Montreal, especially in the Jewish community," but also among English-speaking intellectuals, upper-class youth, and the middle class.[6]

Those who accepted party membership were to become involved in the Workers' Unity League and the National Unemployed Workers' Association, both founded in 1930.[7] Other militants were to involve themselves in public causes, such as the civil liberties union, the committee for the defence of workers' rights, or the consumers' league. Public demonstrations were part of a broad program of public education to convince the masses that the present economic system had collapsed and must be terminated. In November 1947, fifty-six organizations gathered in Montreal to raise awareness of problems with the current economy – including some Catholic organizations. The Communist leaders who attended were from the intellectual, scientific, and professional classes and well educated. These groups included associations of managers, students, religions, youth, professionals, social service, and labour unions. They had sympathizers among doctors, lawyers, professors, journalists, ministers, and film and radio personalities.[8]

Communist activists targeted labour unions and working conditions. Communists directed the smaller unions and the unorganized workers, and their skills were valued and appreciated. Because of their zeal, Communist workers were designated for leadership positions in their unions and quickly came to the leadership of small unions. By 1947 five unions of the Canadian Labour Congress were run by Communists: automakers, foresters, electricians, furriers, and miners.[9] "Undoubtedly the most serious problem confronting it [the Canadian Congress of Labour] in these early years," according to Irving Abella, "was the strength of the Communists and their supporters."[10] The operations of the Canadian Congress of Labour on the West Coast were almost entirely controlled by Communists.[11] Four unions of the Trades and Labour Congress of Montreal were Communist directed: the merchantman, American textile workers, international chemical workers, and garment workers. Northwestern Quebec was a key area in the battle for control between the left-wing miners and the capitalist owners. This was not true, however, of the large Catholic unions such as the Canadian and Catholic Confederation of Labour, which defended itself successfully against infiltration. The fact was that of the more than one thousand unions in Quebec, only twelve were Communist controlled. Dion believes that these figures were reason to be optimistic about the future of the union movement in Quebec.[12]

The Industrial Council of the Labour Progressive party (Communist party) recommended the formation of industrial clubs in the workplace for the workers and their families. The clubs were to be places of encounter for the members and their fellow workers. Marxist education was always an underlying goal of the clubs so that the workers could be trained for the struggle against monopoly capital. Party members were the vanguard in challenging the industry and winning leadership roles among their fellow workers. Newspapers and journals were important tools of persuasion for the workers in these clubs, bringing Communist influence to bear in every factory. The industrial clubs were supposed to foster regular discussion groups to consider problems in the industry so that the workers would be willing to accept party guidance. In the long view, political issues were more important to the party than economic issues, but the overall goal was the formation of a unified working class to strive for political control and social needs.[13]

The popular appeal of the Communist party in Quebec elections was limited. Four candidates ran for the Labour Progressive party in the provincial election of 1936, garnering a total of 1,045 votes; five candidates in the provincial election of 1944 won a total of 7,873 votes, of which Michael Buhay won 6,457; Guy Caron, the only candidate in the election of 1948, polled 4,648 votes. In the federal elections of 1930, 1935, 1943, 1945, and 1949 candidates were entered, but only in the two wartime elections was a Communist, Fred Rose, elected, winning respectively 5,784 and 10,414 votes. Most of the names entered in the election were French or English. In their rejection we can see that Quebec's romance with Communist candidates was short-lived.[14]

The Communists determined to exploit such contentious issues as unemployment, conscription, imperialist wars, anti-union sentiment, inadequate housing, and high prices. For its own purpose the party also employed papal teachings pleading for social justice in society.

The leadership emphasized that, in addressing the needs of the working people and rejecting world fascism, the goals of Christianity and communism were similar. The Communist party directed social workers to embrace the same goals as church workers in defending the oppressed and in the call for justice.[15]

To halt the spread of organized labour in Quebec, the government of Maurice Duplessis passed restrictive labour legislation in 1937, which subjected labour unions to methodical repression. The "padlock law" enabled the attorney general to close locations used for distributing Communist literature. The church, in contrast, took a more inspirational approach by establishing labour schools, founding Catholic unions, and engaging with the needs of the working people. The church emphasized Catholic action, which involved its members in the cooperative movement and adult education with the goal of attaining social justice.[16]

In general, as we have seen, the Communist party in Quebec sought out an élite of intellectuals and workers and "never gained more than a few hundred members and sympathizers," and none outside Montreal.[17] The Communist leadership, well trained at specialized schools, inculcated a strong sense of party goals and party discipline. The Communists were masterly in relating to the needs of the workers and manipulating the media to its purposes. The leadership was focused and persistent, but the Cold War dashed hopes of further expansion. The Communist fortunes in Quebec went into decline after the war and never recovered. Along with governmental repression and cultural incompatibility, the principal reason for the waning of communism, according to Dion and Linteau, was the staunch religious faith of the people of Quebec.[18]

COMMUNISM IN ENGLISH CANADA

The Communist Party of Canada opened its first office at Guelph in 1921. Its membership accepted the twenty-one conditions necessary for admission to the Comintern. This meant acquiescing in Soviet direction of policies of mass-action and revolutionary disruption and preparing for the coming dictatorship of the proletariat. As Russian general W.G. Krivitsky had stated in 1939: "The Communist Parties are nothing more than branch offices of the Russian Communist Party."[19] As noted earlier, Canadian government vigilance made it necessary for the Communist party to change its name a number of times: from 1922 to 1924, it was called the Workers' party; from then until 1943, it used its official title as the Communist party of Canada; after that it was known as the Labour Progressive party.[20]

Quoting from party documents of 1929, Watson Kirkconnell reveals that "although the overwhelming majority of the population is made up of Canadian and French-Canadian workers, 95 per cent of the Party membership is confined to three language groups – Finnish, Ukrainian, and Jewish."[21] His point was that while most native-born Canadians showed little interest in joining the Communist party, eastern Europeans proved to be the most fertile group for recruitment in Canada. Foreign-language federations and their language presses were the access points for Communist recruitment. These federations, thinly disguised as cultural, educational, and athletic organizations, supplied the bulk of Canadian members. The organizations mobilized members and disseminated information to workers to recruit others for the struggle against capitalism and imperialism. Along with the federations, Communist front organizations were also thrown into the fray to espouse public causes, attract members, and communicate Soviet propaganda. One such front organization was the National Council for Canadian-Soviet Friendship, which was initiated in 1943.[22]

It was the custom of the Canadian Communist party to convene annually to mobilize its resources in obedience to the latest directives from Moscow. These directives included assessing the party's performance during the year and assigning tasks for the next year. Cell groups attending the meeting represented a cross-section of Canadian society. They would study the directives and determine discussion topics, which included recruiting, agitation, and espionage. The central committee and secretariat in Toronto directed twelve districts, which in turn guided the cell groups. Members were not to move from one city to another without permission from the party. The National Federation of Labour Youth was also a prominent part of the Communist network.[23] But the primary level of expansion in the early 1930s was the recruitment of labour unions into the Communist-directed Workers' Unity League. After 1935 the policy changed from the recruitment of unions to the infiltration of non-Communist unions. The Canadian Seamen's Union (an American Federation of Labor affiliate) and the United Electrical Workers (a Congress of Industrial Organizations affiliate) were successfully infiltrated and made over into Communist-controlled unions.[24]

The archbishops of Toronto, Neil McNeil and his successor James C. McGuigan, were alert to the determination of the Communist leadership and their successes in Ontario. As we have seen, McNeil encouraged Catherine de Hueck to open Friendship House in downtown Toronto to care for the needy and invited Henry Somerville to return from England to edit the *Catholic Register* and to educate Toronto Catholics in social thought. When he was archbishop of Regina, McGuigan guided the publication of *A Joint Pastoral Letter*, which addressed "the abuses of materialistic capitalism" and called for "a reconstructed social order based on Christian principles." He went on to articulate Catholic thinking and denounce communism as "the avowed enemy of God" and "the gravest menace facing human society today." He urged that study groups be formed to examine *Rerum Novarum* and *Quadragesimo Anno* and to promote their principles throughout the land.[25]

After McNeil's death, McGuigan moved to Toronto and extended his concern for the propagation of Catholic social thought. Father Joseph O'Neill records that after McGuigan took his new position in Toronto he discovered a report on communism that his predecessor had received from the chief of police. It named the labour unions in which Communists were making headway and identified Communist front organizations in the city. In a dispassionate and logical manner Somerville assessed the Communist threat in Toronto for the new archbishop. A year later McGuigan published a pastoral letter warning Catholics that "the virus of Communism is being spread in our midst" and exhorted them to work "for a more equitable Christian Social order." If parishioners were not energetic in responding to the "plight of the working class," he warned, Torontonians might provoke a catastrophe similar to Spain where workers in their "antagonism to religion have burned down churches and murdered hundreds of clergy."[26]

McGuigan launched a program of Catholic Action in the Toronto archdiocese. He listed a number of Catholic organizations under the title of Catholic Action, and among the organizations was the Holy Name Society. The society, a contemporary Catholic men's organization, renewed a medieval devotion to the Holy Name, which Monsignor John Hand in 1903 established at Toronto's oldest parish, St Paul's. By honouring the Holy Name, this men's organization spread quickly to other parishes throughout the diocese. In 1936 McGuigan appointed the energetic Father Thomas Manley as director of Holy Name Union. A Communist candidate at this same time in Toronto won 31,000 votes which shocked the new director. Manley feared that the disaster of the Spanish Civil War could happen in Canada if something was not done about the spread of communism. The Holy Name Society, by affirming Catholics in their faith, would become "a bulwark against Communism." The Society appealed to working-class membership, and "the bulk of its members are of the working class." For him the Holy Name Society was a natural fit to draw Catholic workers away from communism and to lure other workers away from Communist temptation. Archbishop McGuigan, knowing the Holy See was "terribly afraid of Communism," appreciated Manley's zeal.[27]

A high point of the year for the Holy Name Society was the annual demonstration and convention held in Toronto in the middle of June. From 1920s through the 1930s, about twenty-five thousand people would march with a dozen bands from Queen's Park to De La Salle Oaklands on Avenue Road. Thirty thousand people filled the Oaklands grounds in 1937 for the Mass and rally. The speakers rejoiced in the freedom of a country that allowed peaceful demonstrations and condemned Communist countries for prohibiting such gatherings. Archbishop McGuigan avoided political references but urged young people to contribute to "the regeneration of Christian forces and to the upbuilding of the highest ideals of true patriotism." McGuigan's favourite themes called for renewal of the Christian education of youth, study groups for adults on social teachings, and above all, Catholic loyalty to Canada.[28]

In his *Social Message of the Church* published in 1939, McGuigan stressed the "rights of workers," the importance of study clubs, Catholic labour school, and credit unions. A provincewide convention of the Holy Name Society in June of the same year assembled at the Royal York in Toronto. Manley saw it as a rally to strengthen the faith of Catholics at home and in the workplace and to check the spread of communism. McGuigan in a more positive manner saw it as a vehicle to send out a renewed body of faithful to promote a Christian social order. The Holy Name gathering began on Friday night at St Michael's Cathedral with a pontifical High Mass wherein the archbishop called for the Christian education of the youth and the "reconstruction of the social order." On Saturday there were study clubs, instruction on the cooperative movement and social justice, and personal and public renewals. Then on Sunday, forty thousand people marched from Queen's Park to Varsity Stadium and participated in the concluding exercises. Those attending took the Holy Name pledge for personal renewal, which bolstered their resolve to implement Catholic social thought.[29]

To implement social justice on the parish level, the Confraternity of Christian Doctrine and the Holy Name Society agreed to sponsor discussion groups on the social teachings. The CCD arranged mixed groups that went well and continued on for several years. In contrast, the Holy Name all-male discussion groups stalled after a short time. A Speaker's Bureau was then fielded to provide specialists to talk in parishes on the social teachings, but this effort also collapsed. A program that was well received by parishioners was the initiation of parish credit unions. Parish credit unions were popular and mushroomed quickly and, Father Joseph O'Neill concludes, endured well down through the years.[30]

With the encouragement of the archbishop, two Jesuits rose up in Toronto to meet the crisis and confront communism through lectures and the opening of a labour school. In 1930 Father Joseph Keating founded a lecture series called the White Front (as opposed to the Red Front), which continued for eighteen years. The lectures were held weekly in the fall and spring at the Jesuit Seminary in downtown Toronto for about thirty business and professional people from various faiths. In 1950 Father Charles McGuire founded the Toronto Catholic Labour School and convened sessions fall and spring until 1970. Representatives of labour, government, management, and clergy were recruited to teach Catholic social thought and to foster cooperation between labour and management.[31] The Communist menace over twenty-five years challenged the faith of Catholics, but the church responded positively by educating the youth, forming adult study groups, and setting up cooperative organizations.[32]

A Catholic force of determination and inspiration met the Canadian Communist force of like persistence. Canadian Catholics geared up for the twilight struggle with the Communist threat by stressing education and renewed spirituality. The Canadian government exercised its legal right to check subversion and purge trade union membership of Communists. Eight party leaders, Buck, Ewan, Boychuk, Popovich, Carr, Hill, Bruce, and Cacic, were convicted in 1931 of plotting the destruction of the Canadian state and were sent to Portsmouth Penitentiary as treasonous enemy agents. During the phoney war in Europe from 1939 to 1941, the Canadian government declared the Communist Party of Canada illegal, and one hundred and thirty-three leaders of the organization were incarcerated in detention camp. Igor Gouzenko's postwar revelations demonstrated that Soviet spies in Canada were recruited from the Communist party. After a round up of agents, national organizer Sam Carr became a fugitive from Canadian justice, and Fred Rose was incarcerated as a Soviet agent. The Canadian Congress of Labour expelled three of its major left-wing unions after the war.[33] The Communist party was a danger to the Canadian parliamentary system during the 1930s and 1940s, a threat that was creatively dealt with by the Canadian government and, to a lesser degree, by the Catholic clergy and laity.[34]

ITALIAN FASCISM IN TORONTO

During the 1930s in Toronto an informal alliance was struck, according to Luigi Pennacchio, between Canadian Catholicism and Italian fascism to pursue mutually acceptable goals. Both the Holy See and the archdiocese of Toronto were preoccupied with the threat of communism and failed to recognize the less-noxious danger of the friendly fascists. In 1929 the Vatican and the Italian government signed the

Lateran Accords at Rome and extended to each other diplomatic recognition after sixty years of numbing silence. To follow up on this *rapprochement*, King Victor Emmanuel III and Queen Elena visited Pope
Pius XI at Vatican City on 5 December 1929. Reconciliation, which was
prayed for, seemed to be achieved between Pope Pius XI, as leader of
the Catholic church, and Benito Mussolini, as the leader of the Italian
government.[35]

In Toronto, on the same day that the king came calling on the pope
in Rome, the Italian vice-consul, *Cavaliere* Giovanni Ambrosi, visited
Archbishop Neil McNeil. Toronto Italians at this time, as John Zucchi
points out, suffered from an inferiority complex, nostalgic nationalism, and fear for family solidarity – which made them susceptible to information from home.[36] The leading Fascists in the Italian community
made piecemeal arrangements with the clergy in Italian parishes to
combine efforts among fellow Italians to strengthen Catholicism and
Italian culture. Fascist leaders would be allowed to use classrooms in
churches and separate schools to operate *la Scuola Italiana* for the
teaching of the Italian language and Italian nationalism. With the
opening of after-school classes at St Patrick's, St Francis's, St Clem-
ent's, St Paul's, and St Mary's schools, the loss of young Italians to Irish
Catholicism could be halted. The priests would evangelize Italian families, encourage them to attend weekly Mass, and exhort them to perform their regular religious practices.[37] The Fascists and church
leaders in Toronto thus tied Italian nationalism to Italian Catholicism
just as l'abbé Lionel Groulx in Quebec had tied Canadien Catholicism
to Canadien nationalism. First McNeil and then McGuigan, in anti-
Communist moods, accepted this informal alliance between the Toronto church and fascist representatives. In Rome Mussolini had
dreams of world imperial influence and saw Italian Catholics as vehicles for Italian power.[38]

The Italian parishes in Toronto were Our Lady of Mount Carmel,
St Agnes, and St Mary of the Angels. These parishes accepted fascist
delegations and permitted them to influence parish life. Italian priests
Father Peter Truffa of St Agnes Church and Father Settimio Balo of
St Mary of the Angels Church sincerely believed that fascism, by renew-
ing Italian religion and culture, would help to make their parishioners
better Italians and better Catholics. The leakage of Italians to Irish
Catholicism or to Protestant evangelism could thus be staunched.
Some Italian Canadian priests, excited by the promotion of Italian na-
tionalism, helped raise money in 1937 for Italy's colonial adventure in
Ethiopia.[39]

Archbishop McNeil saw the need to assist new Italian immigrants as
they adjusted to Canadian ways. He actively sought priests and sisters

to care for their material needs and to evangelize them. He recruited the Carmelite Sisters of the Divine Heart of Jesus to visit Italian Canadians and "to dispense religious memorabilia and artifacts and to stress to the Italians the importance of baptism and the absolution of sins in the confessional."[40] He sought out St Elizabeth Visiting Nurses to take care of their medical needs. The St Vincent de Paul Society, which had been well established in the archdiocese since the years of Bishop Armand Charbonnel, brought them food, clothing, furniture, and other necessities. McNeil had hoped to entice Italians to embrace the religious practices of the Canadian church and to send their children to the separate schools where they would be Canadianized. He hoped that they would learn English and adopt the devotions of the Toronto church. Few cultural concessions were considered necessary for Italian needs.[44]

In the midst of this cultural stalemate between the established Canadian church and the demands of Italian Catholics, the Italian vice-consul stepped forward and offered a comprehensive solution. The Italian government would support the dissemination of Italian culture in language schools for Italian children and provide funds for adult athletic clubs. He sought and received the support of some of the business leaders of the Italian community. The theme of many events was *Dio e Patria*.[42] Italian officials saw the Catholic parishes as "capable of uniting and nourishing the Catholic and Italian spirit" in the new Canadians. Fascist consular officials were especially wary of Protestant overtures to Italians because Protestant churches often presented themselves as a refuge for anti-Fascists. To attract Italians to Protestantism, the Orange Lodge in 1930 founded the Giuseppi Garibaldi branch. Italians against fascism often provided information about Fascist activities to members of the CCF for debate in Parliament. This caused considerable embarrassment to Fascist party members.[43]

A war of words erupted between the pro-United Church/CCF coalition and the Fascist faction in the struggle to control the loyalty of the Italian community. Archbishop McNeil ignored the issue of Fascist collaboration, preferring to concentrate his energies on checking the spread of communism. The apostolic delegate to Canada, Monsignor A. Cassulo, along with Pius XI, saw atheistic communism as the long-term enemy of Catholicism. Cassulo conveniently overlooked the fact that in Italy since 1931 Fascists had attacked church property, Christian education, and Catholic youth organizations. McNeil, avoiding internecine controversies within Italian parishes, turned over Italian parishes to religious congregations – the Redemptorists, Salesians, and Franciscans – who could bring in Italian clergy to deal with cultural problems in a comprehensible manner.[44]

Archbishop James McGuigan, fearing to give offence to German or Italian Catholics, felt it was necessary to explain away Catholic protest demonstrations against fascism during June 1938 and apologized for these demonstrations. He ignored stories in the *Catholic Register* about the Nazi persecution of Catholics in Germany and Austria, and the Fascist oppression of Catholic youth organizations in Italy.[45]

In the spring of 1939, Archbishop McGuigan was forced to investigate Fascist activities in Catholic schools and churches. Over four hundred children had been enrolled in a network of Italian language classes conducted in parish halls and school buildings. The Italian government funded the textbooks and other expenses of the classes. The children were taught Italian language, culture, geography, and history, all of which were presented through the glossy veneer of national fascism. The children were taught to think of themselves as Italian citizens, members of the Italian Empire, and willing to fight for fascism. In the spring of 1939 war clouds loomed heavy over Europe and presaged a conflict between the Fascist powers and the western democracies.[46]

In March 1939 the Catholic Separate School Board asked the City of Toronto to end Communist instruction in the public schools. The Communists struck back by demanding that the Separate School Board end Fascist instruction in Catholic schools. The Italian consul suddenly withdrew financial support for Italian classes from separate schools and Catholic churches.[47] The issue died down with a sigh of relief by the principals. When the Italian Fascists declared war on the western allies in May 1940, Italy and Canada were automatically at war against each other. The Canadian authorities immediately declared fascist activities illegal and imprisoned over two hundred Italian businessmen who had been associated with such activities.[48] Fascism in Canada was dead, concludes Pennacchio, and the dangerous alliance between Toronto Catholicism and Italian fascism was permanently terminated.[49]

Italian immigrants arriving in Toronto needed the affirmation of a familiar culture amidst the religious and social upheaval they were undergoing. To have those needs mitigated, the new Canadians turned to the Catholic Church. The church in response allowed itself to fall into an informal alliance with the Italian Fascists, who for their own purposes hoped to meet the needs of the new Italian Canadians. The Fascists reinforced Italian culture in a church fashioned by Irish Catholicism. The informal alliance in the 1930s between the Catholic church and the Italian Fascists met the needs of Italian Catholics for language instruction and social gatherings, but it had to be suspended abruptly with the outbreak of the Second World War. The sheer number of Italian immigrants challenged the Ontario church to broaden its cultural base and become more catholic.

THE SPANISH CIVIL WAR AND THE
ENGLISH-LANGUAGE PRESS

During the Spanish Civil War (1936–39), Catholic newspapers traditionally sided with the Nationalists. Art Cawley describes the division
created in the western world by the Spanish war: "Ideology tran-
scended geographic boundaries and people of various religious and
social groupings tended to identify with their Spanish counterparts despite real differences." Catholics in the western world associated with
the persecuted Catholics in Spain, and republicans around the world
associated with comrades trying to break the bonds of the church-state
alliance oppressing them. The Fascists of Europe came to the aid of
the Nationalists, the Communists and secularists to the aid of the Republicans. The Catholic press in Canada laboured mightily to check
Republican propaganda and convince Canadians of the righteousness
of the Nationalist cause.[50]

The English-language Catholic press during the Spanish Civil War
consisted of ten diocesan newspapers, three monthlies, and one bi-
monthly.[51] The combined circulation of 130,000 served a population
of one million English-speaking Catholics. Cawley concludes from
these numbers that only the clergy and lay élites were influenced by
these Catholic publications and that, in fact, the majority of Catholics
had little concern for foreign issues. Reportage on the Spanish Civil
War was reprinted from foreign newspapers and journals, especially
from the United States, and thus had an American hue. The activities
of the American bishops might receive more coverage in Canadian
newspapers than the statements of Cardinal Villeneuve, the primate in
Quebec. The fear of communism and socialism dominated the newspapers more than the fear of fascism. Fascism for its part tolerated religion and did not see it as an unsolvable problem. Fascism was looked
upon less harshly by Catholics as merely reactive to worldwide Communist subversion.[52] This attitude proved to be correct as fascism in two
decades had waxed and waned, but communism proved to have staying power, lasting five decades longer, and was the more virulent threat
to the western world.

The sanguine attitude of the Catholic press to both sides at the outbreak of the Spanish Civil War changed quickly when thousands of
Spanish clergy were murdered and hundreds of churches destroyed.[53]
The editorial tone shifted to reporting the life-and-death struggle between opposing forces, "a war between Christian civilization and Red
barbarism."[54] Pius XI, in his encyclical *Divini Redemptoris,* responded to
the disaster of the Catholics in Spain. He acknowledged the destruction with great sympathy and wrote, "Every church, every religious

house, every trace of the Christian civilization has been beaten to the ground ... the hatred, the barbarity, the unbridled violence with which this horrible butchery is being carried out are such as to be hardly credible in our age."[55] What was not recognized was that the Church, in identifying with the monarchy and the aristocracy, had failed to serve the Spanish people and in fact had abdicated its social mission among the common people. In anger over their abandonment, the people turned against the élites and against the church.

In North America English-speaking popular opinion stood clearly in favour of the Republicans. The Catholic press was under terrific pressure to explain Catholic sympathy for the Nationalists. Catholic publications contended that the civil war was fought to defeat communism. Catholics supported General Francisco Franco's Falangist party, the Catholic news reported, because it was the better of the two forces for Catholics. Further, the Catholic press wrote off the Republican forces as ignorant of the real nature of the conflict and dismissed the secular liberals as anti-Catholic. Toronto Catholics were told that Franco was "a man of destiny" who could take the play away from the Communists. As a foreign correspondent, Catherine de Hueck reported in *The Sign* that "Franco is our general. We also want a new Spain." His forces were lionized in the Catholic press as bringing food and medical assistance to the starving populations. The conflict was described as a life-and-death struggle between the forces of atheistic communism and Catholic Christianity.[56]

Catholics in general lacked interest in the conflict, but dissent emerged among Catholics élites. The new journal *Social Forum*, published in Ottawa, was sceptical about Franco's leadership and admitted it was "hesitant to give the Fascist rebels the Crusader's Cross" when its revolt was "financed by the wealthy landowners and industrialists who saw their economic dictatorship threatened." The journal explained that "the Church of Spain has become identified with reaction and the worker has turned for leadership to the bitterest enemies of the faith."[57]

A second dissenting voice was that of the English convert C.J. Eustace, who published articles in the *Catholic Record* (London) and the *Commonweal* magazine (New York). Like the philosopher Jacques Maritain, Eustace was reluctant to identify the church with Franco and found no justification for Nationalist reprisals. Yet dissent from the Nationalist cause in English Canada was not easily tolerated among Catholics.[58]

Pro-Nationalist Catholic newspapers entered into pitched battles with Republican secular newspapers. The *Beacon* (Montreal) disputed with the Montreal *Star*, the *Catholic Register* with the *Toronto Star*, the *North-west Review* (Winnipeg) with the Winnipeg *Free Press*, and the *Brit-*

ish Columbia Catholic (Vancouver) with the Vancouver *Province.* In one of these disputes, the *Catholic Register* forced the *Toronto Star* to back down. Editor Henry Somerville disputed the verity of writer Van Paassen's supposedly eye-witness dispatches on the civil war to the *Star.* Somerville accused the reporter of having fabricated Nationalist atrocities to sway Canadians to Republican sympathies. The owner of the *Star,* impressed by Somerville's accusations, went to Paris to investigate and dismissed the delinquent reporter on the spot for false reportage. Protestant papers for the most part remained neutral in the conflict.[59]

The Mackenzie-Papineau Battalion was deplored by the Catholic press as "Canadian dupes in the Communist International Army." They were "fighting for Moscow ... fighting for Communism." The *Catholic Register* raised the question whether the partisans of international revolution in Spain should be readmitted to promote class warfare and civil revolution under the guidance of the Communist party. Catholic newspapers called for government investigation of the Mackenzie-Papineau Battalion's legal right to recruit, finance, and transport volunteers to disrupt a friendly state.[60]

To the North American secular eye, the Spanish Civil War appeared to be a fight between the Republicans who represented liberal democracy and the Nationalists who represented totalitarian fascism. To the Catholic press the war was seen as Christian civilization defending itself against atheistic communism. In fact, as Cawley insightfully concludes, the Spanish war really was an internal conflict, "the culmination of an historical process of truly domestic nature and proportions, the ultimate clash between the forces of progress and tradition within Spanish society. The War was not imported from abroad and had little to do with either Communism or fascism."[61]

The Canadian clergy and press defended the Nationalists as they would the Spanish church. What they failed to realize was that the Spanish church, through its close association with the monarchy and the wealthy of Spain, alienated itself from the masses.[62] As the Canadian church had ministered to the needy and was identified with the ordinary people, the Spanish church showed most concern for the upper class and lost touch with the Spanish people. It thus set itself up as a target of the revolutionary forces. The massacre of Catholic religious and clergy at the outbreak of the civil war forced Catholics in Spain and most other countries to sympathize with the Nationalists. Cawley points out that the tightly controlled Canadian Catholic press had little circulation beyond the clergy, and the lay élite had little influence with Catholics at large.

It must be admitted that there was no official Catholic policy on the Spanish Civil War. The Canadian church during the 1930s did not convene annual meetings; hence Catholic bishops had no joint policy on the issue. The bishops did not discuss ecclesial problems and form a united policy on the Spanish Civil War, the CCF, and other issues. Despite the pro-Nationalist attitude of Catholic publications and hierarchy, numerous North American Catholic workers identified with their Spanish comrades who supported the Republicans. Canadian Catholics, like most other Canadians, were isolationist at the end of the 1930s and foreign intervention was far from their minds. Although sympathetic to the Nationalists, Catholics had made little effort to advocate their cause.[63]

VICHY IN QUEBEC

If Catholics in general were less receptive to communism for religious reasons and more sympathetic to fascism for cultural reasons, the Québécois were definitely sympathetic for cultural and religious reasons to the apparent success of fascism in France. The German blitzkrieg on the western front in June 1940 and the consequent collapse of Western Europe left France, Belgium, Holland, and Denmark under the heel of German occupation. Hitler occupied Paris, northern France, and the Atlantic ports and, in the South, set up a collaborationist government under the hero of World War I, Marshall Pétain. As the French nation was convulsed in its defeat by the Nazis, the shock and humiliation rippled outward to penetrate francophones around the world. Those who gloried in French military prowess from the time of Francis I, Louis XIV, and Napoleon to the recent victory over German imperialism in the Great War were pained and shamed by the breakdown of French leadership. Among those who shared the pain were the Québécois, who were shocked by the fear that a wall of isolation would now shut them off from their cultural roots. The vagaries of the Second World War threw them into unwanted proximity with the English in the imperial struggle.[64]

In attitude most Québécois, Paul Couture explains, were either isolationist, regionalist, or totally unconcerned with the cataclysm enveloping the world. Those who perceived the tragedy unfolding divided themselves into the majority group who were sympathetic to Vichy and supported the government of Marshall Pétain, and the minority group who backed General Charles de Gaulle and the Free French.[65]

When the Third Republic collapsed from the weight of its secular decadence, Québécois hoped that the Vichy government would restore France to its grandeur and its religious roots. Widespread sympathy for the government of Marshall Pétain dominated Quebec through these years. Canada, the United States, and the Holy See were among the thirty-three national states that had recognized the new Vichy government. Pétain promised a renewal of traditional authority according to corporatist and professional structures and a *restauration* of the French state as recommended by the teachings of Pius XI. The clerical-nationalists in Quebec saw Pétain liberating France from the excesses of secular democracy, restoring religious education in the schools, and accepting church guidance on affairs of state. He promised "Travail, Famille, Patrie," and it was believed he was pursuing a concordat with the Holy See. The clerical-nationalists in Quebec perceived Pétain's government as a "dynamic new force, predicated upon Catholic orthodoxy, striving to discipline the national energies of a nation which had forgotten her providential mission as the *fille aînée de l'Eglise.*"[66]

The Jesuits of the École sociale populaire and their monthly publication *Relations* accepted the new Vichy government. Cardinal Villeneuve and the editors of *L'Action catholique,* giving guarded support to Pétainists, condemned the underlying Nazi ideology and pointed out that the Allies were fighting for the survival of Christianity. The lower clergy remained sympathetic to the promised restoration of Catholic and traditional values in France and extended their favourable perceptions of the Vichy leadership to the Quebec faithful.[67]

Québécois nationalists and *Le Devoir* commented favourably on Vichy France and at the same time proposed Canadian isolationism and encouraged anti-British attitudes. Editorials expressed positive admiration for the inspiration of right-wing French intellectual Charles Maurras and the support of the right-wing organization L'Action française for Vichy: "le meilleur gouvernement que la France ait jamais eu" (the best government France has ever had). The Vichy leadership, it was believed, was carrying out a national revolution to unite the Latin bloc of France, Spain, Italy, and Quebec in a new order. This new alliance offered to the lonely and isolated Québécois the hope of union with other Christian nations. *Le Devoir* was shocked to see France's former ally, Great Britain, engaged in an imperialistic war against France. The British in July 1940 demonstrated their hostility to France when they sank the French fleet at Mers-el-Kébir and later attacked French colonies. Canada, the Quebec newspaper believed, should ignore British imperialism and remain neutral. The Vichy consuls in Montreal and Quebec City supplied pro-Vichy newspapers to the anti-conscription Quebec nationalists and *Le Devoir.*[68]

The French-language Canadian Broadcasting Corporation showed the Pétain government similar consideration. By contrast, French CBC and *Le Devoir* did not treat the Free French of de Gaulle with similar fairness. The CBC discovered it was unable to dismiss the French CBC head because, as the highest ranking francophone civil servant, his firing would have been tantamount to an attack on the Québécois. Many of the anti-conscriptionists at CBC resented the pro-British attitudes of English Canadians and continued to welcome the propaganda of Vichy France.[69]

When compared with Marshall Pétain, who had been a hero in the First World War, Charles de Gaulle was unknown. The Gaullists were looked upon as political opportunists who deserted France at its collapse to go to the safety of Britain. They were thought to be French-speaking tools of British imperialism, with their self-serving pro-British and anti-French propaganda. The Gaullists failed to offer the vision of Pétain's *restauration*. Pétain promised a corporatist state fashioned according to the spiritual vision of *Quadragesimo Anno* and the hope of a new world order uniting the Latin bloc. Gaullism by comparison was thought to be prosaic and motivated mainly by British racism.[70]

Well-informed Vichy propagandists stressed the close ties between France and Canada. In their broadcasts they described the legal existence of the new government, its autonomy in Europe, its popularity, and how it had overcome the degeneracy of the Third Republic, which had been infiltrated by bolsheviks and Jews. A number of Catholics in France and in Quebec chose to see Jews as devious money lenders who posed a threat to French identity and thus determined to avoid doing business with them.[71] Not everyone, however, perceived Jews in this manner. The Canadian ambassador to France, General Georges Vanier, wrote to Ottawa that Canada had a "wonderful opportunity" to be generous and at the same time benefit from Jewish immigration.[72] The Mackenzie King government remained closed to Vanier's suggestion and later to his efforts to bring Jewish children to Canada.[73]

Vichy emphasized the values of national revolution including religion, family, work, and education. It warmly sympathized with the French Canadians who remained subject to British rule and under the gun on the issue of conscription. The Vichy propagandists succeeded, Couture contends, in giving "official sanction from the French government" to the core attitude of the Québécois – that they were an exploited minority under British imperialism.[74] The Vichy propagandists gained the attention of the Québécois intellectuals and lower clergy and succeeded in restoring the bond of sympathy lost between French Canada and France following the British Conquest. The majority of Québécois were not inspired by either the Communists or the Fascists, but of the two ideologies, we have seen that the latter received the warmer response among the intellectuals and the professional classes.

CONCLUSION

The Communists gained little headway in Quebec with their culturally foreign ideology, but they did attract new Canadians, middle-class youths, and a number of working people. Manifesting considerable effort and skill, the Communist leadership gained control of a number of Canadian unions across Canada and fielded a number of socio-political organizations in the principal urban centres. In response, the Quebec church founded Catholic labour unions to seek worker benefits and family wages within the frame of social harmony and Christian respect for all classes. The Canadian church stressed the need for labour schools to educate the workers and lay involvement in social justice. Communism made few inroads among the Canadian Catholics.

The Fascists demonstrated that among Canadian Catholics they were more successful than the Communists and less dangerous. Canadian Catholics by way of culture and religion proved to be more susceptible to Italian, Spanish, and French fascism than to Russian communism. During the 1930s fascism was taught, along with Italian language and history, in Catholic facilities in Toronto, but this involvement was limited to one ethnic community. During the Spanish Civil War, the hierarchy and Catholic press sided with Franco's Nationalists against the Republicans. During the Second World War Quebec culture showed itself susceptible to Vichy propaganda, but the Canadian hierarchy resisted fraternization with Vichy sympathizers. The Catholic hierarchy and newspapers showed sympathy for the struggle of the Spanish Nationalists, the Toronto Italians learned fascism along with Italian culture, and the Quebec élites espoused the Vichy ideals for a time, but the Canadian Catholic community never embraced fascism. The spirit of fascism was peripheral to the lives of Canadian Catholics. Catholics formed no volunteer brigades or papal zouaves, nor did they send aid and medical supplies to Italy, Spain, or France.

12 Quebecization of Catholicism

The bifurcation of the Canadian church widened during the First World War and continued through the depression and the Second World War. French-speaking Catholics were threatened by the war, conscription, and the expansion of federal power. English-speaking Catholics, travelling in the opposite direction, rallied fully behind the federal government in the war effort and committed their resources to the policy of mobilization. The Canadian church with great difficulty managed to steer a middle course between support for voluntary recruitment and the flat-out support for total war.[1] Church leaders straddled the different feelings of ethnic Catholics – French, English, Irish, German, Italian, Ukrainian, Polish, and Hungarian.

Like a dark cloud hanging over society, the threat of conscription returned to Quebec in 1939 with the outbreak of the European war. The Bloc Populaire Canadien, in fear of Canadian mobilization, promoted neo-nationalism, provincial autonomy, and the secularization of the social network. The outbreak of the postwar labour disputes permanently shattered the harmony of the church and state in Quebec. Canadian labour unions felt free to express their disagreement with wages and working conditions. In 1949 the asbestos strike rocked the province of Quebec and demanded the Catholic church support the workers.

CONSCRIPTION

The contentious issue of national conscription arose for a second time in the first half of the century with the beginning of the Second World

War. The question rooted in the First World War remained fresh in the minds of clergy and Canadiens. In September 1914 Archbishop Paul Bruchési of Montreal had rallied the Quebec episcopacy to publish a collective letter asking the Québécois to be loyal to the British Crown and show commitment to the Canadian nation. The Catholic press echoed the bishops' letter and took it as an attitude of most Canadiens. Quebec Catholics for a time sympathized with Canada's participation in England's struggle.[2]

Yet the Quebec consensus, which the bishop's letter represented, was fragile. Canadiens did not feel obliged to offer more than lip service to the Borden government, which, they felt, hardly represented them. They remained dismayed by Ontario's mean-spirited Regulation 17 (1912), which had shut down bilingual education in that province. The nomination of an English Protestant as the chief recruiting officer in Quebec was taken as a harbinger that the war would be used as a strategy to assimilate Canadiens. The Quebec nationalists were strongly opposed to an open-ended Canadian commitment to the war effort. Henri Bourassa rightly judged that the bishops' letter did not define Catholic doctrine and thus did not bind Canadiens to serve. The bishops of Rimouski and Chicoutimi saw no moral obligation to support the English war, and many thought Canadian bishops were too subservient to the government.[3]

In 1917 the government had created the Commission of National Service to register men for possible service and asked Bruchési to ensure church cooperation. He tried to rally the clergy, but the reaction was mixed. During the summer, the government, without public consultation, passed a bill allowing for military conscription. Always against conscription, Bruchési now felt misled and betrayed. In future the Quebec episcopate would distance themselves from the government and indicated that the war was merely a question of charitable assistance and conscription not one of moral obligation. The bishops still had to negotiate an exemption from conscription for seminarians, religious, and clergy, and in the long run they had to be mindful that Rome, London, Ottawa, and Toronto[4] favoured harmony among the different factions in Canada. Tensions eased temporarily in late autumn of 1918 with the end of the war.[5] Martin Robin summed up the catastrophic effect of conscription on Canadiens: "The Borden régime sought to maximize Canada's war effort through massive compulsory mobilization. The price it paid was the alienation of an increasingly articulate labour leadership in English-speaking Canada as well as the uniform loss of Quebec support."[6]

With the advent of the Second World War in 1939, the Canadien fear of compulsory conscription intensified. The Québécois placed their trust in the hands of the senior minister of Justice, Ernest Lapointe, who restrained the hawkish instincts of Mackenzie King, who wanted to enter immediately into the war on the side of Britain. As long as Lapointe was King's lieutenant for Quebec, the Canadiens knew that their views were represented fairly in the government.

In the summer of 1940 the Commons passed the National Resources Mobilization Act, which allowed the government to assess Canadian resources and labour, and the drama heated up. Only after the Québécois defeated the Union Nationale, elected the Godbout Liberals in Quebec, and endured the shock of the collapse of the French Republic before the German armies was it possible to table such legislation. Yet confidence in the Liberal government collapsed following the death of Lapointe in November 1941.[7] King no longer had a Québécois lieutenant of stature to advise him on Quebec matters and to restrain his Canadian patriotism.

The demand for petrochemicals, steel, aircraft, motor vehicles, and high technology intensified Canadian industrialization and stimulated the Quebec economy. At the same time, the stable society of the 1930s became fluid with internal migration in the early 1940s as Canadians pursued jobs, prosperity, and military service. Social disruption afforded adults new freedoms of work and travel, and the shadow of conscription menaced Canadiens in their new-found prosperity. The attack on Pearl Harbour in December 1941 and the capture of two battalions of Canadian troops at Hong Kong put great pressure on the Canadian government of Mackenzie King to legislate conscription for overseas duty.[8]

In 1942 the government held a referendum asking the people to release it from its promise not to institute conscription. In the ensuing public debate racial antagonisms surfaced in Canadian newspapers. The results of the vote were predictable in that over eighty percent of Canadians voted for conscription while the same percentage of Canadiens voted against it. To Canadiens, the threat of cultural and linguistic assimilation loomed large behind conscription and the centralizing preparations for war.[9]

The Quebec bishops discovered that they and their parishioners were caught between the Canadian government's desire to wage total war and Quebec's resistance to the idea of fighting English foreign wars. The episcopacy, to avoid the entrapment from which Bruchési suffered from the Borden government in 1917, stressed traditional Catholic teachings of submission to valid authority and the moral obligation to free oppressed nations. Their intention was to provide spiritual leadership, without justifying the decisions of politicians. They scheduled a day of prayer "for the return of peace and the triumph of justice" and saw to the appointment of Bishop Charles Leo Nelligan of Pembroke as the ordinary for Catholic chaplains in the military.[10]

Cardinal Villeneuve of Quebec (1931–47) visited Canadian troops at Montmagny in November 1940. (NA)

Other than this token support of the nation, the Quebec bishops were individually free to address the war as they saw fit. Cardinal Villeneuve, believing that fascism posed a real danger to Christianity, asked clergy and laity to support the resources registration of 1940. Bishop Napoléon la Brie of Hauterive followed suit. Bishop F-X Ross of Gaspé refused to support the measure. Bishops Georges Courchesne of Rimouski and Philippe Desranleau of Sherbrooke remained as silent as possible. The new archbishop of Montreal, Joseph Charbonneau, remained in the middle and did not choose sides. At a national day of prayer in February 1941 with troops mustered and colours flying at Notre Dame Basilica in Montreal, Ernest Lapointe invoked God's blessing and Cardinal Villeneuve praised the British war effort. The cardinal continued his active support of the allied war effort and was photographed visiting Canadian troops. Upon seeing this photograph, Desranleau quipped: "It is an imperialist symbol: the cardinal delivering the Canadian church to British imperialism."[11]

The Ontario bishops assured the prime minister of their support for the referendum of April 1942, but it was an opinion that the Quebec bishops did not share.[12] For the remainder of the war, the Quebec bishops refrained from criticizing the war effort and rallied popular sentiment in support of legitimate authority. Only in January 1945 did the bishops publish a pastoral letter on Christian order and contemporary problems.[13] John MacFarlane maintains that, as long as Québécois believed that they were represented in the government, "they were willing to compromise at times and accept the majority decisions even on such important issues as participation in the war and mobilization for the defence of Canada." After Ernest Lapointe's death, however, they no longer felt represented "and could no longer accept the decisions of the English-Canadian majority, most notably the 1942 plebiscite and the 1944 decision to send conscripts overseas." Through the struggle to be represented "French Canadians became Québécois."[14]

BLOC POPULAIRE CANADIEN

The Bloc Populaire Canadien in Quebec, as analysed by Michael Behiels, was not a political party but a coalition of views that, when bound together, revealed little cohesion. The coalition was founded to combat the federal government on two fronts: military conscription for overseas service and acquisition of extensive wartime powers. Because Canadian unity was necessary for the war effort, the federal government appropriated to itself extensive financial, social, and administrative powers. The Bloc responded to federal expansion by uniting various ideologies into a single ethnic and socio-economic protest movement. At the same time, it laid the groundwork in the 1940s for the devolution of traditional social structures.[15]

The protest movement eventually broke down into two factions, the rural conservatives and urban nationalists. The conservative nationalist ideology was Quebec centred and inward looking, and it appealed to the rural Québécois. It hoped to cleanse Quebec nationalism of religious and messianic expectations and emphasized the power of the individual against the power of the federal state. The urban nationalist ideology, by contrast, appealed more to the secularized, more sophisticated Québécois of the Henri Bourassa tradition. The urban nationalists were cosmopolitan and outward looking and made bilingualism and biculturalism their primary goals. Their leaders, André Laurendeau and René Chaloult, trained the first generation of ideologues for the Quiet Revolution. They were to demand radical change in Quebec society and the Catholic church.[16]

André Laurendeau had edited *L'Action nationale* since 1937 and had been the secretary-general of the Bloc since 1943. He had worked to create a political party but had to settle for a coalition. His program, which combined elements of both the old and the new ideologies, was encapsulated in the motto "Le Canada au Canadiens et le Québec aux Québécois!" He sought sovereignty for Canada, autonomy for Quebec, and a secularist vision for the nation and the province.[17]

The Bloc's foreign policy called for Canada to move away from membership in the British Commonwealth and towards the Pan-American

Youthful André Laurendeau edited *L'Action nationale* (1937–44), was secretary-general of the *Bloc Populaire Canadien* and editor of *Le Devoir* (1947–63), and taught Quebec nationalism, ca 1940 (ANQ)

Union. Its social agenda centred on the concept of a just society, which included the avoidance of foreign capital investment. It planned that a Quebec-run society would guarantee fair wages, provide for government intervention in the economy, and advance bilingualism between the founding peoples. For Quebec, in particular, the Bloc promoted autonomy, which would keep it free from uncontrolled federal centralization and overarching federal welfare programs. The autonomous province of Quebec would take control of housing, pensions, unemployment insurance, family allowances, and health insurance. The Bloc was also strongly in favour of the devolution of social welfare programs to the provincial level.[18]

The Bloc did not choose to question the church's opposition to socialism and the CCF. It simply advocated a Christian corporative society that would build on existing structures, such as the Catholic labour unions, Catholic Family Movement, and cooperatives, and then move beyond these structures to modernize Quebec society. What the Bloc sought was a social corporatism that would "destroy the economic dictatorship of monopoly capitalism" and restore small and medium-sized enterprises. They theorized that fifty British and American industrialists owned 8 per cent of Canadian businesses that produced 81 per cent of goods. The restoration of small businesses would stimulate the economy and produce economic and cultural equality.[19]

The two economic instruments for implementing such an egalitarian policy would be cooperatives and nationalization. Producer and consumer cooperatives, which were already common throughout the rural areas, would restore small and middle-sized enterprises. The monopolies would be dealt with by the nationalization of certain key industries. Especially high on the nationalization list were public utilities and telephone companies, pulp and paper, oil and gas, and coal and mining industries. Both policies would give Canadiens greater control over the provincial economy. In 1944 the Bloc supported the province in its takeover of Montreal Light, Heat and Power Consolidated, which became the basis of Hydro-Quebec.[20]

Other problems the Bloc Populaire Canadien addressed were the depopulation of rural Quebec and the lack of a comprehensive social security system for urban workers. It advocated new colonization programs, rural electrification, better health and education facilities, cooperatives and the caisses populaires, and conservation and better management of the forest industry. For urban workers the Bloc proposed a family wage, a comprehensive social security system, assisted housing, free and compulsory education, comanagement of industries, and sharing of profits by owners and workers.[21]

In 1947 an internal power struggle splintered the Bloc into federal and neonationalist factions. The pro-Canadian conservative nationalists, on the one hand, followed Maxime Raymond. They were sympathetic to the Union Nationale. They believed in leaving provincial matters in the hands of Duplessis and directing their energy to reforming federal politics. The neonationalists, on the other hand, under the leadership of André Laurendeau and René Chaloult, wanted to turn the Bloc "into a movement of education for neo-nationalist socioeconomic and political reforms." They opposed the Duplessis regime and articulated their reforms in *Le Devoir* and *L'Action nationale*. In the Bourassa tradition they insisted that social reforms be firmly under the control of Québécois. "While paying lip service to the tenets and values of traditional French-Canadian clerical nationalism, the Bloc Populaire," concludes Behiels, "began the process of articulating a secular, socio-economic, and state-oriented neo-nationalism."[22] In the 1940s the Bloc prepared a seedbed of ideas and trained a new generation of nationalists who in the fifties would redefine Quebec nationalism and initiate the Quiet Revolution.

The Bloc Populaire Canadien promoted the devolution of the Catholic social network. It offered a Canadian way to secularize Quebec culture and prepare it for the post-modern world. In an amiable way, Laurendeau and Chaloult were determined to guide Quebec towards becoming a bilingual and secular society. To do this they inspired the leaders of the Quiet Revolution in secular liberalism but were careful not speak against church activities. Of the different movements within the Catholic church in the late 1930s and early 1940s, the Quebec ferment was the most radical and far-reaching.

THE DUPLESSIS RÉGIME, 1944–59

The Duplessis régime considered itself the bulwark of French Catholicism. Maurice Duplessis was a brilliant deal maker, but lacking a coherent economic policy for the province, he ran his government on patronage. He idealized the farmers and had little sympathy for unionized factory workers. He attracted business by opening up the natural resources to exploitation and keeping labour subdued and wages down.[23] Schools, hospitals, and orphanages conducted by bishops and religious were overburdened with responsibilities and funded inadequately. By means of provincial grants, he manipulated the altruism of religious congregations, which operated the social assistance network. Any protest from religious workers on justice issues would bring speedy reprisals in the form of less funding for their clients.[24]

The opposition, which included Gérard Pelletier and his colleagues, named the postwar period of the Duplessis régime the *Grande Noirceur* (Great Gloom). We learn from Pelletier that the Quebec government employed both legislation and the Quebec Provincial Police to hobble trade unionism. This policy was initiated in 1947 when the provincial police were called out to end a strike at Lachute. Gérard Filion, the editor of *Le Devoir*, responded to the police brutality by writing a scathing editorial entitled "Social Justice Dispensed by the Truncheon." It rallied significant social opposition to the Duplessis régime, and the battle lines were drawn.[25]

The Duplessis government struck back in 1948 with Bill 5, the aim of which was to "straitjacket" the trade unions in Quebec. But the legislation backfired. It only served as a lightning rod to unite American and Canadian labour unions and prompted the Sacerdotal Commission of Social Studies of Quebec to throw its support behind them. Duplessis backed down but only temporarily. In the face of this opposition, he was determined to discredit the union movement.[26]

Quebec wages, according to Gérard Pelletier, were the lowest anywhere in North America. To keep control of the debate, the Duplessis régime attacked socially minded intellectuals, such as Georges-Henri Lévesque, OP, the dean of Social Science at Laval University.[27] Duplessis feared Communists and thought that social assistance networks were communist inspired and restrictive of the free enterprise system. Insular and provincial, Duplessis bragged that he had never read a book since his college years and delighted in attacking freedom of thought at the university.[28]

After the asbestos strike had begun in 1949, students at Laval had collected money for the families of the strikers. The rector, Msgr Ferdinand

Vandry, forbade students to take the strike relief money to the workers. He explained to the student leaders what other religious leaders had already experienced: "Mr Duplessis will take his revenge … He'll take it out on small things – fifty thousand dollars for a laboratory, twenty-five thousand for renovating a lecture-room – small subsidies, I grant you, but they mean serious problems if they are cut off."[29] Vandry also felt the need to apologize to Duplessis for Dean Lévesque's social conscience, his "lack of judgement," and promised to put an end to such indiscretion.[30]

Nor did the Duplessis government tolerate verbal attacks from the media. It offered firms that customarily bought advertising from the critical *Le Devoir* government contracts to advertise elsewhere. To maintain institutions, Quebec bishops and religious superiors felt obliged to play the role of suppliants before *le Chef*. Church officials found their ministries overextended and themselves entrapped into permanent negotiations to finance the services they provided. They did not speak publicly of the oppression they endured but kept the silence that was demanded of them.[31]

During the Duplessis years, highways in ridings that did not vote for *Union Nationale* were not paved. The south shore autoroute between Montreal and Quebec City remained unpaved in Saint-Hyacinthe and the Richelieu Valley because the people had not voted for Duplessis. The town of Shawinigan failed to have its bridge replaced over the Saint-Maurice River because the town's voters foolishly had not cast their ballots for Duplessis. The premier used public funds not for social needs but to maintain power.[32]

Duplessis was paranoid and suspicious of foreigners and foreign products. He feared eggs imported from Communist Poland and disliked the French from France because he believed they were atheists. He would brook no suggestions by foreigners about the running of the province of Quebec.[33]

If Duplessis was suspicious of outsiders, he was exceedingly suspicious of English Canadians and the Canadian government for alleged intrusions into Quebec life. The Canadian government during the war embarked upon a program enlarging federal powers. Even after the war, to prevent a return to the depression, the federal government put in place subsidies to universities, direct taxation, and social programs that included social insurance numbers. Even a nationalist such as Pierre Trudeau protested against the federal government's providing these services – although he acknowledged the need for them.

As a buffer against outsiders, Duplessis loved to wrap himself in the fleur-de-lis of Quebec nationalism and Catholic piety. He had no economic policy and advanced no social programs during the 1940s and

Striking Christian workers during the asbestos strike in 1949 beg help at Sunday Mass from parishioners in Quebec. (ANQ)

1950s, but he decried the federal onslaught against Quebec life and culture.[34] Yet when the Quiet Revolution came, Québécois showed themselves no longer interested in Duplessis's inward-looking culture. The secularization of Quebec society had commenced, and it would not stop until the Québécois transformed the province into a secular Quebec.

THE ASBESTOS STRIKE, 1949

The church had sided with the workers in their parishes but always expounded the need to avoid strikes and societal disharmony. Mindful of the threat of communist unions, the church in the 1920s founded numerous Catholic unions, and labour priests were appointed chaplain-advisors of the Catholic unions.[35] But the asbestos strike of February 1949 forced the church to choose decisively between workers and employers. Many Catholics elected to support the five thousand workers in the Eastern Townships against the mine owners rather than allow themselves to be caught on the side of the owners and the government. There was no middle ground. A choice had to be made.

The mine owners asked the public whether the strike was the beginning of a political revolution. Gérard Dion, a priest on the Sacerdotal Commission of Social Studies, answered concisely that the strike was about workers asking their employers for a family wage, union participation in management, and protection from asbestos fibres in the mines.[36] It was about the survival of workers and their families, not social upheaval. While there was some loose talk about revolution, this was clearly not the direction of the Canadian Catholic Congress of Labour (CCCL). The Catholic church had confidence in the Catholic unions, workers, and their chaplains. In past labour disputes, Quebec archbishops Louis-Nazaire Bégin (1898–1925) and Jean-Marie Villeneuve (1931–47)[37] had personally intervened to give recognition and bring an early resolution to the conflict.[38]

In the asbestos strike, Maurice Duplessis's Union Nationale government took the side of the Johns-Manville Company and the other company owners. In the legislative assembly, it accused labour leaders of being unorthodox Catholics. The union chaplains rushed to the defence of the strikers. The government stated that the strike was illegal, and unless the strikers returned to work, it would not consider intervention.[39]

The asbestos strike was the Rubicon of the Catholic trade union movement in Quebec. Early on union funds were exhausted, and union leaders feared they would have to capitulate to the owners. Surreptitious help from the various dioceses was no longer enough. The union appealed to the bishops in the spring of 1949 for their public support. Archbishop Maurice Roy of Quebec (1947–85) offered a plan for negotiation, but it was rejected by the Duplessis government. The government then proceeded to withdraw legal recognition from the CCCL. At the same time, Johns-Manville began to hire non-union labour and evict workers from company homes.[40]

The company owners also began an advertising campaign against the CCCL and the workers. Quoting the writings of Pope Benedict XV and interpreting them as a condemnation of strike action, full-page newspaper ads accused the workers of wanting more than improvement in wages, hours, and working conditions. They accused the Catholic unions of radical communism. After three months of struggle, the financial and moral resources of the strikers were exhausted. Negotiations at the end of April were deadlocked.[41]

Aware of the tragic nature of the strike, the Sacerdotal Commission of Social Studies decided it was time to make a public statement. They appealed to "everyone, regardless of social class, to show sympathy for the workers and their families" and to give them "the material assistance that they require." They made an urgent appeal to "all associations" to cooperate in "a collection for the stricken families."[42]

Two days later on 1 May at Notre Dame Basilica in Montreal, the Chairman of the Episcopal Committee on Social Issues, Archbishop

Joseph Charbonneau, spontaneously addressed the public statement of the Sacerdotal Commission. He revealed his strong sympathy for the working class, which he described as a "victim of a conspiracy which seeks to crush it." He declared furthermore that "the Church has a duty to intervene," being more concerned with "human beings" than capital, and asked that justice be done. "This is why," the archbishop explained, "the clergy decided to intervene."[43]

Parishes in Quebec collected money and food at the church door every Sunday for the remainder of the strike. The impressive sum of $167,558 was contributed during this period to alleviate the hardship that the strike brought to the workers' families. From Rome Bishop Philippe Desranleau of Sherbrooke wrote a letter supporting the strikers. He stated that those in authority had a duty to support the weak who earn their living. "I wholeheartedly support the asbestos workers in their just demands."[44]

Archbishop Roy of Quebec again offered his services as mediator, and this time his offer was accepted. He demonstrated great skill in the resolution of the dispute and insisted that the company back down on its plans to layoff two hundred workers. After the strike was settled, the newspapers and the CCCL acknowledged the support and diplomacy of Roy, Charbonneau, and the Sacerdotal Commission of Social Studies.[45]

After the resolution of the strike, Gérard Dion considered the question why the church intervened. First, he wrote, the church stepped in on the side of the strikers because the company raised moral arguments impugning the goals of the strikers and the orthodoxy of their Catholic social thought. "A passive attitude on the part of the Church would have been interpreted [by the owners] as an approval of these moral judgments." Second, the very existence of the Catholic trade unions was threatened. The companies made a concerted effort to break the CCCL and crush its strike. Third, the suffering of the workers, their persecution by the police, fear of a breakdown in social order, and deadlock in negotiations – all this demanded a neutral body to re-establish dialogue. Finally, Lewis Brown, the head of Canadian Johns-Manville Company, agreed to have Archbishop Roy as mediator, whom he respected because of his impressive military career during the war.[46]

What were the consequences of church intervention in the asbestos strike? By its intervention the church became the catalyst for union victory. Consequently, the union won the respect of the North American labour movement, but the return to work did not end the struggle. The Quebec Provincial Police continued to slander union chaplains and strikers and provoked Bishop Desranleau to protest publicly. The government and the corporations went so far as to denounce the clergy and Catholic unions to Rome.[47]

Pierre Elliott Trudeau, a founder of the monthly *Cité Libre* and editor of the book *The Asbestos Strike* (1956 in French and 1974 in English), worked for Canadian federalism between 1969 and 1974. (ANQ)

Gérard Pelletier, journalist for *Le Devoir, La Presse*, radio and TV, and federal cabinet minister between 1969 and 1974. (ANQ)

And heads did roll. Charbonneau asked for the removal of Jean D'Auteuil Richard, the editor of the Jesuit magazine *Relations* who had warned miners of the medical danger of silicosis. Dominican Georges-Henri Lévesque was denounced to Rome by certain factions and investigated for heresy.[48] Jesuit Jacques Cousineau was forced off the Sacerdotal Commission of Social Studies and into exile, and "the commission," according to Roberto Perin, "gradually became an empty shell."[49]

The greatest shock, however, was reserved for Archbishop Charbonneau. At the beginning of January 1950, the apostolic delegate invited him to Ottawa where he was ordered to resign without appeal. The apostolic delegate told Charbonneau to be out of Montreal by the end of the month. The church officials denied that Charbonneau's open support of the strikers was the principal reason for his resignation. The Franco-Ontarian Charbonneau wrote that it was the bishop of Rimouski who rallied some Quebec bishops against his ecclesial innovations.[50] Two Montreal bishops were forced to resign within seventy-five years, Bourget because he had been considered too conservative and Charbonneau because he was considered too liberal. But Rome's

Jean Marchand, labour leader in the
Confederation of Canadian Catholic
Workers and president of the
Confederation of National Trade Unions,
between 1969 and 1974. (ANQ)

surgical strike was limited to Charbonneau and did not touch Desranleau, which bolstered the contention that it was not the strike that
caused his dismissal but the changes Charbonneau permitted in his
diocese in response to the early rumblings of the Quiet Revolution. As
Charbonneau was reduced to a parish priest in Victoria, Bishop Philippe Desranleau of Sherbrooke became an archbishop and his diocese
was made a metropolitan see in 1951, while Archbishop Roy of Quebec City was named cardinal in 1965.[51]

The most significant event during the asbestos strike was the
Church's decision to stand clearly with the workers rather than with
the provincial government and international corporations. At the
same time, it acted discreetly so as not to offend the government.[52] Despite Rome's warning to avoid a crippling strike, the Catholic unions
pioneered their own methods of dealing with recalcitrant employers
and demanded their own adaption of Catholic social justice. When the
dust settled after the strike, the Quebec bishops in 1950 issued a pastoral letter in which they declared explicitly that Catholics must side with
human needs over capital interests and support the rights of labour
unions and collective bargaining.[53]

The asbestos strike ended the informal alliance of "cross and crown"
that had existed for over a hundred years. The strike was only a harbinger of greater upheavals to come. But it was the Quiet Revolution, according to Gérard Pelletier, that decisively destroyed twenty years of
the Duplessis régime and clerical-nationalism as a force in Quebec.[54]

The desires of postwar Québécois youth were different from those of their parents who had lived within the slender horizons of the depression. The generation that came into its own after the Second World War had experienced the wartime industrial revolution, and many in the Canadian services had travelled to Europe and elsewhere in the world. Federal militants rose up, among them journalists Pierre Trudeau and Gérard Pelletier, who published *Cité Libre*. Connected with labour leader Jean Marchand, they organized cooperatives[55] and were attacked by the clerical nationalists for their secular, federal, and international vision. The new militants criticized the older clergy for restraining their involvement in church and society but found sympathy for their aspirations among Archbishop Charbonneau and the younger clergy.[56]

CONCLUSION

Conscription loomed like a divisive ogre over the Canadian church. During the First World War, Archbishop Bruchési was drawn in stages into supporting participation and mobilization, which ultimately concluded with Canadian conscription. Embarrassed by this involvement, the Quebec clergy determined to avoid being trapped into the same stance during the Second World War. They felt obliged to support the government in mobilizing to defend Canada and provide Britain with voluntary assistance in men and material. But for the Quebec bishops, conscription for overseas duty was never on the horizon. The "yes but" attitude of the Quebec clergy in the two world wars was unique to the Canadian situation and was adopted in the face of traditional Roman loyalty to civil governments.

The Bloc Populaire Canadien rallied a coalition of Canadiens who were upset with the threat of conscription, the enlargement of the Canadian government, and the church's control of social services. Although politically unsuccessful, they animated an ideology that became the seedbed of the 1950s revolution seeking a new freedom in Quebec society. For fifteen years the nemesis of the Bloc was the dominant Dupressis régime with its parochial, reactionary attitude.

By the early 1950s the tightly woven carpet of Canadian ultramontane Catholicism unravelled. Many Quebec bishops took a stand in favour of the asbestos strikers, and church members sided with the workers. This stand split the French Canadian hierarchy because the rural bishops continued to see the future of Quebec in terms of adherence to law and order as mediated by the mine owners and the Duplessis government. The bishop of Rimouski and some of his colleagues from smaller centres have been given credit for engineering the fall of the archbishop of Montreal. Charbonneau, reading the signs of the times, recognized the early ferment that was leading to the Quiet Revolution. During the asbestos strike, he placed the urban community beside the workers and their families.[57] During the early 1960s, Québécois Liberals took full control of the government and secularized the social network and French Canadian culture. They terminated the Duplessis autocracy and severed the informal alliance of Catholic clericalism and Quebec nationalism. The church changed from being a controlling influence in Quebec society to being a judicious critic of its destiny. As the Quebec church was devolving, the English-speaking church continued to construct Canadian Catholicism outside Quebec.

13 The Canadianization of Catholicism

English-speaking Catholics in the postwar period continued to say their prayers and sing their songs at Sunday Mass, yet the demand for change was evident throughout Canada and especially in Quebec. Canadian religious congregations and laity continued to construct Catholic institutions across Canada by building new schools and hospitals. The Sisters of St Martha (CSM), for instance, expanded their caring ministries at Antigonish to include a variety of professional activities, and the Catholic Women's League (CWL) opened houses across Canada to look after newly arrived immigrant women. The bishops formed an episcopal conference based in Ottawa to adapt church institutions to Canadian needs and to coordinate Canadian policies.

As the Canadians continued to build, Canadiens began dismantling historic social structures in their province. The intellectuals, literati, and liberals were champing at the bit to wrestle Quebec's destiny away from the control of an ultramontane church. Although secularism had challenged Protestants since the turn of the century, it only struck Québécois Catholics in the 1950s and 1960s and English-speaking Catholics in the 1960s and 1970s. The secularization that followed altered the roles of clergy and laity in society. The number of student openings at Catholic colleges remained stable for a decade, but the future of Catholic post-secondary education has now come into question.

RELIGIOUS WOMEN LOOK TOWARDS PROFESSIONALIZED SKILLS

In the Maritime provinces, as elsewhere in Canada, church institutions perpetuated Catholic culture. Problems abounded, however, in the continuance of these institutions. For example, a well-established college like St Francis Xavier at Antigonish, Nova Scotia, despite increasing enrolment, had the greatest trouble staying solvent. To save money and ease the financial burden on Catholics, Archbishop Michael Hannan of Halifax proposed the unification of three Catholic colleges: St Francis Xavier, St Mary's of Halifax, and St Dunstan's of Charlottetown. His proposal was not acted on, and financial difficulties persisted for these colleges. Bishop John Cameron of Antigonish, anxious to reduce costs and improve the quality of housekeeping at St Francis Xavier College, sought help in 1894 from religious sisters. Because religious congregations did not have the personnel to answer this appeal positively, the Sisters of Charity of Halifax, as Sarah MacPherson relates the story, offered to train Antigonish diocesan women to solve the problem for their diocese. The offer was gratuitous as the Charities had recently established an auxiliary branch, the Sisters of St Martha, that would be devoted to the "household management of educational institutions." The Sisters of Charity felt that they could easily include others in this training program.[1] The offer, Cameron believed, would give relief to the needs of the college and the diocese.

For his part, Bishop Cameron asked his parish priests to "look through your congregation for such persons as may be fit" to serve the church in household management at St Francis Xavier. This meant priests were to seek young women between the ages of eighteen and twenty-six who, for two years of novitiate, would be responsible for their own clothes, bedding, and doctors' bills.[2] A number of women volunteered and were sent to the novitiate at Mount St Vincent in Halifax where they were educated and trained as the Congregation of St Martha. From 1894 to 1900, thirty-one women from Antigonish went to Halifax to be trained as Marthas. The Sisters of Charity of Halifax provided a novice mistress to guide spiritual formation and a mistress of work to supply the housekeeping skills necessary for this vocation. Almost immediately the Sisters of St Martha of Antigonish began to develop their own spirituality and customs, which distinguished them from the Charities.[3]

In 1897 ten Sisters of St Martha and three Sisters of Charity of Halifax moved into their new convent on the campus of St Francis Xavier and began their ministry. The sisters organized for 130 students and staff the preparation of regular meals, the cleaning of the buildings, and the nursing in the college infirmary. "The entry of the Marthas [to St Francis Xavier College] marked a new era in hygiene and comfort for the St Francis Xavier students."[4] The dining-room provided balanced and tasty meals, and the residences were well ordered and spotless. During this period, numerous differences arose between the Sisters of Charity and Bishop Cameron about past arrangements and about the future of the Marthas. With the new convent already operating, the bishop did not hesitate in 1900 to sever the tie between the Sisters of St Martha of Antigonish and the Sisters of Charity of Halifax. Thus it was that in the fall, fifteen women gathered at the new convent to perform the work of the college and to train new sisters.[5]

The Sisters of St Martha of Antigonish proceeded to elect their superior and to choose a novice mistress of the four novices. For their first community retreat of 1901, the prominent Jesuit E.J. Devine introduced them to the Spiritual Exercises of St Ignatius Loyola.[6] Afterwards their constitutions of 1897 were adapted to reflect the needs of the sisters and their ministries in the diocese of Antigonish. The sisters were to be governed by their own superior under the direction of the Religious Chapter, that is, an assembly of all sisters under perpetual vows. The bishop was the head of the community in spiritual matters, a college council was to guide their college ministries, and the board of governors of St Francis Xavier College was to direct them in "temporal matters." Each member was allotted room, board, and a wage of two dollars monthly paid to their community.[7]

The resolution of these internal matters completed, the Sisters of St Martha started to look outward to the Antigonish community wherein they might share their ministries and increase their skills. As personnel became available, the sisters responded to needs in communities beyond the college campus. St Joseph's Hospital administration at Glace Bay requested in 1902 that the Marthas undertake its household management, and for the first time sisters moved off campus to accept a new apostolate. In 1906 at the request of the citizens and physicians of Antigonish, the sisters opened a cottage hospital. In 1908 they undertook a retirement home for priests at Mount Cameron. To accomplish these tasks the Congregation began sending sisters for nursing education in 1902. To raise funds for these various new enterprises, the Marthas incorporated themselves in 1907 in the province of Nova Scotia.[8]

Over the next decade the Sisters of St Martha gained autonomy from St Francis Xavier College and opened ministries outside the diocese of Antigonish. The first such request came from a former member of the diocese, Archbishop Neil McNeil of Toronto. He asked the Marthas to provide housekeeping services for the newly founded St Augustine's

Seminary in Toronto. Despite reluctant support from the Antigonish community, nine sisters set out for Toronto in the summer of 1913 to be present for the opening of the seminary.[9] Several years later the sisters at Antigonish began training and educating sisters for the diocese of Charlottetown. Four new sisters from Charlottetown and three Antigonish sisters returned to Charlottetown to establish Marthas in the diocese.[10]

The autonomy the sisters exercised had to be dealt with by the council at St Francis Xavier College. The sisters put their trust in Father Moses Coady to be their advocate at the college council. He was a trusted priest of the diocese and member of the faculty. In 1917 the college council granted the sisters the right to be responsible for their own enterprises and to be financially autonomous. That same year they opened St Mary's Home for orphans and unwed mothers at Sydney. Between 1918 and 1921 they constructed a motherhouse at Antigonish. The Sisters of St Martha accepted teaching positions in the Nova Scotia public schools and became involved in the work of the Antigonish Movement. In 1931 the Congregation of Religious in Rome gave the Sisters of St Martha a pontifical charter. As a papal institution, they could govern their own enterprises and operate charitable apostolates outside the diocese and around the world.[11]

Securely founded, and with expanding ministries in nursing, education, and social work, the Marthas between 1925 and 1937 were invited to exercise their organizational skills beyond Antigonish and Toronto. J.T. Kidd, the former rector of St Augustine's Seminary and bishop of Calgary (1925–31), asked the Congregation of St Martha in 1927 to buy a private hospital in Lethbridge that was available for $65,000. Quickly responding to Kidd's request, the sisters purchased the Brett Sanatorium at Banff and, after revitalizing the dilapidated building for $23,000, renamed it the Mineral Springs Hospital. A low occupancy rate and the depression demanded of the sisters great financial and promotional skills to keep this spectacular site operational.[12] To borrow the necessary funds and to conduct the business of health care outside of Nova Scotia, the sisters incorporated their congregation in the western provinces.[13] The Sisters of St Martha, like other Maritime congregations such as the Sisters of St Anne, the Sisters of the Child Jesus, and the Sisters of Providence, established themselves solidly in western Canada.

Originally recruited for household management at St Francis Xavier College, the Sisters of St Martha upgraded their skills and expanded their horizons across Canada to include the management of church institutions, hospitals, schools, human resources, and social work. They demonstrated that the humble with strong faith can do great things. In the Maritimes and western Canada they aspired to the customary goals of the church and performed the ministries they chose in the traditional way. Maritime Catholics played an important role in the growth of church institutions in the western provinces.

WOMEN STRUGGLE FOR A PLACE
IN THE CANADIAN CHURCH

Pius x and Pius xi, confronted by secularism infiltrating Catholic culture, called upon Catholic parishioners to become involved in Catholic Action to foster devotional piety and social concerns in their communities. The popes invited Catholics to participate in the apostolate of the church through their bishops. Catholic women in Edmonton, according to historian Sheila Ross, responded to this call in 1912 by forming the Catholic Women's League under the guidance of Archbishop Emile A. Legal. He sought women who would attend to single women and families immigrating to the Canadian West, and let them know that Catholics cared about their distress and would help them with their needs. Settlers arriving from the British Isles and eastern Europe endured the cultural shock of the Canadian West, and then of being transported to isolated rural locations far from family, friends, and the necessary links for survival. In their bewilderment they did not have the comfort of religion as clergy and churches were not available in the outlying area of settlements. Practising Catholics in this devotional hiatus were proselytized by established denominations.[14]

Bishop Legal in 1910 organized the Catholic Association of Alberta to extend care to immigrants. The bishop, along with Abbé Casgrain and the author Katherine Hughes, had hoped in 1912 to acquire a hotel to provide new Canadians with temporary accommodation, a community house, and employment bureau but found few funds in a soft economy. The bishop then turned to a larger number of Catholic women to welcome the new Canadians. Casgrain suggested a diocesan women's organization modelled after the Catholic Women's League of London, England. The London league, highly praised by Cardinal Francis Bourne of Westminster at the Eucharistic Congress in Montreal, was connected with Rome, the church hierarchy, and the lay apostolate. An Edmonton Catholic Women's League could then be linked to the London league, which had immigration accommodations for travelling women. The London league was connected to its German equivalent, Katholischer Frauenbund, and to the leagues in France and Italy. As he did with the men's Catholic Association of Alberta, Legal asked that the Edmonton league, sacrifice its own ideology to follow the bishop, collaborate in his apostolate, and be faithful to Catholic values. The Catholic Women's League went into operation under the sponsorship of Bishop Legal and thus avoided the many directions of local pastors.[15]

Katherine Hughes called a meeting of existing women's associations in the Edmonton diocese in November of 1912. These associations were invited to affiliate into a federation of women's societies that would be directed by a central executive board to handle the larger social problems in the community. The hope was to enroll every Catholic woman from the parishes of the diocese. The apostolate of the league was to promote the spiritual welfare of its members and to be engaged in social concerns of the community, especially the care of young girls living away from home. Volunteers were delegated to meet the trains arriving in Edmonton and provide temporary lodgings. A downtown home was purchased as a hostel, and a lay matron was placed in charge of the home. Free employment and fund-raising bureaus were also operated from the home.[16]

Other branches of the Catholic Women's League were formed at Montreal in 1917, Toronto and Ottawa in 1918, and Halifax, Regina, and Sherbrooke in 1919. Edmonton women, especially Katherine Hughes and her sister, Loretta Kneil, a former Edmonton league president and then Immigration department worker in Ottawa, saw the need for the national coordination of good works and the formation of a national organization. They were keenly aware that because they were not a national association, as were other denominations, "Catholic women were not being represented" at government meetings to assist in the settlement of postwar immigrants in Canada. Kneil consulted the minister of Justice, C.J. Doherty, whose wife was a member of the league, and was told to contact the president of the Montreal league, Bellelle Guerin. Recognizing the importance of the message, Guerin invited representatives of the League and other women's groups to meet at Montreal in the early spring of 1920 "to consider the possibilities of federating all existing CWL organizations with a view to standardize our aims and objects that we may become a real power for good."[17]

At the convocation of Catholic women in Montreal in June 1920, the Catholic Women's League was formed "to unite Catholic women ... to secure the influence needed for promotion of Catholic Social Action, Catholic Education, and Racial Harmony within the Catholic Church in Canada." By the nature of their volunteer commitment, members were called upon to transcend the initial goals of personal morality and parish piety to embark upon the self-development necessary for Catholic Action and public service in the civic arena. Member Paula Kane used the term "social feminism" to encapsulate the league's attitude of personal spiritual growth deployed by women to better their society. They wished to be modern women involved in contemporary society while fulfilling the expectation of Catholic women. Bellelle Guerin was selected to be the first national president of the CWL and spoke about the importance of "Catholic feminism." It should guide women to face their problems and, with sound judgment, decide "what is best for our families and ourselves" and carry the women's "influence to the scale of justice whenever righteousness demands."[18]

Immigration increased after the First World War, and the Catholic Women's League once again helped with the settlement of new Canadians. The CWL now had a network of homes from the Maritimes to Alberta in which women could stay. A National Directory of Boarding Homes for Catholic Women was soon compiled. Although the league members espoused the principle of working with all immigrants, the anglophone composition of league members made them more acceptable to the Irish, Scottish, and English working girls. The Edmonton CWL sponsored groups of Hebridean and Irish women coming to the Prairies as house workers. They were able to place women in rural homes where they earned between fifteen and twenty dollars per month, over and above their room and board.[19]

In 1926 the CWL purchased for the Sisters of Service a large house in the city centre to accommodate a Religious Correspondence School. This helped the sisters not only with the Saturday classes in religion they offered but also with the extensive correspondence of religious courses they conducted for rural children for whom schools were not easily available. This gave Catholic farm families direct contact with church personnel. Rural Catholics were pleased to receive the correspondence along with magazines and any other information that was enclosed. From the Edmonton house, it was reported in 1926 that "3,043 catechism lessons had been sent out, and 1,781 corrected; 10,900 papers and magazines had been mailed to the scattered rural Catholic population in Alberta."[20] The sisters engaged in this apostolate believed they contacted more families by correspondence than they would by teaching in rural schools. Recognizing the importance of this western enterprise, the founder of the Laura Secord chocolate stores, Senator Frank O'Connor of Toronto, donated one hundred dollars a month to the correspondence school. Eight years later the school had grown and reported that its teachers had corrected 5,140 lessons, sent 967 personal letters, and mailed out 32,468 papers and magazines to rural Catholics.

The CWL generated its own opposition and competition. While the league boasted thirty thousand national members during the 1920s, many parish priests were not happy with a national organization that drained off personnel and money for faraway causes. The Catholic Church Extension Society, which dealt with the needs of immigrants and of Canadian missions in the West, was competing with the CWL for personnel, money, and mission territory. The CWL was moreover in competition with the fund-raising endeavour of other Christian religions during those years. Its members, however, were not involved in gender issues or temperance activities.[21]

At the Winnipeg national convention in 1922, the Redemptorist Father George Daly arrived from Toronto to plead that the Catholic Women's League should adopt the work of the newly founded Sisters of Service. Known by the acronym of SOS, the congregation was founded by Catherine Donnelly to work with immigrants by bringing them spiritual help and educating their children, especially in outlying areas in the West where facilities were scarce.[22] Daly argued before the CWL that by getting behind the sisters, "by identifying your organization with the SOS, you will help to keep to your organization its national character ... to remain a Catholic Dominion-wide organization." Daly then drafted a motion proposed by Gertrude Lawler, the well-known Catholic and first president of the Toronto league, who stated that the national CWL "heartily endorses this work of the Sisters of Service and willingly adopts it as one of its national works."[23] The convention resolved to form a national committee to study what support should be provided and to ask each member to make a personal contribution to the apostolate.

The Toronto league also agreed to run "a home for young working women, particularly immigrant Catholic girls." In 1923 the CWL temporarily operated a hostel at 2 Wellesley Lane, adjacent to the Sisters' provincial office, until the Sisters were able to take it over. The Toronto, London, and Chatham leagues answered the Sisters' request to clothe the needy by sending "donations of warm clothing, shoes, stockings, and underwear as well as outer garments" so that prairie children would be able to attend school through the winter. They also enclosed some Christmas gifts for each child. League members from eastern Canada and Edmonton packaged books, magazines, and other reading materials to send out to needy families in the West.[24]

In 1924 Winnipeg league members drove sixty miles north of the city to a cabin at Camp Morton located on the edge of Lake Winnipeg where the Sisters of Service were teaching in an isolated school nearby. The women brought "staple food supplies and canned goods, homemade treats of jam, cakes and pies, and books for the library."[25] Two years later, the Winnipeg league purchased a large, attractive, and centrally located house that the Sisters of Service operated as a women's hostel. By 1924 the CWL's 35,000 members had contributed $4,580 to the mission of the Sisters of Service.[26]

The greatest challenge to the Catholic Women's League across Canada came from the fourth bishop of Calgary, Francis P. Carroll. He judged that the shortcomings of the league grew out of a faulty constitutional framework. Carroll, however, had to tread gingerly around the CWL once it won papal approval in 1924. Nevertheless, he believed the women were wandering aimlessly without the firm guidance of the bishops. It was the direction of the hierarchy, Carroll explained, that turned good intentions into works of the church and allowed them officially to be deemed Catholic Action. He proposed that the bishops should choose representation on the CWL governing board.[27]

The Calgary representatives presented his suggestions to the National Convention at Winnipeg in 1941. The league was criticized for overemphasizing the national organization and failing to seek the direction of the bishops. Moreover, money and personnel were drained from parishes without the consent or support of local pastors. The independence of the national council from the clergy made it unable to generate national or local support. On the other hand, with the support of the bishops and pastors, Carroll saw the organization becoming a mass organization of Canadian women with members from every parish.

Two years later, Carroll wrote to Archbishop Duke of Vancouver, paraphrasing a line from John Donne's sonnet *The Anatomy of the World* that showed Donne's discomfort at the impending dissolution of traditional cosmology: "The thing is upside down. The women should not be deciding what is to be done, and then telling the bishops or asking the bishops' permission to do it. The bishops should tell the women what is to be done!"[28]

Carroll proposed two possible alternatives to the CWL constitution. The first would create a separate society operated independently of the church, such as the Knights of Columbus or the St Vincent de Paul Society. The second model would establish parochial units to be operated in conjunction with the parish and then united into a national organization. The national executive would thus inspire its members rather than command them. With the second model, Carroll believed that the CWL's "greatest asset will be its partnership in the life of the Church under the bishops, and therefore, in true Catholic Action. The CWL will not be a distinct society but a federation."[29]

As Carroll expected, he generated firm opposition among the strong-minded women of Alberta. Carroll's proposal's were twice spurned by the women of the CWL. Archbishop Duke thought the league should become a select women's organization like the Knights of Columbus. Archbishop Peter J. Monahan of Regina (1935–47) favoured a diocesan federation of women. The growth of membership stagnated without diocesan and parish support. Dissatisfaction with the constitutions remained unresolved. During the 1940s the league accepted the second model proposed by Bishop Carroll. They shifted to parochial units and autonomous diocesan units, which would then be moulded into the national federation. The Catholic Women's League thus sought integration under the direction of the bishops into the Canadian Catholic ecclesial structure with the expectation that clergy would support them and that they would gain larger membership.[30]

In the postwar period the Catholic Women's League was looking to renew its apostolate for peacetime. Men and women at St Anthony's Parish in Toronto were members of a parish group called Christians for Renewal and sought ways to improve the spiritual climate in Canada. One of the members, Louise Summerhill, a mother of seven children, had been shocked when the Canadian government permitted "the partial legalizing of abortions" in 1967. Inspired by prayerful reflection, she telephoned her pastor, Father Joseph O'Neill, in October 1968 and asked about setting up "a telephone answering service for expectant mothers who needed support in bearing their children."[31]

She sought a positive approach to supporting pregnant women by providing a free service to give help without seeking to have their children adopted or get into political debate. She founded Birthright as an inclusive organization to promote life and soon 600 branches had opened in North America. As a referral agency, Birthright is "concerned with shelter, medical or legal help, and making contacts with social service agencies for financial assistance or professional counselling. It recommends reputable adoption agencies, arranges for maternity and baby clothes, looks after transportation needs and above all provides supportive friendship."[32]

The Catholic Women's League was attracted to Birthright for its positive attitude in supporting life and many of its members volunteered to help. Most CWL members preferred this less-extreme form in promoting life. In the Toronto area CWL members set up parenting centres and residences for expectant mothers.

A second event that recently involved the members of the Catholic Women's League was the construction of the "Green Kit." In 1971 the Canadian bishops began a study on the role of women in the church and sought to converse with Catholic women from both French and English sections of the league. Prominent Toronto league member Mary Matthews represented English-speaking Canadians. The bishops learned that women expected to be regarded as full and equal members in the church, and that the expectation included ordination to the ministry and presence on decision-making bodies. After the study was completed, Vatican documents were published instructing church members that the ordination of women was not to be discussed or even considered by Catholic clergy or laity.[33]

At a 1975 conference, the bishops approved a proposal that women should be permitted as consultants to and members of the offices of the Holy See. Two years later the Vatican countered with a declaration that in fidelity to Christ the church does not consider itself authorized to admit women to the priesthood. To facilitate the dialogue, the Canadian Conference of Catholic Bishops (CCCB) decided in 1984 to publish the Green Kit to foster examination of the role of women by church people. Cardinal Emmett Carter of Toronto saw the Green Kit as unrepresentative, confrontational, negative, and lopsided feminism and reacted strongly against the idea. The following day Cardinal Louis-Albert Vachon saved the project by moving that the bishops approve the kit.[34]

Further objection came from the Women for Life, Faith, and Family who proposed "the Blue Kit," which in their view followed the spirit of the papal encyclicals. The bishops, however, preferred the Green Kit because it promised to raise awareness of women in the church. It proposed that the language of the liturgy be inclusive, that church responsibilities be shared by men and women, that women's voices be heard on church matters and in proclaiming the Word, and that leadership roles also be given to women. The study based its proposals on the Vatican II statements calling for equality, the teaching of the Scriptures about Mary and the female witnesses of the resurrection, and Paul's statement demanding equality as "there is no longer Jew or Greek, there is no longer slave or free, there is no longer male or female."[35] The kit called upon Christians to walk a "journey of reconciliation" by setting up structures for dialogue and understanding.[36]

In 1985 the Catholic Women's League resolved to take the lead in helping the bishops to promote dialogue between men and women by use of the Green Kit. Fifteen thousand kits were distributed, but Father Joseph O'Neill concedes that they were "not a big draw." Initial responses to the Green Kit recorded by the CCCB were 70 positive and 23 negative. Episcopal differences over the kit gave mixed signals to the women, and in a number of dioceses the kit was hardly used.[37]

The attitudes of Catholic women to the Green Kit and to Catholic feminism, according to O'Neill, could be divided among those who feared change, those who welcomed more responsibility, those who saw women's ordination as the issue, and those who wanted a completely level playing field without the disadvantage of hierarchy. Objections to the Green Kit focused on the bibliography, which included the works of Catholic feminist scholars Rosemary Ruether and Elisabeth

Fiorenza. Of the four categories of Catholic women, O'Neill placed most members of the CWL in the second, among those who would welcome more responsibility. An additional few he placed in the third category, among those who worked for the ordination of women. The CWL as a volunteer organization helped raise women's awareness that Catholic life existed beyond home and family and that women's personal skills should be developed and professionalized.[38]

CREATING THE CANADIAN CHURCH: CCCB

Among Canadian Catholics, there was no forum for developing attitudes towards contemporary problems such as trade unions, the CCF, fascism, and communism. In the political sense there was no Canadian Catholic church with ready-made policies. There were a number of dioceses linked directly to the Holy See, but geographically they were grouped together only by their commitment to Canadian Catholicism. Since 1851, plenary sessions of Canadian bishops had been convened to resolve mutual problems. Theologically and jurisdictionally, however, Catholic bishops, as the successors of the apostles, remained entirely independent of one another. In canon law they were responsible only to the Holy See. A Canadian bishop following the Roman canons was free to deal with particular problems in his own way – with or without the agreement of his colleagues. Individual bishops were free to deal on an *ad hoc* basis with particular issues such as supporting labour, or the CCF, or condemning communism and socialism. Many bishops recognized clearly the need for an organization that would provide not only a forum for discussion but also a method by which they would be able to solve problems and formulate policies.

Rome changed the status of the Catholic church of Canada in 1908 from a mission to an established church. Propaganda Fide, which had governed the Canadian mission church since 1622, transferred its responsibility to the Vatican Office of Secretary of State. After this date the Canadian bishops enjoyed direct communication with the Holy See. Coming together in a plenary meeting in Ottawa in 1943, the Canadian bishops struck a committee headed by Archbishop James C. McGuigan of Toronto to deal with the petitions of individual bishops requesting that a permanent episcopal body be established. The committee recommended "the establishment of a permanent organization of the Canadian Episcopate." A plan was thus drawn up in 1943 to establish the Canadian Catholic Conference (CCC) and it was approved at a plenary assembly of forty-four bishops and one abbot.[39] Coincidently, the Canadian Council of Churches (also called the CCC) met within the year to initiate discussions and fellowship.[40]

The Canadian Catholic Conference established a permanent secretariat, and six commissions were struck to study issues of particular interest to the bishops, such as postwar problems, missions, Christian education, works of charity and hospitals, moral and liturgical discipline, and political-religious questions. At a plenary sessions two years later, an administration council composed of the archbishop of Quebec, three French-speaking bishops, and three English-speaking bishops was formed to coordinate the work of the commissions and permanent secretariat.[41] Although the CCC coordinated the activity of its more than one hundred members, it was never considered to be the official voice of the Canadian episcopate. Its decisions were but guidelines for the bishops without having the juridical force of church law.[42]

During the war years Prime Minister Mackenzie King showed new interest in a national health insurance plan. The Catholic Hospital Council of Canada was quickly formed in 1942 to cope with such a radical shift in Canadian social policy. The bishops set up a permanent commission on health. In supporting the Catholic Hospital Council of Canada, they made a point of condemning the spectre of state medicine while being willing to tolerate a federal health insurance plan.[43]

Wartime and postwar immigration caused the bishops great concern. A great number of Chinese males came to Canada and, after the war, a flood of European refugees. The CCC set up a social action department whose functions included looking after immigrants. It worked closely with the government and other immigration agencies. The case load in the postwar period expanded dramatically. In 1952 the Holy See established the International Catholic Immigration Commission in Geneva, which offered the CCC $100,000 in travel loans to assist refugees heading to Canada.

This opportunity challenged the bishops to provide a comparable organization to administer these startup funds. The bishops had two choices: the Winnipeg-based Catholic Immigrant Aid Society (CIAS) or the Montreal-based Rural Settlement Society of Canada (RSSC). They chose the RSSC to administer the $100,000 along with matching grants from the bishops. The federal government recognized the RSSC as one of four church organizations engaged in immigration work and from 1956 to 1958 called upon it to help settle 37,000 Hungarian refugees. In 1957 the RSSC and the CIAS merged to form the Catholic Immigration Service (CIS) with headquarters in Montreal. Catholic immigration work proved to be quite successful. "From 1952 to 1960, assisted by the revolving fund, just over 20,000 people had been moved," concluded Bernard Daly; and "another 11,000 had been helped through other programs." With the immigration crisis over by 1967, the CCC asked CIS to return the $400,000 it had been lent. The

CCC requested payments of $50,000 yearly. The CIS paid off the loan, scaled down its operations, and continued to provide services. The CCC allowed CIS to retain the remaining funds, declaring itself no longer fiscally responsible for the CIS.[44]

Since publication of *Rerum Novarum* and *Quadragesimo Anno*, Catholics were committed to social action, but many had different views on what Catholic social thought involved. In 1934, for instance, Archbishop Georges Gauthier of Montreal (1923–40) condemned the CCF, in spite of the disagreement of other bishops, clergy, and laity. His unilateral condemnation caused much confusion among clergy and laity. It became clear from the incident that the bishops needed a forum in which they could deal decisively with such issues. In 1943 the Canadian Catholic Conference considered and resolved the issue. It instructed Catholics that they were free to vote for the political party of their choice as long as that party stood for the principles of the Canadian nation and Catholic social thought.[45] This action in effect reversed Archbishop Gauthier's condemnation of the CCF.

To increase public understanding of Catholic social thought, the CCC sponsored study days in Toronto in February 1944. The theme was the building of "a Catholic-inspired Canadian social system." L'abbé J.C. Leclaire of Quebec, Henry Somerville of Toronto, and Dr Moses Coady of Antigonish led discussions on urban industrial and rural agrarian problems. Union delegates from Quebec showed the participants how they had constructed Catholic social organizations on the corporatist model of the cooperation of state, industrialist, and worker. They believed appropriate planning would achieve full production and full employment. After the conference Leclaire continued to publish about Catholic action, while Father Francis Marrocco of Peterborough founded the Institute of Social Action at St Patrick's College in Ottawa. The Antigonish model of cooperatives and adult education enjoyed great prominence in the implementation of Catholic social action across Canada. Catholic colleges, seminaries, and parishes used the social models of Quebec and Antigonish and adopted them to the needs of the Canadian church.[46]

The process by which the CCC organized Catholic charities revealed a tension between those at the top of the Catholic establishment, which included Archbishop Paul-Emile Léger (1950–68) and the papally inspired Caritas Canada, and those at the bottom, which included English Catholic social workers. The different approaches were not easily reconciled. To coordinate efforts, the CCC sent a few Quebec and Ontario priests in 1944 to observe the activities of the United States National Conference of Catholic Charities. Their mandate was to devise a plan for a Canadian organization that would set policy and organize fund raising. The Canadian Catholic Welfare Conference was founded in 1951 with English and French sections. Concerned about centralization, a number of bishops dissented and strongly recommended provincial organization rather than federal organization.

Five years later, the Holy See established Caritas Internationalis to coordinate worldwide Catholic charities. It sought the support of dioceses throughout the world including those in Canada. Archbishop Léger was the first Canadian prelate to direct his diocesan resources towards Caritas Internationalis. In 1953 the French section left the Canadian Catholic Welfare Conference and joined Caritas Canada of the Montreal archdiocese to form a single French Canadian front. The English section worked on its own. In both sections, however, the program was becoming redundant. The Canadian provinces had expanded their social services to such a degree that both English and French sections left the work to the provinces and in 1973 closed down.[47] The Canadian dioceses worked independently and found it more desirable to raise and appropriate funds locally for the particular charities in their jurisdiction, or leave this work to the Canadian Catholic Organization of Development and Peace.

Pope Pius XII approved the constitution of the Canadian Catholic Conference in 1955, forty-seven years after the Canadian church had been established under the regular jurisdiction of the Holy See.[48] The growing bureaucracy of the CCC needed a suitable location in Canada. The choices were Quebec City, the primatial see, or Ottawa, the capital. After due deliberation the CCC chose Ottawa, largely because it was accessible to the apostolic delegate in Ottawa. During the 1970s the CCC established offices in the rented space of a modest old building owned by the archdiocese of Ottawa. Some bishops thought this was an "unfortunate decision" for the CCC. They would have preferred that a modern architectural prize be constructed in a new suburb of Ottawa as representative of the new episcopal organization and the large Catholic population of Canada. Modesty prevailed, however, in the choice of office space, and modesty continued to characterize the tone of the Canadian bishops. The name of the CCC was changed in 1977 to the Canadian Conference of Catholic Bishops, or CCCB, to avoid confusion with other groups using the acronym CCC and to emphasize its association with the bishops.[49]

CATHOLICS COPING
WITH SECULARIZATION

The Quebec church proved itself perceptive in not opposing the strong force of nationalism coursing through the Canadiens. This secularizing movement found much support among the lower clergy, religious, and laity. Archbishop Maurice Roy of Quebec and Archbishop Paul-Emile Léger of Montreal conceded the desired changes to the Quebec Liberal government in return for some influence on social services, hospitals, and Catholic schools.[50] The government quickly seized the province's social network and injected it with new funds.

Secularization was not new in Canada, it had been going on at least since the Act of Union of 1841. David Marshall contends that the Protestant faiths were more deeply affected than the Catholic by the secularizing influence of public schools, Darwinian science, biblical criticism, and especially the ministerial clergy.[51] Catholics were protected and sacredized by the devotional revolution going on within Catholicism since the 1840s.[52]

Secularization implies a weakening of the role of religion in individuals, an attenuation of their religious beliefs, and an overall decrease in regular religious observance. A century earlier than Catholics, Protestants were challenged by secularization. It could be argued that the Protestant Reformation and the resulting multiplication of belief systems was a *de facto* agent of secularization. Historians Herbert Butterfield and Owen Chadwick believe that the toleration of religion in Europe led to the cry for religious liberty, which in turn led to secularization.[53]

Neither church nor state found itself able to set the agenda against the powerful force of benign secularism. Here we are not discussing a more virulent form of secularism tainted with anti-clericalism. Secularization occurred simultaneously on different levels of society. Protestant clergy accepted the insights of evolutionary science and biblical criticism without losing their faith, but that acceptance had a devastating effect on their perplexed faithful. The Darwinian revolution and scientific history questioned the credibility of traditional biblical interpretations and threw much doubt on long-held church customs. School boards removed religion from the public schools on the grounds that it was irrelevant, something for private devotion only. Medical and food sciences lessened the anxieties of the faithful about such acts of God as epidemics and famines. Insurance companies replaced fraternal organizations in offering protection to widows and families from death and disaster. Industrial work, shopping, and recreational activities challenged the traditional Lord's Day Sunday observance. The media and entertainment industry pre-empted the time of the Sunday observance, which included time for church, Sunday school, personal prayer, and parish festivals.[54]

French- and English-speaking Canadians, by contrast, practised their Catholicism energetically and enjoyed a strong identity within the

Catholic church. Rather than secularization overwhelming them and their culture, "sacredization" proved a more powerful force in their lives. Ultramontane bishops Bourget of Montreal, Fleming of St John's, and Lynch of Toronto initiated the devotional revolution, believing it was crucial to the survival of Canadian Catholicism. As the devotional revolution gained speed, new religious congregations sprang up first in France and Ireland, and then in Canada and the United States. The combination of parishes and religious congregations spread the Roman devotions of Pius IX and recruited the faithful into pious confraternities. Roman devotions, such as the rosary, processions, pilgrimages, evening vespers, and consecration of the home to the Sacred Heart of Jesus became popular among faithful Catholics. Sensing their new-found solidarity against secularization, Catholics believed that the Church was central for them in education, health care, and social welfare.[55]

The devotional revolution strengthened French- and English-speaking Catholicism.[56] It helped Catholics to cope with the pain of being out of step with secular society. Sacredization proved to be a more powerful force among Catholics than secularization because their community was more circumscribed and their sacramental faith not dependent upon the interpretation of the Word by the university world.[57]

At the same time the devotional revolution allowed Catholics to accept the two most important concepts in modern church life, voluntarism and separation of church and state. The faith in North America depended not upon the European principle of *cuius regio ejus religio* (the post-Reformation principle stating that the prince of the region determined its religion) but upon the free acceptance of a religion by its adherents. Their European predecessors had believed in a symbiotic relationship in which church and state supported one another's goals. Anything less was considered to be indifferent, permissive, and irresponsible to the things of the Lord. However, after 1840 Canadian Protestants abandoned the European concept of the union of church and state. It was inevitable that Catholics would follow. The practice of infant baptism remained strong among Catholics, but it also allowed the faithful, when they became adults, to affirm their chosen faith and freely support this church by involvement and donations.[55]

While benign secularization ebbed and flowed among the Protestant churches, sacredization strengthened the devotional life and faith commitment among Catholics. The secularization of public schools, science, and history weakened Protestantism. During the same period the devotional revolution galvanized the faith of Catholics, and the Catholic sacramental system nourished their faith on a regular basis.

THE RISE AND FALL OF
CATHOLIC HIGHER EDUCATION

Tertullian, a thinker of the early church, raised a key question for Christians: "What has Athens to do with Jerusalem, the Academy with the Church?" Brian Hogan supplies a contemporary answer by stating that Christians, while protecting themselves from secularization, have always opted for the academic forum and the intellectual life. Should Christian studies be focused only on the Scriptures and theology, or should they also include liberal arts, science, and philosophy? Hogan contends that Christians of the early church opted for academic forums and valued the pursuit of knowledge and the truth. The great medieval universities were founded, funded, and protected by the Christian church. The French Revolution secularized these universities, but the private religious colleges became the intellectual cutting edge for the Catholic confrontation with the secular world. In the face of nineteenth-century science and the secularized university, Canadian Catholics chose to send their children for undergraduate education to religious colleges that offered a balanced program of liberal arts, science, religion, and Catholic social teachings.[58]

How do Catholics approach higher education? According to Hogan, papal teachings ask the Christian university to provide the undergraduate with a thorough foundation in the Word of God. They also assert the importance of Catholic social teachings in the course offerings along with the study of liberal arts, scripture, and theology. The church asks that academic freedom be exercised by Catholic scholars in the transmission of the faith in its entirety. Finally, it must be pointed out to the professor that higher education is a mission of service and not necessarily a coherent or articulated system.[60] The Catholic university offers a complex, multicultural, and integrated approach to education with much room for variation. However, because of limited resources, it cannot afford the degree of specialization typical of the secular university.

Hogan selected three Catholic colleges as typical of Catholic higher education: St Francis Xavier of Antigonish, St Michael's of Toronto, and St Thomas More of Saskatoon. I would like to add a fourth of which I have some personal knowledge, St Paul's College at the University of Manitoba in Winnipeg. St Francis Xavier College was founded in 1853 to do two things: educate young men of the diocese for public life and provide suitable candidates for the clergy. As we have seen, the Sisters of Notre Dame affiliated St Bernard's Academy of Antigonish with St Francis Xavier in 1894 and offered women university courses leading to a Bachelor of Arts degree. Four women graduated in 1897.[61] making St Francis Xavier the first Catholic institution in North America to award women a university degree. In 1926 the college opened a Department of Nursing and Health in affiliation with the Sisters of St Martha and the School of Nursing of St Martha's Hospital. A department of St Francis Xavier also offered a Bachelor of Science in nursing. Besides being the first Catholic college to initiate women's education, St Francis Xavier pioneered new ways of sustaining Catholic educational institutions. According to Hogan, "the collaborative involvement of religious communities in developing and sustaining institutions has come to be a common feature of many such institutions in Canada."[62]

St Michael's College in Toronto was opened in 1852 by the Basilian Fathers at the request of Bishop Armand Charbonnel. In the bishop's mind the college's main goal was to educate young men and prospective clergy. In 1908 St Michael's became a federated college of the University of Toronto. It was noted earlier that St Joseph's and Loretto colleges affiliated four years later with St Michael's to offer Catholic women a chance to obtain a university education. St Michael's went on to establish the Pontifical Institute of Medieval Studies in 1929 to explore Thomistic theology and philosophy in a contemporary context and became widely known as a research centre. A graduate department in Theology was opened at St Michael's College in 1955. Along with Regis College, St Augustine's Seminary, and four other Christian colleges, St Michael's was a founding member in 1969 of the Toronto School of Theology of the University of Toronto. On the university campus, St Michael's pioneered cooperation between religious congregations and religious colleges, between Christian colleges and ecumenical theology, and between religious colleges and the secular university.[63] The restructuring of the college system at the University of Toronto in the 1970s, however, has left the religious colleges in serious financial difficulty and in a "hostile environment" for the foreseeable future.[64] The future of the Catholic college on the secular university campus is far from guaranteed.

At Saskatoon in 1926 the Catholic laity founded a Newman Centre at the University of Saskatchewan. Ten years later the laity established St Thomas More College to provide courses and teaching to meet "the broader intellectual needs of the Catholic community." The Basilian Fathers accepted responsibility for the college in 1936 and federated it with the University of Saskatchewan. The initiative of the Catholic laity assured that "the college preceded rather than followed the development of the seminary."[65] A small seminary was added by the diocese in 1966 to house seminarians completing their bachelor degrees. Dealing with financial challenges from without and threats to its autonomy from within, the college reached out for a broad base of community support by including non-Catholics among its governors, faculty, and students. This ecumenical approach permitted St Thomas More to re- solve its financial problems, affirm its federated agreement at the Uni- versity of Saskatchewan, and retain its Catholic character.[66]

Shortly after the founding of St Paul's College in Winnipeg, the En- glish-speaking Jesuits undertook its operation in 1933. It was the sec- ond Jesuit college in Manitoba, the first being St Boniface College established by the French-speaking Jesuits forty-five years earlier. The new Jesuit administration at St Paul's made every effort to raise aca- demic standards in order to compete for students with the other col- leges at the University of Manitoba. Assiduous study and hard work were emphasized as the formula for success. Enrolments rose along with revenue, and Jesuit faculty increased to eighteen along with dioce- san priests and lay instructors.[67] Ten years after the Second World War, St Paul's and the Anglican St John's moved their college divisions to new buildings at the Fort Garry campus giving their students access to the university libraries, science laboratories, and athletic facilities.

From 1958 to 1968, St Paul's and St John's enjoyed their golden age of being autonomous affiliated colleges. They continued to "receive student registration fees, to hire and pay their own faculty, and to determine their own curriculum."[68] These activities were the heart of autonomous religious colleges. The university departments by the Agreement of 1970 took over these college duties and college auton- omy disappeared. University professors formed a faculty union that controlled hiring, tenure, and promotion. The departments opened the colleges up to influences that were at adds with college life, weak- ening student organization and cohesion. Maintenance of the college buildings deteriorated. Not being able to hire its own faculty, St Paul's College became entirely dependent upon university departments for staffing. The departments looked to their own needs, not to those of the colleges. Teaching Jesuits disappeared from the campus, but lay professors and administrators took the helm and fielded new pro- grams that would maintain Catholic tradition and restore university fi- nancial support.[69]

Catholic colleges generally functioned as undergraduate institutions preparing future teachers and other professionals. They had few grad- uate facilities to groom a Catholic intelligentsia. For instance, it was only in the last twenty-five years that research facilities have been ex- panded at St Francis Xavier University, St Paul University in Ottawa, the Toronto School of Theology, and the Newman Theological Centre in Edmonton to offer graduate degrees in theology.

Brian Hogan asks what kind of access do students have if they want to embark on a Catholic university education in Canada. He contends that Canadians have less access today than in the past. His statistics show that in the United States one Catholic institution of higher education exists for every 200,000 Catholics, in India one for every 70,000 Catholics, and in Canada one for every 450,000 Catholics. Between 1970 and 1983, the number of Catholic universities and colleges in Canada has decreased by forty and is currently tallied at seventeen. The closures were brought about by the decrease in government funding for education, especially for small religious colleges, and the lack of religiously committed professors who are able to donate their salaries to the college. Catholics were forced to ask some hard questions: What constitutes a Catholic college? What value do Catholics place on higher education? Are Catholics willing to raise funds and sit on college boards?[70]

Hogan concludes that Christians from the time of the Roman Empire have embraced the academic forum and the intellectual life. Christian scholars founded the great medieval universities and colleges. Christians traditionally selected the best works from the classics. Catholic colleges have communicated the Christian tradition by teaching theology and applying it to Canadian social and economic problems. Catholics believe that the religious college is an important component of Canadian integrated learning, which embodies a balance of intellectual, personal, and communal values.[71]

CONCLUSION

Canadian Catholicism has been going through a learning experience that formed it into the postwar Canadian church. We saw how a religious congregation in the Maritimes and the Catholic Women's League in Edmonton sprang up and, quickly professionalized, extended their horizons to other Canadian communities. Other Catholic religious congregations in English-speaking Canada continued to expand church structures in the traditional way. The bishops, meanwhile, built supra-diocesan structures to sort out the Canadian church policies. The bishops, with the approval of the Holy See, looked to North American models to create the Canadian Catholic Conference as a forum for addressing contemporary problems. Canadian pluralism was by then entrenched, and the Catholic hierarchy included among their numbers French, Irish, Scottish, German, Italian, and Ukrainian bishops. As Canadian bishops constructed and expanded traditional forms of religious life, the Canadien bishops were challenged by the fundamental liberalization of the social and religious structures of their province. Secular liberalism, an overwhelming force in Quebec in the 1950s, only penetrated Anglophone Canada in the second half of the 1960s.

The devotional revolution and the sacramental system protected Canadian Catholics from secularization. Pious practices, separate schools, seminaries, and religious culture insulated Catholics from the mainstream Canadian culture. Catholic colleges were still a haven for a balanced education of intellectual, personal, and communal values. The move of Catholics towards higher studies and specialization exposed their faith to the challenge of the secular sciences. During the 1970s on the university campus, biblical criticism, technological changes, and benign secularization confronted the traditional English Catholic culture. Bruised from encounters with the secular university, Catholic institutions suffered from the reduced numbers of student places and professors, and the colleges lost ground to the secular universities. The Canadian bishops, hoping for insight into the problems of liberalization, secularization, consumerism, mass media, and the sexual revolution, assembled at the Second Vatican Council. Sloughing off the fossilized remains of ultramontane spirituality, the council brought forth a profound *aggiornamento* in Catholic culture. As the bishops during the early 1960s looked to conciliar teachings for understanding and guidance, the Liberal politicians in Quebec City moulded modern Quebec and secularized the church-state relationship.

14   The Second Vatican Council and Its Challenge

Angelo Roncalli, besides having been a parish priest and seminary professor, was the national director for the Italian overseas missions and for twenty-seven years a papal diplomat working during the interwar period and the Second World War in Bulgaria, Turkey, and Greece, and after the war in France. Sometimes dressed in tie and business suit, and sometimes vested in the episcopal soutane with its purple piping, Roncalli carried on the diplomacy of the Holy See and was exposed to the division between eastern and western Christianity. He listened to the voices of Muslims, French Republicans, and world diplomats. He helped to smuggle Jews from Nazi-controlled nations to safe havens elsewhere.[1] In his unpretentious but helpful manner, he looked at Christianity from without and within and saw the need for Catholic renewal, unity of Christians, and dialogue with the modern world. Following his election in 1959 as Pope John XXIII, he did what Christians do when in crisis: he called a church council to assemble in Rome.

As good Pope John began preparations to caulk the leaky planks of the barque of Peter, the new Liberal government of Jean Lesage at the helm of government in Quebec City passed legislation to update the civil machinery of the province. Quebec's speedy renewal of the social network challenged the Church and necessarily involved the restructuring of social institutions. The new subjectivity and freedom of the spirit defied the structures of both church and society.

THE QUIET REVOLUTION

In the early 1950s the Catholic Church in Quebec was perceived by Canadians from outside the province as an archetype of control and power. Cardinal Paul-Emile Léger (1950–1968) turned out to be a popular replacement for Joseph Charbonneau as archbishop of Montreal, and the Québécois appeared to maintain their passionate religious commitment. When appointed the archbishop, Léger was the very model of a pre-Vatican II cleric, intelligent, imposing, and the strong leader of a devoted church. Claude Ryan, editor of *Le Devoir* and onetime Quebec cabinet minister, described the church, which Léger and Archbishop Roy of Quebec guided, as heavily burdened. It operated most of the Quebec lower schools, forty classical colleges, three universities, provincial hospitals, social services, trade unions, and cooperatives and exerted a strong influence on the newspapers and publishers. The Catholic Church in Quebec to English-speaking observers appeared an unfathomable and impregnable fortress.[2]

The bishops and chaplains in Quebec guided the left-leaning Young Christian Workers and the Young Christian Students and encouraged them to reach out to other youth. Through study groups the Quebec youth were well acquainted with a Christian understanding of social justice, and they were encouraged to support workers' organizations and get involved in efforts to strengthen human rights and democracy. In their letters the bishops backed off from condemning socialism and communism and raised more immediate concerns for Christians. The religious leaders in the 1950s proved to be the strongest agents in Quebec for labour reform and social reform.[3]

The external image of a stable church in a secure province did not correspond to reality. Despite the church's many works and ministries,[4] some observers believed that the church's leadership in the early 1950s was out of touch with contemporary Quebec and that the church needed to be rebuilt from the ground up. Attendance at the weekly Mass was declining,[5] and the number of vocations to the priesthood and religious congregations was dwindling. One concerned witness described to a bishops' commission the task of rebuilding the shattered nature of Quebec society: "Our undertaking is like a huge tapestry; it could be refurbished so that the outside observer would see it shine again in all its brilliance, though it appears to be about to fall into tatters, piece by piece, because what holds it together has all but dried up."[6] Some lay leaders clearly saw Canadien Catholicism collapsing and in need of new vision.

Archbishop Léger of Montreal (1950–1968) at a demonstration of the Movement of
Christian Workers, ca 1950 (ANQ)

In a study of students in Quebec during the 1950s, Nicole Neatby
discovered that they were intent upon religious and political reform.
Avoiding political affiliation, they were deeply inspired by the Christian truths of Quebec society and looked for the emergence of a renewed Quebec. They saw Quebec in the postwar period as having
fallen "prey to a corrupt value system, its citizens increasingly dominated by materialistic and selfish goals," rather than sharing their new
wealth with their needy neighbours. The students established work-
shops to inculcate "the Christian idea of service to others."[7]

Students broke into two factions, traditionalist and modernist, that
they might question the *status quo* and implement answers. The tradi-
tionalists believed that the political and religious reforms they sought
were rooted in personal regeneration, deeper understanding of the
church's teaching, fuller participation in the sacraments, and service
of others. They joined Pax Romana, Fédération des étudiants des uni-
versités catholiques du Canada, and the St Vincent de Paul Society to
exercise their concern for the poor. In their ministry they experienced
the immediate needs of the poor but did not question the causes of
poverty.[8]

The modernist students took another approach by preparing an open environment for discussion on campus. They believed that Catholic teachings must be discussed and that "students would develop a stronger and more influential Catholic faith and, in turn, strengthen society's Christian values."[9] Unsympathetic to the traditional students who followed their faith blindly, they believed their faith had to be questioned and took a more critical stance towards the workings of church and state. They would read *Quartier Latin, Cité Libre,* and *Le Devoir* and enjoyed the provocative articles that challenged them to a deeper understanding of the Christian faith. They believed that being authentic in their faith and sincere in their commitment was central to contemporary Christianity. They were sympathetic to secularization and declericalization and demanded access of laity to decision-making positions in education, health care, and social services.[10]

The university administration responded to student reformers with enthusiasm but within set limits. They liked the student involvement in social issues and their concern for the poor but imposed a type of censorship on *Quartier Latin* in that "scandalous articles and inappropriate texts" would have to be approved by two moderators. In the 1950s students were not anxious to alienate the university powers and accepted these restraints. The reforms sought by the modernist students, Neatby concludes, "heralded the debates and changes associated with the Quiet Revolution that would emerge a few years later."[11] Contemporary Catholicism fuelled the student expectations of the 1950s, but Quebec nationalism was to inflame the reforms of the 1960s.

The Quiet Revolution was officially launched in 1960 with the election in Quebec of the Liberal government of Jean Lesage. The laity took full control of the schools and universities, the hospitals and social services, the trade unions and cooperatives, and these institutions were secularized. The public purse was used to professionalize and expand these services. The civil servants quickly replaced clerics in managerial positions. Cardinals Léger and Roy and the religious superiors who operated most of these institutions reacted "with relative serenity" and did not overtly challenge the changes. The church thus allowed the revolution to remain quiet.[12] The right-of-centre journal *Tradition et Progrès,* published from 1957 to 1962, argued that religion should continue to have a role to play in the schools and universities, and that the state and the Church are a natural team in Quebec history.[13] But the bishops knew it was time to relinquish the heavy financial burden of upgrading the social network and to let the professionals and bureaucrats direct it.[14]

Sympathizing with the national aspirations of Québécois, the clergy affirmed the pursuit of democracy, modernity, freedom, and justice.

Church doctrine by the time of Vatican II embraced people's right to fashion their own political future.[15] The bishops now played the role of societal goads rather than overlords and cautioned the Quebec majority that they should respect minority groups such as anglophones, allophones, and native people.[16]

In view of the conflicts within Quebec society at that crucial juncture, Claude Ryan, longtime editor of *Le Devoir,* believed the Quebec church sincerely renewed itself and made a radical review of its relationship to society. The social undertakings of Catholics were streamlined and traditional institutions were downsized. New projects were launched for the poor, weak, and underprivileged. Believers and nonbelievers coexisted in Quebec society and open confrontation was allowed to erupt in public. In the wake of its radical review of church policy, according to Ryan, the Catholic community sought a deeper understanding of itself as it strove to respect the freedom of all individuals and set about reorganizing its service to the poor and underprivileged. The amicable secularization of social services in church-run institutions allowed Catholics to retain a pastoral presence in those institutions. A humbler, more modest and receptive church continued to support the people's right to determine their own political future.[17]

The old Catholic ideology centring on "rural values, ethnic solidarity, religion, and a rejection of politics and the state" was quickly swept away and replaced by a modern church that supported a multicultural and democratic society. A new nationalism based on social democracy rose up to free the Québécois from the anglophone business élite and Roman regulation and control. In the face of this new force, the bishops accepted the spirit of modernity flowing in the Quebec church and the importance of implementing social justice in Quebec society. In 1965, to ensure Christian involvement in the movement towards self-determination, the bishops accepted the Quebec independence movement. By 1970 Catholic groups had given way to secular reorganization in the formation of the new Quebec.[18]

Some traditional Catholics resisted these fast-moving changes. In November 1965 François-Albert Angers and Jesuit Jean Genest protested in the pages of *l'Action nationale* against the rapid expansion of state powers and feared the anti-clericalism of the Liberal government. At the same time their article "Le bill 60 et la démocratie totalitaire," published in the Jesuit *Relations,* protested the government's legislation as destroying the school system by modernizing and secularizing it. The article envisioned a factory-like school system that would create dehumanized and rootless students similar to machines with interchangeable parts.[19] Traditional Catholics hoped the school system would avoid this outcome by remaining[19] the way it was.

New professional teachers took a different view. They contended that during the interwar and wartime years the Quebec Catholic public school system was badly neglected by the Catholic school commission. Wendy Johnston has shown that because of a stronger tax base and politically more astute leaders, the Protestant school board was able to levy more funds for the development of its schools than were the Catholic boards. She contends that the resources available to the Catholic system were less than equal to those available to the Protestant boards. She also points out that Catholics who were better off sent their children to private schools run by religious congregations and were less interested in voting extra funds to Catholic public schools.[20] The fragmentation of the Quebec schools, despite efforts at centralization in the interwar period,[21] prevented the formation of a unified system for the generation of funds and teachers. But the ascendancy of the new professionals in the Catholic system meant that the neglected schools of the Catholic majority in Quebec would finally be suitably funded and organized.[22]

Catholics committed to modernizing society rallied and affirmed the direction of the Quiet Revolution. The Dominican magazine *Maintenant* through the 1960s encouraged the modernization of Quebec and the reform of the educational system. The magazine supported the autonomy of the political state, respect for the individual conscience, democratic structures in the church, and interreligious dialogue. It advocated state intervention hoping that the Québécois would participate more fully in the new nation, and through their participation avoid injustice, sexism, racism, imperialism, and exploitive capitalism.[23]

The new editor of the Jesuit magazine *Relations* backed the faith and justice movement within Quebec society. The magazine advocated political liberation, democratization of the church, liberty of conscience, and new forms of Christian expression. Christian Marxism was discussed in the magazine, along with the liberation theology of Latin America and self-determination of Quebec.[24]

At the end of the 1960s the church was disestablished and accepted a new role with the people of Quebec as *compagnon de route*. In future bishops would not control society but be friendly critics speaking to the moral issues of "unemployment, regional disparity, aboriginal rights, the plight of refugees and immigrants, and the environment."[25] The bishops advocated working for the collectivity while respecting minority distinctions. The church remained a significant but non-political presence in Quebec society. During the independence referendum of 1980, for example, the bishops asked the clergy to remain neutral and not to sway voters to one side or the other. The church,

David Seljak surmises, retained "its moral authority and public presence by creating a sustained ethical critique that integrated its traditional commitment to Quebec society with the new social teaching coming from Rome, Europe, and Latin America." Catholicism's enthusiasm in the 1980s "for democratic participation, responsible citizenship, and individual liberty," Seljak concludes, set the Quebec Catholic community off by "centuries" from the church of the 1950s.[26] A Canadian Catholic democratic ideology was being forged to meet the needs of Canadians in the twenty-first century.[27]

PRECONCILIAR CONSULTATION

Curial officials, bishops, and theologians in Rome earnestly began preparing the agenda for the opening sessions of the Second Vatican Council.[28] *Vota et consilia*, or agenda items, were requested from Catholic bishops and theologians around the world. The bishops were advised to prepare their responses in secret. Thinking of themselves more as branch-plant managers than successors of the apostles, many of the bishops sent perfunctory replies forwarding only traditional questions and answers to the preparatory commission. The Canadian bishops sent sixty replies in Latin to Rome – except for Cardinal Léger who sent nineteen pages in the vernacular.[29] As it turned out, "the Canadian bishops were mainly concerned by legal, disciplinary and, to some extent, liturgical questions."[30] Eighty-eight percent of the Canadian bishops responded to the commission, but the quality of the answers revealed limited vision.[31] According to Bishop De Roo, "First, the pope's call wasn't taken up very seriously [by the bishops]. Then, when the heads of the various Vatican congregations [in Rome] finally got down to work, they proposed and defended their own agendas. Later, the various Roman universities got into these turf wars."[32] In fact, little creative theology was contributed at this point on the major issues of the Church, such as ecclesiology, ecumenism, Christian unity, Scripture, lay apostolates, the roles of bishops, and women in the church.

The *vota* of the English-speaking bishops revealed an inadequate theological heritage that had marked the church from the First Vatican Council to the death of Pius XII in 1958. During this period pious and loyal bishops were chosen over scholarly bishops. The concept of episcopal collegiality was absent, and there was little incentive to consult the faithful or university savants. Yet the *vota* proved to be the first step in raising the episcopal consciousness of a world church that harboured great theological and liturgical diversity. Especially stimulating was contact with the theology of the postwar period, such as at the Institute Catholique in Paris and the University of Louvain in

Belgium,[33] which was rooted in the return of Catholic institutions to the biblical, patristic, and liturgical sources.

The *vota* of the anglophone bishops were one or two pages in length and gave little indication that the laity had been consulted. The topics dealt with the housekeeping chores of clerical dress, vernacular recitation of the breviary, reform of the Index of Forbidden Books, easing fasting rules, eliminating stipends, and the need for a universal catechism. Some bishops requested greater conformity among Eastern rite Catholics to the "Canadian way" and suggested that it should be made easier for them to become Latin rite.[34]

The Ukrainian eparch of Toronto, Isidore Borecky, submitted "the most far-reaching and profound submission." A sound theologian with a vision of a world church, he divided his recommendations into six: revision of the constitution of the church, proper designation of the church as "Catholic," not Roman Catholic, equality of the eighteen rites of the Catholic church, evangelization of unbelievers, reunion of Christian churches, and adaption of discipline to current needs. He expressed his concern that the Latin church was lording it over the Eastern church and that Western Catholics were assimilating Eastern Catholics. His was the only Canadian *vota* that proposed the visionary reunion of the Eastern and Western churches. Both Borecky and Archeparch Maxim Hermaniuk of Winnipeg showed a great sensitivity to the catholicity of the church, and as a result many of their recommendations were incorporated into the decrees of the Second Vatican Council.[35]

Eleven preparatory commissions were set up in June 1960 to which fifteen Canadian bishops and eleven priests were named. Cardinals McGuigan and Léger, and Archbishop Paul Bernier of Gaspé were appointed to the central coordinating committee. Archbishops Roy of Quebec City and Hermaniuk of Winnipeg were named to the theology commission. Archbishop Flahiff of Winnipeg was named to the commission for religious life. Coadjutor Archbishop Philip Pocock of Toronto was appointed to the commission for clergy and lay people. Bishop Alexander Carter and G.E. Bourgeois were consultants for the lay apostolate. Theologian Gregory Baum was consultant for the secretariat promoting Christian unity. The appointed commissions were to compress the *vota* from bishops and universities around the world and reduce them to two thousand pages, or nineteen booklets, presented to the bishops upon their arrival.[36]

Eighty-five per cent of the bishops of the province of Quebec sent in their *vota* to Rome. This response totalled seventy-four pages, of which Cardinal Léger, as mentioned, contributed nineteen pages, eight bishops contributed three to six pages, and the remaining thirteen one to two pages each. The bulk of the Quebec responses came from the metropolitan centres of Montreal, Quebec City, Ottawa, Saint-Jean, and Valleyfield. Responses were prepared with little consultation among fellow bishops. The exceptions to the rule were the submissions of Sherbrooke and Nicolet, Valleyfield and Montreal auxiliary, and Sault-Ste-Marie and Joliette, for which separate reports had been prepared in common with each other. Bishop Charles Parent of Rimouski appointed a diocesan commission of three, Roy of Quebec City sought help from theologians asking that a diocesan committee be struck, and Lemieux of Ottawa consulted clergy at the seminary, in parishes, and at *l'Action catholique*.[37] In all, thirteen Quebec bishops structured mechanisms for consultation within the diocese.[38]

The Quebec *vota* recommended mitigation of fast and abstinence regulations, renewal of sacraments, use of the vernacular, a renewed understanding of the church, enhancement of episcopal power, lay apostolates, consideration of the relationship between Scripture and tradition, and ecumenism. Léger himself suggested that non-Catholic observers be allowed at the council. An interested and intelligent participant, Léger placed himself apart from the other Quebec bishops. His *vota* were extensive, clearly organized, and well thought out, and they revealed his unique exposure to *nouvelle théologie*. Archbishop Maurice Roy of Quebec, in his prudent manner, elaborated questions for the council but without imposing his own judgments. Bishop J.A. Martin of Nicolet, revealing his intellectual gift for patristics, was sensitive both to the Eastern tradition and modern problems. Archbishop M.J. Lemieux of Ottawa and Bishops G.M. Coderre of Saint-Jean and Paul Bernier of Gaspé were notable contributors to the preparation of the council.[39]

The Quebec *vota* expressed pastoral concerns and avoided the contentiousness of theological disputation. They acknowledged a decline in Catholic culture since the turn of the century and looked forward to a more flexible church that would make proper adjustment to the contemporary world. They sought the rechristianization of society through the use of renewed liturgical and sacramental forms. The Quebec *vota* reflected the theological trends of Belgium and Europe more than those of North or South America. The *vota* revealed, writes Gilles Routhier, not polished theological thinking, not an analysis of the social change that was breaking upon Quebec, but the beginning of an awakening of the Quebec church to the loaded meaning of the Quiet Revolution.[40]

Quebec Catholics nibbled on European theological renewal from a distance, but it was rather their concern for social justice that convinced them to embrace the conciliar *aggiornamento*. The preconciliar consultation caused disturbances among clergy and laity and began the awakening of the Quebec church. University professors, union leaders, Catholic Action, and the intelligentsia injected new experiences from the contemporary world and broadened the outlook of the clergy. Catholics resolved to confront the modern world and the contemporary media. The scenario on the diocesan level of collegial consultation became firmly rooted among the faithful.[41]

A bishop and theological team that must be singled out was that of Archbishop Maurice Baudoux of Saint-Boniface. Responding in 1959 to the request for reflections on the upcoming council, the archbishop gathered a council of nineteen priests living within the archdiocese to prepare a response for the preparatory commission. Many of these youthful consultants later become bishops in their own right: Remi De Roo at Victoria (1962), Antoine Hacault at Saint-Boniface (1964), Edouard Gagnon at Saint-Paul (1969), and Noël Delaquis at Gravelbourg (1973). The team prepared submissions, met periodically, and began selecting appropriate problems to submit to the council.[42]

The most important and creative contributions to the preparatory stages of the council came from the Canadian post-secondary institutions in Montreal, Quebec City, Ottawa, and Toronto. The Faculty of Theology at the University of Montreal recommended a contemporary explication of the relationship between Scripture and tradition, clarification of the meaning of ordinary magisterium, and elucidation of modern christology taking into account the theories of psychology. The Faculty of Political-Social Sciences asked for a theology of lay spirituality – which later emerged in the council documents *Gaudium et Spes* and *Lumen Gentium*. The dean of Commercial Studies of the University of Montreal suggested that the council be open to the findings of sociology, economics, anthropology, and political science and allow some experts in these fields to be on the preparatory theological commissions. They wanted to shed light on some of the key contemporary questions of the period. Michael Fahey says of the three "remarkable" academic submissions from Montreal that they "can be placed on a par with some of the finest theological reflection underway in Europe at that time especially in France and Belgium."[43]

The University of Ottawa provided important contributions in four sections: *de ecclesia*, dissemination of Catholic teaching, liturgical renewal, and canonical reform. It questioned the encyclical *Humani Generis,* which equated the Roman Catholic church with the mystical body of Christ and asked that its membership be more lucidly explained. It asked further for a clarification of the differing roles of bishops and laity.[44]

The second section of the Ottawa submission asked that Catholic theology confront the new sciences of psychology and psychoanalysis. It asked that teachers and students be allowed to read necessary material currently prevented by the Index of Forbidden Books. The third section requested that liturgy be reformed and the vernacular employed. The final section called for revision of canon law by the council rather than by a papal commission.[45]

Laval University made a brief submission of a page and a half under five headings: constitution, clerics, religious, sacraments, and "sacred times." In regard to the constitution of the church, it asked that a better balance be found between papal primacy, episcopal authority, and the role of the laity. They proposed uniformity of clerical dress and a reduced exemption for order priests. They also recommended that the Eucharistic fast should be reduced, concelebration considered, and mixed marriages permitted in church. The Pastoral Institute suggested to the council that liturgical readings be in the vernacular, eucharistic prayer in an audible voice, and the lectionary cycle be renewed.[46]

The Pontifical Institute of Mediaeval Studies at the University of Toronto submitted two pages recommending higher qualifications for the professors of Catholic colleges and seminaries. It stressed the importance of students and professors having access to literature on the Index and of encouraging them to publish the fruit of the academic research. The submission suggested that clergy should be well educated and exposed to Canadian culture in order to minister to laity who were increasingly cultured and better educated. It recommended that the Vatican library be kept open during summer for the use of scholars. In short, writes Michael Fahey, "what was submitted by the four Canadian Catholic centres of learning is a fitting tribute to their health and creative vision."[47]

The submissions from the dioceses, scholars point out, were not theologically strong, although the Ukrainian and Canadien *vota* had more weight than the anglophone *vota*. The Catholic colleges were more in touch with the directions of world Christian theology than the dioceses and proved more helpful in providing the preparatory commission with vision for the future. The preparation of the *vota* was a wake-up call to the Canadian church to leave textbook theology behind it and begin to discern the signs of the times.

CONCILIAR AGGIORNAMENTO

Eighty Canadian cardinals and bishops arrived at Rome to become involved in the commissions and regular sessions of the Second Vatican Council. They joined 2,460 other council fathers checking into hotels and religious houses.[48] If one were to choose three Canadian stars of the council, they would have to be Cardinal Léger of Montreal, Archbishop Baudoux and his St Boniface team, and the Ukrainian duo Archeparch Maxim Hermaniuk of Winnipeg and Eparch Isidore Borecki of Toronto. Many others deserve recognition for their work, but these three contributed in special ways. To begin with, Léger made 24 interventions on the floor of the council, second only to Cardinal Ruffini who intervened 36 times. The prominent cardinals Frings and Bea each intervened only 18 times, and Cardinals Alfrink and Suenens only 17 times.[49] Hermaniuk spoke 8 times. Baudoux addressed the council 7 times but also submitted 23 written texts to the council, as opposed to only four submitted by Léger. Baudoux was president of the Canadian bishops' conference at the beginning of the council and during the sessions was succeeded by Archbishop George Flahiff who spoke once at the council. Both represented the Canadian bishops at the Inter-Conference Group of national bishops who held regular caucuses to discuss the conciliar issues.[50]

Cardinal Léger spoke on religious life, the Virgin, marriage, the teaching function of bishops, the life of priests, and the peace of the kingdom. His most significant act before the first session was a letter written to John XXIII in September 1962 addressing the deficiencies of the conciliar program. Graciously alerting the pope to the poverty of the main schemas prepared for the council, Léger called for a genuine *aggiornamento* of Catholic institutions and thought. He asked that in faithfulness to Christ the council not reconstruct past ecclesial structures but address the needs of all people in a complex and multicultural world. He asked that authentic human values be respected even in the event of error and that the church put itself at the service of humanity. Léger believed that theological traditions should be recognized for what they are – one tradition among many.[51]

The Roman dicasteries (agencies of the Roman Curia), Léger recommended to John XXIII, might cooperate with scholars and hand over difficult questions to Catholic universities for research and reflection. For Léger, God's revelation went beyond the church. He proposed that the church not overuse and thus abuse the gift of infallibility. He asked that the church be humble in its pursuit of truth and remain within its field of competence. Gaining outside authority for his letter, Léger won the support of six principal cardinals, Liénart of Lille, Suenens of Brussels, Frings of Cologne, König of Vienna, Döpfner of Munich, and Alfrink of Amsterdam, who affixed their signatures to the document. Montini of Milan was approached but, although sympathetic, did not sign. In this move, Léger struck one of the first crucial blows at the council to liberate the council fathers from curial control and thus shape the conciliar coalitions for the upcoming sessions.[52] Sharing Pope John's vision, Léger, Montini, the cardinals mentioned above, and the majority of residential bishops gave the council a whole new thrust.[53]

After the opening Mass at St Peter's Basilica, the bishops were scheduled to approve the membership of the commissions and begin work. Cardinal Liénart stood up and moved that time be allowed for consultation and study of the list of the commissioners. His motion was immediately seconded by Cardinal Frings. This was a crucial turning point, and the Council began to reinvent itself.[52] Archbishop Baudoux quickly organized the Canadians to put together lists of Canadian nominees to the commissions, and then began to collect nominees from other national conferences to compile lists of commissioners from around the world. Eleven Canadians were elected and two appointed. Canadians, who comprised two percent of the membership, received four percent of commission seats. Commissioners included Léger, Roy, and Georges Pelletier of Trois-Rivières assigned to faith and morals, Marius Paré of Chicoutimi and John Cody of London assigned to seminaries and Catholic education, Martin of Nicolet assigned to liturgy, Lemieux of Ottawa to government of dioceses, Pocock of Toronto to discipline, Flahiff to religious life, Valérien Bélanger of Montreal to sacraments, Baudoux to oriental churches, and Hermaniuk to the Secretariat for Promoting Christian Unity. National conference presidents, including Baudoux, organized themselves into the Inter-Conference Group, which met on Friday afternoons to compare notes and plan strategy.[55]

A second Quebec bishop who was prominent for his contribution was G.M. Coderre of Saint-Jean. He asked the council to exercise consultation and cooperation in the process of renewal. He made three interventions during the sessions of 1963, 1964, and 1965. In the first he asked for more openness to the needs of the Eastern bishops. In his second intervention, he spoke in favour of church support for the presence of women in various roles at the council, in the church, and in society. He pointed out that because of their pride, men alone were not able to discern God's will for women. In his third intervention Coderre asked for a declericalization of the church and for the episcopate not to dominate the community it served. He asked the church to engage in ecumenical dialogue, which, he pointed out, was the necessary stage between former condemnations and future Christian unity. He hoped that the Church, through collegial consultation, would be de-Italianized and internationalized.[56]

The team of Archbishop Baudoux deserves special recognition for its work both before and during the council. Ukrainian eparchs

Borecki and Hermaniuk must be acknowledged for their international vision of church. Borecki is singled out for this groundbreaking pre-conciliar letter seeking equality of Eastern and Western cultures and the ecclesial union of Eastern and Western churches as discussed above.[57] Hermaniuk is placed in the conciliar constellation for the eight interventions he made with his usual finesse (one more than Baudoux and seven more than Flahiff).[58]

As a member of the commission on religious life, Archbishop Flahiff wrote long letters to friends about the happenings of the council. He remarked that while the speakers were limited to ten minutes the acoustics in the huge nave of St Peter's were excellent and without echo. Flahiff spoke to the council on the historical aspects of Christian divisions, which, he believed, might be looked at as a dynamic allowed by God for the awakening and conversion of the people of God. Schisms remind the church that "she is not yet as holy as she should be and not yet perfectly obedient to her vocation to be catholic."[59]

In regard to the document on religious life, Flahiff regretted that by the autumn of 1964 it was not ready for submission. He wrote that the second draft "has been sadly truncated as a result of successive reductions on orders from higher authorities and now lacks both organic unity and inspiration, dealing as it does with a limited number of more or less unconnected practical aspects of our life."[60] He was cheered, however, that religious life found a place at the centre of the Church in the important document *Lumen Gentium,* published in November 1964. *Lumen Gentium* was prepared by Belgian theologians under the direction of Cardinal Suenens. Yet it was not until the following year at the final session in October 1965 that Flahiff and the other members of the commission saw *Perfectae Caritatis* on religious life win council approval.[61]

Bernard Daly highlights four Canadian bishops who contributed to the decrees on the lay apostolate: Alexander Carter of Sault Ste Marie, William Power of Antigonish, Paul-Émile Charbonneau of Hull, and Remi De Roo of Victoria. Carter served as a consultant to the council's preparatory commission on the lay apostolate and kept in touch with the members of the council commission of the lay apostolate and social communications. He forcefully intervened concerning the first draft: "You know, reading this draft I could come to only one conclusion. We are afraid, scared stiff in fact, of the laity and we do not want to allow them, in any way, shape or form, to share in any creative action in the Church. They are there just to listen and to obey. This will not do."[62] He asked that the document be rewritten, and it passed through several more drafts. In October 1964 he intervened at council on the third draft by criticizing it for being negative, "composed solely by clerics," and asked that the role of the laity in the mission of the church be broadened.[63]

Charbonneau, De Roo, and Power, living in the same residence and coordinating their activities, worked also on the document of the lay apostolate. They seconded Carter's view asking that the draft be rewritten so that the instruction would reflect the wish of the laity for "a dynamic invitation to follow a vocation rooted in authentic biblical theology of the People of God." De Roo recommended that the people of God be called "through baptism and confirmation to co-operate with Christ in the restoration of all things according to the divine plan of redemption." The laity and the clergy worked together in both the temporal and spiritual orders.[64]

Charbonneau complemented De Roo's recommendations by asking that the laity incarnate themselves in their communities so that "the Church … [might] be the world moving towards the perfect realization of God's whole plan for it, at the level of both creation and redemption." The laity were to immerse themselves in the theological life of Christ and share religious reality with those around them. They could be mandated in their work by the episcopal guidance of Catholic Action.[65]

Power described how the laity should be formed to be living witnesses of Christ and participate in the mission of the church. Their formation should develop human gifts, involve them in the world, lead into the mystery of Christ, encourage them through group action, and maintain their contact with the bishop.[66]

The work of these four Canadian bishops can be seen in the council documents. The specific role for the laity in the mission of the church was identified in *Lumen Gentium* (sections 31–3), *Gaudium et Spes* (section 43), and *Apostolicam Actuositatem* (Lay Apostolate). This last decree in its second section describes the laity as having "in the Church and in the world their own assignment in the mission of the whole people of God." The third section identifies the "twofold vocation" of evangelization and sanctification of humanity. Apostolic formation (sections 28–32) talks about the development of human gifts, involvement in the world, entry into the mystery of Christ, and relations with the bishops. "It is not to claim too much," Daly writes, "to conclude that Carter, Charbonneau, De Roo and Power had a major role in bringing the decree of the lay apostolate into agreement with what other major Council texts said as an historic innovation, about the place of the laity in the divine plan for creation and redemption."[67]

The conciliar decrees gave new energy to Catholics in regard to Scriptural renewal, liturgical reform, vernacular, collegiality, lay involvement, and interfaith dialogue. Questions that remain for future church people to consider are whether Catholics as a church can employ conciliar organization rather than the monarchical model; whether synods will have deliberative rather than consultative powers (as Hermaniuk proposed); whether women, who make up more than fifty percent of parishioners, will be permitted to be part of the governing structure; and whether revelation can be uncovered primarily in the local church rather than at head office. These questions and others must be seriously dealt with by any Christian body.

For four years the bishops commuted back and forth between their home dioceses and Rome. Meeting with delegates of all races and nations from around the world enlarged their vision of the church and its mission. The council strengthened the bishops in the bonds of world Christian fellowship and enriched the Canadian bishops in their understanding of Canadian Christianity. Returning to North America in the late fall of 1965, they discovered a revolution of popular consciousness underway in Canadian Catholicism and, within their own dioceses, a much broader concept of lay ministry.[68]

THE CHALLENGE OF SUBJECTIVITY

At the plenary assembly in 1985, Julien Harvey, sj, asserted to the Canadian bishops that the Roman church since the Reformation lived in an objective world that presumed the existence of linear time and a body of objective knowledge. The members at the Second Vatican Council believed Christian time had a definite beginning at the creation of the world, a middle with the life, death, and resurrection of Jesus Christ, and the end time with God's final coming. For the Christian, life proceeds from the experience of faith in dealing with our past, through the good and loving acts of the present, and towards the hope that elucidates our future. Christians since the disciplinary and doctrinal formulations of the Council of Trent learned to believe in the existence of objective models and demanded conformity to them. Catholic institutions were perceived to be localities of discipline and schools places of order and learning, where catechisms were to be memorized and rules kept. The Tridentine decrees made Catholic life uniform around the world, and in nineteenth-century Canada, ultramontane spirituality inspired the observance of Catholic devotion, which was easily recognized and seriously followed.[69]

In the worldwide romantic revolution of the 1960s, existentialists, phenomenologists, poets, and literati challenged church-going, duty-bound Catholics anew. The subjective universe emphasized affectivity, authenticity, personal growth, and the creation of human solidarity. Powered by this new subjectivity, many Catholics challenged the objective world out of which the council, its teachings, and the church sprang.

Expatiating on the spiritual conversions outlined by Canadian theologian Bernard Lonergan, Fred Crowe explains the importance of subjective conversion for objective understanding. Conversion, in Crowe's view, is the basis of dialogue among religious people and among religious groups. A fourfold conversion of soul, mind, heart, and emotion is necessary before the reunion of divided Christian denominations might take place.[70]

Communications after the council slackened between Ottawa and Rome just when Canadians hoped contacts would be enhanced. The Canadian bishops wrote letters during this period on various topics, including *Humanae Vitae* and the decentralization of the church, and the Vatican bureaucracy perceived the Canadian bishops as progressive. The result was that their requests for the laicization of priests and for decisions on marriage cases received a delayed response from the Roman Curia. Rome, it became obvious, decided without listening either to special consultants or bishops' conferences. This ecclesial blindness left the Canadian bishops apprehensive about Roman methodology on other problems.

In 1967 the apostolic delegate, Archbishop Emanuele Clarizio, expressed interest in establishing closer ties with the Canadian bishops through regular meetings, interviews, and consultations between his office and the Canadian Catholic Conference. At a plenary meeting of the bishops in 1969, the delegate, in an un-Roman fashion, cast aspersions upon the Canadian bishops, using strong words like "revolt" and complaining of his sufferings at their hands. Cardinals Roy and Flahiff immediately wrote to Rome giving assurances to Paul VI in the name of the Canadian bishops. In 1969, to ensure open communications in the future, the president and vice-president of the CCC resolved to make annual visits to the Holy See to facilitate a direct exchange of their views with Roman officials.[71] They hoped by this pilgrimage to "comment, suggest, present requests, and to assess the life and work of the Canadian church."[72] They also considered installing a permanent representative in Rome and inviting Roman officials to visit Canada. Although the communication problems resolved themselves, they realized Roman officials viewed the Canadian church as a kingdom to be ruled and local dioceses as provinces to be governed.

For political reasons, Prime Minister Pierre Trudeau sought diplomatic recognition from the Holy See and the exchange of ambassadors. Thus, the apostolic delegation in Ottawa was raised to the rank of a pro-nunciature in October 1969. The government named an Irish Canadian Catholic, Everett Robbins of Manitoba, as its first ambassador to the Holy See. After receiving the news of the pro-nuncio's appointment, the president of the CCC announced apologetically, especially for the benefit of other Christian clergy, that bishops had not sought "a change of status and had not wished a privileged situation," and that they would continue their ecumenical activity "on the basis of equality, respect, and fraternal love."[73]

In the mid-1980s Restorationists from around the world, reacting to the romantic extremes of the 1960s, struck back. They reasserted traditional neoconservative values, restricted the interpretations of council documents, and condemned liberation theologians from the Third World. Their lay colleagues in the public forum advanced a neo-liberal political agenda of free enterprise, deregulation, and curtailment of social programs. Transnational corporations sought the advantage of law and order on a world scale. It was now that the G7 nations would determine the economic rationalization for the northern as well as the southern nations. Taking a different tack, the Church opted to align itself with the poor and the marginalized around the world. The Second Vatican Council had called upon Catholics everywhere to affirm this option by seeking justice in society and the compassion of good works.[74] In countries of the southern hemisphere liberation theology inspired people in their struggle to bring forth the kingdom of God in this world.[75]

The impact of the council on Catholics has been dramatic, and it was received by Catholics in three ways.[76] The faithful first received the council by means of liturgy and catechesis. The liturgy, sacraments, responses, and hymns were translated into vernacular languages so that they could be readily understood and adopted by the congregation. In the Eucharist the laity saw, as in the early church, the priest facing them from the altar in the front of the sanctuary and directly addressing them in prayer and word. The parishioners participated in this "work of the people" as lectors, servers, ushers, and ministers of communion.[77]

For renewing the catechesis, the *Come to the Father* series was employed after the council and used into the 1980s. Many lay teachers were involved in discussions that helped to shape the catechetical method and content. Memorization was abandoned as a principle method of instruction so that teaching could be centred on helping the children to love Jesus and to understand their religious commitment. The dysfunction of the family in Canadian society demanded that the catechetical initiation of the student to God the Father be shifted to Jesus Christ who shares his Father with us. Responding to this new social phenomenon, the *Born of the Spirit* (elementary level) and *We Are Strong Together* (intermediate level) series emerged during the 1980s and 1990s.[78] The renewal of liturgy in the churches and catechetics in the schools revived for many faithful Catholics their personal prayer life, their friendship with God, and their commitment to Christianity.[79]

A second way in which the faithful received the council was through the outpouring of the Spirit, which aroused inner subjectivity in their lives. The notion of the fundamental option in moral decisions helped to deepen a sense of personal conscience. There was a new effort to strive for authenticity by the four conversions of religion, morality, understanding, and psychic integration. The charismatic renewal brought into many people's lives the experience of the Spirit for which they yearned. The reception of the message of the council by many Catholics renewed their inner life.

The local churches received the council in a third way. They welcomed the *aggiornamento* in the administration of the diocese and began to reform local church structures. The CCC expanded its consultations to include laity and other believers. Senates of priests and parish councils emerged to widen grass-roots participation in the administration of the Canadian church. The council documents stressed collegiality among the bishops and the importance of their mutual participation in the life of the international community.[80] In regard to overseas missions, the bishops were disappointed that they were not encouraged by the Holy See to extend direct help between various national churches without first going through the demeaning exercise of seeking permission. The council documents were received publicly by the exercise of liturgy and catechesis, personally in subjective and individual growth, and structurally in the effort to encourage participation of the faithful in the work of the church.[81]

Christ's presence in the church and the church's presence in the world meant, according to Julien Harvey, a Christian emphasis on human rights. To form a compassionate society, the church put much emphasis on the option for the poor.[82] It meant resisting alliances with the neo-liberalism of self-help and the law-and-order Christian Right.[83] The Canadian church becomes the sacrament of human rights when it acts justly and associates with those who are marginalized by our society, that is, Amerindians, immigrants, refugees, the elderly, and women. Renewed ministries in the church were for the benefit of all. They were involved in the renewal of human solidarity (*koinonia*) and the service of the disadvantaged (*diakonia*), and they acted as an advocate of cooperative society.[84]

At the risk of being called "naive," the church, Harvey concludes, must continue to speak for the marginalized. Daily contact with the hungry, the homeless, and the suffering must force the church to intervene on behalf of the poor. The church must deepen its sensitivity to the weak and its authenticity in living the Christian gospel. The mission of the local church is to speak out at diocesan and world synods. As the council has directed and recent popes have written, the church must strive to transform the hard-nosed attitude of materialists into a more compassionate vision for the progress of society.[85]

CHARISMATIC RENEWAL

The Spirit of God not only visited the theologians and clergy engaged in dialogue during the council but it also poured its power into the hearts of the Christian community. During the three decades since the Second Vatican Council, charismatic renewal has spread across Canada and profoundly moved a sizeable number of Catholics. The twofold movement was both positive and negative: it was a response to the reading of the Word of God but also a reaction against the secularization and liberalization of Canadian society.

The renewal began in the United States at Duquesne University in 1967. By the following year, according to James Hanrahan, Basilian professor of church history, it had spread to Madonna House at Combermere, Ontario. Catherine de Hueck, the founder of Combermere, felt that the Latin church lacked awareness of the Spirit, and thus she welcomed the freeing expression of the Spirit within her community. "The release of the Holy Spirit" brought much awe, joy, and forgiveness to the Madonna House community.[86]

Beginning in Canada at Combermere in August 1968, the renewal spread quickly to the principal cities of all the provinces and to countless other Canadian communities. Although free of the bureaucratic structure of the Catholic church, charismatics were ready to accept the spiritual direction of the church. The movement continued to spread rapidly among Canadian Catholics during the last decades of the twentieth century and became a source of vocations to priesthood and religious life.

The Catholic experience of the Spirit was not quite the same as that of the Pentecostal churches. The Pentecostal churches placed great emphasis on the expression of the gift of tongues as the public manifestation of the true baptism of the Holy Spirit.[87] By contrast, the Catholic experience would place praying in tongues among the many gifts of the Spirit, such as peace of soul amidst troubles, a hunger for the Scriptures, a deep appreciation of the sacraments, and a conversion of life. Catholic tradition recognized the gift of tongues in the context of other gifts of the Spirit. The charismatic movement brought to the members of Madonna House an openness to others, an ability to exercise new ministries, and a healing power among the participants.[88]

Father Jim Duffy convened a charismatic prayer group at the Marian Centre in Regina in 1969. He held regular meetings, and the numbers began to increase. At one point during the year, he counted sixty-five names. By the beginning of 1970, an average of twenty-six attended the weekly meetings. In the spring attendance rose to sixty. Outside influences on this group came from Ann Arbor, Michigan, and Madonna House in Ontario. Father Duffy was transferred to the West Indies in the fall of 1970 and left that charismatic prayer group well established.[89]

Other charismatic prayer groups popped up across Canada. Groups were initiated at Vancouver in 1969, Edmonton in 1971, Winnipeg in 1973, and Ottawa in 1975. In Ontario groups were organized in 1969 at St Mary's College in Sault Ste Marie, and at Holy Rosary Church in Toronto, Holy Redeemer College and Assumption Church in Windsor. In Toronto Jean Vanier gave a faith and sharing retreat and inspired a group to meet in 1970 at St Augustine's Seminary for Scripture study and shared prayer. Influenced by the Full Gospel Business Men's Fellowship, two more charismatic prayer groups were formed in Toronto. One, named Emmanuel Prayer Group, met in the crypt of St Basil's Church and the other met at Holy Rosary Church. From these two groups other charismatic prayer groups sprang up throughout Toronto.[90]

In Ottawa Fr Bob Bedard encountered students in 1975 who asked that he introduce the charismatic renewal to St Pius X High School. Not entirely sympathetic, as Bedard tells it, he nevertheless attended a Life in the Spirit seminar to learn about the movement and to experience the Spirit. He received the "baptism of the Holy Spirit," and from this pivotal event came the gift of personal prayer. He rejoiced in this new gift and willingly placed his future in God's hands.[91]

At St Pius X, Bedard guided the lives of young students to solid Catholic piety, and a number of them entered the seminary. He also gave spiritual direction and personal healing to disillusioned seminarians who were ready to abandon their vocations to the priesthood. While Bedard was pastor of St Mary's Parish in Ottawa, a number of his young friends were ordained. With the approval of the archbishop of Ottawa, this small group founded the Companions of the Cross. By the middle of the 1990s, the Companions had attracted over fifty seminarians of which over twenty were ordained. They now direct six parishes in the Ottawa area and have requests to open parishes in Canada, the United States, and abroad.[92]

In Quebec the charismatic renewal began in 1969 when Sr Flore Crête returned to Montreal from Notre Dame University in Indiana. When permission to start a group at the motherhouse of the Sisters of Providence was refused, she founded a group in her family home. The following year, Father Jean-Paul Regimbal returned from Phoenix, Arizona, and was appointed director of the Trinitarian retreat house at

Granby, Quebec. His charismatic prayer influenced retreatants. Some were healed amidst great excitement, and almost instantly prayer groups started up. At Loyola College, Montreal, in the summer of 1973, Father Regimbal held a charismatic conference attended by five thousand, half anglophone and half francophone. The following summer sixty-five hundred participated at Laval University. In 1977 twenty thousand participated at a French-speaking charismatic renewal held at the Olympic facilities in Montreal.[93] It was estimated that by 1978 charismatic Catholics in Quebec numbered between forty thousand and sixty thousand.[94]

English-speaking Quebec was alerted to the renewal by Oblate father Joe Kane. On sabbatical from mission work, he was inspired by charismatic groups in Seattle. After some work with renewal groups in Vancouver, Father Kane went to Montreal where several prayer groups emerged. Along with other English and French clergy, he played a significant role in the development of charismatic renewal in Quebec.[95]

Charismatic renewal was interesting but also threatening to the Québécois. It threatened because it was inspired by English-speaking culture offering what appeared to be new forms of worship and a new spirituality that might be contemptuous of church authority and Canadien culture. To deal with these fears, the charismatic leaders of Quebec asked Archbishop Paul Grégoire of Montreal in 1972 for his permission to conduct a seminar at the Grand Séminaire for the priests and religious. They acquainted the priests and religious with "information about the charismatic renewal, its history, the experience involved, and its developing theology."[96] The seminar was a success, the clergy accepted the presentations earnestly, and in six months the numbers of those involved in charismatic renewal doubled.

The renewal was based upon experiencing the peace of God in one's life. The movement contended that those who knew the presence of God in their lives experienced inner peace and avoided despair. Inner peace for the charismatic is rooted in a personal encounter with the Lord. God takes the initiative in loving those who welcome him in their hearts. To receive this interior peace, recipients must place themselves in the hands of God and abandon themselves to the power of the Lord.[97]

The diocesan seminar on charismatic renewal resolved the cultural fear among Québécois, but two very serious problems arose: the shortage of priests familiar with charismatic expression and the inability of an unstructured movement to cope with rapid growth. The lack of priests available for prayer groups left a gap in the charismatic experience especially in the areas of prayer instruction and sacramental life. The average priest, moreover, was slow to take the new seekers seriously and deal with their hunger for prayer when their theology and ecclesiology were limited. Prayer groups grew rapidly in Quebec during the 1970s. By 1979, 822 prayer groups existed with 38,000 members, whereas in the rest of Canada, 500 prayer groups thrived with 20,000 members.[98]

In the summer of 1970, Father John McLeod returned from Ann Arbor, Michigan, to Cape Breton and began prayer groups in his New Waterford parish. Oblate fathers Joe Kane and Fred Miller arrived in Charlottetown to give a retreat to the Sisters of St Martha. In the evening they held ecumenical charismatic prayer services, which were open to the clergy and laity of the area. Fathers Faber MacDonald and Gerry Tingley attended the meetings.[99]

In response to requests from the Halifax laity in 1971, Archbishop James Hayes (1967–91) asked Fathers MacDonald, Tingley, and Ted Butler to meet with interested parishioners. These meetings continued in different homes until the group settled at St Thomas Aquinas Church. In 1973 Father Phil Lewis of Newfoundland attended a charismatic leadership session in Charlottetown and then returned to his parish in Freshwater near Placentia to initiate a charismatic prayer group. That same year, Redemptorist father Bill Comerford invited Fathers MacDonald and Tingley to help him begin a charismatic prayer group in Saint John, New Brunswick, while at Maison Ste Croix in St Joseph, New Brunswick, Father Oscar Melanson founded an Acadien group.[100]

An attempt in 1973 to set up an Atlantic Pastoral Committee at Charlottetown to direct the movement collapsed because participants feared being controlled. There was a desire among Catholic charismatics to let the Spirit flow freely without interference from ecclesial structures. A second effort in Halifax in 1976 was more successful, and the Atlantic Service Committee was established. Charismatic conferences were organized for Charlottetown, Halifax, Moncton, Saint John, Antigonish, and Sackville. In the western provinces and in Ontario and Quebec, similar structures emerged, giving direction but being careful not to exercise control.[101]

Another characteristic feature of the renewal has been its contact and cooperation with the Canadian bishops and clergy. Archbishop Hayes of Halifax was one of the earliest bishops to be active in the movement. Other bishops, such as auxiliary bishop M. Pearse Lacey of Toronto, attended meetings and kept the CCCB informed of activities. Lay leaders guided the movement, but Catholic clergy were always available and supportive. In 1975 the Canadian bishops published *Charismatic Renewal* and challenged members to involve themselves in parish life, study, and reflection on the Scriptures and to assist in the renewal of the church. It cautioned them to avoid the excesses of sensationalism, emotionalism, and fundamentalism.[102] Young people were inspired by charismatic renewal to serve the Christian community as committed lay people, clergy, and religious.[103]

The renewal's rapid dissemination across Canada in the 1970s and 1980s was a sign of hope that the reception of the Spirit would be a successful instrument in the renewal of the church. Yet concerns about the future of the movement, Hanrahan wrote in 1983, still remain among its more than sixty thousand members. Is it heir to the sound teaching and wisdom of the Christian tradition?[104] Why are leaders so slow to emerge? How can the swinging-door syndrome among some members be dealt with? Charismatic renewal is not pretentious, and it perceives itself realistically as a weak instrument in the hands of God to renew the church.[105] The movement has renewed the hearts of many Catholics, but it appears unable to renew the whole church. It can stir the hearts of some faithful, but it does not seem to have the force to bring about the conversion of the corporate church.

CONCLUSION

In Quebec the secularization of social services and urban culture freed the Catholic church to commit itself more fully to the spiritual needs of the people. After the Quiet Revolution, the church no longer wielded political power but rather relied on the mystery of the sacramental life, the presence of the Spirit, and the inspiration of the Word of God to give spiritual direction to Québécois. The Second Vatican Council inspired Christians and other believers around the world with its mystical belief that Jesus Christ was the sign of the living church. The Canadian bishops at the council perceived more clearly the potential of the church to be an expression of God's love, that is, a sacrament of human rights to build a more humane Canada. The Canadian bishops hoped to transform the free-enterprise, neo-liberal society confronting Canadian Catholics into a more compassionate one.

Members of the community at Combermere were touched by the charismatic enthusiasm from Duquesne and Notre Dame universities. Inspired by the Word, they reacted against the secularization and materialization of Canadian society and supported the spread of spiritual renewal across the country. This Christian renewal was transported into Canada from the United States, yet the renewal, with little structure of any sort, had no colonial shadow. It proved to be an excellent example of clean Christian inculturation into the Canadian and the Quebec cultures. Inspired by the love of God, the charismatic movement exercised considerable independence but within the guidelines of the Canadian bishops. The new openness and concern of the Christian community for the rights of all meant new involvements in the ecumenical and social justice issues of women and native peoples.

15 Contemporary Dynamics

Early in the twentieth century the Canadian Catholic church became greatly involved in the social issues and the labour questions facing parishioners. Catholic trade unions were organized, adult education initiated, and cooperatives launched. As prosperity returned during and after the Second World War, world missions linked Canadians with the economic and social problems of other nations and the Canadian Catholic Organization for Development and Peace was established to offer assistance. The Canadian bishops raised questions on economic justice in Canada, development in the North, and restoration of world solidarity. In dealing with social justice, Catholics discovered the need to coordinate their efforts with other believers. Christians in Canada began to study their common faith commitment and to share in the good works of one another. Collaborative organizations such as Plura were formed to deal with poverty in Canada, while Ten Days for World Development addressed unfair transnational structures and international trade inequalities.

During the Second World War, Canadian women were recruited from their homes to work in war-related factories and businesses. After the war they were expected to make room for the returning soldiers by returning to non-paying jobs in the home, or to lesser-paying jobs as secretaries and menial workers. Having tasted a living wage and the social life of the workplace, many women refused to step back into anonymity and poverty. Instead, some went to university during the postwar period, earned degrees, and emerged as teachers, lawyers, doctors, and other professionals. Yet it was not until the end of the

1960s that the major universities became officially coeducational and recruited women students in equal numbers. The professionalization of women's work challenged the post-Vatican II church to welcome the new professionals into its offices and sanctuaries.

The native people during the war fought overseas for the great victory over the Axis powers. They returned to the Canadian shore decorated with ribbons, medals, and honours, but they soon rediscovered the same discrimination they suffered before the war. They had fought for freedom, equality, and human rights only to find that back on the reserve they had little chance of finding well-paying jobs like other Canadians. They were thus condemned to live an impoverished life without even the benefit of voting. Energized by their disappointment, native people sought the vote, and in the 1960s they received it. With the experience of that empowerment, the native people next demanded control over their own lives and the education of the children. In the 1970s they set up their own school boards and looked forward to governing their own affairs.

SOCIAL JUSTICE

Peering down from the Vatican walls in 1891, Leo XIII launched a thunderbolt into the capitalist and Marxist camps by insisting that they espouse a more humane system of work and production. Pope Leo published *Rerum Novarum*, which placed the church on the side of the employed, underemployed, and the unemployed. He challenged labour, management, and capital to cooperate in the production of goods and in the payment of a living wage. He challenged the Communists to allow workers the freedom of religious worship, private property, and personal rights. This giant step forward in labour-industrial relations placed the church squarely on the side of the workers and asked that government act reasonably when regulating disputes. Papal teaching offered Catholics and the world a model well beyond the dream of restored Christendom and beyond the sterility of the separation of church and state.[1]

Acting on papal teaching, the Jesuits in 1912 founded at Montreal the *École sociale populaire* and eight years later Joseph Papin Archambault, SJ, initiated annual conferences on social teaching, called the Semaines Sociales du Canada. The explosion in the number of Catholic labour unions in Quebec following the First World War led to formation of the Canadian and Catholic Confederation of Labour in 1921 (CCCL). In 1928, as we saw earlier, father Jimmy Tompkins, Father Moses Coady, and A.B. Macdonald established the Antigonish Movement at St Francis Xavier University. After the Second World War

Fr F.A. Marrocco founded the School of Social Action at St Patrick's College in Ottawa. Following Vatican II, the Canadian bishops formed the Social Affairs Commission, which included the laity and clergy and met on a regular basis to plan social strategy.[2]

The laity and bishops in 1970 formed the Canadian Catholic Organization for Development and Peace (CCODP) in response to the call of Vatican II for personal involvement in the plight of the needy and the disfavoured. CCODP launched an education program that proved successful, but few Canadians, beyond making small contributions, were able to leave their work, travel, and personally assist the people of developing nations. Most parishioners found themselves locked into employment patterns and could not get leave from their work to bring their skills to developing countries. By 1987 CCODP piloted over 230 groups that met across Canada promoting the experience of solidarity with suffering people in the far corners of the earth.[3]

After the Second Vatican Council, the Canadian church began downsizing its institutional commitments. No longer did it seek to dominate the social weal but rather raised questions about Canadian lifestyle. The church desired to expand a parochial vision to the plight of world nations on other continents. In the Third World, as in the first, transnational corporations were dismantling national economies. Cardinal George Flahiff of Winnipeg presented *Education for Justice* to the World Synod in Rome in 1971. It contributed to *Justice in the World* and became one of the key post-conciliar documents on social justice. He urged personal solidarity with the poor and the marginalized as a way of working out a program of social justice. "Unless we are in solidarity with the people who are poor, marginal or isolated," Flahiff believed, "we cannot even speak effectively about their problems."[4]

In 1975 the CCCB published the Labour Day statement, *Northern Development: At What Cost?* The bishops called upon Euro-Canadians to advocate social justice for native people and to be responsible stewards of Canadian energy sources. The Canadian bishops called specifically for a just settlement of Native land claims before the launching of industrial projects, a statement that "generated public discussion far beyond church circles."[5]

During the downturn of the early 1980s the Social Affairs Commission of the CCCB issued *Ethical Reflections on the Economic Crisis* (1983). The bishops asked that economic priorities for Canadians be reestablished provoking vigorous dialogue with the business community. "Labour, antipoverty, women's and farm groups responded positively to the call to create a new social movement or coalition."[6]

At the Roman Synod in 1985, Bernard Hubert, president of the Canadian bishops, admitted the problem of motivating both clergy and laity to become engaged in social justice. He asked the synod "how to assure better participation on the part of our Catholic communities and specialists in evolving, preparing and finally welcoming ... [social justice]; how to help our people go beyond a purely individual ethic and defend the moral dimensions of all human activity, economic, political, religious, scientific, cultural or military." Of Christians he asked the full acceptance of *Gaudium et Spes* by embracing responsibility for the welfare of the world.[7]

Meanwhile, large corporations set a different pace by automating production, slashing expenses, and dismissing thousands of wage earners at home and abroad, and as a result of this anti-social activity, the stock market rewarded them with higher share prices and the lofty praise of the business community. At the same time corporation lobbyists pressured politicians to reduce the number on welfare and to trim the amount paid out on unemployment insurance. It became apparent that neoliberal monetarism thrives on permanent underemployment and shrinking social benefits, and in the process, destroys the Christian family and human solidarity. In future only the United Nations, international labour organizations, and international churches can question the sway of sovereign corporations. The restoration of human solidarity demands from Christians the formation of cooperatives, self-help groups, and communal reconciliation. Living in a free society, the Canadian bishops point out that Christians are ultimately responsible for making prudent decisions to rebuild human solidarity and to base it on the prophetic principles of the Bible.[8]

ECUMENICAL ACTIVITY

The bishops returning from the Second Vatican Council carried with them the refreshing words of *Unitatis redintegratio* exhorting church people to restore the "unity among Christians." Paul VI and Patriarch Athenagoras of Constantinople withdrew mutual medieval excommunications in 1965, and dialogue has continued on a low level. Healing has recently been slowed by the Patriarchate of Moscow who refused to continue the dialogue, accusing Rome of proselytism when in the western Ukraine Rome asked for return to the pre-bellum status quo. At the same time, the Ukrainian and Romanian Greek Catholics asked for return of their churches, which the Soviet NKVD had forced them to hand over to the Orthodox after the Second World War.[9] Currently the Patriarchate of Moscow delays these just requests and protests concessions granted to Eastern Rite Catholics by the Russian government.[10]

Canadian Christians, inspired by the reconciling tone of the council, began to talk about their shared faith and good works. This fellowship, as the council urged in *Nostra aetate*, was quickly extended to other religious believers such as the Jews, Muslims, and Hindus. The Christian Pavilion at Expo '67 in Montreal was the result of ecumenial collaboration between seven Canadian Christian churches. Among the visitors it welcomed were four large canoes of Christians from Sainte Marie among the Hurons, of whom I was one of twenty-four Jesuits, bringing the ecumenical message that the teaching of Christ first preached by seventeenth-century Jesuits along the Canadian waterways was still heard and lived along the banks of Georgian Bay and the French, Mattawa, Ottawa, and St Lawrence rivers. More significant in the year after Expo '67, the Canadian Council of Churches and the Canadian bishops established the Joint Working Group to foster Christian fellowship and ecumenical activity. They initiated a common understanding of baptism, pastoral care in ecumenical marriages, and a week of prayer for Christian unity. Canadian Catholics welcomed this new openness, and Canadien Catholics, completing the secularizing of Quebec, adjusted to the new circumstances in a province that now included numerous non-Catholics. Interdenominational marriages had become common among Catholics and Protestants. Catholic children in Canada often attended schools with Protestant neighbours.[11]

The interfaith dialogue arose from this new spirit of ecumenism. Paul VI and Archbishop Michael Ramsey initiated Anglican-Catholic discussion in 1966, and within four years the Anglican-Roman Catholic International Commission (ARCIC) had been established to resolve the problems of ministerial orders and church authority and to build mutual *koinonia*. ARCIC published its *Final Report* in 1981.[12] Dr George Carey and John Paul II asked that a second commission meet in 1997–98 to clarify the understanding of universal primacy in *The Gift of Authority*.[13]

Catholics and Anglicans in Canada entrusted their discussion to eight representatives from each church who met three times yearly. Nine bishops from each church met annually to iron out pastoral problems and to discuss the progress of ARCIC between Canterbury and Rome. Guidelines were published for ecumenical marriages and for clergy moving from one communion to another.[14]

Catholics and Lutherans have communicated on the international level since the early 1970s and established a series of discussion groups outlining a basic consensus on justification by faith through grace. Since 1986 representatives of the CCCB have met with the Evangelical Lutheran Church of Canada seeking mutual understanding on the theological issues of ordination, priesthood, eucharist, and episcopacy. The summary report was published in 1999.[15] Since 1986 the CCCB accepted associate membership in the Canadian Council of Churches by reason of not overwhelming the Canadian Council of Churches with its large numbers (Canadians are forty-five percent Catholic and thirty-six percent Protestant). The Canadian Catholic church was admitted to the CCC with full membership in 1999 but accepted a limited number of representatives. Discussion between the Catholic and United churches began in 1974 with six members from each church meeting twice yearly. Discussion centred on abortion, evangelization, and the methods of appropriate dialogue.[16]

From 1962 to 1987 Gregory Baum of the Faculty of Theology, St Michael's College, at the University of Toronto edited the *Ecumenist,* which was published by Paulist Press. Well-known scholars in the journal extended the frontiers of Catholic thinking into scholarly discussions about disarmament, refugees, women in the church, ecumenical approaches to abortion and decolonization, and the redistribution of wealth. This slim fascicle served the useful function of sharing common interests in interdenominational dialogue.

Other working groups arose from ecclesial discussion groups, among them Plura and Ten Days for World Development. Plura, a Canadian Catholic church initiative, grew in 1968 out of a workshop that also included the Presbyterian, Lutheran, United, and Anglican churches. The goal of the workshop was to address poverty in Canada. The churches quickly realized that together they were a much stronger force, and that by focusing on the needs of Canadians, they could more successfully recruit resources from private and public donors. From this cooperative insight Plura emerged (the acronym Plura comprises the first letter of the participants, Presbyterian, Lutheran, United, Roman, and Anglican) with Roméo Maione as its chair from 1971 to 1973. The churches donated $500,000 in startup money to deal with domestic poverty and asked the government to contribute a matching grant. Plura's goal was not to grant hand-outs to individuals but rather "to enable self-help groups to take on the struggle of domestic poverty."[17]

Plura should be decentralized, it was agreed, by leaving decisions on the regional level. Local groups would be much better able to attack the root causes of poverty in Canada. Plura wanted to enter into partnership with low-income groups that were being impoverished and marginalized by the corporate agenda of free trade, privatization and deregulation. It proposed that low-income self-help groups participate in finding solutions to their problems through research, analysis, and education. The churches continued to provide funding proportional to revenues, and one commentator depicted Plura as "a remarkable ecumenical achievement in which the churches have truly passed 'from words to actions.'"[18]

Plura's decentralized structure allowed eastern Canadians to concentrate on social analysis and "conscienticization" by looking into
working conditions and adequate wages. In Ontario Plura supported
the unemployed who needed sustenance until they could find work. In
New Brunswick Plura mobilized church people to help the needy transcend their poverty and construct a more just society. In Montreal, as
in New Brunswick, Plura sought to have church people working with
the deprived to give them hope and analyse the root causes of their
plight. The Alberta Plura decided to support the Calgary Poverty Protest group, launching demonstrations against the widespread poverty
that the government would not acknowledge. Plura listened to the
marginalized, helping them to help themselves, and avoided creating
more dependency. Plura's decentralized working groups succeeded in
linking interchurch coalitions with self-help groups in the fight to
moderate the destructive side of free trade, privatization, and
deregulation.[19]

A second interfaith group that emerged in the aftermath of the
Second Vatican Council was Ten Days for World Development. It came
together in 1970 in the wake of meetings between Catholic and Protestant members of the Inter-Church Consultative Committee for Development and Relief. It dealt with the Third World and resolved "to
foster further co-operation of our churches in the whole field of development." Cooperation became the cornerstone of its activities. The
Catholic church, along with the other churches, contributed both
funds and personnel to the group. Teach-ins were held across Canada
to acquaint Canadians with the plight of Christians around the globe.
Once again, Roméo Maione, a strong force behind the coalition, initiated the key exercise of Ten Days for World Development.[20]

Ten Days for World Development was first unveiled between 8 and
19 March 1970. Leading church figures were asked to participate in a
long-term education program. Archbishop Ted Scott, primate of the
Anglican church of Canada, Bishop William Power, president of the
CCCB, Dr John Zimmerman, president of the Lutheran Council in
Canada, Dr Max Putnam, moderator of the Presbyterian church in
Canada, and Dr Bruce McLeod, moderator of the United Church of
Canada visited various Canadian cities, met government officials and
labour leaders, were briefed by John Dillon of the GATT-Fly Project,
and met the press. In the process of the ten days, church leaders put
together a statement of concern, *Development Demands Justice*, to persuade government officials and the people of Canada to concern
themselves with the Third World. They asked government policy
makers to consult the Canadian people in the formation of public
policy and to ensure Third World participation in deliberations. The

Canadian media responded to the issues raised by the principal Canadian churches, and study groups emerged across the country.[21]

For the education program, different themes evolved: trade inequities, the new international economic order, and the popular topic of world food. Eighty committees emerged across the country to animate discussion and motivate church groups and other community members. The various groups maintained a decentralized structure, and each was encouraged to elect representatives for the national committee planning sessions. Visitors from the Third World were invited to provide input, and the members realized that the resolution of these issues demanded political involvement. For the members, failure to be political and the neglect of organized local support meant losing the battle for Third World peoples. As the program was geared for action, many Canadian policies dealing with Third World countries had to be changed. Participants sent letters to the Prime Minister's Office, Foreign Affairs, and Canadian banks. They asked for understanding on Latin American issues and sympathy for the debt crisis of poor nations. Business-community churchgoers criticized pastors for preaching the church's "option for the poor." However, inroads had been made among the middle class, and "a network of local committees ... assumed a mantle of leadership" in being responsible on moral issues. Canadian Christians at the grassroots level took increased responsibility for challenging corporate and government structures when they acted unfairly.[22]

Protestants and Catholics on the ecclesial and the secular level combined efforts to fashion a better society at home and abroad. They focused on their common beliefs and shared needs and worked to reign in corporate abuses in society. Other coalitions such as Gatt-Fly and Project North were organized to promote human rights and corporate responsibility. Christians left doctrinal differences for another day because their strength before the poor, the media, and the public lay with their own cooperative unity.

EXPANDING MINISTRY FOR WOMEN

Work is not a new enterprise for women. Women have always worked, performing the "three generic occupations" of production, reproduction, and maintaining the family.[23] Likewise Christian ministries are not new for women. Women at different times have exercised the Christian ministries, such as mothering, teaching, nursing, and also served as deacons, caring for the needs of Christian community. Yet history ignores the activity of women and native people and makes them the objects of history rather than its creative agents. The history of western civilization until recently has been the preserve of white male scholars who have written little about women, aboriginals, or the marginalized peoples of the world.[24]

One major paradigm shift in historical thinking is the change in focus from androcentric to all-inclusive human history. According to this view of history, equality and democracy must replace patriarchy, domination, and exploitation. Ellen Leonard raises the question: is the church sexist? She answers diplomatically that, as the Catholic church has embraced the "preferential option for the poor," it has embraced concern for the well being of women and children. She believes that this preferential option must begin with the real poor, that is, it must begin with women and their children.[25]

Canadian women have been coming into their own, first as socially active volunteers, and then as career persons. The ministry of the Catholic church is to make salvation available to all, and if the church is to be comprehensive in its ministries, it must include all people. Women point out that, given the opportunity, they would enrich male ministry with compassion and inclusivity. Incorporated into the Church's ministry, women would transform the sectarian history of Catholicism into a world view and would help the Greco-Roman church stough off its exclusiveness and open itself to universality.[26]

At the Roman Synod on the Ministerial Priesthood in 1971, Cardinal George Flahiff of Winnipeg raised the issue of women in the church on behalf of the Canadian bishops. Flahiff asked that passages in the code of canon law reflecting the natural inferiority of women be eliminated and that the council teachings of *The Church in the Modern World* and *The Decree on the Apostolate of Lay People* condemning discrimination against women in the church be implemented. He urged that a papal commission be struck to study these questions so that the church did not lag behind the reforms of secular society. Professor Mary Ellen Sheehan of the Faculty of Theology at St Michael's College sees Flahiff's intervention as a watershed for the CCCB on the women's issue.[27]

At the Synod on Reconciliation in Rome twelve years later, Archbishop L.A. Vachon of Quebec City stated that the church was not credible "unless the recognition of women as full members becomes simultaneously a reality within the church itself." He asked that bishops "recognize the ravages of sexism and our own male appropriation of church institutions" and be open to dialogue, conversion, and change.[28]

At a subsequent synod on the laity in 1987, Archbishop James Hayes of Halifax spoke on behalf of lay involvement in the decision-making bodies of the church. The laity would help to resolve problems of violence, discrimination, injustice, and exclusion within the church. A more comprehensive synodal body, Hayes explained, would help the church achieve *communio*, that is, the communal interplay of Christian life. On the same occasion, Bishop J.-B. Hamelin of Rouyn-Noranda pointed out that, although women are the majority of those active in the church, they do not participate in ecclesial decision making because of exclusionary regulations. He maintained that the credibility of the church will suffer if women are not treated fairly.[29]

The CCCB set up an ad hoc committee on women in the Church between 1982 to 1984 to examine the issues and make recommendations. Consulting over one thousand women, the committee, composed of women and bishops, identified twelve issues "as a continuing agenda for the Canadian Church." The agenda included denunciation of injustices against women, use of inclusive language in the liturgy, pastoral appointments of women equal to those of men, scholarship funding for lay women in ministry, gender equality on church committees and commissions, and a long-term program of full membership for women. The committee, along with the CWL, prepared the Green Kit, discussed earlier, for educational use in parishes and among diocesan groups. The CCCB endorsed these measures.[30]

In the same year Bishop Bernard Hubert wrote a letter to all the members of the diocese of Saint-Jean on the equality of women. He pointed out that Jesus respected the equality of all people including women because they were made in the image of God. The equality of the three persons of the Trinity was an analogy of how men and women might relate. As the three persons of the Trinity were completely equal in relation to each other, so should all persons be completely equal with regard to others. Hubert encouraged women to continue to enrich church members by sharing their experience of inequality, and he urged pastors to strive to change the attitudes of the faithful by employing the Green Kit.[31]

A meeting at Montreal between lay people and Quebec bishops in 1986 concluded with a number of proposals to improve the status of women in the church. Among them were the participation of women in decision making, placing paid coordinators for women's issues in every diocese, equality in liturgical celebration, inclusive language, just pay, women seminary professors, and continuing openness on the question of the ordination of women.[32]

In the same year Bishop Remi De Roo of Victoria asked for an investigation of church structures to lay bare value-laden assumptions of the patriarchal system. He believed the church was caught in a dualism condoning both private and public ethics. While inviting more participation of women in church offices, De Roo called for an in-depth social analysis of the church's tradition on women. He believes that church people have to begin an extensive program of bridge building and commitment to bring about a huge cultural reversal.[33]

After examining the various policies of the Canadian bishops on women in the church, Mary Ellen Sheehan concludes with some critical reflections. Pope John XXIII, Vatican II, and CCCB called for personal conversion to end inequality in the church and to overcome racism and sexism of every type. The CCCB has denounced sexism and challenged itself and others to change. Sheehan continues, however, that the issues the bishops have not addressed are numerous. The CCCB has not considered that church teachings and authority operate from "patriarchal assumptions and practices." Roman congregations have recently rejected the horizontally inclusive language used in the New Standard Revised Version of the Bible and the American Bible Translation used in the Catechism of the Catholic Church, which have been approved by the episcopal conferences. The message formulated in these Roman decisions was only too clear to women. As long as one group was subordinated to another group, exclusion would continue and problems linger unresolved. The question might be raised about how to cleanse the hierarchy of patriarchy, of the discrimination against one group by another. Can democratic reforms on some levels be introduced into the hierarchical church? Will an egalitarian relationship of men and women in the church replace the current practice of reciprocal complementarity?[34]

Sheehan asks whether the bishops will "acknowledge publicly the beginnings of an alternate theological view" on the suitability of women for ordination. The bishops have to implement their own teachings that women are fully equal before God and in the church. Church women with grievances about discrimination do not have the due process available to them in democratic societies. Church leaders, then, must be pro-active in raising the consciousness of church members. If the church is to play a prophetic role in society, it must first liberate the Spirit of God within itself. In a self-corrective process, the Spirit will redirect values that give witness to gender equality.[35]

Since the 1970s the Canadian bishops have raised in Rome the question of women's equality in the church, including the admission of women to public ministry. The CCCB has worked against sexism in the Canadian church and promoted women to church offices. The Green Kit was prepared to raise awareness of women's equality among Catholics. Bishops have yet to cleanse the patriarchal structures from the hierarchical system, raise further consciousness of inequality, and introduce egalitarian partnership between men and women. The prophetic witness of the church depends on the basic truth of equality among the members. The women's movement and native rights are the cutting edge of the churches in Canada today. These movements are transforming graces for the Christian churches, and their resolution will open the churches to the future.

DISSENT TO THE RIGHT AND TO THE LEFT

Catholic dissenters from the right are centred in Opus Dei, Comunione e Liberazione, Focolare, and the pro-life movement. Opus Dei is a secular institute of clergy and laity founded in Spain in the late 1930s by Msgr Josemaría Escrivá de Balaguer and approved by the Holy See. It is committed to the sanctification of its members and society but is highly criticized for being secretive and autocratic and for teaching rigorous spirituality. Odan (Opus Dei Awareness Network) looks on Opus Dei as "a cult with questionable recruitment practices" and offers "education, outreach and support to those adversely impacted by Opus Dei." Comunione e Liberazione is a Catholic renewal movement established in Italy to foster communion with the church as the basis for Christian liberation. Often the movement found itself in conflict with the Italian bishops and the spirit of the Second Vatican Council. It is considered the Italian equivalent of the Spanish Opus Dei. Focolare was approved by the Holy See in 1962 as a religious community of celibates and associated marrieds who are involved in secular pursuits for the transformation of the world according to the gospel ideals.

For the sake of brevity let us focus on the pro-life movement. Michael Cuneo investigated the paradoxical nature of the movement and discovered within the Catholic Church a "discordant chorus of contentious voices." The Canadian bishops at Winnipeg in September 1968 prepared a pastoral letter interpreting Paul VI's *Humanae Vitae*. They instructed Catholics to embrace the spirit of the encyclical by taking a pro-life stance but at the same time allowed the faithful, in application of this principle, to follow the informed dictates "in good conscience."[36] "In other words," Cuneo contends, "the bishops presented *Humanae Vitae* as an ideal rather than a binding requirement for Catholic sexual conduct." The pro-life movement later in the 1970s resurrected this letter as evidence, in its view, of the absence of the bishops' firm commitment to papal teaching arising from the Canadian episcopate.[37]

It happened that not many clergy were involved in pro-life activities. It was also evident that the laity in the 1970s were polarized into pro-life and pro-social-justice devotees. The pro-lifers quickly progressed from the Alliance for Life, with its diverse membership of middle-class women supported by the Catholic Women's League and the Knights of Columbus to the Coalition for Life. The coalition included such groups as Anglicans, left-wing members of the New Democratic Party, and working-class and pro-family Catholic women, and it later evolved into the well-organized and confrontational Campaign for Life in 1978. Campaign for Life seized the vanguard of the movement, believing that the Canadian bishops and the Catholic faithful were dragging their feet. They saw the willingness among certain Catholics to tolerate contraceptives as the thin edge of the wedge ultimately leading to promiscuity, secularism, feminism, and abortion. These revivalists saw themselves as the true leaven inspiring a lethargic and secularized church. They saw themselves as a "distinct society within the Canadian church," which, during the 1980s and 1990s, led to the factional division of Canadian Catholicism.[38]

Social justice Catholics, emphasizing the other side of the issue, aligned themselves with the Second Vatican Council and the Canadian bishops and soon became involved in ecumenical enterprises with believers of other faiths. They enjoyed the presence of large numbers, the guidance of the bishops in social justice, and the advantage of an international church with eyes, ears, and hands around the world. The Canadian bishops, sympathetic to the social justice Catholics, operated with them in the larger context of an "ecumenical consensus." Only moderate protests were mounted against government laws allowing choice in reproductive matters.[39]

Perhaps most significant in the early years of the Pro-Life Movement was the initiative of Louise Summerhill to found a non-political organization, Birthright, in Toronto. Her purpose was not to picket or correct the political and social climate but to provide sympathetic support for pregnant women who needed help. "I was convinced," Summerhill mystically pondered, "that abortion is entirely destructive, but it is so easy to become deeply and emotionally involved in 'lobbying' against the legalization of abortion in government, and overlook the humane concern of our opponents for the suffering and despair of distraught pregnant women." Under her compassionate guidance hundreds of Birthright centres opened throughout North America, and the movement has been a Canadian success story.[40]

Catholic dissenters from the left included many Catholic women and religious sisters who decided that Catholic Christianity must transcend the narrowness of Rome on gender discrimination. As card-carrying Catholics since their baptism, they were not going to leave the church over a disagreement. They choose to remain as dissenters in their church. They have been joined in ignoring Roman supervision on gender issues by Catholic men, gays and lesbians, and other marginalized peoples. The dissenters argue that they were born Catholic, raised Catholic, and cannot be anything else but Catholic, whether the Roman church acknowledges gender equality or not. They resolve to dissent in place and not move.

Joanna Manning is one such Christian who was born and raised Catholic, was some years a religious sister, and completed a doctorate in theology from Regis College in Toronto. She carefully read the papal encyclicals, including John Paul II's *Mulieris Dignitatem,* and analysed their teachings. She concluded from her research that John Paul II has manifested his militancy against the movement for women's equality. Manning perceived that the pope, when describing women as "equal but different," really meant that women should be dependent, passive, and remain below men in the chain of being. Manning also points out the pope's failure to consult women, to whom he directs his lengthy instruction, and his lack of familiarity with the recent findings of anthropology, psychology, and biology. [41]

Manning contends that the arrogant aggression of the Vatican towards women has alienated women in Canada and elsewhere, and that many rather than remain passive to such browbeating are drifting from the church. She writes, "The ferocity of John Paul II's 1994 pronouncement against women's ordination left me stunned; I even contemplated leaving the Catholic Church." The papal instruction also forced Professor Mary Malone of St Jerome's College to decision. She became an example of a well-educated and well-loved committed Catholic who fell into loose union with Rome because she experienced it as endemically patriarchal. She perceived it to be an oppressive institution and preferred to pursue God in freedom outside its restrictive embrace. [42]

If women can leave the church after mature reflection and prayer, young women in Toronto can leave because they feel that their presence is not desired and their views are not respected. A young woman by the name of Cristina, who was inspired in school by John Paul's *Concern for the Social Order,* tactfully questioned the expenditure of a bequest in her parish on marble and statues. Her pastor reacted, "Just who do you think you are!" and proceeded to humiliate her in front of her friends. Her ideas, which came from the papal letter, were labelled "feminist," and her name was removed from the list of parish lectors. Cristina felt that she and her concerns were not taken seriously and ceased looking to the church for guidance. [43]

The Ontario Catholic Women's League, meeting in Waterloo in July 2000, voted in favour of supporting the World March of Women 2000. Their bishop advisor asked the CWL to dissociate itself from the march. The Ontario president reproved the advisor for intervening in an internal women's matter and explained to members that the CWL was always pro-life; by its involvement in the women's march, the CWL was engaged in its traditional ministry of addressing "poverty and violence in our communities." In doing this the Ontario CWL confirmed the decision of the CCCB, national CWL, Canadian Religious Conference (CRC), and CCODP in favour of the march. The CCCB endorsed 57 provisions of the women's march but excused itself from supporting the provision on reproductive rights and same-sex marriages. The national CWL approved this resolve in siding with other Catholic organizations and overlooked the advice of dissenters denouncing the March of Women 2000.[44]

To Joanna Manning the corporate culture of the Catholic church is against the equality of women and against women in the priesthood. The church espouses the human rights of the United Nations but "has ruthlessly and systematically denied any discussion of the advancement of these same rights within the Church." The procedures of the church of Rome deny human rights to clergy and laity who are part of the loyal opposition. Manning, who operates the Anne Frank House for students and refugees and prepares a weekly breakfast for the hungry, finds "cognitive dissonance" in the pursuit of human rights by a pope who guides the church with an iron fist. She sees the Catholic church withdrawing into a fortress mentality wherein things are sacred on the inside and secular on the outside.[45] She sees the future in small faith communities that build alternatives outside denominational structures. They will be "both autonomous and connected, as well as inclusive and ecumenical."[46]

Another dissenter is Tony Clarke. He was codirector of the CCCB social affairs department for more than twenty years (1972–94) when letters on the substantive issues of Catholic social justice were formulated. In December 1992, while advisor of the CCCB, Clarke challenged Prime Minister Brian Mulroney on national television to stop deceiving the Canadian people about the heavy price paid in their standard of living for the Free Trade Agreement. He was concerned that the government, in conforming to the requirements of the agreement, was facilitating the corporate agenda of layoffs and reduced benefits. Two years after this event Clarke left the CCCB because the bishops wanted wider consultation with the laity. Clarke at the same time was in conflict as speaker for the CCCB on social issues and speaker for on NGO coalition against North American free trade. He responded by pointing out that the CCCB had relinquished its "moral leadership" on economic and social policy issues. He found it "difficult to understand how the churches can sleepwalk through this massive overhaul of our social system without raising some profound moral challenges."[47] Clarke recommended that the Catholics, along with other believers, should build lively faith communities to challenge unfair social systems and to reveal

Christ's love to people struggling in a competitive world. In fact, the church was willing to speak to these societal changes but found Clarke could not speak for it on moral attitudes and for NGOs on trade issues without confusing religious and secular messages. These dissenting voices raise issues with which an international church must deal.

NATIVE RESIDENTIAL SCHOOLS

Key to the church's relationship with the First Nations is the resolution of the residential schools issue. The historian must try to balance three pertinent viewpoints. First, from the view of Catholic religious who volunteered to serve on the Canadian missions, the native residential schools were a heroic enterprise to educate and deepen the spirituality of the First Nations. Second, for many of the native youths who attended them, the schools were a prison they had to endure until the age of sixteen when they could leave. Third, for the federal administrators who were trying to trim budgets, the schools were a source of irritation because the school principals and native people were continually demanding adequate funding when the government was trying to cut costs. The government felt no urgency to provide funds because there were no native votes at the election polls. These three viewpoints about native residential schools leave gaps in our understanding and are hardly reconcilable, but it is still premature to expect a definitive history.[48]

Catholic religious congregations from 1860 to 1960 operated about fifty-seven of the 101 native residential schools in Canada, or 60 percent of the total.[49] This was a period of classical evangelization and cultural insensitivity. The Missionary Oblates of the Mary Immaculate took responsibility for the main body of these schools.[50] Their purpose was to educate the native children and foster spiritual growth. The Euro-Canadian curriculum, which embraced the Western values of objectivity, regularity, discipline, and study,[51] conflicted with the native world of subjectivity, spontaneity, and visionary dreams.

Upon the objective world of Western civilization, the world of spiritual and cultural subjectivity dawned in the 1960s. A romantic revolution, which included the Quiet Revolution in Quebec, the Kennedy New Frontier in the United States, and Trudeaumania in Canada, also included the native world of subjectivity and dreams. The native world soon replaced the objective knowledge of the schools with the subjective knowledge and interests of the students. The focus of education now transformed itself to the pursuit of personal growth and cultural roots. It became urgent for us all to appropriate our gifts, engage the universe bravely, and seek self-transcendence. We had to strive to be authentic and real before our peers. The demands of subjective education seriously undermined the objective education of the last century. Native residential schools were passé, based as they were on the foundation of Euro-Canadian objective education. The subjective values of knowing one's roots, language, culture, and nation pointed to a new type of education.

In the 1880s the Canadian government, in an effort to honour its commitment to the education to the native people, began funding native residential schools operated by the Christian churches of Canada.[52] The government recognized that the churches had found a funding formula for native schools providing a modest education at a minimal cost. Once the government took over the financing of these schools, it imposed its own agenda, which included English-only as the language of instruction. The government's agenda of assimilation did not go down well with the French-speaking Oblates and Jesuits, who operated the Catholic residential schools. The government wished to assimilate the native people into Canadian society and believed that a working knowledge of English was a necessary skill. However, as money spent on Euro-Canadian schools increased with growing populations, the money spent on native schools decreased in spite of growing populations.[53] Balancing the budget at residential schools became even more impossible when attendance of native children was made compulsory in 1920.[54]

The effect of residential schools on native children is the subject of intense debate among scholars. David Nock contends that residential schools were a prime example of "cultural replacement," that is, the replacement of native culture by Euro-Canadian culture.[55] John Milloy points to the dilemma between the culture of the school and the home in which the native people found themselves, while being given little help to resolve the contradiction.[56] Other scholars argue that the schools functioned as a "cultural synthesis" that enabled native culture and rites to survive. Jacqueline Gresko argues realistically that the haphazard discipline of native residential schools allowed native people to preserve native culture. Many schools allowed the use of native languages for religious instruction, services, and recreation.[57] Martha McCarthy found that there was a cultural exchange between Oblates and the tribes comprising the Dene in the North, and the Oblates translated catechisms and hymns into the native languages, travelled in canoes and on snowshoes, and felt "at home" in the native villages.[58] Robert Carney demonstrates that the Oblates in the Northwest Territories educated native children for different life choices: traditional, non-traditional, or some combination of both. He shows that it was the Oblates who were first among non-native groups to advocate native control over their own affairs. [59]

The government commissioned the Hawthorn Report in 1966–67 to review native residential schools and make recommendations. The report recommended that residential schools be closed and native children sent to provincial schools. The hidden agenda was secularization of denominational schools. To prevent this, the Catholic bands in the 1970s took over the operation of the Dogrib, Blue Quills, and Qu'Appelle schools.[60] Evaluation of the new native-run schools made it clear that the Oblate ideal of native schools approximated more closely the preferences of band-operated, on-reserve schools. Native children were educated near home in the faith of their parents.[61] In the Northwest Territories, they were provided with an education that offered them choices for their future.[62] From this brief examination, it becomes clear that David Nock's concept of cultural replacement was too limited. It cannot explain the cultural the synthesis experienced in Catholic residential schools, which more accurately revealed what happened for many, that is, that native parents and children adapted parts of Euro-Canadian culture according to their own needs and at their own pace. Current scholars are more appreciative of the role that native people played in their own destiny.[63] Robert Choquette points out that the mission churches and schools gave the native people "the wherewithal to survive in the alien but conquering Euro-Canadian culture."[64]

For the native people, the residential school was a mixed experience. Isabelle Knockwood provided a devastating account of life at the Shubenacadie residential school, characterized by hardship and abuse, a high dropout rate, sickness, sabotage, and absenteeism.[65] The relentless discipline of the schools alienated children from their native communities. Endemic underfunding undermined the schools' ability to generate a more generous and insightful adaptation to native education. In 1924, seventy-three native residential schools received on average only $21,700 each to operate their schools.[66] The underfunded residential schools, John Milloy makes clear, made them unhealthy for both students and staff.[67]

The schools also produced some positive experiences. In *Indian School Days* Basil Johnston shows an interesting and humorous side to the residential school.[68] He attended the Spanish Residential School in Ontario in the postwar period. It offered secondary education as a new element in native education. The principals of a number of Oblate schools had pressed for government funding to include the secondary level but had received an indifferent response.[69] Generally, the missionaries and school staffs were interested in native languages and cultures. They produced 141 dictionaries in 27 different native languages, 74 grammars of native languages, and many studies, journals, and liturgical books on native culture.[70] In the end, the residential schools eased the onslaught of Euro-Canadian culture that swept over native cultures and allowed a cultural synthesis between Euro-Canadian culture and the religious customs of native parents.[71]

Aboriginal issues are on the cutting edge of Catholic social thought today. Pope John Paul II, while visiting the native people in the Canadian North in 1984 and 1987, exhorted Canadians to respect native rights, initiate reconciliation concerning past wrongs, and support them in the renewal of their faith and culture through gospel solidarity. Euro-Canadians must make common cause with the goals of native people if native people are to be welcomed fully into Canadian communities and if they are to share their faith with Euro-Canadian Christians.[72]

Native residential schools were collapsing under the force of new educational values in the 1960s and 1970s. They were given the final push in the 1980s by the sexual abuse scandals that surfaced and made their operation indefensible.[73] The native values of culture, religion, and language soon replaced the traditional Euro-Canadian values of discipline, rules, and rote learning. Christians seek reconciliation with native people over the emotional, physical, and sexual abuse of the residential schools and support them in their struggle to educate their children in their own traditions.[74]

LET JUSTICE FLOW

The Canadian bishops in *Let Justice Flow like a Mighty River* (1993) acknowledged that Catholics have not always recognized native people as their bothers and sisters, "as another people of water and the Spirit." They promise that Catholic Christians will do better in the future.[75]

During the nineteenth century, the bishops acknowledged that a symbiotic relationship developed between church and state for Canadian nation building. This relationship encouraged a sense of cultural and spiritual superiority that the missionaries assumed over the native people. They also protected native rights in the face of a parsimonious federal government and taught native children in day and residential schools. The church people and Native people during the past four centuries have shared many joys and many sufferings. The nineteenth-century missionaries sadly failed to recognize the native peoples as people of water and Spirit and thus contributed to the weakening of the native spirit. According to the bishops, Catholics in future must demonstrate a greater appreciation of the aboriginal peoples. They must become partners with native people in common projects and support them in their quest to be architects of their own future.[76]

Church-run residential schools have caused much suffering to native peoples. One in six native people have attended a residential school for a period of a few years. The bishops have recommended that all dioceses seek a process of disclosure and the healing of wounds caused by physical or sexual abuse. They propose that healing conferences and school reunions be occasions to express a sense of loss and shame and to initiate the healing of "brokenness in Native communities and Native families." The government must be brought into the healing process because it was responsible for the deliberate underfunding of the schools and the consequent use of student labour to operate them. The aboriginal spirit speaks to all religious people advocating the restoration of the universal circle of humanity. This spirit calls for the renewal of the meaning of life, work, generosity, and relationship of natives and non-natives.[77]

Admitting past mistakes and looking to rebuild its relationship with the native people, the Canadian church encourages victims to move beyond the victim stage and begin the healing process. The Church urges all to "trust in the strength, skills and inner power of the native people ... [and] in the power of the Spirit to change" all our hearts. The bishops invite all Canadians to affirm the strength and dignity of the native people. The affirmation of native spirituality strengthens the First Nations and Christianity. The Catholic church affirms the supremacy of conscience in matters of religion and cultural heritage. Native prayer, culture, and experience offer the basis of a native Christian theology. Such a theology would emphasize justice, healing, and the use of the sacred pipe, vision quest, fast, and sweat lodge. The Canadian church encourages dialogue between Christian and native spiritualities.[78]

The importance of preserving native spirituality brought together in 1975 members of the Anglican, Catholic, and United Church to form Project North. The goal of this interchurch dialogue was to build support and solidarity with native organizations. The Canadian Conference of Catholic Bishops published two letters, *Northern Development: At What Cost?* in 1975 and *A Cry for Justice from the North* in 1981. Both letters questioned the need for development at the expense of the Aboriginal people. The CCCB asked Prime Minister Pierre Trudeau in 1981 to recognize aboriginal treaty rights in the new Canadian Constitution. At the time of the Meech Lake Accord in 1987, the CCCB and the other churches asked Canadians to enter into a "new covenant" with aboriginal peoples to ensure native rights, to recognize the First

Nations as a distinct people, and to guarantee them an adequate land base and the power of self-determination. Governments must not only support the principle of native self-government but also the social and economic renewal of native communities.[79]

The CCCB concludes *Let Justice Flow Like a Mighty River* by making a commitment to stand with the native people in their struggle. The bishops agreed to educate Catholics on the subject of native rights and on the support for the social and economic renewal of native communities. They pledged to affirm the spirituality of the native people and to collaborate with them in the disclosure of abuses and the formation of healing circles. They asked Catholics to travel with the native people in their joys and sufferings and welcome their leaders to church meetings and into church structures. The bishops promised to maintain ecumenical solidarity to further the economic, social, and constitutional justice for native peoples. "The undermining of aboriginal culture has left all of us less whole, less human." Catholics, say the bishops, must struggle along with the native people "for the heart and soul of our Nation." The bishops urged Canadians "to rebuild the foundation of Canada" on the basis of this mutual trust.[80]

Achiel Peelman, a Catholic theologian and influential church person from deep within the Oblate tradition, goes one step further by suggesting that the First Nations, in dialogue with other Catholics, have to be allowed to form a church in their own tradition. They have to be allowed to rediscover their own spiritual traditions – the sacred pipe, medicine wheel, tree of life, vision quest, sun dance, and sweat lodge – to come to a richer appreciation of Christianity. Through their traditions, the native people are rediscovering the importance of Jesus Christ for the preservation of their native religion and culture. Peelman believes that the native people have to be given the space to go beyond ecclesial confrontation and create a more adequate theology of the Christ of creation, the cosmic Christ of the future.[81]

CONCLUSION

Social justice, interfaith ecumenism, Canadian women, and native people are meaningful dynamics in today's church. The way Catholics address themselves to the marginalized, women's rights, believers of other faiths, and native people will directly affect the Catholic Church's ability to make it through the next century as the world-class church it claims to be. The Catholic church must address itself to the issues of fair labour practices, world missions, human solidarity, justice in Canada and the world. Catholics have found solidarity with their colleagues in the beliefs and good works they share in common.

Shared organizations have raised consciousness of the mutual concern for the needy and the marginalized that underpins any challenge to unjust economic and political structures.

Christian women ask for the support of the church in their struggles. While some women consider the church the hand of the past and an instrument of oppression, most Canadian women are willing to engage in dialogue with the church in the hope that a conversion experience will renew the Christian vision and inspire all to service. The laity have been hired in church offices, schools, and colleges, and women hold many of these positions. The Canadian bishops have continued to educate clergy and laity on the importance of eliminating sexism and racism in the church as a positive sign of God's love in the world. The CCCB has raised a number of times with the Holy See the issue of women in the ministerial apostolates. Canadian women and native people, by their presence on the decision-making bodies of the church, can make those bodies truly catholic in their composition and truly ecumenical in their decisions. Women have the special gifts of survival, empowerment, and pluralism with which to enrich the Catholic community.

Native people have asked their fellow Catholics to give a sympathetic hearing to the cultural displacement they have endured. They have requested help from church people as they reclaim their dignity, strengthen their families, stabilize communities, and launch educational programs. A genuine reconciliation is necessary. Euro-Canadian Catholics are called by their leaders to seek reconciliation with their Native brothers and sisters and welcome them onto parish and diocesan boards. native people contribute their love of God through closeness to nature and their commitment to the land. Women, the marginalized, and native people, given a chance, will help to universalize, energize, and organize the Catholic church in the twenty-first century.

Epilogue

The overarching themes explored in this volume were Gallicanism, focusing on missions and diplomacy; Romanism, examining structural growth and ultramontane spirituality; and Canadianism, reviewing multicultural cooperation, social justice, interfaith sharing, women issues, and native Catholicism. Other themes might have been developed, but in this brief history of Canadian Catholics, it seemed more apropos to deal with the principal themes and leave the rest for other studies.

Gallican Catholicism in Canada entrenched seventeenth-century missionary roots, and Catholics since that time have continued to exercise missionary activity to the present day. French spirituality in the challenging environment of Canada inspired, among others, Jean de Brébeuf, Marie de l'Incarnation, François de Laval, Kateri Tekakwitha, and Joseph Chihwatenha and led them into mystical union with God.

The British military occupation after the middle of the eighteenth century taught Canadien Catholics the advantage of quiet diplomacy as a better way of dealing with a victorious colonial power. The Crown of England subjected seventy thousand French Catholics to the rule of a Protestant nation. However, to keep Catholics secure from the revolution in the American colonies, the Crown granted them the temporary practice of the "Romish religion." In accordance with such tolerance, the English government permitted a Canadien priest to be ordained bishop and thus secured to Quebec episcopal succession, public worship, and the collection of revenue for church government. The British rulers worked out a *modus vivendi* with their Catholic subjects. The most important result was that the impoverished church, devoid of support from France, became truly Canadian and discovered its own support structures. The diplomacy of getting along with the civil state became a central activity for the Catholic bishops.

At the end of the eighteenth century the Scots and the Irish came to Newfoundland and the Maritimes. They received only sporadic attention from the Quebec clergy and demanded their own Gaelic- and English-speaking bishops and priests. With inspiration from the clergy, they built their own churches, schools, and colleges. Maritime Catholics voted for Confederation in the hope that they would be granted separate schools. The Scots and the Irish added the first elements of pluralism to the Canadien church, and the bishops meeting at Quebec began a trilingual dialogue. This effectively broke the Canadien control of the Catholic church in Canada. Propaganda Fide in Rome proposed a twofold plan to organize North America under the sees of Quebec for French-speaking Catholics and Baltimore for the English-speaking Catholics. Yet different ethnic groups emerging in the United States and British North America forced the acceptance of a more chaotic and multicultural tradition on the continent.

As the European churches rose from the ashes of the French Revolution, church leaders in Quebec, inspired by Roman spirituality, restructured the Canadian church to keep in step. The romanticism of ultramontane spirituality spread like wildfire and romanized the Canadian church. It championed loyalty to Roman spirituality and sought international union for Catholics under the leadership of the pope. The Holy See encouraged the popular new devotions, wrested the reins of national churches in Europe from their monarchs, and directed episcopal sees around the world. Education and piety went hand in hand in the restoration of an international Catholic culture that the French Revolution had destroyed. Two leading European laymen, de Maistre and Veuillot, inspired Canadian bishops Bourget and Laflèche to embrace papal leadership.

The devotional revolution motivated both French-speaking and English-speaking Catholics. Regular attendance at Mass became the norm in Canadian parishes by the late nineteenth century. The Oblate fathers extended ultramontane devotions to Central Canada and opened missions and schools across the Canadian Northwest to nourish the faith of the native people.

Catholic support for Confederation was late but timely. It was late because French- and English-speaking Catholics feared that a unitary federal government controlled by the Protestant majority would be used to impose a Protestant culture and school system on Catholics. It became apparent to Maritime Catholics that if they wanted their own schools, they would have to support two systems – the public schools with their taxes and the Catholic schools with their fees. The Fenian invasions of 1866 and the fear of a victorious Union army marching north encouraged Catholics to overlook this unfairness and to get behind the Canadian confederation plan. It would unify the provinces and provide a solid wall of protection against American republicanism. Catholics hoped, at the same time, that the Tory plan for Confederation would establish separate schools in the Maritimes.

Within the rich soil of ultramontane institutions of the nineteenth and early twentieth centuries, the seeds of a more open spirituality began to sprout and flower. The winds of church affairs shifted from blessing ultramontane spirituality to blessing new openness within the church. In the 1870s Elzéar Taschereau was ordained to the see of Quebec and a pontifical university charter was granted to Laval University. Ten years later, Rome further affirmed a more open direction for the Canadian Catholics by making Taschereau the first Canadian cardinal. The political winds in Canada also shifted away from the Tories with the election of Liberals Honoré Mercier as premier of Quebec and Wilfrid Laurier as prime minister. The apostolic delegate, Merry Del Val, reporting on his visit to Canadians in the spring of 1897, praised the Laurier government and urged the clergy to be restrained in their political criticism of the government. Pope Leo XIII's letter, which followed Merry Del Val's visitation, cautioned the clergy against involvement in politics and asked them to accept Prime Minister Laurier's leadership on the Manitoba schools issue. After the turn of the century, the conservative bastion, resisting societal change, began to break down, and Catholic women's colleges opened in Antigonish, Montreal, and Toronto. They offered women a solid education and career opportunities outside the home.

Spreading Catholicism to the Canadian Northwest expanded the rivalry of French- and English-speaking Catholics across the nation. Canadiens were the first to settle the West, yet English-speaking settlers soon dominated the church. French-speaking Catholics formed communities in Saskatchewan and Alberta. The Catholic Extension Society hoped to anglicize western immigrants and assimilate them into the English-speaking church. Striving to form a national missionary effort by extending English Catholic culture to the West, the Extension Society destroyed its own credibility in the minds of the Canadiens, who obviously could not support such a misguided effort. The arrival of Central and Eastern European immigrants on the western prairies helped to moderate tensions and make Canadians more tolerant of one another. These later immigrants canadianized a bicultural church into a multicultural church.

The Latin Rite French and Irish hierarchs at first showed the Eastern Rite Ukrainian immigrants little understanding. Confronted with their seepage from the Catholic church, Archbishop Langevin and the other Canadian bishops reversed direction and sought a Ukrainian bishop who would understand and guide Ukrainian Catholics. Canadian bishops supported Bishop Budka in his effort to organize the first Ukrainian diocese in Canada with clergy, parishes, schools, and newspaper. Among the different language groups in western Canada, English soon became the dominant language. By 1930 English-speaking bishops had responded to this change and had replaced French-speaking bishops.

As bishops dealt mainly with the urban apostolate, the religious congregations such as the Oblates, the Sisters of St Ann, and the Sisters of St Martha spread throughout the Canadian Northwest. They opened Catholic schools, orphanages, and hospitals to deepen the spirituality of the native people. This ministry proved helpful in the short run but in the long run showed itself not to be sensitive to the needs of the native people and the native culture. Since the 1970s the First Nations have taken over responsibility for native education, and the bishops and Oblates have continued to work with native leadership to create an Amerindian church. Unity in diversity has been and will continue to be a bedrock principle of the Canadian Catholic church.

When the world trading markets collapsed in 1929, Canadians, like others, suffered from dramatic financial reverses. Papal encyclicals inspired the Canadian responses of the Antigonish Movement, Action libérale nationale of Quebec, the *Catholic Register* in Toronto, and a pro-CCF movement on the Prairies. Tompkins and Coady inspired farmers, fishers, and miners to educate themselves and form credit unions. They encouraged a depressed people to accept the findings of science and become democratically involved in building a fairer society. The Action libérale nationale drew inspiration from Catholic social thought, President Franklin Roosevelt's New Deal, and French Canadian nationalism and put together a political platform that won seats in the Quebec legislature. The ALN understood the importance to Québécois of being masters in their own house and makers of their own destiny and saw little relevance for the CCF in *la belle province*. Henry Somerville and Murray Ballantyne pointed out that Catholic social justice had much in common with the CCF and that the bishops should not condemn the party. Father Cullinane defended the CCF by saying that its combination of British parliamentary democracy and the Canadian cooperative movement had produced an authentic Canadian political party in sympathy with Catholic social thinking.

During the interwar and postwar periods, as church leaders and their congregations renewed themselves, the desire for a more authentic Canadian church intensified. Religious, clergy, and laity continued to extend and shape regional church structures. Religious congregations continued to run schools, hospitals, and social services. Church people made efforts to reach out to native people in Canada and to new immigrants from Italy, Hungary, and elsewhere. Yet the response of church leaders to these two groups was entirely inadequate. Thus, to deal with diocesan and extradiocesan problems on a national level, the Canadian bishops formed the Canadian Catholic Conference in 1943. The conference set up committees to deal with Canadian ecclesial, social, economic, and multicultural problems. While the organizing of church structures proceeded apace in other provinces, in Quebec the Bloc Populaire Canadien began the process of deconstruction and established the foundation of the Quiet Revolution. It demanded the secularization of church-operated hospitals, schools, social, and cultural institutions and educated a generation of Quebec youth to carry out a devolution of the Catholic social network.

Catholics in English-speaking Canada, largely unaware of the political and religious upheaval in Quebec, continued to say their prayers and sing their songs as if the tidal wave of the romantic revolution was not coming. However, the demand for change in Quebec soon spread to the rest of Canada. In the asbestos strike, the churches in Montreal and Sherbrooke sided with the workers and distanced themselves from the Duplessis government. The Quiet Revolution soon followed in the 1950s and 1960s, and the Quebec Liberals secularized the schools, hospitals, and social and cultural institutions. Secularism during the following decade challenged not only the Québécois but also the smugness of English-speaking Catholics. Secularized social welfare systems, medical services, life insurance policies, and burials removed the church from its traditional role of assisting the faithful through the major passages of life. The number of student places at Canadian Catholic colleges was decreasing. Balanced education offered by the Catholic college was challenged by specialization and technology at the secular university.

To address the stresses, strains, and rapid changes of the postwar world, Pope John XXIII convoked the Second Vatican Council in 1962. The universal church had to face the challenge of secularization, liberalization, and subjectivization, which was already well advanced in Western Europe and the Americas. For its part the Canadian church had to face the demand for social justice, Quebec sovereignty,

First Nations autonomy, and women's rights. Subjective authenticity was important to the post-Vatican II church. Students, workers, and the middle class for the first time were seeking their roots. The church supported the right of a distinct people in Quebec to determine their own future. The Canadian church in general had to be authentic and genuine to enter into dialogue with other churches. The charismatic movement was a popular expression of subjectivity and authenticity. After the Second Vatican Council, Catholics stove with new enthusiasm to become more authentic Canadian Christians.

The emergence of social justice, interfaith issues, women's rights, and native claims after the Second Vatican Council demanded that the church listen to and be more affirmative towards fellow Christians and minority groups. Ecumenical coalitions were set up to improve relations between Christians, minister to Canadians below the poverty line, and give help to Third World nations around the world. Following the war, it was difficult for native people to return to the reserve and for women to go back to the home. In church affairs they sought their rights and a future for themselves and their families. They sought to participate as equals in liturgical and administrative functions. The bishops, acknowledging the church's shortcomings in regard to native people, have laid out a policy for full acceptance of native people for the future. The bishops have raised the question of women in public ministry in Rome and informed Catholics in Canada on women's grievances and charisms. The CCCB recommended that Catholic institutions hire women in schools, colleges, and administration.

The main themes of this study – Gallicanism, Romanism, and Canadianism – manifest a Trinitarian ecclesiology whereby the Spirit inspired Catholics in their formation of the Catholic churches in Canada, which were then guided in their Canadian evolution by the universal Catholic church. As Catholics during four centuries became rooted in Canada, the universal church helped them to avoid parochialism and nationalism. These themes have reinforced themselves and become the frame for a synthetic history of Canadian Catholics and the basis of a Canadian Catholic ecclesiology. Canadian Catholics have yet to construct a particular Canadian ecclesiology that would include missions, interlinkages and Roman linkages, multicultural cooperation, social thinking, inner subjectivity, secular interface, Catholic women, and native people.[1]

At the beginning of this study, I stated that the overall goal of the analysis was to identify from published research the emerging themes in Canadian Catholicism. I maintain that the journals and monographs used for this purpose reflect accurately the similarities and dis-similarities, strengths and weaknesses in Canadian Catholic history. The study knits these themes into a historical vision of Canadian Catholics. I trust that the reader has found that this synthesis sheds light on the complex bond that welded very dissimilar Canadian Catholics into one believing community.

Notes

INTRODUCTION

1 Campeau, *The Jesuit Mission*, 295–8; McGrory, "Full Circle," 343. McGrory's sources are native leaders Joe Couture and Harold Cardinal.
2 I use the term Catholic rather than Roman Catholic so as to include Ukrainian Catholics and the other sixteen eastern rites of the Catholic church.
3 Sir Samuel Leonard Tilley (1818–96), the premier and lieutenant governor of New Brunswick, selected this passage from Psalm 72:8; *Dictionary of Canadian Biography*, s.v. "Sir Samuel Leonard Tilley."
4 Sheridan, *Love Kindness*, 338–42, and *Do Justice!*, 275–86 and 239–49.
5 Trigger, in *Natives and Newcomers*, 5–7, sums up and questions this tradition.
6 Jaenen, *Church in New France*, ix–x.

CHAPTER ONE

1 Jaenen, *Church in New France*, 3–4.
2 *Gentlemen and Jesuits*, 141–2, 165–78, 229–41; *Dictionary of Canadian Biography*, s.v. "Jessé Fléché."
3 Jaenen, *Church in New France*, 13–16.
4 Campeau, *La Mission des Jésuites chez Le Hurons*, 44.
5 *Dictionary of Canadian Biography*, 1, s.v. "Jean Dolbeau," "Joseph Le Caron," "Denis Jamet," and "Pacifique Duplessis."
6 Axtell, *The Invasion Within*, 49–50.
7 The Holy See in 1622 placed Propaganda Fide in charge of all Catholic missions, but national monarchies in previous centuries had appropriated

much of this power. The French Revolution destroyed the power of national monarchies in the missions, and thus Propaganda Fide acquired by default full direction of mission work around the world. Schatz, *Papal Primacy*, 131, 135–8.

8 Jaenen, *Church in New France*, viii.
9 Post-Tridentine spirituality refers to the crusading spirituality after the Council of Trent (1545–63), which renewed the discipline and spiritual life of the Catholic church.
10 *Dictionary of Canadian Biography*, 1, s.v. "Charles Lalemant."
11 Ibid., s.v. "Jean de Brébeuf."
12 Ibid., s.v. "Énemond Massé."
13 Axtell, *The Invasion Within*, 62.
14 Jaenen, *Church in New France*, 40–1.
15 Campeau, *La Mission des Jésuites chez Le Hurons*, 266–7.
16 Eccles, *France in America*, 27–8.
17 Axtell, *The Invasion Within*, 43.
18 Dickason, *The Myth of the Savage*, 254–70.
19 Jaenen, *Church in New France*, 25–6.
20 Axtell, *The Invasion Within*, 56–7; Crowley, "The French Regime to 1760," 22–3.
21 Crowley, "The French Regime to 1760," 11–12.
22 *Dictionary of Canadian Biography*, 1, s.v. "Marie Guyart, *dite* Marie de l'Incarnation"; Noel, *Women in New France*, 4–5.
23 Inculturation is a post-Vatican II term that describes the process by which the gospel message should be adapted to particular cultures. Evangelism in this sense consists not in imposing religious culture from without but in animating the sense of God from within the neophyte. Through the seventeenth century Jesuits in China, Vietnam, India, and elsewhere indigenized Christianity in various cultures. In New France they learned the Huron language, ate Huron food, travelled in Huron canoes, and were accepted as band associates. The gospel was translated into Huron through catechisms, hymns, and prayers.
24 Boucher, *Le Visage de l'Eglise du Canada*, 23.
25 Axtell, *The Invasion Within*, 46–7.
26 Eccles, *France in America*, 24–5.
27 Axtell, *The Invasion Within*, 72–4.
28 Vecsey, *The Paths of Kateri's Kin*, 29; Axtell, *The Invasion Within*, 78–9.
29 Noel, *Women in New France*, 7.
30 Axtell, *The Invasion Within*, 85–9.
31 Ibid., 80.
32 Vecsey, *Paths of Kateri's Kin*, 23–30.
33 Ibid.
34 Axtell, *The Invasion Within*, 120.

35 The Jesuit Order at this time was well versed in the practice of inculturation and stressed learning languages and accommodating to cultures. Matteo Ricci became a Chinese Mandarin, wore the square bonnet and silk robes of the scholar and served in the court of Beijing. Roberto de Nobili became a Indian Brahmin, dressed in the saffron robe and wooden clogs, maintained the vegetarian diet of the *sannyasi* (holy man), and served in Madura. Ricci wrote in Chinese, and de Nobili in Tamil. Jesuits on other missions, such as Alexandre de Rhodes in Vietnam, followed these enterprising examples. See Spence, *The Meaning Palace of Matteo Ricci*, and Cronin, *A Pearl to India*.

36 Nish, ed., *The French Régime*, 1: 157. *Jesuit Relations* was published between 1632 and 1673 to gain vocations and financial support for the missions.

37 Vecsey, *Paths of Kateri's Kin*, 31–2.

38 Campeau, *Mission des Jésuites chez les Hurons*, 353–4.

39 Trigger, *Natives and Newcomers*, 262–6.

40 Ibid., 266–72; *Dictionary of Canadian Biography*, 1, s.v. "Jean Brébref," and "Jérôme Lalemant."

41 *Dictionary of Canadian Biography*, 1, s.v. "Joseph Chihwatenha" Vecsey, *Paths of Kateri's Kin*, 61–2.

42 *Dictionary of Canadian Biography*, 1, s.v. "Joseph Chihwatenha."

43 Campeau, *Mission des Jésuites chez les Hurons*, 104.

44 Ibid., 231–4.

45 Ibid.

46 Campeau, *The Jesuit Missions among the Hurons* 294.

47 *Dictionary of Canadian Biography*, 1, s.v. "Kateri Tekakwitha."

48 McGrory, "Full Circle," 281.

49 Campeau, *Mission des Jésuites chez les Hurons*, 256–7, 269.

50 Axtell, *The Invasion Within*, 125–7.

51 Vecsey, *Paths of Kateri's Kin*, 67–8.

52 Ibid., 68–9, 83–5; Jaenen, *Church in New France*, 34–6.

53 Campeau, *The Jesuit Missions among the Hurons*, 297–98.

54 Axtell, *The Invasion Within*, 277–9.

55 Jaenen, "Amerindian Responses to French Missionary Intrusion," 3–8.

56 Jaenen, "Amerindian Responses to French Missionary Intrusion," 8–14.

57 Henri Béchard, *Jérôme Le Royer de la Dauversière*, 142–50

58 Adair, "France and the Beginnings of New France," 246–50; Eccles, *New France in America*, 25–6.

59 Adair, "France and the Beginnings of New France," 252–63 and 269.

60 Eccles, *France in America*, 48, 51.

61 Adair, "France and the Beginnings of New France," 268–9, 272–3.

62 Simpson, *Marguerite Bourgeoys and Montreal*, 89, 101.

63 Crowley, "The French Regime to 1760," 11–12.

64 *Dictionary of Canadian Biography*, 1, s.v. "Jeanne Mance."

65 Axtell, *The Invasion Within*, 59.

66 Simpson, *Marguerite Bourgeoys and Montreal*, 46–57.

67 Ibid., 148–9.

68 Ibid., 153.

69 *Dictionary of Canadian Biography*, 1, s.v. "Marguerite Bourgeoys"; Rapley, *The Dévotes*, 100–12; Jean, *Évolution des Communautés Religieuses de Femmes*, 27–35.

70 *Dictionary of Canadian Biography*, 1, s.v. "Marguerite Bourgeoys."

71 Simpson, *Marguerite Bourgeoys and Montreal*, 171–2.

72 Ibid., 122–3, 178–9.

73 Crowley, "The French Regime to 1760," 43.

74 Simpson, *Marguerite Bourgeoys and Montreal*, 171–2.

75 *Dictionary of Canadian Biography*, s.v. "Gabriel Thubières de Levy de Queylus."

76 Adair, "France and the Beginnings of New France," 274–7.

77 Johnston, *Life and Religion at Louisbourg*, 11, 33.

78 Ibid., 3–4.

79 Ibid., 4.

80 Crowley, "The Inroads of Secularization," 6–7.

81 Crowley, "Church and People at Louisbourg," 8–9.

82 Ibid., 9–11.

83 Johnston, *Life and Religion at Louisbourg*, 102, 106–8.

84 Ibid., 67–8, 81.

85 Ibid., 84–5.

86 Crowley, "The French Regime to 1760," 24–7; Johnston, *Life and Religion at Louisbourg*, 152–4.

87 Crowley, "The French Regime to 1760," 19.

88 Falardeau, "The Role and the Importance of the Church in French Canada," 344; Jaenen, *Church in New France*, 83–4.

89 Crowley, "The French Regime to 1760," 22–3.

90 *Dictionary of Canadian Biography*, 2, s.v. "François de Laval."

91 Bokenkotter, *A Concise History of the Catholic Church*, 242–4. Bokenkotter explains the Four Gallican Articles as prescribing that the bishop of Rome does not have power over kings or general councils, was not infallible on his own, and that papal documents have to be received by the Church for validity. Jaenen, *Church in New France*, 41–2.

92 Nish, *The French Régime*, 1: 51; Eccles, *France in America*, 69–71.

93 Falardeau, *French-Canadian Society*, 1: 344–5.

94 Axtell, *The Invasion Within*, 64–7.

95 Nish, *The French Régime*, 1: 69–70; Eccles, *France in America*, 71.

96 Jaenen, *Church in New France*, 77–8.

97 Nish, *The French Régime*, 1: 75–7.

98 Falardeau, *French-Canadian Society*, 1: 24–6, 345–6.

99 Jaenen, *Church in New France*, 84.

100 *Dictionary of Canadian Biography*, 2, s.v. "Jean-Baptiste de la Croix"; Jaenen, *Church in New France*, 32–3.

101 Falardeau, *French-Canadian Society*, 1: 344.

102 Cliche, "Dévotion populaire," 17–34.

103 Thomas, "Quebec's Bishop as a Pawn," 151.

104 *Dictionary of Canadian Biography*, 2, s.v. "Jean-Baptiste de la Croix."

105 Falardeau, *French-Canadian Society*, 1: 343–4.

106 Jaenen, *Church in New France*, 68.

107 Crowley, "The French Regime to 1760," 52–3.

108 Axtell, *The Invasion Within*, 286.

109 Crowley, "The French Regime to 1760," 48.

110 Ibid., 50–3; Jaenen, *Church in New France*, 150–6.

CHAPTER TWO

1 Zoltvany, ed., *The French Traditions in America*, 189.

2 *Dictionary of Canadian Biography*, 3, s.v. "Henri-Marie Dubreil de Pontbriand."

3 Waite, ed., *Pre-Confederation*, 2: 46–8; Falardeau, "The Role and Importance of the Church," 346; Griffiths, *The Acadians*, 65–85; Lemieux, *Histoire du Catholicisme québécois*, 2, 1: 14.

4 Egremont to Governor Murray, 13 August 1763, 169, and Instructions to Governor Carleton, 3 January 1775, 602, in Shortt and Doughty, eds., *Documents*.

5 *Dictionary of Canadian Biography*, 3, s.v. "Henri-Marie Dubreil de Pontbriand," and "Jean-Olivier Briand."

6 Instructions to Governor Murray, 7 December 1763, 169, and Instructions to Governor Carleton, 3 January 1775, Shortt and Doughty, eds., *Constitutional History of Canada*, 603–6.

7 Brunet, *Les Canadiens après La Conquête*, 117.

8 Waite, eds., *Pre-Confederation*, 2: 48–50.

9 Brunet, *Les Canadiens après La Conquête*, 122–3.

10 *Dictionary of Canadian Biography*, 2, s.v. "Henri-Marie Dubreil de Pontbriand," 197–8; Lemieux, *Histoire du Catholicisme québécois*, 2: 1, 18–19.

11 Report of Lords Commissioners for Trade and Plantations Relative to the State of the Province of Quebec, 10 July 1769, Shortt and Doughty, eds., *Constitutional History of Canada*, 389–90.

12 Instructions to Governor Carleton, 3 January 1775, Shortt and Doughty, eds., *Constitutional History of Canada*, 603–5.

13 Neatby, *Quebec: The Revolutionary Age*, 121–2.

14 Instructions to Governor Carleton, 3 January 1775, Shortt and Doughty, eds., *Constitutional History of Canada*, 613; Brunet, *Les Canadiens après La Conquête*, 127–8, 136.

15 *Dictionary of Canadian Biography*, 4, s.v. "Jean-Olivier Briand."

16 Ibid.

17 Ibid. "The Conquest and Its Aftermath," in *A Concise History of Christianity in Canada*, edited by Terrence Murphy and Roberto Perin (Toronto: Oxford University Press, 1996), 58; Lemieux, *Histoire de catholicisme québécois* 2:1, 16.

18 *Dictionary of Canadian Biography*, 4, s.v. "Jean-Olivier Briand."

19 Ibid.

20 Brunet, *Les Canadiens Après La Conquête*, 126–27.

21 Chaussé, "The Conquest and Its Aftermath," 58 and 66.

22 Shortt & Doughty, *Constitutional History of Canada*, 387–88, Report of Lords Commissioners for Trade and Plantations Relative to the State of the Province of Quebec, 10 July 1769: Gilles Chaussé, "French Canada from the Conquest to 1840," in *A Concise History of Christianity in Canada*, edited by Terrence Murphy and R. Perin (Toronto: Oxford University Press, 1996), 58.

23 Joseph Cossette, "Jean-Joseph Casot," *DCB* 4: 134–35.

24 Shortt & Doughty, *Constitutional History of Canada*, 604, Instructions to Governor Carleton, 3 January 1775: Gilles Chaussé, "The Conquest and Its Aftermath," 58.

25 Brunet, *Les Canadiens Après La Conquête*, 128.

26 Shortt & Doughty, *Constitutional History of Canada*, 604, Instructions to Governor Carleton, 3 January 1775.

27 Neatby, *Quebec: The Revolutionary Age*, 120–22, 138–41.

28 Shortt & Doughty, *Constitutional History of Canada*, 191, Instruction to Governor Murray, 7 December 1763.

29 Shortt & Doughty, *Constitutional History of Canada*, 383, Report of the Lords Commissioners For Trade and Plantations Relative to the State of the Province of Quebec, 10 July 1769.

30 The bishop signed "Desgly." See *Dictionary of Canadian Biography*, 4, s.v. "Louis-Philippe Mariauchau d'Esgly."

31 Lemieux, *Histoire du Catholicisme québécois*, 2, sec. 1: 26.

32 Cramahé to Dartmouth, 22 June 1773. Shortt and Doughty, eds., *Constitutional History of Canada*, 484.

33 *Dictionary of Canadian Biography*, s.v. "Louis-Philippe Mariauchau d'Esgly."

34 Murphy, "James Jones," 26–7.

35 *Dictionary of Canadian Biography*, s.v. "Jean-Olivier Briand," and "Louis-Philippe Mariauchau D'Esgly."

36 *Dictionary of Canadian Biography*, s.v. "Jean-Olivier Briand," 4: 95, 97–8; Crowley, "The French Regime to 1760," 54

37 The Quebec Act, 1774, Shortt and Doughty, eds., *Constitutional History of Canada*, 572–5.

38 Neatby, *Quebec: The Revolutionary Age*, 139–41, 146.

39 Waite, ed., *Pre-Confederation*, 2: 56–7.

40 Chaussé, "The Conquest and Its Aftermath," 75.

41 Lemieux, *Histoire du Catholicisme québécois*, 2, sec. 1: 32.

42 Chaussé, "The Conquest and Its Aftermath," 74.

43 Ibid., 101.

44 Ibid., 68–9.

45 Ibid., 90–1.

46 Choquette, *The Oblate Assault on Canada's Northwest*, 30–2.

47 Chaussé, "The Conquest and Its Aftermath," 58.

48 Brunet, *Les Canadiens après La Conquête*, 139.

49 Voisine and Hamelin, eds., *Les Ultramontains Canadiens-Français*, 73–4, 122–3, and 134.

50 Falardeau, "Role and the Importance of the Church," 346–7.

51 Chaussé, "The Conquest and Its Aftermath," 61–2.

52 Ibid., 66–7.

53 Ibid., 83.

54 Waite, ed., *Pre-Confederation*, 2: 64–5.

55 Chaussé, "The Conquest and Its Aftermath," 76–7.

56 Ibid., 78–9.

57 Lemieux, *Histoire du Catholicisme québécois*, 2, sec. 1: 11; Chaussé, "The Conquest and Its Aftermath," 84–6.

58 Chaussé, "The Conquest and Its Aftermath," 86–7.

59 Ibid., 87.

60 *Dictionary of Canadian Biography*, 6, s.v. "Joseph-Octave Plessis."

61 Lemieux, *Histoire du Catholicisme québécois*, 2, sec. 1: 36–8.

62 *Dictionary of Canadian Biography*, 6, s.v. "Joseph-Octave Plessis."

63 Ibid.

64 Ibid.

65 Ibid.

66 Ibid.

67 Ibid.

68 Chaussé, "The Conquest and Its Aftermath," 80–1.

69 *Dictionary of Canadian Biography*, 6, s.v. "Joseph-Octave Plessis."

70 Lemieux, *Histoire du Catholicisme québécois*, 2, sec. 1: 49–50.

71 *Dictionary of Canadian Biography*, 6, s.v. "Joseph-Octave Plessis."

72 Chaussé, "The Conquest and Its Aftermath," 89.

73 *Dictionary of Canadian Biography*, 6, s.v. "Joseph-Octave Plessis."

74 Brunet, *Les Canadiens après La Conquête*, 128–9.

75 *Dictionary of Canadian Biography*, 6, s.v. "Joseph-Octave Plessis."

76 Lemieux, *Histoire du catholicisme québécois*, 2, sec. 1: 84–6.

77 *Dictionary of Canadian Biography*, 6, s.v. "Joseph-Octave Plessis."

78 *Dictionary of Canadian Biography*, 6, s.v. "Joseph-Octave Plessis."

79 Chaussé, "The Conquest and Its Aftermath," 94–95.

80 *Dictionary of Canadian Biography*, 6, s.v. "Jean-Jacques Lartigue."
81 Lemieux, *L'Établissement de la Première Province Ecclésiastique au Canada*, 497–9. It is interesting that six years after Quebec became a metropolitan province, the archdiocese of Westminster in London was created as the first metropolitan province in England. Edward Norman, *The English Catholic Church in the Nineteenth Century* (Oxford: Clarendon Press, 1985), 124–7.
82 Between 1755 and 1758 the British forces rounded up 6,000 to 10,000 Acadians, men first but women and children later, and loaded them onto transport ships to disperse them through the unprepared and unwelcoming English colonies. Many former Acadians after a time returned to French territories or to inland Acadia.

CHAPTER THREE

1 Bumstead, "Scottish Catholicism in Canada," 79–81.
2 Codignola, "The Policy of Rome," 100–2.
3 Ibid., 107–8.
4 Murphy, "James Jones," 26–7, and "The Emergence of Maritime Catholicism," 33; *Dictionary of Canadian Biography*, 5, s.v. "James Jones."
5 *Dictionary of Canadian Biography*, 5, s.v. "James Louis O'Donel."
6 *Dictionary of Canadian Biography*, 6, s.v. "Angus Bernard MacEachern."
7 Codignola, "The Policy of Rome," 106–7.
8 Ibid., 111–12.
9 Ibid., 113–16.
10 Chapeau et al., eds., *Canadian RC Bishops, 1658–1979*.
11 Codignola, "The Policy of Rome," 117.
12 Lahey, "Catholicism and Colonial Policy in Newfoundland," 51.
13 Byrne, ed., *Gentlemen-Bishops and Faction Fighters*, 9
14 Ibid., 9–10.
15 *Dictionary of Canadian Biography*, 5, s.v. "James Louis O'Donel."
16 Lahey, "Catholicism and Colonial Policy in Newfoundland," 52–3.
17 *Dictionary of Canadian Biography*, 5, s.v. "James Louis O"Donel."
18 Lahey, "Catholicism and Colonial Policy in Newfoundland," 53–4; *Canadian RC Bishops*.
19 O'Donel to Troy, 8 December 1792, Byrne, *Gentlemen-Bishops and Faction Fighters*, 120–2.
20 O'Donel to Plessis, 14 May 1800, Byrne, *Gentlemen-Bishops and Faction Fighters*, 171–3 and 144–5.
21 Lahey, "Catholicism and Colonial Policy in Newfoundland," 54.
22 *Dictionary of Canadian Biography*, 5, s.v. "James Louis O"Donel"; Byrne, *Gentlemen-Bishops and Faction Fighters*, 21.

23 Lahey, "Catholicism and Colonial Policy in Newfoundland," 56 and 63.

24 Byrne, *Gentlemen-Bishops and Faction Fighters*, 234–5; Lahey, "Catholicism and Colonial Policy in Newfoundland," 57; *Dictionary of Canadian Biography*, s.v. "Patrick Lambert."

25 Byrne, *Gentlemen-Bishops and Faction Fighters*, 297.

26 *Dictionary of Canadian Biography*, 5, s.v. "Thomas Scallan."

27 Lahey, "Catholicism and Colonial Policy in Newfoundland," 58–9; *Dictionary of Canadian Biography*, 5, s.v. "Thomas Scallan."

28 Lahey, "Catholicism and Colonial Policy in Newfoundland," 63–5; *Dictionary of Canadian Biography*, 5, s.v. "Thomas Scallan."

29 Lahey, "Catholicism and Colonial Policy in Newfoundland," 65–7; *Dictionary of Canadian Biography*, 5, s.v. "Thomas Scallan."

30 Lahey, "Catholicism and Colonial Policy in Newfoundland," 68.

31 Cameron, " 'Erasing Forever the Brand of Social Inferiority,' " 50; Bumstead, "Scottish Catholicism in Canada," 83–5.

32 Bumsted, "Scottish Catholicism in Canada," 86.

33 Akenson, *Small Differences*, 98–107.

34 Bumsted, "Scottish Catholicism in Canada," 89–90.

35 Choquette, *L'Église catholique*, 20, 27.

36 *Dictionary of Canadian Biography*, 7, s.v. "Alexander McDonell," 545–6, and s.v. "The Emergence of Maritime Catholicism," 47–9.

37 Lambert, "The Face of Upper Canadian Catholicism," 10–11.

38 Ibid., 14–15.

39 Ibid., 14.

40 *Canadian Encyclopedia*, s.v. "Alexander Macdonell."

41 Lambert, "The Face of Upper Canadian Catholicism," 17–18, 22.

42 James D. Cameron, *For All the People*, 12–13.

43 Bumstead, "Scottish Catholicism in Canada," 91–4; Chapeau et al., eds, *Canadian RC Bishops*.

44 *Dictionary of Canadian Biography*, 8, s.v. "William Fraser."

45 Wilson, *The Irish in Canada*, 9–12.

46 Houston and Smyth, *Irish Emigration and Canadian Settlement*, 189–217; Wilson, *The Irish in Canada*, 3–7. Some of the effects of the penal laws on church life in Ireland are described by Patrick J. Corish in "The Irish Catholics at the End of the Penal Era," *Religion and Identity* (St John's: Jesperson, 1987), 1–2.

47 Terrence Murphy, *Religion and Identity*, 68–78.

48 *Dictionary of Canadian Biography*, 5, s.v. "James Jones."

49 Murphy and Stortz, *Creed and Culture*, 130–1.

50 *Dictionary of Canadian Biography*, 5, s.v. "Edmund Burke."

51 Ibid.

52 Terrence Murphy, "The Emergence of Maritime Catholicism," 45–6.

53 *Dictionary of Canadian Biography*, 8, s.v. "William Fraser."

54 Murpphy and Stortz, *Creed and Culture*, 131–2.

55 *Dictionary of Canadian Biography*, 8, s.v. "William Fraser."

56 Ibid., s.v. "William Walsh."

57 A.A. Johnston, *Catholic Church in Eastern Nova Scotia*, vol. 2: 188–91.

58 Murphy and Stortz, *Creed and Culture*, 133.

59 Johnston, *Catholic Church in Eastern Nova Scotia*, II: 205–12.

60 Murphy and Stortz, *Creed and Culture*, 134.

61 Johnston, *Catholic Church in Eastern Nova Scotia*, vol. 2: 212–15.

62 MacLean, "An Outline of Diocesan History," 7.

63 Cameron, *For All the People*, 76–8, 96–7.

64 Cameron, " 'Easing forever the brand of social inferiority,' " 49–64.

65 *Dictionary of Canadian Biography*, 12, s.v. "Peter McIntyre."

66 MacDonald, *The History of St. Dunstan's University*, 114–15; Shook, *Catholic Post-secondary Education*, 35–45.

67 Shook, *Catholic Post-secondary Education*, 57–61.

68 Cameron, *For All the People*, 71–2.

69 Johnston, *Catholic Church in Eastern Nova Scotia*, 2: 504–5; Cameron, *History of St Francis Xavier University*, 66–7.

70 Johnston, *Catholic Church in Eastern Nova Scotia*, II: 507–09.

CHAPTER FOUR

1 Lebrun, *Joseph de Maistre*, 235–6.

2 Ibid., 239, 246.

3 Bokenkotter, *Church and Revolution*, 43–4.

4 Ibid., 52–4.

5 Ibid., 55–6.

6 Misner, *Social Catholicism in Europe*, 57.

7 Bokenkotter, *Church and Revolution*, 59–60, 76.

8 Ibid., 77.

9 Ibid., 77–80.

10 Ibid.

11 Chaussé, "Un Évêque mennaisien au Canada," 105, 110–11.

12 Ibid., 105–6; Bokenkotter, *Church and Revolution*, 43–4.

13 Bokenkotter, *Church and Revolution*, 44–5.

14 Chaussé, "Un Évêque mennaisien au Canada," 119.

15 *Dictionary of Canadian Biography*, 6, s.v. "Jean-Jacques Lartigue."

16 Lemieux, *Histoire du Catholicisme québécois*, 2, sec. 1: 18–19, 64–9; *Dictionary of Canadian Biography*, 6, s.v. "Jean-Jacques Lartigue."

17 Chaussé, "The Conquest and Its Aftermath," 101.

18 *Dictionary of Canadian Biography*, 6, s.v. "Jean-Jacques Lartigue."

19 Galarneau, "Monseigneur de Forbin-Janson au Québec," 134–7.

20 Monet, "French-Canadian Nationalism," 43–4.

21 Caulier, "Vie Spirituelle," 113.

22 Ibid., 110.

23 Monet, "French-Canadian Nationalism," 43–4.

24 Voisine and Hamelin, *Les Ultramontains Canadiens-Français*, 94.

25 Sylvain, "Libéralisme et ultramontanisme au Canada français," 1: 114–15.

26 Sylvain, "Libéralisme et ultramontanisme au Canada français," 112–14.

27 Chaussé, *Jean Jacques Lartigue*, 16, 139–40, 144–5, 201; Monet, *The Last Canon Shot*, 128–9, 249–50.

28 Dubeau-Legentil, "*Le Petit Catéchisme*," 237–55.

29 Caulier, "Vie Spirituelle," 109–11.

30 Ibid., 112.

31 Marraro, "Canadian and American Zouaves," 83–99.

32 Voisine and Hamelin, *Les Ultramontains-Canadiens-Français*, 76.

33 Choquette, *The Oblate Assault on Canada's Northwest*, 17.

34 *Dictionary of Jesuit Biography*, 55–9; Fay, "What Manner of Men Are These?, 4–5.

35 Laverdure, *Redemption and Renewal*, 1–2, 8, 29–60.

36 Iwicki, *Resurrectionist Charism*, 1: 164–7.

37 Jean, *Évolution des communautés religieuses de femmes*, 85–8.

38 Coffey, "George Edward Clerk," and "*The True Witness and Catholic Chronicle*," Report 1, 46–59, Report 4 (1937–38): 33–46; *Dictionary of Canadian Biography*, 10, s.v. "George Edward Clerk."

39 Coffey, "*The True Witness and Catholic Chronicle*," Report 1, 30.

40 Bowen, "Ultramontanism in Quebec," 299–301; *Dictionary of Canadian Biography*, 11, s.v. "Ignace Bourget."

41 Perin, "French-Speaking Canada from 1840," 224.

42 Perin, "Troppo Ardenti Sacerdoti," 285.

43 Voisine and Hamelin, *Les Ultramontains-Canadiens-Français*, 85–6; Perin, *Rome in Canada*, 43, 106–7, 121, and "French-Speaking Canada from 1840," 223–24.

44 Perin, "Troppo Ardenti Sacerdoti," 297.

45 Dolan, *The American Catholic Experiencest*, 436.

46 Sylvain, "Libéralisme et ultramontanisme au Canada français," 121–2 and 128–9.

47 Ibid., 236–44.

48 Byrne, *Gentlemen-Bishops and Faction Fighters*, 27.

49 *Dictionary of Canadian Biography*, 7, s.v. "Michael Anthony Fleming."

50 FitzGerald, "Michael Anthony Fleming," 64 (1998): 34.

51 FitzGerald, ibid., 41–4.

52 Ibid., 32–5. FitzGerald, "Michael Anthony Fleming and Ultramontanism," 32–5. The "Yellowbellies" from Wexford, Ireland, were an élite who

established themselves in St John's and won favour in Newfoundland's mercantile and colonial ascendancy prior to 1830. Known as "Yellowbellies" in Ireland and Newfoundland for the yellow sashes that members of County Wexford hurling teams often wore, they were eclipsed in political influence in Newfoundland after 1836 by a new Catholic élite from County Waterford known as "Wheybellies." Discontented with the élite accommodation between the British officials in Newfoundland and the Yellowbellies, the Waterford faction sought political equality for Catholics, supported Daniel O'Connell's drive for Catholic emancipation and repeal of the union, and associated themselves with the vicar apostolic of Newfoundland, Bishop Michael A. Fleming, who desired a more arduous and uncompromising ultramontane Roman Catholicism.

53 Murphy, "Trusteeism in Atlantic Canada: The Struggle for Leadership among the Irish Catholics of Halifax, St John's, and Saint John, 1780–1850," *Creed and Culture*, 136–39.
54 FitzGerald, "Michael Anthony Fleming," 35–7.
55 Byrne, *Gentlemen-Bishops and Faction Fighters*, 298.
56 FitzGerald, "Michael Anthony Fleming," 44.
57 *Dictionary of Canadian Biography*, 7, s.v. "Michael Anthony Fleming."
58 *Dictionary of Canadian Biography*, 6, s.v. "John Thomas Mullock."
59 Ibid.
60 Ibid.
61 Burns, "From Freedom to Tolerance," I: 465–6.
62 Ibid., 466–7.
63 Ibid., 468.
64 Ibid., 469.
65 Ibid., 470.
66 Ibid., 470.
67 Ibid., 471.
68 Ibid., 472–3.
69 Cottrell, "Irish Catholic Political Leadership in Toronto," 261. The Fenians were a militant Irish-American society organized in 1859 to promote Irish independence. Many Irish, fighting for the victorious Union forces in the American Civil War, lingered in the east coast states to swell the ranks of a Fenian army and prepare attacks on British forces in Canada. In 1866 Fenian raids were made over the border into New Brunswick, Quebec, Ontario, and, in 1870, into Manitoba but were repulsed by joint British and Canadian Forces.
70 Burns, "D'Arcy McGee," 475–6.
71 *Dictionary of Canadian Biography*, 7, s.v. "Michael Power."
72 Clarke, *Piety and Nationalism*, 9–11.
73 Donald Akenson would support Clarke's contention. See *The Irish in Ontario*, 27–8, 45–7.

74 Clarke, *Piety and Nationalism*, 9. The Irish roots of ultramontanism are sketched out by Murphy, *A Concise History of Christianity in Canada*, 169–71. For the formation of parallel voluntary organizations in Germany, please see von Arx, ed., *Varieties of Ultramontanism*, 27.

75 Clarke, *Piety and Nationalism*, 45–8.

76 Ibid., 52–3.

77 Ibid., 56–60.

78 Stortz, "Archbishop John Joseph Lynch," 4–9.

79 *Dictionary of Canadian Biography*, 11, s.v. "John Joseph Lynch."

80 Ibid.

81 Clarke, *Piety and Nationalism*, 61.

82 Choquette, *The Oblate Assault on Canada's Northwest*, 81, 2, 14–15.

83 *Dictionary of Canadian Biography*, 8, s.v. "Joseph-Norbert Provencher."

84 *Dictionary of Canadian Biography*, 12, s.v. "Alexandre-Antonin Taché."

85 Estelle Mitchell, *The Grey Nuns*, 29–31.

86 Choquette, *The Oblate Assault on Canada's Northwest*, 82–6.

87 *Dictionary of Canadian Biography*, 12, s.v. "Alexandre-Antonin Taché."

88 Ibid.

89 Ibid.

90 Perin, *Rome in Canada*, 31; *Dictionary of Canadian Biography*, 12, s.v. "Alexandre-Antonin Taché."

91 Choquette, *The Oblate Assault on Canada's Northwest*, 88–9.

92 MacGregor, *Father Lacombe*, 216–41.

93 Choquette, *The Oblate Assault on Canada's Northwest*, 90–3.

94 *Dictionary of Canadian Biography*, 10, s.v. "Modeste Demers."

95 McNally, *The Lord's Distant Vineyard*, 25–8, 192–5.

96 *Dictionary of Canadian Biography*, 11, s.v. "Louis-Joseph d'Herbomez"; McNally, *Lord's Distant Vineyard*, 92–3, 125–6.

97 Choquette, *The Oblate Assault on Canada's Northwest*, 94–7.

98 Roberto Perin provides an excellent description of the ultramontane devotions in Quebec. See "French-Speaking Canada from 1840," 198–202.

99 Perin, *Rome in Canada*, 43, 67, 92, 124.

CHAPTER FIVE

1 Cameron, "'Easing Forever the Brand of Social Inferiority,'" 49.

2 Alexander, *The Antigonish Movement*, 54.

3 Cameron, "Easing Forever," 52–3.

4 Ibid., 55–9.

5 McGowan, "Conspicuous Influence," 11.

6 Cameron, *History of St Francis Xavier University*, 97–8.

7 Cameron, "Easing Forever," 60–1.

8 Ibid., 63.

9 Ibid., 63–4.
10 Paul Cullen was a most influential Irish and Roman ecclesial official during the middle of the nineteenth century. His positions included agent for the Irish and Australian bishops, rector of the Irish College in Rome, temporary rector of the College of Propaganda during the Roman crisis of 1849–50, archbishop of Armagh (1850–52), and archbishop of Dublin sequentially (1852–78), as well as apostolic delegate and Irish cardinal, 1866–78. During these last years he was instrumental in framing the definition of papal infallibility at the First Vatican Council. *Catholic Encyclopedia* (1966) and Bowen, "Ultramontanism in Quebec and the Irish Connection," 1: 297–9.
11 Corcoran, *Mount Saint Vincent University,* 6–7; O'Gallagher, "The Sisters of Charity of Halifax," 57–9.
12 O'Gallagher, "Sisters of Charity of Halifax," 61–3.
13 MacLellan, "Nova Scotia," 13–14; A. A. Johnston, *History of the Catholic Church in Eastern Nova Scotia,* 2: 420–3.
14 *Dictionary of Canadian Biography,* 11, s.v. "Michael Hannan."
15 Hanington, *Every Popish Person,* 140.
16 *Dictionary of Canadian Biography,* 11, s.v. "Michael Hannan."
17 Corcoran, *Mount Saint Vincent University,* 11–13.
18 O'Gallagher, "Sisters of Charity of Halifax," 63.
19 *Dictionary of Canadian Biography,* 12, s.v. "Joanna Harrington."
20 Hanington, *Every Popish Person,* 148.
21 O'Gallagher, "Sisters of Charity of Halifax," 63–4.
22 Vaillancourt, *Papal Power,* 267–97; Dolan, *The American Catholic Experience,* 189–90.
23 *Dictionary of Canadian Biography,* 13, s.v. "Cornelius O'Brien."
24 Hanington, *Every Popish Person,* 155–7.
25 O'Gallagher, "Sisters of Charity of Halifax," 64–7.
26 Corcoran, *Mount Saint Vincent University,* 181.
27 Ibid., 18; O'Gallagher, "Sisters of Charity of Halifax," 65–6; Conwell, *Contemplation in Action.*
28 O'Gallagher, "Sisters of Charity of Halifax," 66.
29 Ibid., 67. An alternative view of the work of the sisters at the Shubenacadie residential school has been written by Isabelle Knockwood in *Out of the Depths.* Knockwood described the confusion of native children arriving at the school, the studies, student labour, the punishments that were meted out, and the long-term effects of schooling upon them. The book is a severe if melodramatic indictment of the way the school was operated.
30 McGahan, "The Sisters of Charity of the Immaculate Conception," 101–7.
31 Hennessey, "New Brunswick," 8–9.
32 McGahan, "The Sisters of Charity of the Immaculate Conception," 109–11.
33 Ibid., 117.
34 Ibid., 116.

35 Ibid., 117–22.

36 Ibid., 123–4.

37 Ibid., 124–5.

38 Ibid., 125–6.

39 Ibid., 126–30.

40 Ibid., 132–3.

41 Grace, "For a Reinterpretation of the History."

42 Dolan, *The American Catholic Experience*, 293. Dolan recounts that the first Catholic women's college, the College of Notre Dame of Maryland, opened in 1896. Trinity College in Washington, DC, followed in 1900. By 1915 nineteen women's colleges existed in the United States.

43 Huntley-Maynard, "Catholic Post-secondary Education for Women in Quebec," 37–8.

44 McKee, "Quebec," 18–19; Trofimenkoff, *The Dream of Nation*, 121.

45 Huntley-Maynard, "Catholic Post-secondary Education for Women in Quebec," 38–9.

46 Ibid., 39.

47 Ibid., 40–1.

48 Danylewycz, *An Alternative to Marriage*, 13–20.

49 Huntley-Maynard, "Catholic Post-secondary Education for Women in Quebec," 41–2.

50 Ibid., 43–4.

51 Ibid., 44–5.

52 Ibid., 45–6.

53 Ibid., 46–8.

54 Danylewycz, *Taking the Veil*, 144–50, 155–7.

55 In *Lamentabili* (1907) and *Pascendi Dominici Gregis* (1907) Pope Pius X condemned the teaching of those who were generically called "modernists." Loisy, Tyrell, Le Roy, Dimnet, and Houtin were accused in their argumentation of using rationalism to explain sacred theology and Scripture. This condemnation of Catholic scholars ended the study of creative theology, Scripture, and church history for three decades.

56 Walker, *Catholic Education*, 55.

57 Ibid., 44–9.

58 Stobo, *Historical Development*, 2–3.

59 Stortz, "Separate But Never Equal," 66–7.

60 Walker, *Catholic Education*, 318–31; Stortz, "Separate But Never Equal," 66–7; Stobo, *Historical Development*, 2–3.

61 Cameron, *For the People*, 97–9.

62 Other comparisons might include the Cobourg Ladies Academy, 1847, and St Hilda's College, Toronto, 1893, and the well-known American institutions Vassar College, 1861, and Radcliff College, 1879; Shook, *Catholic Post-secondary Education*, 159.

63 Smyth, "Developing the Powers of the Youthful Mind," 105–6.

64 Rapley, *The Dévote*, chapters 4 and 5.

65 Smyth, "Developing the Powers of the Youthful Mind," 104–05.

66 Ibid., 109–11.

67 Ibid., 114–16.

68 Ibid., 117.

69 M. Margarita, "The Institute of the Blessed Virgin Mary," 79; Carr, "The Very Reverend J.R. Teefy, CSB, LLD," 94–5; Shook, *Catholic Post-secondary Education*, 155.

70 Smyth, "Developing the Powers of the Youthful Mind," 119–20, 122; Shook, *Catholic Post-secondary Education*, 157–9.

71 Smyth, "Developing the Powers of the Youthful Mind," 119, 122.

72 Ibid., 121.

73 Smyth, "Christian Perfection," 43.

74 Smyth, "Developing the Powers of the Youthful Mind," 123.

75 Ibid., 124–5.

76 Wahl, "Father Louis Funcken's Contribution," 513.

77 Ibid., 514–15.

78 Ibid., 516–18, 529; Iwicki with Wahl, *Resurrectionist Charism*, 242–7.

79 Wahl, "Father Louis Funcken's Contribution," 520–3.

80 Ibid., 526.

81 Ibid., 525–6.

82 Ibid., 527–30.

83 Choquette, *L'Église catholique dans l'Ontario français*, 314.

CHAPTER SIX

1 Careless, *The Union of the Canadas*, 210–12.

2 Winks, *Canada and the United States*, 371–2.

3 Flemming, "Archbishop Thomas L. Connolly," 68–9.

4 Johnston, "Popery and Progress," 152–4. Joseph Howe unleashed "one of the most cutting merciless attacks against the Irish" denouncing them as disloyal and as "promoters of turbulence and disloyalty."

5 Flemming, "Archbishop Thomas L. Connolly," 72–3.

6 Ibid., 73–5.

7 *Dictionary of Canadian Biography*, 12, s.v. "Peter McIntyre."

8 Hanington, *Roman Catholicism in Nova Scotia*, 122.

9 Flemming, "Archbishop Thomas L. Connolly," 75–9.

10 Ibid., 77, 80, 83–4.

11 Baker, "An Irish-Catholic Journalist-Politician," 5–12.

12 Ibid., 13–14.

13 Flemming, "Archbishop Thomas L. Connolly," 75.

14 Baker, "An Irish-Catholic Journalist-Politician," 15.

15 Ibid., 17–19.
16 Baker, *Timothy Warren Anglin*, 146.
17 Ibid., 148, 153.
18 Ibid., 147.
19 Thériault, "The Acadianization of the Catholic Church in Acadia," 297.
20 Baker, *Timothy Warren Anglin*, 154.
21 Ibid., 175.
22 Ibid., 179–81.
23 Baker, "An Irish-Catholic Journalist-Politician," 20–2.
24 Ibid., 22–3.
25 Ullmann, "The Quebec Bishops and Confederation," 48–9.
26 Ibid., 48–9, 52–4.
27 Ibid., 61–4.
28 Ibid., 66–9. Translation by T. Fay.
29 Stobo, *Historical Development*, 3.
30 Toner, "The New Brunswick Schools Question," 88; Silver, *The French-Canadian Idea of Confederation*, 2d ed., 54–5.
31 Toner, "The New Brunswick Schools Question," 88–9.
32 Ibid., 89–90.
33 Ibid., 90–1.
34 Silver, *The French-Canadian Idea of Confederation*, 91–2.
35 Toner, "The New Brunswick Schools Question," 91–2.
36 Silver, *The French-Canadian Idea of Confederation*, 52–4, 97–100.
37 Ibid., 97.
38 Ibid., 88–90.
39 Hennessey, "New Brunswick," 8–9.
40 Stanley, "The Caraquet Riots of 1875," 23–4 and 170–2.
41 Silver, *The French-Canadian Idea of Confederation*, 97–100.
42 Ibid., 103–4, 236.
43 Stanley, "The Caraquet Riots of 1875," 24–5.
44 *Dictionary of Canadian Biography*, 12, s.v. "Timothy Warren Anglin."
45 Toner, "The New Brunswick Schools Question," 93–5.
46 Stanley, "The Caraquet Riots of 1875," 37–8.
47 Hennessey, "New Brunswick," 10–11.
48 Toner, "The New-Brunswick Schools Question," 86, 94–95; Stanley, "The Caraquet Riots of 1875," 21 and 37.
49 Morton, *Manitoba*, 141–2, 186; Friesen, *The Canadian Prairies: A History*, 125–6.
50 Silver, "French Canada and the Prairie Frontier," 12.
51 Morton, *Manitoba*, 247–8.
52 Crunican, *Priests and Politician*, 33–43.
53 Morton, *Manitoba*, 279–80; Crunican, *Priests and Politician*, 237–9.
54 McLaughlin, " 'Riding the Protestant Horse,' " 44–6.

55 Crunican, *Priests and Politician*, 250–2.

56 Ibid., 256–8.

57 Ibid., 265–8; Crunican lists historians Willison, Sketon, Lower, McInnis, Wade, Schull, Rumilly, David, and Proulx (277–8) and newspapers Toronto *Mail and Empire*, Toronto *Globe*, London *Times*, and Boston *Journal* (301–6); also see 287.

58 Ibid., 274–6.

59 Ibid., 276–7.

60 Ibid., 274.

61 Ibid., 278–84.

62 See Edgar McInnis's popular textbook *Canada: A Political and Social History*, 432. McInnis falls into this misunderstanding when he describes a Catholic's vote for Laurier as "disobedience to the bishops and thus a mortal sin." Crunican, *Priests and Politician*, 287.

63 Crunican, *Priests and Politician*, 287–306.

64 Clarke, "English-Speaking Canada from 1854," 302–3.

65 Crunican, *Priests and Politician*, 317–18.

66 Ibid., 319–23.

67 Perin, *Rome in Canada*, 153–7; Rusak, "The Canadian 'Concordat' of 1897," 232–4.

CHAPTER SEVEN

1 McGowan, "Rethinking Catholic-Protestant Relations in Canada," 11–2 and 26–8.

2 Miller, "Anti-Catholicism in Canada," 26–28.

3 Moir, "Toronto's Protestants," 315.

4 Ibid., 314, 325.

5 Miller, "Anti-Catholicism in Canada," 28–30.

6 Johnston, "Popery and Progress," 146.

7 Johnston, "Popery and Progress," 146–8.

8 The Know-Nothings belonged to an American third party of the 1850s who, when asked for the purpose of their party, replied "I know nothing." The party was a grass-roots, red-neck nativist movement that disliked foreign-born immigrants, and in particular just after the potato famine, Irish Catholics. Carrying only the state of Maryland in the federal election of 1856, the party disintegrated once and for all.

9 Johnston, "Popery and Progress," 149–54.

10 Ibid., 150.

11 Ibid., 150.

12 Ibid., 155–159.

13 See, *Riots in New Brunswick*, 62–4.

14 Ibid., 186–7.

15 Ibid., 149.

16 Ibid., 128, 141, 150–1, 173–4.

17 Ibid., 201.

18 Ibid., 186–7.

19 Conacher, "The Politics of the 'Papal Aggression' Crisis," 13–27. When Pius IX created Nicholas Wiseman as the cardinal archbishop of Westminster along with four other English Catholic dioceses, Protestant publications cried out "papal aggression," yet in the British North American provinces, the English government had already approved ten dioceses and an archdiocese.

20 Miller, "Anti-Catholicism in Canada," 31–7.

21 Laverdure, "Charles Chiniquy," 50–3.

22 Miller, "Anti-Catholicism in Canada," 37.

23 Guindon, *Quebec Society.*

24 Galvin, "The Jubilee Riots in Toronto, 1875," 93–107. Protestant men and boys in Toronto on two Sunday afternoons, 26 September and 2 October 1875, rioted to stop Catholics marching in peaceful pilgrimage from St Paul's to St Michael's Cathedral, St Patrick's and St Mary's churches, and then back again.

25 Miller, "Anti-Catholicism in Canada," 38–9.

26 Morton, *Manitoba*, 123–48; Flanagan, *The Diaries of Louis Riel*; Friesen, *The Canadian Prairies*, 227–35.

27 Miller, "Anti-Catholicism in Canada," 40–1.

28 Moir, "Canadian Protestant Reaction," 80–5; Miller, "Anti-Catholicism in Canada," 40–1.

29 Moir, "Canadian Protestant Reaction," 80–1.

30 Ibid., 81–2.

31 Ibid., 92–3.

32 Ibid., 84–6.

33 Ibid., 88.

34 Ibid., 87–90.

35 Miller, "Anti-Catholicism in Canada," 41–2.

36 McGowan, "To Share in the Burdens of Empire," 191.

37 Moir, "Toronto's Protestants," 314, 325.

38 Miller, "Anti-Catholicism in Canada," 41–2.

39 McGowan, "Rethinking Catholic-Protestant Relations in Canada," 12–14.

40 Ibid., 15–16.

41 Ibid., 17.

42 Ibid., 18.

43 Ibid., 19–20.

44 Hryniuk, "Pioneer Bishop, Pioneer Times," 28–30; McGowan, "Rethinking Catholic-Protestant Relations in Canada," 22.

45 McGowan, "Rethinking Catholic-Protestant Relations in Canada," 25–7.

46 Careless, "Limited Identities in Canada," 1–10.

47 McGowan, "Rethinking Catholic-Protestant Relations in Canada," 29–31.

48 Mitchell, *The Grey Nuns of Montreal,* 222–7.

49 Hanington, *Every Popish Person,* 155–7.

50 MacPherson, "Religious Women in Nova Scotia," 105.

51 McDonald, *For the Least of My Brethren,* 13, 18–23, 38, 47–8; Dwyer, "Sisters of St Joseph," 75–78.

52 Ibid., 63.

53 McDonald, *For the Least of My Brethren,* 50–2, 55, 61–5.

54 Ibid., 77–8, 80, 82–3, 85–6.

55 Cellard and Pelletier, *Faithful to a Mission,* 38–42, 68–70, 91, 107, 113.

56 Daly, *Remembering for Tomorrow,* 22–3.

57 Cellard and Pelletier, *Faithful to a Mission,* 114.

58 Ibid., 170.

59 Cellard and Pelletier, *Faithful to a Mission,* 183, 192–215.

60 Ryan, "Economic Development," 385, 389.

61 Ibid., 387–9.

62 Ibid., 390–2.

63 Ibid., 392–3.

64 Ibid., 394–5.

65 Ibid., 396–7.

66 Ibid., 397–8.

67 Ibid., 398–9.

CHAPTER EIGHT

1 Silver, *The French-Canadian Idea of Confederation,* 232–7.

2 Choquette, "English-French Relations," 3–4.

3 Ibid., 4–5.

4 Ibid., 7–8.

5 Ibid., 8.

6 Ibid., 8.

7 Ibid., 8–9.

8 Ibid., 9–11.

9 Ibid., 11–13.

10 *Dictionary of Canadian Biography,* 13, s.v. "Alexander Macdonell."

11 Choquette, "English-French Relations," 13–14.

12 MacDougall, "St. Patrick's College: Ethnicity and the Liberal Arts in Catholic Education," *CCHA Study Sessions* 49 (1982): 56.

13 Farrell, "Michael Francis Fallon," 87–8.

14 Choquette, "English-French Relations," 14.

15 Ibid., 15–19.

16 Huel, "The Irish French Conflict," 51–70.

17 Also consult I.A. Silver's view of French-Canadian messianism in *The French-Canadian Idea of Confederation*, 232–7 and 264–8.

18 Choquette, *Language and Religion*, 2.

19 McGowan, "The De-greening of the Irish," 126–41; *The Waning of the Green*, 286–91.

20 Choquette, *Language and Religion*, 9–12.

21 Ibid., 13–14.

22 Ibid., 15–16

23 Ibid., 16–17.

24 Ibid., 18.

25 Ibid., 19–20.

26 Ibid., 25–32.

27 Ibid., 33–4.

28 Ibid., 34–7.

29 Ibid., 43

30 Huel, "Gestae Dei Per Francos," 39–40.

31 Choquette, *The Oblate Assault on Canada's Northwest*, 228–32.

32 Mitchell, *The Grey Nuns*, 17–27.

33 Huel, "Gestae Dei Per Francos," 43–4.

34 Lalonde, "Archbishop O.E. Mathieu," 45–7.

35 Dolan, *The American Catholic Experience*, 179–80.

36 Lalonde, "Archbishop O.E. Mathieu," 47–9.

37 Ibid., 49–50.

38 Ibid., 50–1.

39 Ibid., 51–3.

40 Ibid., 54–7.

41 Ibid., 58–9.

42 Huel, "The Anderson Amendment," 5–21.

43 Lalonde, "Archbishop O.E. Mathieu," 58–9.

44 McGowan, "Religious Duties and Patriotic Endeavours," 107–8.

45 *Dictionary of Canadian Biography*, 14, s.v. "Fergus Patrick McEvay."

46 See also McGowan, *The Waning of the Irish*, 231.

47 McGowan, "Religious Duties and Patriotic Endeavours," 108–9, 111, and *The Waning of the Green*, 232–3. And see Duff Crerar's comment on Burke, "the eccentric monsignor" claiming to be the chief of Catholic chaplains as found in *Padres in No Man's Land*, 36.

48 McGowan, "Religious Duties and Patriotic Endeavours," 109–10.

49 *Dictionary of Canadian Biography*, 14, s.v. "Adélarde Langevin."

50 McGowan, "Religious Duties and Patriotic Endeavours," 111–12.

51 Ibid., 113–14.

52 Ibid., 115–16.

53 Ibid., 116–17; also see Duff Crerar, *Padres in No Man's Land*, 36, 42, 50–1 in regard to Burke's role as military chaplain.

54 McGowan, "Religious Duties and Patriotic Endeavours," 118–19.

55 Farrell, "Michael Francis Fallon," 73–4.

56 Power, "The Mitred Warrior," 22.

57 Farrell, "Michael Francis Fallon," 75–7.

58 Fiorino, "The Nomination of Bishop Fallon," 36–46.

59 Farrell, "Michael Francis Fallon," 78–9.

60 Ibid., 82–3.

61 Ibid., 84–5.

62 Ibid., 86.

63 Ibid., 87.

64 Ibid., 87–8.

65 Ibid., 88.

66 Cecillon, "Turbulent Times in the Diocese of London," 372–4.

67 Cecillon, "Turbulent Times in the Diocese of London," 377–86; Power, "Fallon versus Forster," 49–66.

68 Farrell, "Michael Francis Fallon," 89–90.

69 Armstrong, *The Crisis of Quebec, 1914–1918* 58–62; see also, Granastein and Hitsman, *Broken Promises*, 69–70, 86–9, and *Conscription 1917: Essays* viii.

70 Burns, "The Montreal Irish and the Great War," 67–9.

71 Ibid., 70–2.

72 Ibid., 73–4.

73 Ibid., 77–81. Trihey's figure of 150,000 British troops suppressing the Irish people was inflated by the shock of the repression of the Easter Rising. Before the Rising, the Irish volunteers were outnumbered by the British establishment two or three to one. At that time Britain had 6,000 soldiers in Ireland in addition to an armed Royal Irish Constabulary of 9,500. Troops poured into Dublin throughout the week, and within forty-eight hours the odds had changed to twenty to one. This puts the number of British forces at 40,000 to 50,000. Artillery quickly and ruthlessly swept the barricades from the streets as high explosives and firepower won the day. Vaughan, ed., *A New History of Ireland*, 214–15.

74 Akenson, *Small Differences*, 98–107.

75 McGowan, " 'To Share in the Burden of Empire,' " 178–9.

76 Ibid., 185–7.

77 Ibid., 179–81.

78 Ibid., 182; Crerar, *Padres in No Man's Land*, 41–2.

79 McGowan, "To Share in the Burdens of Empire," 190–1.

80 McGowan, *The Waning of the Green*, 281–3.

81 McGowan, "To Share in the Burdens of Empire," 191–2.

82 Choquette, *Creed and Culture*, 20–1.

CHAPTER NINE

1 Huel, "Epilogue: Redefining Church and Spirituality," 269–89; Peelman, *Christ Is a Native American*, 193–223.
2 Marunchak, *The Ukrainian Canadians*, 99.
3 Martynowych, *Ukrainians in Canada*, 182. The Union of Brest in 1596 united the Orthodox metropolitan province of Kiev (western Ukraine) with the Catholic church. The Eastern language and liturgy were respected but at the same time they acknowledged union with the Holy See in Rome.
4 Bociurkiw, *The Ukrainian Greek Catholic Church*, 10–12.
5 Perin, *Rome in Canada*, 166.
6 Darlington, "The Ukrainian Impress on the Canadian West," 142–5.
7 Hryniuk, "Pioneer Bishop, Pioneer Times," 21–2.
8 Ibid., 23–4.
9 Martynowych, *Ukrainians in Canada*, 184–5.
10 Perin, *Rome in Canada*, 167–8.
11 Marunchak, *The Ukrainian Canadians*, 104–5.
12 Ibid., 106–7; Martynowych, *Ukrainians in Canada*, 202–6.
13 Martynowych, *Ukrainians in Canada*, 194–5.
14 Hryniuk, "Pioneer Bishop, Pioneer Times," 21, 28–9.
15 Ibid., 25.
16 Ibid., 26.
17 Marunchak, *The Ukrainian Canadians*, 112–13; McGowan, "A Portion for the Vanquished," 220.
18 Laverdure, *Redemption and Renewal*, 146–8.
19 Hryniuk, "Pioneer Bishop, Pioneer Times," 30–3.
20 Laverdure, *Redemption and Renewal*, 146.
21 Dolan, *The American Catholic Experience*, 186–8. Uniates are Eastern rite Christians in union with the bishop of Rome.
22 Hryniuk, "Pioneer Bishop, Pioneer Times," 37–8.
23 Bociurkiw, *The Ukrainian Greek Catholic Church*, 200, 202.
24 Hryniuk, "Pioneer Bishop, Pioneer Times," 39–41.
25 McGowan, "A Portion for the Vanquished," 230–1.
26 Perin, *Rome in Canada*, 185–6.
27 McGowan, "A Portion for the Vanquished," 218.
28 Ibid., 237.
29 McLaughlin, *The Germans in Canada*, 3.
30 McLaughlin, *The Germans in Canada*, 4–7.
31 Ibid., 8–9.
32 Giesinger, *From Catherine to Khrushchev*, 360–1.
33 Ibid., 361.
34 McLaughlin, *The Germans in Canada*, 10–11.

35 Windschiegl, *Fifty Golden Years, 1903–1953* 11–19; see also Windschiegl, *A Journey of Faith.*

36 Hubbard, "St Peter's," 365–6.

37 Ibid., 157–8.

38 Ibid.; White, "Language, Religion," 84–98.

39 Avery and Fedorowicz, *The Poles in Canada,* 3–4.

40 Radecki and Heydendorn, *A Member of a Distinguished Family,* 21–7.

41 Avery and Fedorowicz, *The Poles in Canada,* 6–7.

42 Ibid., 7–8.

43 Radecki and Heydendorn, *A Member of a Distinguished Family,* 157–60.

44 Ibid., 30; Avery and Fedorowicz, *The Poles in Canada,* 7–9.

45 Avery and Fedorowicz, *The Poles in Canada,* 8–10.

46 Ibid., 11.

47 Ibid., 12.

48 Ibid., 19.

49 Patrias, *The Hungarians in Canada,* 2–3.

50 Ibid., 5–6.

51 Kovacs, "The Saskatchewan Era, 1885–1914," 66.

52 Ibid., 66–9.

53 Ibid., 69–70; Dreisziger, "The Years of Growth and Change," 120.

54 Kovacs, "The Hungarian School Question," 336–51.

55 Patrias, *The Hungarians in Canada,* 8–9; Dreisziger, "The Years of Growth and Change," 96–7.

56 Dreisziger, "The Years of Growth and Change," 98–108.

57 Huel, "The Irish French Conflict," 53–4.

58 Ibid., 55–6.

59 *Dictionary of Canadian Biography,* 14, s.v. "Émile-Joseph Legal."

60 Choquette, "English-French Relations," 17.

61 Huel, "The Irish French Conflict," 57–8.

62 Ibid., 59–61.

63 Ibid., 61–3.

64 Ibid., 63–4.

65 Ibid., 64–5.

66 Ibid., 65–6.

67 Bérard, "A Cardinal for English Canada," 90–100.

68 Huel, "The Irish French Conflict," 67–9.

69 McNally, "Fighting City Hall," 149–50.

70 Ibid., 155.

71 Ibid., 151–2.

72 Ibid., 152–3.

73 Ibid., 154.

74 Ibid., 157–8.

75 Ibid., 155–6.
76 Ibid., 158–61.
77 Dolan, *The American Catholic Experience*, 295.
78 McNally, "Fighting City Hall," 161–2.
79 Ibid., 162–3.
80 Ibid., 163–4.
81 Ibid., 165–6.
82 Huel, *Proclaiming the Gospel*, 269–71; Peelman, *Christ Is a Native American*, 193–223.
83 Huel, *Proclaiming the Gospel*, 272.
84 Ibid., 273.
85 Ibid., 274–9.
86 Ibid., 280–1.
87 Peelman, *Christ Is a Native American*, 14.
88 Huel, *Proclaiming the Gospel to the Indians and the Métis*, 282–84.
89 Canadian Conference of Catholic Bishops to the Royal Commission on Aboriginal Peoples, *Justice Flow Like a Mighty River*, 33–5.
90 Milloy, "*A National Crime*," 295–305.
91 Huel, *Proclaiming the Gospel*, 284–9.

CHAPTER TEN

1 Forbes and Muise, eds., *The Atlantic Provinces in Confederation*, 234–7.
2 Linteau et al., *Quebec: A History*, 306–7, *Quebec Since 1930*, 1–2.
3 Forbes and Muise, eds., *The Atlantic Provinces in Confederation*, 235–9.
4 Lotz and Welton, *Father Jimmy*, 25–34.
5 Edwards, "The MacPherson-Tompkins Era," 62–4.
6 Lotz and Welton, *Father Jimmy*, 35–54; Cameron, *For the People*, 212.
7 Lotz and Welton, *Father Jimmy*, 63–4.
8 Ibid., 67–74.
9 Ibid., 97–100.
10 Ibid., 103–8.
11 Ibid., 137–50.
12 Laidlaw, ed., *The Man from Margaree*, 13–14; Alexander, *The Antigonish Movement*, 67–8.
13 Cameron, *For the People*, 218–22.
14 Laidlaw, *Man from Margaree*, 14, 18; Alexander, *The Antigonish Movement*, 20, 26.
15 Cameron, *For the People*, 222, 226, 290–1; Alexander, *The Antigonish Movement*, 92–4, 147–54.
16 Laidlaw, *Man from Margaree*, 125–6; Alexander, *The Antigonish Movement*, 35–6, 39–40; Lotz and Welton, *Father Jimmy*, 117–21, 130–5.

17 O'Brien and Shannon, eds., *Catholic Social Thought*, 12–38.

18 Laidlaw, *Man from Margaree*, 11–13, 128; Alexander, *The Antigonish Movement*, 89–92; 97–100; O'Brien and Shannon, eds., *Catholic Social Thought*, 40–77.

19 Baum, *Catholics and Canadian Socialism*, 200–2.

20 Cameron, *For the People*, 287–9.

21 Laidlaw, *Man from Margaree*, 11–12.

22 Ibid., 18–20.

23 Hamelin and Gagnon, *Histoire du Catholicisme québécois*, 3, sec. 1: 276–7.

24 Ibid., 277–8.

25 Vigod, *Quebec before Duplessis*, 32–3, 45; Hamelin and Gagnon, *Histoire du Catholicisme québécois*, 3, sec. 1: 197.

26 Hamelin and Gagnon, *Histoire du Catholicisme québécois*, 3, sec. 1: 194–5; Vigod, *Quebec before Duplessis*, 50–2, 58.

27 Vigod, *Quebec before Duplessis*, 102–4, 116–19; Hamelin and Gagnon, *Histoire du Catholicisme québécois*, 3, sec. 1: 194.

28 Hamelin and Gagnon, *Histoire du Catholicisme québécois*, 3, sec. 1: 220–2.

29 Critics questioned whether the Jocists weren't too idealistic and élistist. 420–5.

30 Vigod, *Quebec before Duplessis*, 200–1.

31 Lévesque later saw many of the goals of the CCF as being compatible with Catholic social thinking and changed his attitude. In 1938 he founded the Faculty of Social Studies in Quebec City and became an advisor to Archbishop Charbonneau. He had a great influence on the archbishop and the archbishop's benign outlook toward the CCF.

32 Baum, *Catholics and Canadian Socialism*, 178. The anarchy of production is a Marxist term to describe the unplanned production for profit of the capitalist system, which pays little attention to people's needs. A current example would be the overproduction of expensive condos when affordable housing for low-income people is greatly needed.

33 Baum, *Catholics and Canadian Socialism*, 99–100, 177–80; Hamelin and Gagnon, *Histoire du Catholicisme québécois*, 3, sec. 1: 227–9, 439–40.

34 Linteau et al., *Quebec since 1930*, 78.

35 Baum, *Catholics and Canadian Socialism*, 181–2.

36 Ibid., 183–5.

37 Vigod, *Quebec before Duplessis*, 217–18.

38 Dirks, *The Failure of l'Action libérale nationale*, 98–9.

39 Dirks, *Failure of l'Action libérale nationale*, 115–17.

40 Baum, *Catholics and Canadian Socialism*, 185–6.

41 L'abbé Groulx and those who followed him in Quebec offered another response to the depression. See Senese, "*Catholique d'abord!*, 154–77.

42 Moir, "The Problem of a Double Minority," 53–67.

43 McGowan, *The Waning of the Green*, 9–12 and 57; Beck, "Henry Somerville and Social Reform," 92–3; Moir, "The Problem of a Double Minority," 53–67.

44 Beck, "Henry Somerville and Social Reform," 93–4.

45 Ibid., 95–9.

46 Ibid., 98–9.

47 Grant, *A Profusion of Spires*, 201.

48 Beck, "Henry Somerville and Social Reform," 104–6.

49 Ballantyne, "The Catholic Church and the CCF," 34–41; Hamelin, *Histoire du catholicisme québécois*, 3, sec. 2: 43–4.

50 Doherty, *Fragments of My Life*, 105–7.

51 Ibid., 107–8.

52 Ibid., 109.

53 Ibid., 110.

54 Ibid., 110–13; Duquin, *The Life of Catherine de Hueck Doherty*, 146–8.

55 When Catherine met Eddie Doherty, he was reported to be "the highest paid reporter in America," women liked him, and he was considered to be "charming and attractive." Duquin, *Life of Catherine de Hueck Doherty*, 192–3.

56 Doherty, *Fragments of My Life*, 173–5; Duquin, *Life of Catherine de Hueck Doherty*, 206–7, 233–4.

57 Doherty, *Fragments of My Life*, 174–6.

58 Ibid., 175–7.

59 Ibid., 181–3.

60 Hanrahan, "Nature and History," 309–10.

61 Baum, *Catholics and Canadian Socialism*, 147–8.

62 Cottrell, "John Joseph Leddy," 43–7; McGowan, *Waning of Green*, 281–3.

63 Gorman, *Père Murray and the Hounds*, 122–5.

64 Kambeitz, "Relations between the Catholic Church and CCF," 62.

65 Baum, *Catholics and Canadian Socialism*, 149–50.

66 Kambeitz, "Relations between the Catholic Church and CCF," 61, 63–4; Baum, *Catholics and Canadian Socialism*, 153–8.

67 Daly, "A Priest's Tale," 12–17.

68 Baum, *Catholics and Canadian Socialism*, 160–5; Kambeitz, "Relations between the Catholic Church and CCF," 66–7.

69 Baum, *Catholics and Canadian Socialism*, 164–5.

70 Hamelin, *Histoire due catholicisme Québécois*, 2: 43–4.

71 Baum, *Catholics and Canadian Socialism*, 168.

72 Daly, "A Priest's Tale," 17–21.

73 Baum, *Catholics and Canadian Socialism*, 169–73.

74 Kambeitz, "Relations between the Catholic Church and CCF," 68.

75 Ibid., 67–9.

CHAPTER ELEVEN

1 Dion, "Le communisme dans la province de Québec," 37–8.
2 Kirkconnell, "Communism in Canada and the USA," 44–5.
3 Dion, "Le communisme dans la province de Québec," 38–9.
4 Linteau et al., *Quebec Since 1930*, 71.
5 Dion, "Le communisme dans la province de Québec," 40.
6 Linteau et al., *Quebec Since 1930*, 74; Betcherman, *The Swastika and the Maple Leaf*, 33–4.
7 Linteau et al., *Quebec Since 1930*, 73.
8 Dion, "Le communisme dans la province de Québec," 41.
9 Ibid., 42.
10 Abella, *Nationalism, Communism, and Canadian Labour*, 66–7.
11 Ibid., 80.
12 Dion, "Le communisme dans la province de Québec," 42–3.
13 Ibid., 44–6.
14 Ibid., 46–8; Linteau et al., *Quebec Since 1930*, 86.
15 Dion, "Le communisme dans la province de Québec," 49–50.
16 Ibid., 50.
17 Linteau et al., *Quebec Since 1930*, 74.
18 Dion, "Le communisme dans la province de Québec," 51; Linteau et al., *Quebec Since 1930*, 75.
19 Kirkconnell, "Communism in Canada and the USA," 42–5, 49.
20 Ibid., 50.
21 Ibid., 43–4.
22 Ibid., 48.
23 Ibid., 46–8.
24 Ibid., 48–9.
25 O'Neill, "Archbishop McGuigan of Toronto," 61–2.
26 Ibid., 63.
27 Ibid., 64–6.
28 Ibid., 67.
29 Ibid., 67–9.
30 Ibid., 70–1.
31 *Dictionary of Jesuit Biography*, 163, 227–8.
32 O'Neill, "Archbishop McGuigan of Toronto," 75–6.
33 Abella, *Nationalism, Communism, and Canadian Labour*, 167.
34 Kirkconnell, "Communism in Canada and the USA," 50.
35 Pennacchio, "The Torrid Trinity," 233. After the seizure of the remainder of the Papal States in 1870, Pope Pius IX and his successors remained prisoners in the Vatican until the Lateran Accords were signed in 1929.
36 Zucchi, *Italians in Toronto*, 169.
37 Ibid., 181–3.

38 Pennacchio, "The Torrid Trinity," 233–4.

39 Ibid., 236–7.

40 Ibid., 237.

41 Ibid., 237.

42 Zucchi, *Italians in Toronto*, 169.

43 Pennacchio, "The Torrid Trinity," 238–9.

44 Ibid., 240–1.

45 Ibid., 241–2.

46 Ibid., 242–3.

47 Zucchi, *Italians in Toronto*, 183–4.

48 Ibid., 192.

49 Pennacchio, "The Torrid Trinity," 243–4.

50 Cawley, "The Canadian Catholic English-Language Press," 25–7.

51 The ten diocesan newspapers included the *Casket* (Antigonish), *New Freeman* (Saint John), *Beacon* (Montreal), *Canadian Freeman* (Kingston), *Catholic Register* (Toronto), *Catholic Record* (London), *North-West Review* (Winnipeg), *Prairie Messenger* (Muenster), *Western Catholic* (Edmonton), *British Columbia Catholic* (Vancouver); the three monthly magazines were *Eikon* (Redemptorist, Montreal), *Social Forum* (lay controlled, Ottawa), *Canadian Messenger of the Sacred Heart* (Jesuit, Toronto); the bi-monthly was *The Third Order Bulletin* (Franciscan, Ottawa); Cawley, "The Canadian Catholic English-Language Press," 28.

52 Ibid., 29–31.

53 Callahan, *The Catholic Church in Spain*, 358; Thomas, *The Spanish Civil War*, 173.

54 Cawley, "The Canadian Catholic English-Language Press," 31–3.

55 Ibid., 32.

56 Ibid., 34–6.

57 Ibid., 38–9.

58 Ibid., 38–9.

59 Ibid., 40–2.

60 Ibid., 45–6.

61 Ibid., 47; Sánchez, *The Spanish Civil War as a Religious Tragedy*, 103–4.

62 Sánchez, *The Spanish Civil War as a Religious Tragedy*, 51–2.

63 Cawley, "The Canadian Catholic English-Language Press," 47–50.

64 Couture, "The Vichy–Free French Propaganda War in Quebec," 200–1.

65 Ibid., 202, 215.

66 Ibid., 202–4.

67 Ibid., 202–5; Adrien Dansette, *Religious History of Modern France* II, 251–2, 283, 380.

68 Ibid., 205–7.

69 Ibid., 208–9.

70 Ibid., 209–11.

71 Langlais and Rome, *Jews & French Quebecers*, 88–9, 94–100.

72 Abella and Troper, *None Is Too Many*, 76–7, 102–3, 195, 211–12.

73 Ibid., 105–24.

74 Couture, "The Vichy–Free French Propaganda War in Quebec," 212–15.

CHAPTER TWELVE

1 Linteau *et al.*, *Quebec Since 1930*, 63.

2 Hamelin and Gagnon, *Histoire du Catholicisme québécois*, 3, sec. 1: 300–1.

3 Ibid., 301–5.

4 McGowan, *The Waning of the Green*, 250–84.

5 Hamelin and Gagnon, *Histoire du Catholicisme québécois*, 3, sec. 1: 305–8.

6 Robin, "Registration, Conscription," 118.

7 MacFarlane, "Mr Lapointe, Mr. King," 29–30.

8 Hamelin, *Histoire du Catholicisme québécois*, 3, sec. 2: 11–13.

9 Ibid., 13–14.

10 Ibid., 14–15.

11 Ibid., 16–17.

12 Ibid., 17–18.

13 Ibid., 19–20.

14 MacFarlane, "Mr Lapointe, Mr. King," 31.

15 Behiels, "The Bloc Populaire Canadien," 487–8.

16 Ibid., 488–90.

17 Ibid., 491–2.

18 Ibid., 492–6.

19 Ibid., 497–501.

20 Ibid., 501–4.

21 Ibid., 505–7.

22 Ibid., 510–11.

23 Trofimenkoff, *The Dream of Nation*, 245–7.

24 Pelletier, *The Years of Impatience*, 35–41; Conrad Black in *Duplessis* (509–10) has a marvellous description of the routines Duplessis played with the bishops.

25 Pelletier, *The Years of Impatience*, 41–2.

26 Ibid., 42–3.

27 Black, *Duplessis*, 546–8; Trofimenkoff, *The Dream of Nation*, 242, 291–2.

28 Pelletier, *The Years of Impatience*, 44–6.

29 Ibid., 47–8.

30 Black, *Duplessis*, 547–8.

31 Pelletier, *The Years of Impatience*, 48–51; Black, *Duplessis*, 509–10.

32 Pelletier, *The Years of Impatience*, 52.

33 Ibid., 53–8.

34 Ibid., 59–60.

35 The Catholic trade unions in Quebec were organized by bishops, religious, and the workers to strive for safe working conditions and a family wage. The Canadian Catholic Congress of Labour was secularized in 1960, dropping the word "Catholic" and adopting the new name of Confederation of National Trade Unions. Linteau et al., *Quebec Since 1930*, 224–6. Also see Hamelin and Gagnon, *Histoire du Catholicisme québécois*, 3, sec. 1: 217–18, 286–7.

36 Linteau et al., *Quebec Since 1930*, 224.

37 Perin, "French-Speaking Canada from 1840," 207, 237.

38 Dion, "The Church and the Conflict in the Asbestos Industry," 205–6.

39 Ibid., 205.

40 Ibid., 207–8.

41 Ibid., 208–10; Hamelin, *Histoire du catholicisme québécois*, 3, sec. 2: 98.

42 Dion, "The Church and the Conflict in the Asbestos Industry," 211; Hamelin, *Histoire du catholicisme québécois*, 3, sec. 2: 99.

43 Dion, "The Church and the Conflict in the Asbestos Industry," 211; Perin, "French-Speaking Canada from 1840," 252; Linteau et al., *Quebec Since 1930*, 224.

44 Dion, "The Church and the Conflict in the Asbestos Industry," 212.

45 Ibid., 212–13.

46 Ibid., 214–15; Black, *Duplessis*, 563–4.

47 Dion, "The Church and the Conflict in the Asbestos Industry," 217–18.

48 Trofimenkoff, *The Dream of Nation*, 292.

49 Perin, "French-Speaking Canada from 1840," 255.

50 Carter, *Alex Carter: A Canadian Bishop's Memoirs*, 110–16; Black, *Duplessis*, 526–34; Hamelin, *Histoire du catholicisme québécois*, 3, sec. 2: 21–2.

51 Dion, "The Church and the Conflict in the Asbestos Industry," 218–19.

52 Hamelin, *Histoire du catholicisme québécois*, 3, sec. 2: 100.

53 Dion, "The Church and the Conflict in the Asbestos Industry," 218–19.

54 Pelletier, *The Years of Impatience*, 30–1.

55 Linteau et al., *Quebec Since 1930*, 255–7.

56 Pelletier, *The Years of Impatience*, 32–4. See the interesting description of Charbonneau by Black in *Duplessis*, 526–8, 538.

57 Carter, *A Canadian Bishop's Memoirs*, 110–16.

CHAPTER THIRTEEN

1 MacPherson, "Religious Women in Nova Scotia," 89–90.

2 Cameron, *And Martha Served*, 6.

3 MacPherson, "Religious Women in Nova Scotia," 90–1.

4 Cameron, *For the People*, 100–2.

5 MacPherson, "Religious Women in Nova Scotia," 92–3.

6 For reference to E.J. Devine as a prominent Jesuit, please see Fay, "E.J. Devine," 9–26; *Dictionary of Jesuit Biography*, s.v. "Edward J. Devine"; and *Dictionary of Canadian Biography*, s.v. "Edward J. Devine."

7 MacPherson, "Religious Women in Nova Scotia," 93–4.

8 Ibid., 94–5.

9 Jackman, OP, *The First Seventy-Five Years*, part I, 8–9; Cameron, *And Martha Served*, 50–2.

10 MacPherson, "Religious Women in Nova Scotia," 95–6.

11 Ibid., 98–101.

12 Cameron, *And Martha Served*, 112–15.

13 MacPherson, "Religious Women in Nova Scotia," 101–2.

14 Ross, "For God and Canada," 89.

15 Ibid., 90–1.

16 Ibid., 92–3.

17 Ibid., 96.

18 Ibid., 97–8.

19 Ibid., 98.

20 Beck, *To Do and to Endure*, 158–9, 197.

21 Ross, "For God and Canada," 100.

22 Beck, *To Do and to Endure*, 65–7.

23 Ibid., 105–6, 110–11.

24 Ibid., 87, 109, 164, 197.

25 Ibid., 125.

26 Ibid., *To Do and to Endure*, 116, 125, 138.

27 Ibid., Ross, "For God and Canada," 103.

28 Ibid., 103–4.

29 Ibid., 105.

30 Ibid., 106–7.

31 O'Neill, "The Catholic Women's League," 1–4.

32 Ibid., 4–5.

33 Ibid., 6.

34 Ibid., 6–7.

35 Gal 3: 28, Holy Bible, New Revised Standard Version, Catholic ed.

36 O'Neill, The Catholic Women's League in the Archdiocese of Toronto, 8–10.

37 Ibid., 10.

38 Ibid., 11–13.

39 Daly, *Remembering for Tomorrow*, 20–1.

40 Puxley, "Chronicle: Ecumenism in Canada," 398–9.

41 Daly, *Remembering for Tomorrow*, 20–1.

42 Prince, "Foundation of the Episcopal Conference in Canada," 104–7.

43 Daly, *Remembering for Tomorrow*, 22–3.

44 Ibid., 23–6.
45 Ibid., 28–9.
46 Ibid., 29–32.
47 Ibid., 34–6.
48 Price, "Foundation of the Episcopal Conference in Canada," 104–7.
49 Daly, *Remembering for Tomorrow*, 14n., 37–9.
50 Hamelin, *Histoire du Catholicisme Québécois*, 3, sec. 2: 243–67.
51 Marshall, "Canadian Historians," 64–5. Christie and Gauvreau in *A Full-Orbed Christianity*, xi–xiii, 244–6, "take issue with the central assertion of the secularization thesis," which David Marshall contends in *Secularizing the Faith* and Ramsey Cook asserts in *The Regenerators*.
52 Marshall, "Canadian Historians," 80–1.
53 Marshall, *Secularizing the Faith*, 7–8, 22–3, 249–50.
54 Marshall, "Canadian Historians," 70–80.
55 Ibid., 64–6.
56 Clarke, *Piety and Nationalism*, 45.
57 Marshall, "Canadian Historians," 67.
58 Ibid., 67–8.
59 Hogan, "'The Word' and the University World," 58–9.
60 Ibid., 59–61. These views are shared by Dennis Murphy in "Expectations," 42–3, where he asks that the colleges be the cutting edge for Catholic culture. For Murphy, the Catholic colleges should seek "a sense of coherence" in a pluralist society to give direction and support to the elementary and secondary levels of Catholic education.
61 Cameron, *For the People*, 97–8.
62 Hogan, "'The Word' and the University World," 63.
63 Ibid., 64.
64 Reford, "St Michael's College," 193–4.
65 Hogan, "The Word' and the University World," 65.
66 Sanche, "A Matter of Identity," 213–14.
67 Fay, "Autonomy Lost," 184–6.
68 Ibid., 186.
69 Ibid., 203–5.
70 Hogan, "The Word and the University World," 66–70.
71 Ibid., 71.

CHAPTER FOURTEEN

1 Blet, *Pius XII and the Second World War*, 176, 181, 186, 199–200.
2 Claude Ryan, "The Church in Quebec," 17–18.
3 Ibid., 20–1.
4 William F. Ryan, *The Clergy and Economic Growth in Quebec*, 271–301; Seljak, "Why the Quiet Revolution Was Quiet," 123.

5 Bibby, *Fragmented Gods*, 20.

6 Claude Ryan, "The Church in Quebec," 18.

7 Neatby, "Student Leaders at the University of Montreal," 74–7.

8 Ibid., 78–9.

9 Ibid., 79.

10 Ibid., 80–4.

11 Ibid., 86–8.

12 Seljak, "Why the Quiet Revolution Was Quiet," 110–11.

13 Gélinas, "Le droit intellectuelle et la Révolution tranquille," 383–5.

14 Claude Ryan, "The Church in Quebec," 18–19; Trofimenkoff, *The Dream of Nation*, 301–2; Hamelin, *Histoire du Catholicisme québécois*, 3, sec. 2: 243–67; Bibby, *Fragmented Gods*, 20–1.

15 Irani, *The Papacy and the Middle East*, 30, 44–5.

16 Claude Ryan, "The Church in Quebec," 23.

17 Ibid., 22–4; Linteau et al., *Quebec Since 1930*, 476–80.

18 Seljak, "Why the Quiet Revolution Was Quiet," 113–16.

19 Ibid., 116–17.

20 Johnston, "Aux sources du développement inéqal," 54–5.

21 Heap, "Urbanization et éducation," 152–4.

22 Johnston, "Aux sources du développement inéqal," 75–8.

23 Seljak, "Why the Quiet Revolution Was Quiet," 118–19.

24 Ibid., 119–20.

25 Ibid., 121.

26 Ibid., 121–4.

27 Fisher in *The Catholic Counterculture in America*, 249–50, 253–4, explains that a similar disintegration of traditional Catholicism occurred during the 1950s in the United States.

28 Alberigo and Komonchak, eds. *History of Vatican II*, 1: 500–1.

29 Daly, *Remembering for Tomorrow*, 41.

30 Rejean Plamondon, "Bishops Feared Voicing Opinions before the Council," *Catholic Register*, 11 November 1996, 17.

31 Fahey, "A Vatican Request," 62–3.

32 Daly, Daly, and De Roo, *Even Greater Things*, 8.

33 Fahey, "A Vatican Request," 63–4, and Grootaers, "Le catholicisme du Québec," 465–6.

34 Fahey, "A Vatican Request," 67–8.

35 Ibid., 68–70.

36 Daly, *Remembering for Tomorrow*, 42.

37 Routhier, *L'Église canadienne*, "Les *vota* des évêques des diocèses du Québec," 25–31.

38 Serré, "Les consultations préconciliaires," 117–18.

39 Routhier, *L'Église canadienne*, "Les *vota* des évêques des diocèses du Québec," 31–53.

40 Ibid., 54–9.
41 Routhier, *L'Église canadienne*, Introduction, 12–16, and Serré, "Les consultations préconciliaires," 141.
42 Routhier, *L'Église canadienne*, "Introduction," 10–11.
43 Fahey, "A Vatican Request," 73–5.
44 Ibid., 76.
45 Ibid., 77.
46 Ibid., 78.
47 Ibid., 79.
48 Daly, *Remembering for Tomorrow*, 43.
49 Grootaers, "Le catholicisme du Québec," 458.
50 Bernard Daly, "Canadian Voices Resounded at Vatican II," *The Catholic Register*, 11 October 1999, 12a.
51 Naud, "Le cardinal Léger," 238–49.
52 Ibid., 250–63.
53 Daly et al., *Even Greater Things*, 5.
54 Zizola, *The Utopia of Pope John XXIII*, 258–62.
55 Daly, *Remembering for Tomorrow*, 43–4.
56 Robillard, "Msgr Gérard-Marie Coderre," 265–75; Daly et al., *Even Greater Things*, 5.
57 Fahey, "A Vatican Request," 68–9; Rejean Plamondon, "Bishops Feared Voicing Opinions before Council," *Catholic Register*," 11 November 1996.
58 Bernard Daly, "Canadian Voices Resounded at Vatican II," *Catholic Register*, 11 October 1999, 12a; Tillard, "L'épiscopat canadien francophone au concile," 291–2.
59 Platt, *Gentle Eminence*, 92, 101.
60 Ibid., 101.
61 Ibid., 101–2.
62 Carter, *Alex Carter*, 174; Daly, "Four Canadian Interventions," 278.
63 Carter, *Alex Carter*, 174; Daly, "Four Canadian Interventions," 279–80.
64 Ibid., 281–2.
65 Ibid., 283–4.
66 Ibid., 285–6.
67 Ibid., 287–90.
68 Dolan, *The American Catholic Experience*, 437.
69 Harvey, "The Church in Canada," 282–3.
70 Crowe, *Son of God, Holy Spirit*; Lonergan, *Collected Works*, 7–8, 227–8.
71 Hamelin, *Histoire du Catholicisme québécois*, vol. 3, sec. 2: 341–3.
72 Ibid., 343–4.
73 Ibid., 345–8.
74 Flannery, ed., "The Church and the Modern World," 975–6.
75 Harvey, "The Church in Canada Twenty Years after Vatican II," 284–5.
76 McBrien, *Catholicism*, 668–9.

77 Theresa Kudirka, Department of Religious, Toronto Catholic School Board, 1998.
78 Ibid.
79 Harvey, "The Church in Canada," 285.
80 Flannery, "*The Church in the Modern World*," 374–6, 998–1,000.
81 Harvey, "Church in Canada," 286–7.
82 "Option for the poor" first entered church documents in 1979 at the Puebla Conference in Mexico presided over by John Paul II. An entire section of the Puebla document was entitled, "A Preferential Option for the Poor" which explained its biblical roots and the love of God for the poor and the oppressed. John Paul II further developed the Catholic commitment to the needy during a talk in Brazil in 1980 and, the following year, in his encyclical, *Labor Exercens*. Dorr, *Option For the Poor*, 209–13, 223–6, 245–51.
83 Clarke, *Behind the Mitre*, 5–21.
84 Harvey, "The Church in Canada, 288–9.
85 Ibid., 289–90.
86 Hanrahan, "The Nature and History of the Catholic Charismatic Renewal in Canada," 307–10.
87 Rawlyk and Noll, eds., *Amazing Grace*, 176–8, 345–6.
88 Hanrahan, "The Nature and History of the Catholic Charismatic Renewal in Canada," 310.
89 For an update on the charismatic renewal in the Canadian West, see Marc Vella's "Gifts of the Spirit," 35–6.
90 Hanrahan, "The Nature and History of the Catholic Charismatic Renewal in Canada," 315–17.
91 N.a. "Fr Bob Bedard," 16–17.
92 Laurence, "Blundering into Renewal," 14–16.
93 Chagnon, *Les Charismatiques au Québec*, 10–11.
94 Hamelin, *Histoire du Catholicisme québécois*, 3, sec. 2: 358–9.
95 Hanrahan, "The Nature and History of the Catholic Charismatic Renewal in Canada," 318.
96 Ibid., 319.
97 Chagnon, *Les Charismatiques au Québec*, 167–70.
98 Hanrahan, "The Nature and History of the Catholic Charismatic Renewal in Canada," 319–21.
99 Ibid., 321.
100 Ibid., 321–2.
101 Ibid., 322.
102 Sheridan, *Love Kindness*, 389–403; Hanrahan, "The Nature and History of the Catholic Charismatic Renewal in Canada," 322–23.
103 Laurence, "Blundering into Renewal," 14–16.
104 Champion, "Uncertainty over Renewal," 33.

105 Hanrahan, "The Nature and History of the Catholic Charismatic Renewal in Canada," 323–4.

CHAPTER FIFTEEN

1 Beaudin, "You will be Called Breach-Mender," 78–80.
2 Sheridan, *Do Justice*, 32–3; Linteau et al., *Quebec: A History*, 414–15.
3 Sheridan, *Do Justice*, 31–2, 142–8.
4 Ibid., 24–5.
5 Lind and Mihevc, *Coalitions for Justice*, 19; Sheridan, *Do Justice*, 275–86.
6 Lind and Mihevc, *Coalitions for Justice*, 108.
7 Sheridan, *Do Justice*, 29.
8 Baum, "Are We in a New Historical Situation?" 33–7; Beaudin, "You will be Called Breach-Mender," 86–9.
9 Bociurkiw, *The Ukrainian Greek Catholic Church*, 102- 88; Chadwick, *The Christian Church in the Cold War*, 204–6.
10 Zenit News Agency, 20 July 2000.
11 McGowan, "Ecumenism," 224; Flannery, *Vatican Council II*, 452–70, 738–49.
12 Anglican-Roman Catholic International Commission, *The Final Report.*
13 The Second Anglican-Roman Catholic International Commission, *The Gift of Authority.*
14 Daly, *Remembering for Tomorrow*, 56.
15 *Justification by Faith Through Grace.*
16 Daly, *Remembering for Tomorrow*, 56–7; McGowan, "Ecumenism," 24–5; 1991 Census, *Canada Year Book* (Ottawa: Statistics Canada, 2001), 89.
17 Boyd, "PLURA," 135–7.
18 Ibid., 138–41.
19 Ibid., 142–5, 148–50.
20 Moffat, "Ten Days for World Development," 151–5.
21 Ibid., 156.
22 Ibid., 157–68.
23 Kinnear, *Daughters of Time*, 2–3, 113, 117–19.
24 Leonard, "Women in Ministry," 36–7; Rahner, "Towards a Fundamental Theological Interpretation of Vatican II," 9–21.
25 Leonard, "Women in Ministry," 38–9.
26 Ibid., 45–51; Rahner, "Towards a Fundamental Theological Interpretation of Vatican II," 9–21.
27 Sheehan, "Recent Statements," 434.
28 Ibid., 435.
29 Ibid., 435–6.
30 Ibid., 436–7.
31 Ibid., 437–8.

32 Ibid., 438–9.

33 Ibid., 439–40.

34 Ibid., 440–2.

35 Ibid., 444–5.

36 CCCB Statement on the Encyclical *Humanae Vitae*, 27 September 1968 in Sheridan, *Love Kindness!*, 147.

37 Cuneo, *Catholics against the Church*, 35–7; see also accounts by Daly in *Remembering for Tomorrow*, 126–131; Carter, *Alex Carter*, 199–200.

38 Cuneo, *Catholics against the Church*, ix–xii, 6–8, 10–11, 21–2, 26–8, 98–9, 149.

39 Ibid., 173–5, 177–8, 215–16.

40 Ibid., 9–10.

41 Manning, *Is the Pope Catholic?* 8–9, 14, 76, and 179.

42 Ibid., 9–10.

43 Ibid., 129–31.

44 *The Catholic Register*, week of 24–31 July 2000, 14, and week of 21–28 August 2000, 3.

45 Manning, *Is the Pope Catholic?* 195–9.

46 Manning, *Is the Pope Catholic?* 221.

47 Clarke, *Behind the Mitre*, xx–xxi, 180, 185, 193.

48 Shanahan, "The Spanish Residential School," 351–62; Miller, *Shingwauk's Vision*, 414–17.

49 National Library of Canada, *Annual Report of the Department of Citizenship and Immigration*, 1950s.

50 Huel, *Proclaiming the Gospel*, 272, 283.

51 Fay, "A Historiography," 79–80.

52 Milloy, *A National Crime*, 53–4.

53 Fay, "A Historiography," 81.

54 Milloy, *A National Crime*, 70–1.

55 Nock, *A Victorian Missionary*, 151–3.

56 Milloy, *A National Crime*, 292–5.

57 Gresko, "White 'Rites' and Indian 'Rites,'" 173–4, 179–81, "Creating Little Dominions," 96, 100, 102.

58 McCarthy, *From the Great River*, 183–7.

59 Fay, "A Historiography," 82–5.

60 Milloy, *A National Crime*, 236–7.

61 Huel, *Proclaiming the Gospel*, 280; Milloy, *A National Crime*, 235–8.

62 Fay, "A Historiography," 86–7.

63 McCarthy, *From the Great River*, xxi, 97–106; Miller, *Shingwauk's Vision*, 79–88; Coates, *Best Left as Indians*, 133–4.

64 Choquette, *The Oblate Assault on Canada's Northwest*, 235.

65 Knockwood, *Out of the Depths*, 153–9.

66 Fay, "A Historiography," 88–92.

67 Milloy, *A National Crime*, 66–7, 106–7, 125–6, 273–5.

68 Johnston, *Indian School Days*.

69 Milloy, *A National Crime*, 229–30; Fay, "A Historiography," 90–2.

70 Bishop Fred Henry, "Wrong Policy, Then and Now," *The Catholic Register*, week of 24–31 July 2000, 5.

71 Huel, *Proclaiming the Gospel*, 272–2; Fay, "A Historiography," 90–2.

72 Fay, "A Historiography," 95–6.

73 Milloy, *A National Crime*, 295–8.

74 Ibid., 155, 109–12, 293–8.

75 Canadian Conference of Catholic Bishops (CCCB), *Let Justice Flow*, 1.

76 Ibid., 2–5.

77 Ibid., 6–11.

78 Ibid., 12–15.

79 Ibid., 16–22.

80 Ibid., 23–8.

81 Peelman, *Christ Is a Native American*, 195–223; Huel, *Proclaiming the Gospel*, 282–5; also Bosch, *Transforming Mission*, 506.

EPILOGUE

1 Wood, "The Church as Communion," 174–6, and Scanlon, "The Ecclesial Dimension of Anthropology," 207–11.

Bibliography

Abella, Irving M. *Nationalism, Communism, and Canadian Labour: The CIO, the Communist Party, and the Canadian Congress of Labour, 1935–1956*. Toronto: University of Toronto, 1973.

Abella, Irving M., and H. Roper. *None Is Too Many: Canada and the Jews of Europe, 1933–1948*. Toronto: Lester and Orpen Dennys, 1983.

Adair, E.R. "France and the Beginnings of New France." *Canadian Historical Review* 25 (September 1944): 246–78.

Akenson, Donald H. *The Irish Diaspora: A Primer.* Toronto: P.D. Meany, 1993.

– *The Irish in Ontario: A Study in Rural Ontario*. Montreal: McGill-Queen's University Press, 1984.

– *Small Differences: Irish Catholics and Irish Protestants, 1815–1922*. Montreal: McGill-Queen's University Press, 1988.

Alberigo, Giuseppe, and J.A. Komonchak. *The History of Vatican II, 1959–1965: Volume I: Announcing and Preparing Vatican II: Toward a New Era in Catholicism.* Leuven/Maryknoll, NY: Peeters/Orbis, 1996.

Alexander, Anne. *The Antigonish Movement: Moses Coady and Adult Education Today*. Toronto: Thompson Educational Publishing, 1997.

Allen, R.A. "The Social Gospel and the Reform Tradition in Canada, 1890–1928." *Canadian Historical Review* 49 (December 1968), 381–99.

Armstrong, Elizabeth H. *The Crisis in Quebec, 1914–1918*. New York: AMS Press, 1967.

Avery, D.H. and J.K. Fedorowicz. *The Poles in Canada*. Canada's Ethnic Groups. Ottawa: Canadian Historical Association, 1982.

Axtell, James. *The Invasion Within: The Contest of Culture in Colonial North America*. New York: Oxford University Press, 1985.

Bagiackas, Joseph. *The Future Glory: The Charismatic Renewal and Implementation of Vatican II.* South Bend, IN: Charismatic Renewal Service, 1983.

Baker, William M. *Timothy Warren Anglin, 1822–96: Irish Catholic Canadian.* Toronto: University of Toronto Press, 1977.

Ballantyne, Murray. "The Catholic Church and the CCF." *Canadian Catholic Historical Association (CCHA) Report* (1963):33–45.

Baum, Gregory. *Catholic and Canadian Socialism: Political Thought in the Thirties and Forties.* Toronto: James Lorimer, 1980.

– "Joe Burton: Catholic and Saskatchewan Socialist," *The Ecumenist* 14 (July/August 1976):70–7.

Bea, Augustin. *Ecumenism in Focus.* London: Chapman, 1969.

Béchard, Henri. *Jérôme Le Royer de la Dauversière: His Friends and Enemies.* Bloomingdale, OH: Apostolate for Family Consecration, 1991.

– *Kaia'tanó: ron Kateri Tekakwitha.* Translated by Antoinette Kinlough. Quebec: Kateri Center, 1994.

Beck, Jeanne R. *To Do and to Endure: The Life of Catherine Donnelly, Sister of Service.* Toronto: Dundurn, 1997.

Behiels, Michael D. *Prelude to Quebec's Quiet Revolution: Liberalism versus Neo-Nationalism, 1945–1960.* Montreal: McGill-Queen's University Press, 1985.

Berkouwer, Gerrit C. *The Second Vatican Council and New Catholicism.* Grand Rapids: Eerdmans, 1965.

Black, Conrad. *Duplessis.* Toronto: McClelland and Stewart, 1977.

Bociurkiw, Bohdan R. *The Ukrainian Greek Catholic Church and the Soviet State, 1939–1950.* Edmonton: Canadian Institute of Ukrainian Studies Press and University of Alberta, 1996.

Bokenkotter, Thomas. *A Concise History of the Catholic Church.* Toronto: Doubleday Image, 1990.

– *Church and Revolution: Catholics in the Struggle for Democracy and Social Justice.* Toronto: Image Doubleday, 1998.

Bosch, David J. *Transforming Mission: Paradigm Shifts in Theology of Mission.* Maryknoll, NY: Orbis, 1997.

Boucher, Ghislaine. *Le Premier Visage de L'Eglise du Canada.* Montréal: Bellarmin, 1986.

Bowen, Desmond. "Ultramontanism in Quebec and the Irish Connection." In *The Untold Story: The Irish in Canada*, edited by Robert O'Driscoll and L. Reynolds. Toronto: Celtic Arts of Canada, 1988.

Boyle, George. *Pioneer in Purple: The Life and Work of Archbishop Neil McNeil.* Montreal: Palm, 1951.

Brodeur, Raymond, and Brigitte Caulier, eds. *Enseigner Le Catéchisme: Autorités et Institutions, XVIᵉ-XXᵉ Siècles.* Quebec: Les presses de l'Université Laval, 1995.

Brodeur, Raymond, and Jean-Paul Rouleau, eds. *La Production des catéchismes en Amérique Française.* Saint-Foy, QC: Éditions Anne Sigier, 1986.

Brunet, Michel. *Les Canadiens après la conquête: De la Révolution canadienne à la Révolution américaine.* Montréal: Fides, 1969.

Buckner, Phillip A., and John G. Reid, eds. *The Atlantic Region to Confederation: A History.* Fredericton: Acadiensis Press, 1994.

Bumsted, J.M. *The Scots in Canada.* Canada's Ethnic Groups, Booklet 1. Ottawa: Canadian Historical Association, 1982.

– *The People's Clearance: Highland Emigration to British North America, 1770–1815.* Winnipeg: University of Manitoba Press, 1982.

Burns, Robin. "The Montreal Irish and the Great War," *Historical Studies* 52 (1985): 67–81.

Byrne, Cyril J., ed. *Gentlemen-Bishops and Faction Fighters: The Letters of Bishops O Donel, Lambert, Scallan and Other Irish Missionaries.* St John's: Jesperson Press, 1984.

Cameron, James D. *For All the People: A History of St Francis Xavier University.* McGill-Queen's University Press, 1996.

– *And Martha Served: History of the Sisters of St. Martha, Antigonish, Nova Scotia.* Halifax: Nimbus Publishing, 2000.

– " 'Easing Forever the Brand of Social Inferiority:' Saint Francis Xavier University and the Highland Catholics of Eastern Nova Scotia." *Historical Studies* 59 (1992): 49–64.

Campeau, Lucien. *The Jesuit Mission among the Hurons, 1634–1650.* Translated by William Lone and George Topp. Bridgetown, NS: Gontran Trottier, 2000.

– *La Première Mission d'Acadie, 1602–1616.* Monumenta Novae Franciae, t. 1, Rome/Québec, "Monumenta Hist. Soc. Jesu"/Presses de l'Université Laval, 1967.

– *La Mission de Jésuites chez les Hurons, 1634–1650.* Montreal: Bellarmin, 1987.

– *L'Evêché de Québec (1674).* Quebec: Soc. Hist. de Québec, 1974.

Canadian Conference of Catholic Bishops (CCCB). *Let Justice Flow Like a Mighty River: Brief to the Royal Commission on Aboriginal Peoples.* Ottawa, 1993.

Carr, Anne. *Transforming Grace.* New York: Harper and Row, 1988.

Carter, Alex. *Alex Carter: A Canadian Bishop's Memoirs.* North Bay: Timiko Publications, 1994.

Cawley, Art. "The Canadian Catholic English-Language Press and the Spanish Civil War." CCHA *Study Sessions* 49 (1982): 25–51.

Cecillon, Jack. Turbulent Times in the Diocese of London: Bishop Fallon and the French-Language Controversy, 1910–18. *Ontario History* 87, no. 4 (December 1995): 369–89.

Cellard, André, and Gérard Pelletier, *Faithful to a Mission: Fifty Years with the Catholic Health Association of Canada.* Translated by David R. Miller. Ottawa: Catholic Health Association of Canada.

Chadwick, Owen. *The Christian Church in the Cold War.* London: Penguin, 1993.

Chagnon, Roland. *Les Charismatiques au Québec.* Montréal: Éditions Québec/Amérique, 1979.

Chapeau, André, OSB, et al., eds. *Canadian RC Bishops, 1658–1979.* Ottawa: Research Centre of Religions History of Canada, St Paul University, 1980.

Chaussé, Gilles. "French Canada from the Conquest to 1840." In *A Concise History of Christianity in Canada,* edited by Terrence Murphy and Roberto Perin. Toronto: Oxford University Press, 1996.

– *Jean-Jacques Lartigue, Premier Evêque de Montréal.* Montreal: Fides, 1980.

Choquette, Robert. L'Église catholique dans l'Ontario français du dix-neuvième siècle. Ottawa: Éditions de l'Université d'Ottawa, 1985.

– *Language and Religion: A History of English/French Conflict in Ontario.* Ottawa: University of Ottawa, 1975.

– *The Oblate Assault on Canada's Northwest.* Ottawa: University of Ottawa Press, 1995.

Christie, Nancy, and Michael Gauvreau. *A Full-Orbed Christianity: The Protestant Church and Social Welfare in Canada.* Montreal: McGill-Queen's University Press, 1996.

Clark, Lovell. *The Manitoba School Question: Majority Rules or Minority Rights.* Issues in Canadian History. Toronto: Copp Clark, 1968.

Clarke, Tony. *Behind the Mitre: The Moral Leadership Crisis in the Canadian Catholic Church.* HarperCollins Publishers, 1995.

Clarke, Brian. *Piety and Nationalism: Lay Voluntary Associations and the Creation of an Irish-Catholic Community in Toronto, 1850–1895.* Montreal: McGill-Queen's University Press, 1993.

Cliche, Marie-Aimee. "Dévotion popularie et encadrement clérical en Nouvelle France: la croyance au miracle dans la région de Québec," *Étude d'histoire religieuse* 52 (1985): 17–34.

Coady, Moses M. *Masters of Their Own Destiny.* New York: Harper, 1939.

Coates, Ken S. *Best Left as Indians: Native-White Relations in the Yukon Territory, 1840–1973.* Montreal: McGill-Queen's University Press, 1991.

Conacher, J.B. "The Politics of the 'Papal Aggression' Crisis, 1850–1851," *Study Sessions* 26 (1959): 13–27.

Conscription 1917. Toronto: Canadian Historical Readings, University of Toronto Press, n. d.

Cook, G.R. "Church, Schools and Politics in Manitoba, 1903–1912." *Canadian Historical Review* 39 (March 1958): 1–23.

Corcoran, Theresa. *Mount Saint Vincent University: A Vision Unfolding, 1873–1988.* Lanham MD: University Press of America, 1999.

Cottrell, Michael. Irish Catholic Political Leadership in Toronto, 1855–1882: A Study of Ethnic Politics. PhD dissertation. University of Saskatchewan, 1988.

Couture, Paul M. "The Vichy–Free French Propaganda War in Quebec, 1940–1942." Canadian Historical Association (CHA) *Historical Papers* 1978: 200–15.

Crerar, Duff. *Padres in No Man's Land: Canadian Chaplains and the Great War.* Montreal: McGill-Queen's University Press, 1995.

Cronin, Vincent. *A Pearl to India: The Life of Roberto de Nobili.* London: Hart-Davis, 1959.

Crowe, Frederick E. *Son of God, Holy Spirit, and World Religions: The Contribution of Bernard Lonergan to the Wider Ecumenism.* Toronto: Regis College Press, 1985.

Crowley, Terry. "The Inroads of Secularizing in Eighteenth-Century New France: Church and People at Louisbourg." CCHA *Historical Studies* 51 (1984): 5–27.

– "The French Regime to 1760." In *A Concise History of Christianity in Canada,* edited by Terrence Murphy and Roberto Perin: Oxford University Press, 1996.

Crunican, Paul. *Priest and Politicians: Manitoba Schools and the Election of 1896.* Toronto: University of Toronto Press, 1974.

Daigle, Jean, ed. *The Acadians of the Maritimes: Thematic Studies.* Moncton, NB: Centres d'études acadiennes, 1982.

Daly, Bernard M. *Remembering for Tomorrow: A History of the Canadian Conference of Catholic Bishops, 1943–1993.* Ottawa: *Canadian Conference of Catholic Bishops,* 1995.

– "Four Canadian Interventions Helped to Shape Vatican II Decree on the Lay Apostolate." In *L'Église canadienne et Vatican II,* ed. by Gilles Routhier. Saint-Laurent, Québec: Fides, 1997.

Daly, Bermard M., May Daly, and Remi J. DeRoo, *Even Greater Things: Hope and Challenge after Vatican II.* Ottawa: Novalis, 1999.

Daly, George. *Catholic Problems in Western Canada.* Toronto: Macmillan of Canada, 1921.

Dansette, Adrien. *Religious History of Modern France, II: Under the Third Republic.* 2 vols. Edinburgh and London: Nelson, 1961.

Danylewycz, Marta. *Taking the Veil: An Alternative to Marriage, Motherhood, and Spinsterhood in Quebec, 1840–1920.* Toronto: McClelland and Stewart, 1987.

Dictionary of Canadian Biography. 14 vols. Toronto: University of Toronto Press, 1966–.

Dictionary of Jesuit Biography: Ministry to English Canada, 1842–1987. Toronto: Canadian Institute of Jesuit Studies, 1991.

Dion, Gérard. "Le communisme dans la province de Québec." La société canadienne d'histoire de l'Église catholique (SCHEC) *Rapport* 15 (1947–48): 37–52.

Dirks, Patricia. *The Failure of the l'Action libérale nationale.* Montreal: McGill-Queen's University Press, 1991.

Doherty, Catherine de Hueck. *Fragments of My Life.* Notre Dame, IN: Ave Maria Press, 1979.

Dolphin, Frank J. *Indian Bishop of the West: Vital Justin Grandin, 1829–1902.* Ottawa: Novalis, 1986.

Dreisziger, N.F. et al. *Struggle and Hope: The Hungarian-Canadian Experience.* Toronto: McClelland and Stewart, 1982.

Duggan, John, and Terry Fay, eds. *Spiritual Roots: Historical Essays on the Roman Catholic Archdiocese of Toronto at 150 Years of Age*. Toronto: Lourdes, 1991.

Dumont, Micheline. *Girls' Schooling in Quebec, 1639–1960*. Ottawa: CHA Historical Booklet, 49, 1990.

– *L'Histoire des femmes au Québec depuis quatre siècles*. Montreal: Éditions Le Jour, 1982.

Dumont, Micheline, and Nadia Fahmy-Eid. *Les couventines: L'éducation des filles au Québec dans les congrégations religieuses enseignantes, 1840–1960*. Montreal: Boréal, 1986.

Duquin, Lorene Hanley. *They Called Her the Baroness: The Life of Catherine de Hueck Doherty*. New York: Alba House, 1995.

Eccles, W.J. *France in America*. Toronto: Fitzhenry and Whiteside, 1972.

Edwards, William X. "The MacPherson-Tompkins Era at St Francis Xavier University." *Report* 20 (1953): 49–65.

Falardeau, Jean-Charles. "The Role and the Importance of the Church in French Canada." In *French-Canadian Society*, edited by Marcel Rioux and Yves Martin. Vol. 1, Carleton Library No. 18. Toronto: McClelland and Stewart, 1964.

Farrell, John K.A. "Michael Francis Fallon, Bishop of London, Ontario – Canada, 1909–1931." *Study Sessions* 35 (1968): 73–90.

"Fr Bob Bedard: No Big Car, but He's Happy (Companions of the Cross)." *Catholic Insight* 5, no. 6 (July-August 1997): 14–16.

Fay, Terence J. Research director. *Dictionary of Jesuit Biography: Ministry to English Canada, 1842–1987*. Toronto: Canadian Institute of Jesuit Studies, 1991.

– "Autonomy Lost: St Paul's College and the University of Manitoba." In *St Paul's College, University of Manitoba: Memories and Histories*, edited by Gerald Friesen and Richard Lebrun. Winnipeg: St Paul's College, 1999.

– "E.J. Devine and the Influence of the Canadian Messenger of the Sacred Heart." *Historical Studies* 64 (1998): 9–26.

– "A Historiography of Recent Publications on Catholic Native Residential Schools." *Historical Studies* 61 (1995): 79–97.

– "What Manner of Men Are These? The Inculturation of Jesuits into Multicultural Canada, 1843–1963." Unpublished ms.

Fiorenza, Elizabeth S. *In Memory of Her: A Feminist Theological Reconstruction of Christian Origins*. New York: Crossroad, 1983.

Fitzgerald, John Edward. "Conflict and Culture in Irish-Newfoundland Roman Catholicism, 1829–1850." Dissertation. University of Ottawa, 1997.

– "Michael Anthony Fleming and Ultramontanism in Irish-Newfoundland Roman Catholicism, 1829–1850." *Historical Studies* 64 (1998): 27–45.

Flanagan, Thomas. *Louis David Riel: Prophet of the New World*. Toronto: University of Toronto Press, 1979.

Flannery, Austin, ed. "The Church and the Modern World." *Vatican Council II: The Conciliar and Lost Conciliar Documents*. Northport, NY: Costello, 1975.

Forbes, E.R., and D.A. Muise, eds. *The Atlantic Provinces in Confederation.* Toronto: University of Toronto Press and Acadiensis Press,1993.

Fraser, James A. *By Force of Circumstance: A History of St Thomas University.* Miramichi Press, 1970.

Friesen, Gerald. *The Canadian Prairies: A History.* Toronto: University of Toronto Press, 1984.

Galvin, Martin A. "The Jubilee Riots in Toronto, 1875." *Study Sessions* 26 (1959): 93–107.

Gélinas, Xavier. "Le droit intellectuelle et la Révolution tranquille: le cas de la revue *Tradition et progrés, 1957–62." Canadian Historical Review* 77 (September 1996): 353–87.

Gerus, O.W., and J.E. Rea. *The Ukrainians in Canada.* Canada's Ethnic Groups. Ottawa: Canadian Historical Association, 1985.

Giesinger, Adam. *From Catherine to Khrushchev: The Story of Russia's Germans.* Battleford, SK: Marian Press, 1974.

Gorman, Jack. *Père Murray and the Hounds: The Story of Saskatdchewan's Notre Dame College.* Sidney, BC: Gray's Publishing, 1977.

Granatstein, Jack, and J.M. Hitsman. *Broken Promises: A History of Conscription in Canada.* Toronto: Copp Clark Pitman, 1985.

Grant, Agnes. *No End of Grief: Indian Residential Schools in Canada.* Winnipeg: Pemmican Publications, 1996.

Gresko, Jacqueline. "White 'Rites' and Indian 'Rites': Indian Education and Native Responses in the West, 1870–1910." In *Western Canada Past and Present,* edited by Anthony W. Rasporich. Calgary: University of Calgary Press, 1975.

– "Creating Little Dominions within the Dominion: Early Catholic Indian Schools in Saskatchewan and British Columbia." *Indian Education in Canada.* Vol. 1, ed. by Jean Barman et al. Vancouver: University of British Columbia Press, 1986.

Griffiths, Naomi. *The Acadians: Creation of a People.* Toronto: Frontenac Library, McGraw-Hill Ryerson, 1973.

Guentzel, Ralph P. "The Centrale de l'Enseignement du Québec and Quebec Separatist Nationalism, 1960–80." *Canadian Historical Review* 80 (March 1999): 61–82.

Hamelin, Jean, ed. *Les Catholiques d'expression française en Amérique du Nord.* Belgium: Brepols, 1995.

Hamelin, Jean, et Nicole Gagnon. *Histoire du catholicisme québécois: Le XXe siècle.* Vol. 1, 1898–1940. Montreal: Boréal, 1984.

Hamelin, Jean, and Nicole Gagnon. *Histoire due Catholicisme Québécois, Vol. 3: Le XXe siècle, Sec. 1, 1898–1940.* Montreal: Boréal Express, 1984.

– *Histoire due Catholicisme Québécois, Vol. 3: Le XXe siècle, Sec. 2: De 1940 à Nos Jours,* directed by Nive Voisine. Montreal: Boréal Express, 1984.

Hanington, J. Brian. *Every Popish Person: The Story of Roman Catholicism in Nova Scotia and the Church of Halifax, 1604–1984.* Halifax: Archdiocese of Halifax, 1984.

Hanrahan, James."The Nature and History of the Catholic Charismatic Renewal in Canada." CCHA *Historical Studies* 50 (1983): 307–24.

Harvey, Julien. "The Church in Canada Twenty Year after Vatican II." *Luman Vitae* 41, no. 3 (1986): 282–3.

Heap, Ruby. "Urbanization et éducation: la centralisation scolaire à Montréal au début de XXe siècle." *Historical Papers/Communications historiques (1985)*: 132–55.

Hebblethwaite, Peter. *Introducing John Paul II: The Populist Pope.* London: Collins/Fount, 1982.

– *John XXIII: Pope of the Council.* London: Chapman, 1984.

– *Paul VI: The First Modern Pope.* London: HarperCollins, 1993.

Hoffman, George. "Saskatchewan Catholics and the Coming of the New Politics." In *Religion and Society in the Prairie West*, edited by Richard Allen. Regina: Canadian Plains Research Centre, University of Regina, 1974.

Horn, Michiel. *The League for Social Reconstruction: Intellectual Origins of the Democratic Left in Canada, 1930–1942.* Toronto: University of Toronto Press, 1980.

Houston, Cecil J., and W.J. Smyth. *Irish Immigration and Canadian Settlement: Patterns, Links, and Letters.* Toronto: University of Toronto Press, 1990.

Hryniuk, Stella. "Pioneer Bishop, Pioneer Times: Nykyta Budka in Canada." *Historical Studies* 55 (1988): 21–41.

Huel, Raymond. *Proclaiming the Gospel to the Indians and the Mètis: The Missionary Oblates of Mary Immaculate in Western Canada, 1845–1945.* Edmonton: University of Alberta Press. 1996.

– "The Irish-French Conflict in Catholic Episcopal Nominations: The Western Sees and the Struggle for Domination within the Church." CCHA *Historical Studies 42 (1975): 51–70.*

Huntley-Maynard, Jean. "Catholic Post-secondary Education for Women in Quebec: Its Beginning in 1908." CCHA *Historical Studies* 59 (1992): 37–48.

Iacovetta, Franca et al., eds. *A Nation of Immigrants: Women, Workers, and Communities in Canadian History, 1840s-1960s.* Toronto: University of Toronto Press, 1998.

Iwicki, John, with James Wahl, *Resurrectionist Charism: A History of the Congregation of the Resurrectionist.* Vol. 1 (1838–1886). Rome: Gregorian University, 1986.

Jackman, Rev. Edward, OP. *The First Seventy-Five Years of St Augustine's Seminary of Toronto, 1913–1988.* Edited by Karen Bootz. Toronto: St Augustine's Seminary Alumini Association, 1988.

Jamet, Albert. *Marguerite Bourgeoys, 1620–1700.* 2 vols. Montreal: La Presse catholique panaméricaine, 1942.

Jaenen, Cornelius J. *The Role of the Church in New France.* The Frontenac Library. Toronto: McGraw-Hill Ryerson, 1976.

– "American Responses to French Missionary Intrustion, 1611–1760: A Categorization." In William Westfall et al., eds. *Religion/Culture: Comparative*

Canadian Studies, edited by William Westfall et al. Ottawa: Association for Canadian Studies, *Canadian Issues* series, vol. 7, 1985.

– *The Belgians in Canada*. Canada's Ethnic Groups Series. Ottawa: Canadian Historical Association, 1991.

Jean, Marguerite. *Évolution des Communautés Religieuses de Femmes au Canada de 1639 à nos Jours*. Montreal: Fides, 1977.

Johnston, Angus A. *A History of the Catholic Church in Eastern Nova Scotia*. 2 vols. Antigonish: St Francis Xavier University, Press, 1960.

Johnston, A.J.B. *Life and Religion at Louisbourg, 1713–1758*. Montreal: McGill-Queen's University Press, 1996.

– "Popery and Progress: Anti-Catholicism in Mid-Nineteenth-Century Nova Scotia." *Dalhousie Review* 64 (Spring 1984): 146–63.

Johnston, Wendy. "Aux sources du développement inéqal: le financement de l'enseignement public à Montréal de 1920 à 1945." *Canadian Historical Review* 76 (March 1995): 43–80.

Jolicoeur, Gérard. *Le Jésuites dans la vie manitobaine, 1885–1922*. St Boniface: Centre d'études franco-canadiennes de l'Ouest, 1985.

Kambeitz, Teresita. "Relations between the Catholic Church and CCF in Saskatchewan, 1930–1950," *Study Sessions* 46 (1979): 49–69.

Kent, Peter, and J.F. Pollard. *Papal Diplomacy in the Modern Age*. Westport, CT: Praeger, 1994.

Kirkconnell, Watson. "Communism in Canada and the USA" CCHA *Report* 15 (1947–48): 41–51.

Knockwood, Isabelle. *Out of the Depths: The Experiences of Mi'kmaw Children at the Indian Residential School at Shubenacadie, Nova Scotia*. Lockeport, NS: Roseway, 1992.

Kovacs, Martin L., ed. *Ethnic Canadians: Culture and Education*. Regina: Canadian Plains Research Centre, 1978.

Lambert, James. "The Face of Upper Canadian Catholicism: Culture and Metropolitarism in the Establishment of the Roman Catholic Church in Upper Canada, 1850–1825." CCHA *Historical Studies* 54 (1987): 5–25.

Landrigan, Lawrence. "Peter McIntyre, Bishop of Charlottetown, PEI" *Historical Studies* 20 (1953): 81–92.

Langlais, Jacques, and D. Rome. *Jews and French Quebecers: Two Hundred Years of Shared History*. Waterloo: Wilfrid Laurier University Press, 1991.

Lascelles, Thomas A. *Roman Catholic Indian Residential Schools in British Columbia*. Vancouver: OMI in British Columbia, 1990.

Lebrun, Richard. *Joseph de Maistre: An Intellectual Militant*. Montreal: McGill-Queen's University Press, 1988.

Lemieux, Lucien. *L'Établissement de la Première Province Ecclésiastique au Canada, 1783–1844*. Montreal: Fides, 1967.

– *Histoire du catholicisme québécois: Les XVIIIe et XIXe siècles. Vol. 1: Les années difficiles (1760–1839)*. Montréal: Boréal, 1989.

Leonard, Ellen. "Women in Ministry." *Grail* 6, no. 2 (June 1990): 34–53.

Lind, Christopher, and Joe Mihevc, eds. *Coalitions for Justice: The Story of Canada's Interchurch Coalitions.* Ottawa: Novalis, 1994.

Linteau, Paul-André et al. *Quebec: A History, 1867–1929.* Toronto: James Lorimer, 1983.

– *Quebec Since 1930.* Toronto: James Lorimer, 1991.

Lonergan, Bernard, *Collected Works.* Vol. 4. Edited by Frederick Crow and Robert M. Dovan. Toronto: University of Toronto Press, 1993.

Luciuk, Lubomyr, and Stella Hryniuk, eds. *Canada's Ukrainians: Negotiating an Identity.* Toronto: University of Toronto Press with Ukrainian Canadian Centennial Committee, 1991.

Lupul, Manoly R. *The Roman Catholic Church and the North-West School Question: A Study of Church-State Relations in Western Canada, 1875–1905.* Toronto: University of Toronto Press, 1974.

McBrien, Richard P. Catholicism. Minneapolis: Winston Press, 1980.

McCarthy, Martha. *From the Great River to the Ends of the Earth: The Oblates and the Dene, 1847–1921.* Edmonton: University of Alberta Press, 1995.

MacDonald, G. Edward. *The History of St Dunstan's University, 1855–1956.* Charlottetown: St Dunstan's University and Prince Edward Island Museum and Heritage Foundation, 1989.

McDonald, Irene. *For the Least of My Brethren: A Centenary History of St Michael's Hospital.* Toronto: Dundurn Press, 1992.

McGahan, Elizabeth W. "The Sisters of Charity of the Immaculate Conception: A Canadian Case Study." *Historical Studies 61 (1995): 99–133.*

McGowan, Mark, and B. Clarke, eds. *Catholics at the "Gathering Place:" Historical Essays on the Archdiocese of Toronto, 1841–1991.* Toronto: CCHA, 1993.

McGowan, Mark G. *The Waning of the Green: Catholics, The Irish and Identity in Toronto, 1887–1922.* Montreal: McGill-Queen's University Press, 1999.

– "The De-greening of the Irish: Toronto's Irish-Catholic Press, Imperialism, and the Forging of a New Identity, 1887–1914." CHA *Historical Papers* (1989): 118–45.

– "To Share the Burden of Empire: Toronto's Catholics and the Great War, 1914–1918." In *Catholics at the Gathering Place": Historical Essays on the Archdiocese of Toronto, 1841–1991,* edited by Mark G. McGowan and B. Clarke, 177–207. Toronto: CCHA, 1993.

– "Rethinking Catholic-Protestant Relations in Canada: The Episcopal Reports of 1900–1901." CCHA *Historical Studies* 59 (1992): 11–32.

– "A Portion for the Vanquished: Roman Catholics and Ukrainian Catholic Church." In *Canada's Ukrainians: Negotiating an Identity,* edited by Lubomyr Luciuk and S. Hryniuk. Toronto: University of Toronto Press, 1991.

McGrory, Barry. "Full Circle." Unpublished manuscript, 1997.

MacGregor, James G. *Father Lacombe.* Edmonton: Hurtig, 1975.

Maclean, Dr. Ray. "As Outline of Diocesan History." *The Casket* (Antigonish; 26 April 1995).

MacLean, R.A. *Bishop John Cameron: Piety and Politics.* Antigonish: Casket Printing and Publishing, 1991.

MacLellan, Haidee Patricia. "Nova Scotia." In *Catholic Schools in Canada.* Toronto: Canadian Catholic School Trustees' Association, 1977.

McLaughlin, K.M. *The Germans in Canada. Canada's Ethnic Groups.* Ottawa: Canadian Historical Association, 1985.

McNaught, Kenneth. *A Prophet in Politics: A Biography of J.S. Woodsworth.* Toronto: University of Toronto Press, 1959.

MacPherson, Sarah. "Religious Women in Nova Scotia: A Struggle for Autonomy. A Sketch of the Sisters of St Martha of Antigonish, Nova Scotia, 1900–1960," *Historical Studies* 51 (1984): 89–106.

Marshall, David. *Secularizing the Faith: Canadian Protestant Clergy and the Crisis of Belief, 1850–1940.* Toronto: University of Toronto Press, 1992.

– "Canadian Historians, Secularization and the Problem of the Nineteenth Century," *Historical Studies* 60 (1993–94): 57–81.

Martynowych, Orest T. *Ukrainians in Canada: The Formative Period, 1891–1924.* Edmonton: Canadian Institution of Ukrainian Studies Press, University of Alberta, 1991.

Marunchak, Michael H. *The Ukrainian Canadians: A History.* Winnipeg: Ukrainian Free Academy of Sciences, 1970.

Maurutto, Paula. "Private Policing and Surveillance of Catholics: Anti-Communism in the Roman Catholic Archdiocese of Toronto, 1920–1960," *Labour/Le travail* 40 (Autumn 1997): 113–36.

Miller, J.R. *Shingwauk's Vision: A History of Native Residential Schools.* Toronto: University of Toronto Press, 1996.

Milloy, John S. *A National Crime: The Canadian Government and the Residential School System, 1879–1986.* Winnipeg: University of Manitoba Press, 1999.

Misner, Paul. *Social Catholicism in Europe: From the Onset of Industrialization to the First World War.* New York: Crossroad, 1991.

Mitchell, Estelle. *The Grey Nuns of Montreal and the Red River Settlement, 1844–1984.* Private publication, n.d.

Moir, John. *The Church in the British Era.* Toronto: McGraw-Hill Ryerson, 1972.

– "The Problem of a Double Minority: Some Reflections on the Development of English-speaking Catholic Church in Canada in the Nineteenth Century." *Histoire Sociale/Social History* (April 1977): 53–67.

Monet, Jacques. *The Last Canon Shot: A Study of French-Canadian Nationalism, 1837–1850.* Toronto: University of Toronto Press, 1969.

Muir, Elizabeth Gillan, and Marilyn Färdig Whiteley, eds. *Changing Roles of Women within the Christian Church in Canada.* Toronto: University of Toronto Press, 1995.

Murphy, Dennis. "Expectations of Catholic Education." *Grail* 6, no. 4 (December 1991): 29–44.

Murphy, Francis Xavier. *Pope John XXIII Comes to Vatican II*. New York: R.M. McBride, 1959.

Murphy, Terrence. "The Emergence of Maritime Catholicism, 1781–1830." *Acadiensis* 13, no. 2: 29–49.

Murphy, Terrence, and Roberto Perin, eds. *A Concise History of Christianity in Canada*. Toronto: Oxford University Press, 1996.

– "James Jones and the Establishment of Roman Catholic Church Government in the Maritime Provinces." *Historical Studies* 48 (1981): 26–42.

– *Religion and Identity: The Experience of Irish and Scottish Catholics in Atlantic Canada*. St John's: Jesperson, 1987.

Murphy, Terrence, and G. Stortz. *Creed and Culture: The Place of English-Speaking Catholics in Canadian Society, 1750–1930*. Montreal: McGill-Queen's University Press, 1993.

Naud, André. "Le cardinal Léger au concile et la conduite de l'intelligence chrétienne." In *L'Église canadienne et Vatican II*, edited by Gilles Routhier. Saint-Laurent, Québec: Fides, 1997.

Neatby, Hilda. *Quebec: The Revolutionary Age, 1760–1791*. Canadian Centenary Series. Toronto: McClelland and Stewart, 1977.

– "Student Leaders at the University of Montreal During the Early 1950s: What Did Students Want? *CCHA Historical Studies* 62 (1996): 73–88.

Noel, Jan. *Women in New France*. Ottawa: Canadian Historical Association, 1998.

Nish, Cameron, ed. *The French* Régime. Vol. 1. Canadian Historical Documents Series. Scarborough: Prentice-Hall, 1965.

– *Quebec during the Duplessis Era, 1935–1959: Dictatorship or Democracy?* Toronto: Copp Clark, 1970.

Norman, Edward. *The English Catholic Church in the Nineteenth Century*. Oxford: Clarendon Press, 1985.

O'Driscoll, Robert, and L. Reynolds. *The Untold Story: The Irish in Canada*. 2 vols. Toronto: Celtic Arts of Canada, 1988.

O'Neill, Joseph H. "Archbishop McGuigan of Toronto and the Holy Name Society: Its Role as a Force against Canadian Communism." *Historical Studies* 55 (1988): 61–77.

– "The Catholic Women's League in the Archdiocese of Toronto: A Post-Vatican II Study of Its Reaction to Issues about Women." Unpublished paper read at the Canadian Catholic Historical Association meeting, Brock University, 3 June 1996.

Oury, Guy-Marie. *L'Homme qu a conçu Montréal: Jérôme Le Royer, Sieur de la Dauversière*. Montreal: Méridien, 1991.

Owram, Doug. *Promise of Eden: The Canadian Expansionist Movement and the Ideal of the West, 1856–1900*. Toronto: University of Toronto Press, 1980.

Peelman, Achiel. *Christ Is a Native American.* Ottawa: Novalis-Saint Paul University, 1995.

Penner, Norman. *The Canadian Left: A Critical Analysis.* Toronto: Prentice-Hall of Canada, 1977.

Pelletier, Gérard. *Years of Impatience.* Toronto: Methuen, 1984.

– "An Interview with Gerard Pelletier," *Grail* 7: 2 (1991): 40–58.

Pelletier-Baillargeon, Hélène. *Marie Gérin-Lajoie.* Montreal: Boréal, 1985.

Pennacchio, Luigi. "The Torrid Trinity: Catholicism, Fascism and Toronto's Italians, 1929–1960." In *Catholics at the "Gathering Place": Historical Essays on the Archdiocese of Toronto, 1841–1991,* edited by Mark G. McGowan and B. Clarke. Toronto: Canadian Catholic Historical Association, 1993.

Perin, Roberto. *The Immigrants's Church: The Third Force in Canadian Catholicism, 1880–1920.* Ottawa: Canadian Historical Association, Booklet 25, 1998.

– "French-Speaking Canada from 1840." In *A Concise History of Christianity in Canada,* edited by Terrence Murphy and Roberto Perin. Toronto: Oxford University Press, 1996.

– *Rome in Canada: The Vatican and Canadian Affairs in the Late Victorian Age.* Toronto: University of Toronto Press, 1990.

– "Troppo Ardenti Sacerdoti: The Conroy Mission Revisited." *Canadian Historical Review* 61 (1980): 283–304

Plante, Guy. *Le rigorisme au XVIIe siècle: Mgr de Saint-Vallier et le sacrement de pénitence, 1685–1727.* Gembloux: Duculot, 1971.

Platt, W. Wallace. *Gentle Eminence: A Life of Cardinal Flahiff.* McGill-Queens University Press, 1999.

Pouliot, Leon. *Mgr Bourget.* 5 vols. Montreal: Beauchemin, 1955.

Power, Michael. "Fallon versus Forster: The Struggle over Assumption College, 1919–1925." *Historical Studies* 56 (1989): 49–66.

– "The Mitred Warrior: A Critical Reassessment of Bishop Michael Francis Fallon, 1867–1931." *Catholic Insight* 8, no. 3 (April 2000): 18–26.

Prince, Bernard A. "Foundation of the Episcopal Conference in Canada." *Studia Canonica* I (1967): 98–109.

Prang, Margaret. "Clerics, Politicians, and the Bilingual Schools Issue in Ontario, 1910–1917." *Canadian Historical Review* 41, no. 4 (December 1960): 281–307.

Radecki, Henry, and Benedykt Heydendorn. *A Member of a Distinguished Family: The Polish Group in Canada.* Toronto: McClelland and Stewart, 1976.

Rapley, Elizabeth. *The Dévotees: Women and Church in Seventeenth Century France.* Montreal: McGill-Queens' University Press, 1990.

Rea, James E. *Bishop Alexander Macdonell and the Politics of Upper Canada.* Toronto: Ontario Historical Society, 1974.

Reford, Alexander. "St Michael's College at the University of Toronto, 1958–1978: The Frustrations of Federation." *Historical Studies* 61 (1995): 171–94.

Report of the Royal Commission for Higher Education in New Brunswick, Fredericton, NB, 1962.

Rhodes, Anthony. *The Vatican in the Age of Dictators, 1922–1945.*

Richard, Lucien et al., eds. *Vatican II: The Unfinished Agenda.* New York: Paulist Press, 1987.

Rioux, Marcel, and Yves Martin, eds. *French-Canadian Society.* Vol. 1. Carleton Library No. 18. Toronto: McClelland and Stewart, 1964.

Ross, Sheila. "For God and Canada: The Early Years of the Catholic Women's League in Canada." CCHA *Historical Studies* 62 (1996): 89–108.

Rousseau, Louis, and F.W. Remiggi. *Atlas Historique des Pratiques Religieuses: Le Sud-Ouest du Québec au XIXe siècle.* Ottawa: Les Presses de l'Université d'Ottawa, 1998.

Routhier, Gilles, ed. *L'Église canadienne et Vatican II.* Saint-Laurent, Québec: Fides, 1997.

– Les *votas* des évêques des diocèses du Québec." In Gilles Routhier. *L'Église canadienne et Vatican II.* Saint Laurent, PQ: Fides, 1997.

Ruether, Rosemary R. *Sexism and God-Talk: Toward a Feminist Theology.* Boston: Beacon, 1983.

Rusak, Stephen T. "The Canadian 'Concordat' of 1897." *Canadian Historical Review* 77 (April 1991): 209–34.

Ryan, William F. *The Clergy and the Economic Growth in Quebec, 1896–1914.* Quebec: Les Presses de l'Université Laval, 1966.

– "Economic Development and the Church in French Canada." *Industrial Relations* 21, no. 3 (1966): 381–405.

Rynne, Xavier. *Vatican Council II.* New York: Orbis, 1999.

Sanche, Margaret F. *Heartwood: A History of St Thomas More College and Newman Centre at the University of Saskatchewan.* Muenster, SK: St Peter's Press, 1986.

– "A Matter of Identity: St Thomas More College at the University of Saskatchewan, 1961–1977." *Historical Studies* 61 (1995): 195–214.

Sanchez, José. *The Spanish Civil War as a Religious Tragedy.* Notre Dame, IN: University of Notre Dame, 1987.

Savard, Pierre. *Aspects du Catholicisme canadien-français au XIXe siècle.* Montreal: Fides, 1980.

Scanlon, Michael J. "The Ecclesial Dimension of Anthopology." In *The Gift of the Church: A Textbook on Ecclesiology,* edited by Peter C. Phan. Collegeville, MN: The Liturgical Press, 2000.

See, Scott W. *Riots in New Brunswick: Orange Nativism and Social Violence in the 1840s.* Toronto: University of Toronto Press, 1993.

Seljak, David. "Why the Quiet Revolution was 'Quiet': The Catholic Church's Reaction to the Secularization of Nationalism in Quebec after 1960." CCHA *Historical Studies* 62 (1996): 109–124.

Shanahan, David. "Spanish Residential School." Unpublished manuscript, 1997.

Sheridan, Edward F. *Do Justice! The Social Teaching of the Canadian Catholic Bishops*. Sherbrooke: Éditions Paulines, 1987.

– *Love Kindness! The Social Teaching of the Canadian Bishops (1958–1989)*. Montreal: Éditions Paulines, 1991.

Shook, Laurence K. *Catholic Post-Secondary Education in English-Speaking Canada*. Toronto: University of Toronto Press, 1971.

– "Pontifical Institute of Mediaeval Studies: An Historical Survey." In Gerald Mulligan. *Were the Dean's Windows Dusty?* Montreal: s.n., 1966, T1-T31.

Shortt, Adam, and Arthur G. Doughty, eds. *Documents Relating to the Constitutional History of Canada, 1759–1791*. Ottawa: J. de L. Taché, 1918.

Silver, A.I. *French Canadian Attitudes toward the North-West and North-West Settlement, 1870–1890*. Montreal, 1966.

– *French-Canadian Idea of Confederation, 1864–1900*. Toronto: University of Toronto Press, 1982.

Simpson, Patricia. *Marguerite Bourgeoys and Montreal, 1640–1665*. Montreal: McGill-Queen's University Press, 1997.

Slattery, T.P. *Loyola and Montreal*. Montreal: N.p., 1962.

Smillie, Benjamin G., ed. *Visions of the New Jerusalem: Religious Settlement in the Prairies*, Edmonton: NeWest Press, 1983.

Smyth, Elizabeth. "Christian Perfection and Service to Neighbours: The Congregation of the Sisters of St Joseph, Toronto, 1851–1920." In *Changing Roles of Women within the Christian Church of Canada*, edited by Elizabeth Gillan Muir and Marilyn Färdig Whiteley, 38–54. Toronto: University of Toronto Press, 1995.

– " 'Developing the Powers of the Youthful Mind': The Evolution of Education for Young Women at St Joseph's Academy, Toronto, 1854–1911." CCHA *Historical Studies* 60 (1993–1994): 103–25.

Spence, Jonathan. *The Meaning Palace of Matteo Ricci*. Toronto: Penguin, 1985.

Stogre, Michael. *That the World May Believe: The Development of Papal Social Thought on Aboriginal Rights*. Ottawa: Éditions Paulines, 1992.

Stone Soup: Reflections on Economic Injustice. Montreal: Paulines, 1998.

Stortz, Gerald J. "Archbishop John Joseph Lynch and the Anglicans of Toronto, 1860–1888." *Journal of the Canadian Church Historical Society* 27 (April 1995): 3–17.

Sylvain, Philippe. "Libéralisme et ultramontanisme au Canada français: affrontement idéologique et doctrinal, 1840–1865, I and II." In *Le bouclier d'Achille*, edited by W.L. Morton, 111–38, 220–55. Toronto: McClelland & Stewart, 1986.

Taves, Ann. *The Household of the Faith: Roman Catholic Devotions in Mid-Nineteenth Century America*. Notre Dame, IN: University of Notre Dame Press, 1986.

Thériault, Léon. "The Acadianization of the Catholic Church in Acadia." In *The Acadians of the Maritimes: Thematic Studies*, edited by Jean Daigle. Moncton, NB: Centres d'études acadiennes, 1982.

Thomas, Hugh. *The Spanish Civil War.* London: Readers Union/Eyre and Spottiswoode, 1962.

Thomas, James H. "Quebec's Bishops as a Pawn: Saint-Vallier's Imprisonment in England, 1704–1709." CCHA *Historical Studies* 64 (1998): 151–60.

Thwaites, R.G., ed. *Jesuit Relations and Allied Documents, 1610–1791.* Cleveland: Burrows 1896–1901. 73 vols.

Tillard, J.M.R. "L'épiscopat canadien francophone au concile." In *L'Église canadienne et Vatican II,* edited by Gilles Routhier. Saint-Laurent, PQ: Fides, 1997.

Toomey, Kathleen M. *Alexander Macdonell: The Scottish Years, 1762–1804.* Toronto: Canadian Catholic Historical Association, 1885.

Toupin, Robert. *Arpents de neige et Robes Noires.* Montreal: Bellarmin, 1991.

Trigger, Bruce G. *Native and Newcomers: Canada's "Heroic Age" Reconsidered.* Montreal: McGill-Queen's University Press, 1985.

Trofimenkoff, Susan Mann. *The Dream of a Nation: A Social and Intellectual History of Quebec.* Toronto: Gage, 1983.

Trudeau, Pierre E. *The Asbestos Strike.* Toronto: James Lorimer, 1974.

Vaughan, W.E., ed. *A New History of Ireland VI: Ireland under the Union, II, 1870–1921.* Oxford: Clarendon Press, 1996.

Vecsey, Christopher. *The Paths of Kateri's Kin.* Notre Dame, IN: University of Notre Dame Press, 1997.

Vidler, Alexander R. *A Century of Social Catholicism, 1820–1930.* London: SPCK, 1964.

Vigod, Bernard. L. *The Jews in Canada.* Canada's Ethnic Groups. Ottawa: Canadian Historical Association, 1984.

– *Quebec before Duplessis: The Political Career of Louis-Alexandre Taschereau.* Montreal: McGill-Queen's University Press, 1986.

Voisine, Nive, dir. *Histoire du catholicisme québécois.* Vol. 2: Les XVIIIe et XIXe siècle. Montreal: Boréal, 1989–91. Tome 1 par Lucien Lemieux and Tome 2 par Philippe Sylvain et Nive Voisine.

Nive, Voisine et Jean Hamelin, dir. *Les ultramontains canadiens-français.* Montreal: Boréal, 1985.

Von Arx, Jeffrey. *Varieties of Ultramontanism.* Baltimore: Catholic University of America Press, 1997.

Wade, Mason. "Relations between the French, Irish, and Scottish Clergy in the Maritime Provinces, 1774–1836." *Historical Studies* 39 (1972): 9–33.

Waite, P.B., ed. *Pre-Confederation.* Vol. 2. Canadian Historical Documents Series. Scarborough: Prentice-Hall, 1965.

Wahl, James A. "Father Louis Funcken's Contribution to German Catholicism in Waterloo County, Ontario." CCHA *Historical Studies* 50 (1983): 513–32.

Walker, Franklin A. *Catholic Education and Politics in Ontario.* Toronto: Thomas Nelson and Sons, 1964.

Wallot, J.P. "The Lower Canadian Clergy and the Reign of Terror (1810)." CCHA *Historical Studies* 40 (1973): 53–60.

Walsh, H.H. *The Church in the French Era: From Colonization to the British Conquest.* Toronto: Ryerson, 1966.

Ward, W. Peter. *The Japanese in Canada.* Canada's Ethnic Groups. Ottawa: Canadian Historical Association, 1982.

White, Clinton. "Language, Religion, Schools and Politics among German-American Catholic Settlers in St Peter's Colony, Saskatchewan, 1903–1916." *Study Sessions* 45 (1978): 81–99.

Wilson, David A. *The Irish in Canada.* Canada's Ethnic Groups, Booklet 12. Ottawa: Canadian Historical Association, 1989.

Windschniegl, Peter. *Fifty Golden Years, 1903–1953.* Meunster, SK: St Peter's Press, ca. 1953.

– *A Journey of Faith: St Peter's Albany, 1921–1996.* Muenster, SK: St Peter's Press, 1996.

Wood, Susan K. "The Church as Communion." In *The Gift of the Church: A Textbook on Ecclesiology,* edited by Peter C. Phan. Collegeville, MN: Liturgical Press, 2000.

Woodcock, George. *Gabriel Dumont: The Métis Chief and his Lost World.* Edmonton: Hurtig, 1995.

Wynn, Wilton. *Keepers of the Keys: John XXIII, Paul VI, John Paul II, the Three Who Changed the Church.* New York: Random House, 1988.

Young, Brian. *In Its Corporate Capacity: The Seminary of Montreal as a Business Institution, 1816–1876.* Montreal: McGill-Queen's University Press, 1986.

Zizola, Giancarlo. *The Utopia of Pope John XXIII.* Translated by Helen Barolini. Maryknoll, NY: Orbis, 1978.

Zoltvany, Yves F. *The French Tradition in America.* Columbia, SC: University of South Carolina Press, 1969.

Zucchi, John E. *Italians in Toronto: Development of a National Identity, 1875–1935.* Montreal: McGill-Queen's University Press, 1988.

Index